KU-749-521

MAKE YOUR OWN

SOFT FURNISHINGS

CUSHIONS * COVERS * CURTAINS

MAKE YOUR OWN

SOFT FURNISHINGS

CUSHIONS * COVERS * CURTAINS

the complete step-by-step guide to creating stylish cushions, loose covers, curtains, blinds, table linen and bed linen, shown in over 900 colour photographs

dorothy wood

LORENZ BOOKS

This edition is published by Lorenz Books

Lorenz Books is an imprint of Anness Publishing Ltd
Hermes House, 88–89 Blackfriars Road, London SE1 8HA
tel. 020 7401 2077; fax 020 7633 9499
www.lorenzbooks.com; info@anness.com

© Anness Publishing Ltd 2000, 2005

UK agent: The Manning Partnership Ltd, 6 The Old Dairy, Melcombe Road, Bath BA2 3LR; tel. 01225 478444; fax 01225 478440
sales@manning-partnership.co.uk

UK distributor: Grantham Book Services Ltd, Isaac Newton Way
Alma Park Industrial Estate, Grantham, Lincs NG31 9S
tel. 01476 541080; fax 01476 541061; orders@gbs.tbs-ltd.co.uk

North American agent/distributor: National Book Network
4501 Forbes Boulevard, Suite 200, Lanham, MD 20706
tel. 301 459 3366; fax 301 429 5746; www.nbnbooks.com

Australian agent/distributor: Pan Macmillan Australia
Level 18, St Martins Tower, 31 Market St, Sydney, NSW 2000
tel. 1300 135 113; fax 1300 135 103;
customer.service@macmillan.com.au

New Zealand agent/distributor: David Bateman Ltd, 30 Tarndale Grove
Off Bush Road, Albany, Auckland; tel. (09) 415 7664; fax (09) 415 8892

All rights reserved. No part of this publication may be reproduced, stored in a retrieval system, or transmitted in any way or by any means, electronic, mechanical, photocopying, recording or otherwise, without the prior written permission of the copyright holder.

A CIP catalogue record for this book is available from the British Library.

Publisher **Joanna Lorenz**

Project Editor **Simona Hill**

Photographer **Paul Bricknell**

Step-by-step Photographer **Rodney Forte**

Stylist **Juliana Leite Goad**

Designer **Lisa Tai**

Editorial Reader **Kate Humby**

Production Controller **Steve Lang**

Previously published as *The Practical Encyclopedia of Soft Furnishir*

1 3 5 7 9 10 8 6 4 2

HAMPSHIRE COUNTY LIBRARY
646.21
0754815633
C013897635

contents

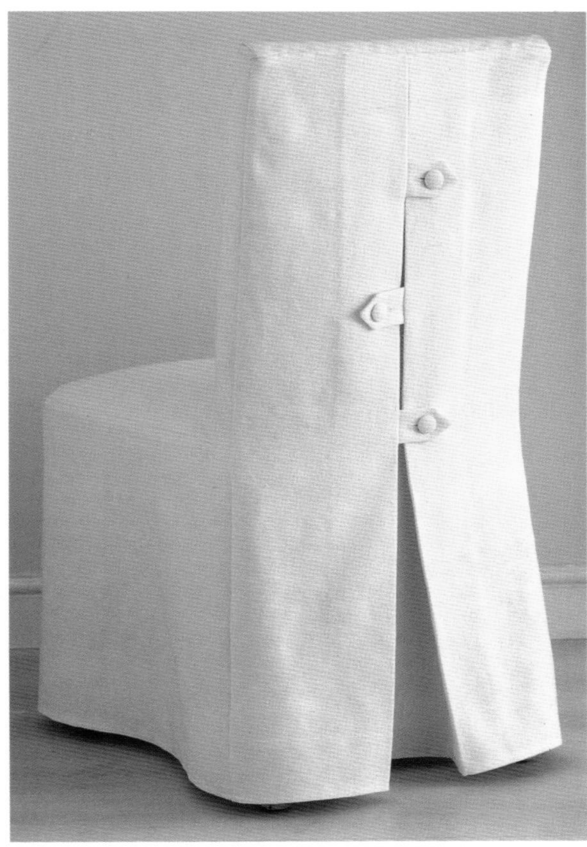

introduction

Soft furnishings make our homes comfortable and attractive, transforming bare walls and furniture into appealing room schemes with style, character and comfort.The tactile qualities of fabric softens the hard edges of walls, floors, and wooden furniture, be it cosy woollen blankets, crisp linen chair covers or luxurious, formal velvet drapes.

As well as having a practical purpose, soft furnishings are decorative, bringing colour, pattern and texture into our homes. Soft furnishings help to establish the style of a room; the colours and design of the fabric can dramatically alter the ambience of a room. Whether it is a single accessory such as a cushion or a major item such as a pair of curtains, your choice of fabric will reflect the type of person you are and the style of surroundings you want to live in.

Curtains and blinds block out draughts, screen light and provide privacy, while sheer voile curtains diffuse the light and make the window into an attractive focal point. Easy-care bed linen and bedcovers ensure a warm and comfortable night's sleep. Stylish table linen can be tailored to match china, or the style of dinner party you are hosting.

Slipcovers protect furniture as well as transform worn or faded chairs, and plump scatter cushions add accent colours to a room's colour scheme and bring appealing warmth and comfort to chairs and sofas.

Changing the decor in a room can produce remarkable results but you will need to take into consideration how much time and money you are able to invest. Wrapping fabric around a curtain pole or tossing a throw over a sofa are quick and easy remedies that cost little in terms of time or money; but making soft furnishings on a grand scale can be costly, so take time over your fabric choices and ensure you will be happy to live with the finished articles for many years.

The Practical Encyclopedia of Soft Furnishings is a comprehensive guide to making the most popular soft furnishing items, and includes many projects suitable for every level of expertise, from easy-to make cushions, pillowcases and sheets, to more complex projects such as chair covers, and swags and tails for formal window treatments.

1 furnishing styles

Whether you are looking for a complete revamp or want to freshen up an existing room, the following pages will provide plenty of inspiration with colours, styles and fabrics to look at. Put a story-board of colours and fabrics together then tailor it to fit your space and lifestyle.

choosing colours

Fabrics are available today in so many colours and patterns that the sheer number probably fills the majority of people with dread. The huge choice does provide tremendous scope for creativity, but it is not easy to create a colour scheme from scratch and many people will have no idea where to begin. Having an idea of the position of the colours in a colour wheel and knowing a little colour theory is always a help, but even interior designers get much of their inspiration and ideas from other people's work. Look in shops and in interior design magazines at different room sets and try to find something you like. Single-colour schemes are the easiest as long as the tones of colour all match, but try to include different textures and scales of pattern in your furnishing accessories to ring the changes, or inject a little pizazz by adding cushion covers, or lampshades or curtains in a bright or daring colour from the opposite side of the colour wheel.

Whether you are changing the entire colour scheme or only replacing one item, you should find the photographs on the following pages inspiring.

neutral tones

Many people find it difficult to see the "big picture" when it comes to choosing a colour scheme and cannot visualize large expanses of colour or its possible effect on a room. As a result, many of us go for safe, neutral colours that we know will work together. Cream, beige and grey tones are comfortable to live with and always stay in fashion, and it is easy to add a splash of colour with a cushion or throw in a warm, complementary shade.

right Unusual cushions will often become a focal point in a room. Bold appliqué designs can be used to introduce different design motifs or to add accent colours that will complement other soft furnishings in the room.

below right An assortment of stripes and checks adds interest to the subtle colour scheme in this room. The warm colour of the tile floor is picked up in the cushions and curtains.

below left Three different styles of fabric blend together harmoniously because of their neutral tones. A dark cream curtain is backed with striped ticking and the effect is softened by the sheer fabric draped behind.

above left The light blue colour on the walls is echoed in the accessories around the room. The dark brown rug adds depth to the otherwise pale colour scheme.

neutrals

shades of green

Green is a calm and tranquil colour to live with, but it is not always easy to find different shades of green that go well together. Choose tones that come from the same part of the colour wheel and mix weaves, stripes and checks together to add visual interest. For example, there are innumerable shades of leaf green, or aqua blue-green that are reminiscent of the sea and vibrant lime greens from the Mediterranean region. Green works well with many other colours – with neutrals for a peaceful room scheme or lime and yellow for a bright, modern look.

above A little zing and freshness is injected into the subtle, almost neutral, tones of this pale green colour scheme by hanging bright green curtains at the large windows. **below left** Different checks and patterned fabrics work well together because they are all based on the same green shades. Red is opposite green on the colour wheel and therefore adds interest and "lifts" the colours in the room. **centre left** Large-scale floral patterns are easy to live with when blended with solid complementary colours. **top left** The dark green check of this chair cover is enhanced by the matching plain deep blue-green cushion. The warm-looking chenille fabric makes the chair instantly appealing.

shades of blue

Blue and white is a classic combination for interiors, often associated with holiday homes and rooms with sea views. Blue-and-white checks invariably appear in the stores in spring teamed with fresh yellows and whites. But there is a wide range of alternative blue fabrics that give a completely different look. Rich blue velvets or satin stripes will create a sumptuous interior in an elegant room, while wonderful homespun checks add a touch of country style.

blues

above An assortment of blue-and-white check cushions shows up beautifully against a deep blue curtain.
below right Bold striped Roman blinds make a striking feature in this thoroughly modern sitting room. The dark blue sofa in a toning shade of blue is enhanced by the pale neutral stripes in the cushion covers.
below left Cushion covers provide an excellent opportunity to mix and match furnishing fabrics and introduce colours and patterns on a small scale.
above left Co-ordinating bed linen with the wallpaper gives a room a very professionally decorated appearance.

shades of yellow

The colour of sunshine, yellow is a very warm and welcoming colour to use for decorating the home. It can be as pale as sand, in wonderful deep creamy shades or as bold and vibrant as the sun, with innumerable shades in between. Alter the mood in a yellow room by using accessories in a harmonious or acid green or use the complementary colour purple for a bold and rich effect. Cheerful yellow works particularly well in kitchens and living rooms, or to brighten up a cool north-facing bedroom.

yellows

top A deep yellow striped Roman blind shades the bright sunlight, allowing a soft warm glow to filter into the room.
above Zingy lime and yellow work well on this bright, appliqué cushion cover.
below right Warm yellow checks and pretty prints combine to make a very welcoming room in a country house.
below left Purple is the complementary colour to yellow, and using the two colours together creates a bold, exciting colour scheme.
above left Green and yellow together bring a touch of the countryside into the home. Pick out the colours in contrasting prints for added interest.

shades of red

Red is a strong, vibrant colour that can produce stunning results in soft furnishings. Bright red looks quite exotic and theatrical in rich velvet and exquisite silk fabrics, whereas paler pinks and coral reds are much subtler colours that can have a calming effect in a room. Be bold and use deep red on the walls and furnishings, as the Victorians did, or just add an accent of red with some well-chosen accessories or trims and ties on curtains.

reds

top right Create a sumptuous, exotic look with rich red silk fabric and stunning tassels.
centre right A variety of bold striped fabrics creates a theatrical effect in this dining room. Flamboyant interlined silk curtains with a dramatic pelmet are a strong focal point.

right Pretty gingham and striped chair covers suggest a warm welcoming country look.
left Choose a selection of different red fabrics to make a collection of cushions to brighten up a neutral sofa or day bed.
above left Traditional chintz prints look modern when mixed with solid red fabrics.

choosing styles

Decorating a home in a manner that you like has never been easier. There is such a diversity of different styles that are considered to be contemporary, each with its own range of fabrics, furnishings and colours. Before deciding, consider your lifestyle and family needs. Furnishing a room with white sofas and chairs may look very sleek, but in a home with children it is not a very practical solution to day-to-day living requirements.

To recreate a particular style, choose items within certain parameters or the overall effect may be lost. This is not as drastic or as difficult as you may think, and it should not be necessary to refurnish a room completely – a change of colour or fabric can completely alter the appearance of an existing piece of furniture, and replacing curtains with blinds or vice versa will help to produce the look that you want to achieve.

The following pages will give you ideas for a range of different styles, from the simple, minimalist scheme using plain lines and neutral tones to the exotic, eclectic look where wonderful colours and exquisite fabrics create a busier, more opulent feel.

minimalist

Simple lines and an uncluttered overall appearance typify the minimalist style. It is by no means cold or stark as natural materials such as plain wood and simple cotton fabrics rather than metal and plastic are used. In the same way, the minimalist style is not necessarily ultramodern and traditional furniture can simply be re-covered in plain, neutral fabrics. It is usually necessary to scale down the window treatments, opt for simple blinds or simply do without. Choose furnishings you really love, since a minimalist interior will ensure they are always on display.

above Exposed beams and an open wooden staircase add warmth to the neutral upholstery fabrics in this barn conversion. A large modern painting and a collection of cushions add a touch of colour to the scheme.

above right Simple roller blinds provide privacy at night, but roll up to create the uncluttered appearance that typifies the minimal look. A few well-chosen accessories add interest to the simple interior.

below right Plain white bed linen and stark, white walls complement each other in this modern bedroom setting.

country

There are a number of styles that come under the label "country", but each has similar roots, albeit from a different country in the world. Over the last few years, country styles from places as diverse as New England, Scandinavia and France have been very popular. Although each has a distinct look, they are all based on a rustic style, with the emphasis on practicality. Think of country style and you immediately conjure up images of soft comfy sofas, small rooms and plenty of paraphernalia, but the modern country look is much more refined – you don't necessarily need a small rural cottage to achieve this look as long as the furnishings and wall coverings are carefully chosen.

left A pretty floral striped fabric makes a wonderful quilt for this unusual iron bed. Plain white bed linen and a charming rug on a polished wooden floor add to the country style.

below right *Toile de jouy* is a glazed cotton print that is typical of the French country style. Traditionally all the surfaces such as walls and curtains are covered in the same print, but it is possible to vary the scale for cushions and wall coverings.

below left Make a pretty tie-on frilled cushion to add a bit of extra comfort to a traditional country chair. The rustic look is completed with accessories made from natural materials such as wicker, rush and wood.

traditional

The traditional style is similar to country style in many ways but it is usually associated with town houses rather than cottages. High ceilings and tall windows allow the decor to be on a much grander scale, allowing greater scope for furnishings and accessories. Although it aims to achieve the same "lived-in" look as the country style, with well-worn colours of faded chintz, the furniture is usually antique rather than simply old and aspires to tasteful grandeur.

right A traditional corona adds height and a touch of elegance to the square lines of this Scandinavian-style bedroom furniture. Antique accessories complete the look.

below right The height of these windows has been subtly lowered by clever draping of the pretty curtains to create a dining room that is both elegant and informal.

below left Traditional country fabrics have been used on a grand scale to create this stunning room, where the emphasis is on comfort rather than formality.

eclectic style

Those of us who favour the eclectic style tend to be individualists who like to collect and display unusual objects and artefacts. It is a style that combines the best ideas from several different sources, mixing and matching them to create a unique look. Fabrics and furniture that have been sourced from antique markets or bric-à-brac shops and holidays abroad are displayed together in a theatrical way, reminiscent of an Oriental bazaar.

left A brightly patterned kilim rug was the inspiration for this Middle Eastern colour scheme. A collection of unusual furniture and artefacts sits comfortably beside the exotic array of cushions that pick out the strong pink and yellow colours in the rug.

below right Fabrics collected from travels abroad have here been made into an assortment of stunning cushions to create an unusual low settee.

below left Use new fabrics and trimmings to make harder-wearing cushion covers. Display them with antique accessories to create the typical eclectic look.

eclectic

contemporary

Bold colours, trendy, modern shapes and strong, clearly defined prints characterize the contemporary look. Geared to the young at heart, this look is not for the faint-hearted, or those unsure of their taste. As new looks come and go, so your furnishings and accessories will need to change to accommodate the latest fashions and trends. But limiting colours and shapes to two or three will provide balance. Choose accessories wisely – introducing different styles will distract from the look.

above left Solid coloured cushions and a large-scale pattern throw work well together in vibrant and clashing tones. Limiting the number of colours helps to hold the design scheme together.
above right Minimal accessories and strong angular lines create a thoroughly modern look that is welcoming.
right This trendy shaped sofa needs space around it to be viewed to best effect. The red fabric is complemented by a single purple cushion and lime walls, to ensure it makes a strong design statement.

contemporary

choosing fabrics

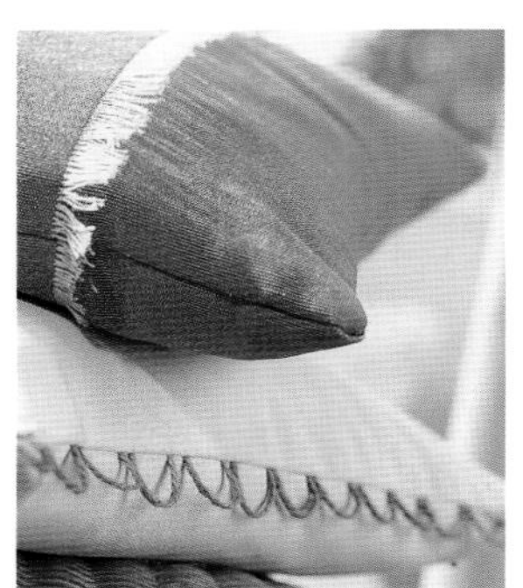

Fabric choice is often instinctive but will undoubtedly be influenced by the furnishing style that you want to achieve. Your personal taste will be a major factor in the choice of fabric and inevitably so will the budget. Think carefully before splashing out on an expensive fabric, and enlist the help of store assistants who are specially trained to help you mix and match colours, patterns and textures, and will be available to advise on the suitability of the fabric for the required purpose. Soft furnishings use large amounts of fabric and the cost can be substantial but there are ways to economize. You can buy fabrics at discount prices by mail order or choose an inexpensive fabric such as plain cotton calico and dress it up with trimmings. Whatever fabric you choose, it must suit the type and style of soft furnishing you are making. Check that the fabric will do what you want. Does it crease badly, will it drape, can it be pressed into pleats, will it gather into soft folds? For large projects, it is a good idea to borrow a fabric sample to hang or drape in your room for a day or two to see if you like it and to ensure that it complements your existing furnishings.

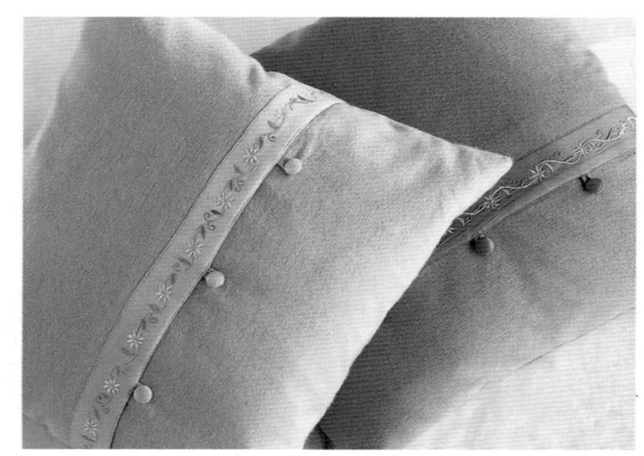

patterns & prints

Patterned fabrics are available in every conceivable style and colour. Some, such as animal prints and bold Bauhaus geometrics, go in and out of fashion, whereas floral chintzes and *toile de jouy* are classics that never seem to date. The scale of the pattern is crucial when you are buying fabric for soft furnishings, and you will need to allow extra for matching and positioning large designs and motifs, particularly on items such as curtains and cushions. Small-scale prints used for curtaining often read as a solid colour in large rooms, while prints that are too large for the scale of the room may become a distracting focal point. Mixing the scales and patterns will help create a balance.

patterns & prints

left and above Bold prints are offset with plain coloured cushions and plain walls. Fabric patterns look best when they can be seen without other prints and colours competing for attention.

textures & weaves

Texture can be introduced to soft furnishings with a fabric that has an interesting weave, such as corduroy, velvet, jacquard and bouclé. These fabrics are frequently made by manufacturers to complement their ranges of print fabrics. Embellishing fabrics with handicraft techniques such as quilting, appliqué, knitting or embroidery will also add texture to fabrics. These items tend to be softer and don't wear as well as plain-woven fabrics and so their practical use is restricted, but they are ideal for accessories, such as cushions and throws.

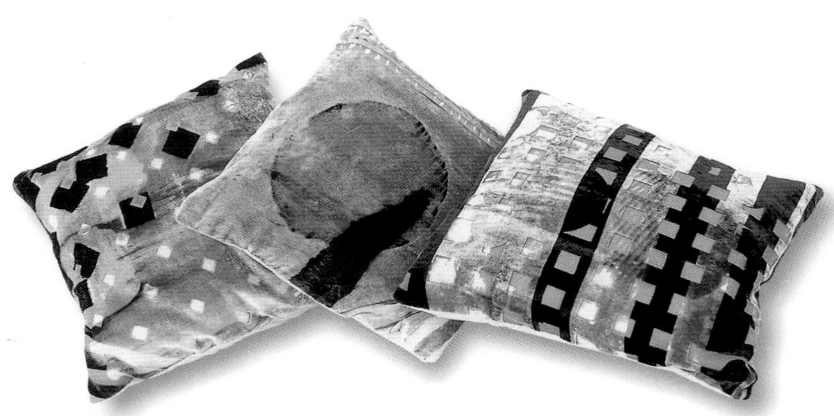

textures & weaves

above Using exquisite fabrics such as hand-made devoré velvet to make a few stunning cushions will add a touch of class to otherwise plain furnishings.

above right Transform plain fabrics with appliqué and quilting techniques. Quilting softens the fabric and makes it crease-resistant.

below right A knitted cushion is warm, soft and comfortable and innumerable textures can be created from the simple plain and purl stitches.

left A wide range of embroidery techniques can be used in soft furnishing. Here a stunning crewel work pattern covers the entire cushion.

stripes & checks

Stripes and checks never really go out of fashion. Stripes add formality to a room, particularly broad bands of stripes, whereas checks add a homely feel to furnishings. Pinstripes are good for small rooms and the smallest checks such as gingham are suitable for children's rooms. Recently utility fabrics such as ticking and homespun checks have become very popular and are a good economic source of furnishing fabrics, but whether you are looking to create an informal country style or to decorate a formal room with elegant curtains you will almost certainly be able to find a stripe or check to suit.

top This unusual and striking combination of stripes and checks work well together without competing. The pale walls and light floor provide a visual rest.

above Traditional tartans work well in many room settings.

right A bold tartan check fabric makes quite an impact in this richly decorated room. Match the check pattern carefully across the width of the curtains for a professional finish.

leather & fur

Leather and fur are wonderful fabrics to use in soft furnishings, but they do tend to go in and out of fashion and can look out of place in the wrong setting. Both are available as natural skins, but there are also many lookalike fabrics that are extremely realistic or you can buy faux fur just for fun. These fabrics make simple and striking footstools and cushions to add a very individual touch to a living room. Try a black and white print cushion on a lime sofa or use pale suede fabric to add decorative details to furnishings.

leather & fur

left and below left Faux fur is made in a variety of textures and colours. The bulky fabrics look best made into large, simple shapes such as this collection of cushions.
right Appliqué is an ideal technique for leather and suede as these materials do not fray. The skins are dyed in a wide range of bright and bold colours. Simply cut out the shape and stitch close to the edge.

sheer fabrics

Sheers and voiles are the latest fabrics to receive attention from manufacturers. Once regarded as frumpy because of their uniform white colour and bland design, sheer curtains and fabrics have become the lastest must-have accessories, and are now widely available in a riot of colours, as well as a range of interesting weaves and prints. Because they are so delicate, sheer fabrics are ideal for creating a romantic or feminine style. They can be used, for example, to make beautiful curtains that provide privacy while still allowing the sunlight to filter through. Sheer fabrics can also be interlined or backed with a plain fabric for stability so that you can still use them when making heavier-weight curtains or matching cushions.

above Modern geometric designs incorporate different tones of colour and can be chosen to colour-co-ordinate with curtains and cushions.
below right Sheer cushion casings decorated with silk and satin ribbons are the perfect feminine accessory for a pastel coloured bedroom.
below centre White sheer curtains are a good choice in small rooms or where plenty of light is required.

sheers

2 cushions & chair covers

There is an abundance of beautiful fabrics that can be made into cushions and loose covers to transform a room, adding a splash of colour to contrast with, or match your decor. Whatever your style, from plain piped cushions to shaped loose covers, there are ideas to suit all tastes.

cushions

Cushions are the accessories in a decor theme and as such add the finishing touch to a room. They can be made in almost any fabric and are one of the most creative aspects of soft furnishing. Cushions in contrasting colours enliven an otherwise flat colour scheme, and are the perfect opportunity to add an accent colour to a room. They add warmth and comfort to a sofa or armchair, and soften the hard edges of furniture. A single scatter (throw) cushion or bolster can inspire the entire interior scheme for a room, or cushions can be carefully chosen at the end to complete the decorating process with touches of colour and textures of fabrics you may not have had the opportunity to use.

above left Cushions can be made in almost any fabric and in any shape and can be finished with a variety of complementary trims and decorative buttons.
below left A wonderfully plush fringing can transform beautiful fabrics into something quite exotic and luxurious.
above Scatter (throw) cushions and a bolster piled on top of a large footstool make a comfortable day bed. The different-shaped cushions are made from an assortment of fabrics and the co-ordinating colour scheme links them all together.

Cushions come in practically any shape or size and can be used in any room in the house. Because there is such a myriad of styles, cushions are one of the most creative aspects of soft furnishing. It is possible to use almost any fabric for a cushion if it is purely decorative and so you can really let your imagination run riot.

Scatter (throw) cushions are versatile – they can be tossed on to a bed, piled on the floor or propped in the corner of an armchair to add a little extra comfort. It is better to make them fairly large if you want to group them, as lots of little cushions can look rather cluttered.

Cushions are the easiest item of soft furnishing to make and the complete novice can tackle the simpler styles. In this chapter there are lots of different styles to choose from and different methods of inserting the cushion pad. Which you choose is often personal preference but each style of cushion cover has been made with the easiest and most suitable method. The openings can also be decorative – a row of buttons down one edge, some pretty ribbon ties or, for an unusual nautical look, cord laced through eyelets.

You can also add a touch of individuality with some unusual trimmings, making the variations on the basic scatter cushion almost endless. It is not only the edges of the cushions that can be decorative; the large area on the front of the cushion cover is the ideal shape for some beautiful handiwork. Simple machine-embroidered motifs repeated over the surface often look most effective, or a larger design can be embroidered using crewel work, Mountmellick embroidery or cross stitch. Fabric crafts such as patchwork and appliqué are also suitable. These techniques can be used to make the cushions as modern or traditional as you like.

The majority of cushions may be square or rectangular but cushion pads are available in an amazing assortment of shapes and sizes, including circles and hearts. Square cushions range from the small 30cm/12in size to the extra-large 55cm/22in which is suitable for a Japanese-style floor cushion. There is plenty of choice in rectangular pads too. Some are almost square and others very long and thin. If you can't find the shape you are looking for, it is quite easy to make your own pad using foam chips, polyester stuffing or feathers. The most expensive filling is feathers, but it lasts much longer than other types and does not go lumpy or flat. The casing on a feather cushion pad should be made from heavyweight

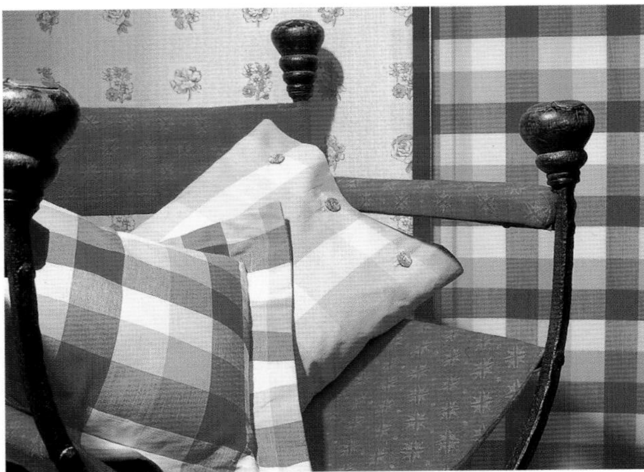

above left Large-scale cushions always look substantial and make a chair more appealing.

above Small motifs, stitched in a contrasting thread, make an Oxford cushion special. Keeping the border area stitch-free gives the cushions a fuss-free look.

left All sorts of fabrics can be used to make cushions. This windowseat cushion has been made from linen dish towels. The tie quilting helps to hold the feather stuffing in position and adds a subtle finishing touch.

calico that helps prevent the ends of the feathers from escaping.

Box-style cushions are similar to scatter (throw) cushions but they have a gusset running around the edge. Feather-filled, box-style cushion pads are available but you can also use a specially cut piece of foam instead. These cushions are ideal for softening a wicker chair or wooden bench or they can be made in extra-large sizes for seating in a child's bedroom or as a bed for a pet. The most suitable filling for larger floor cushions is polyester bead filling, obtainable from most haberdashery stores. The fabrics used for this style of cushion are generally more practical as the cover will need to be removed for cleaning. Even so there are lots of possibilities, from crisp linen or cotton ticking to warm fleece fabrics.

Bolster cushions add an elegant touch, tucked into the arm of a sofa or used as a day pillow on a couch or chaise longue. Depending on how they are going to be used, bolsters can be purely practical or highly decorative. At its most basic, a bolster cushion cover is simply a long tube tied at either end of the cushion pad. This may sound rather plain, but when it is made in crushed organza, the result is a stunningly stylish cushion. More formal bolster cushion covers have a classic piped edge, and covered buttons or luxurious tassels at each end.

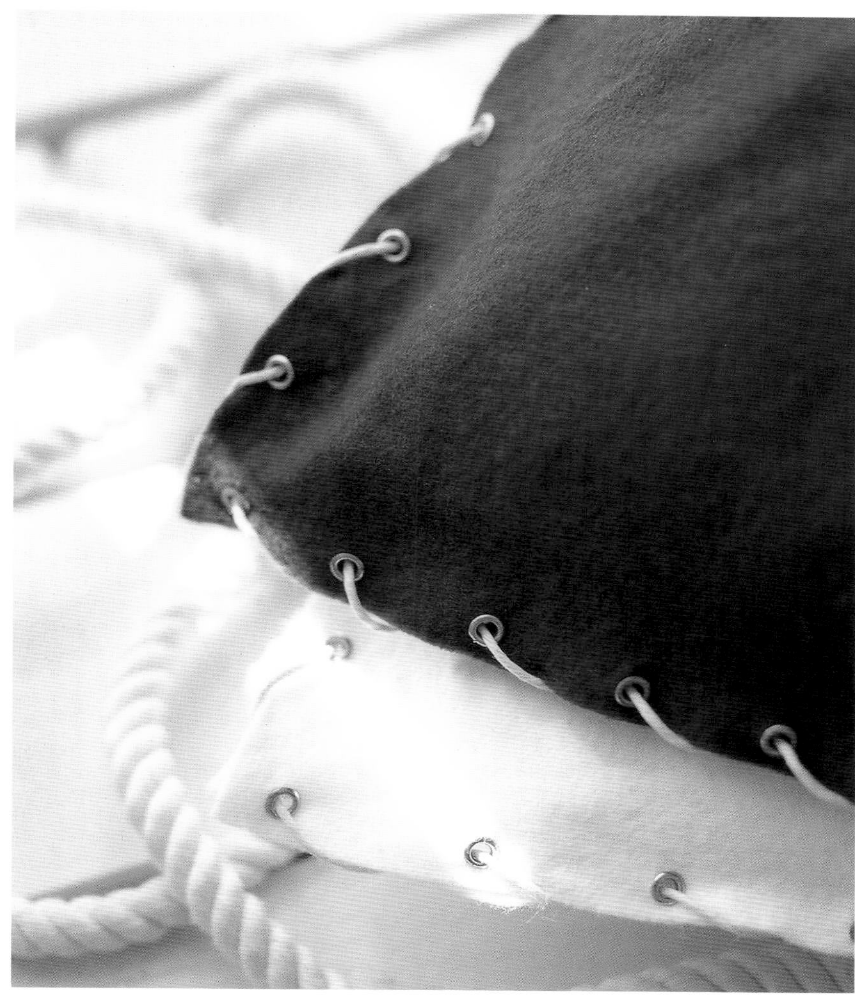

above Crisp blue-and-white canvas cushions trimmed with eyelets and white cord create a distinctive nautical look.

left A variety of checked and striped fabrics work well together in co-ordinating colours. Some of the striped fabrics have been joined diagonally to make unusual cushion panels.

basic cushion with a zipper

A zipper is a practical fastener for a cushion cover. Depending on the shape and size of the cushion, it can be placed in a seam, partway down the back, or in the centre of the back. Concealing a zipper in a seam makes sense, but is only suitable if the seam is straight. Zippers are best placed along the bottom edge of a square cushion, or in a side seam on a rectangular cushion. Choose a strong dressweight zipper that matches the fabric colour; a shade darker will be less visible than a lighter one. To add interest to a basic cushion, use different fabrics for the front and back or insert a contrast panel.

you will need

- **paper and pencil for template**
- **cushion pad**
- **fabric A, for the cushion front**
- **fabric B, for the cushion front**
- **fabric C, for the cushion back**
- **dressweight zipper**
- **sewing kit**

tip for basic cushion with a zipper

Buy a zipper 5–10cm/2–4in shorter than the side seam.

1

2

3

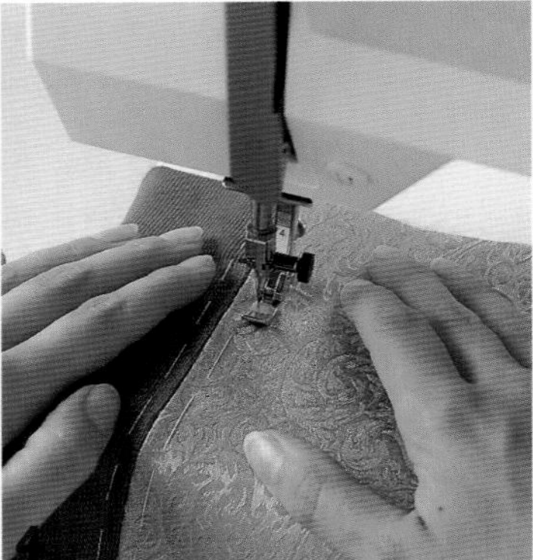

1 Draw a paper template the same size as the cushion pad and fold it in three. Use the folded template to cut out the front panels, adding a 1.5cm/⅝in seam allowance all around. Unfold the template and cut out a cushion back. With right sides together, pin and stitch each front panel to the next along the long edge. Press the seams away from the lightest colour fabric.

2 With right sides together, pin the front and back together down one short side. Centre the zipper on the side seam and mark the position. Stitch up to the marks at each end. Reinforce the stitching by working a reverse stitch at the zipper tab end. Tack (baste) the seam together between the stitches.

3 Press the seam open. Place the cushion cover right side down on a flat surface. Pin the zipper right side down along the tacked seam.

4 Tack along the zipper tape on both sides of the zipper, then mark each end of the zipper teeth with tacking stitches. Working from the right side and using a zipper foot, stitch just inside the tacking stitches, close to the zipper. Pull out the tacking threads and open the zipper slightly. Fold the cushion cover in half, with right sides together, and pin the other seams. Stitch each in place using a 1.5cm/⅝in seam. Trim across the corners and turn through. Ease out the corners from the right side, press, and insert the cushion pad.

basic cushion with a concealed zipper

If a square or rectangular cushion has any attachments such as tassels, braid or cord that could get caught in the zipper teeth, it is better to fit the zipper on the back panel and the braids around the front panel.

you will need

- paper and pencil for template
- cushion pad
- fabric A, for the cushion front
- fabric B, for the cushion back
- dressweight zipper
- 4 tassels, 5–8cm/2–3in long
- sewing kit

tips for basic cushion with a concealed zipper

When using bold patterned fabric, match the pattern along the seam lines of the back panels.

1

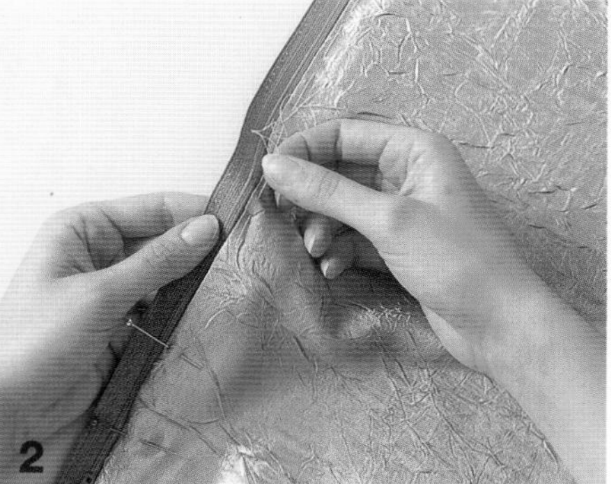

2

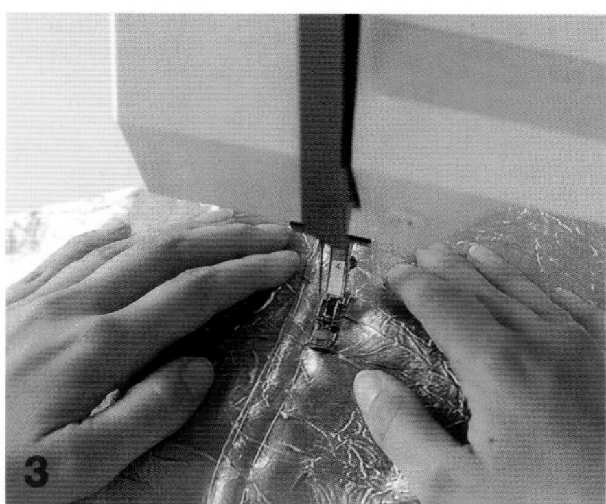

3

4

1 Cut out a cushion front the same size as the cushion pad plus 1.5cm/⅝in seam allowance all around. Draw a paper pattern the same size as the cushion pad and mark a line from side to side about one-quarter of the way down. Cut the pattern along the line. Cut out two fabric pieces for each side of the cushion back, adding 1.5cm/⅝in seam allowance all around. Press under 1cm/½in along the top long edge of the large panel and 2cm/¾in along the long lower edge of the smaller panel. Zigzag-stitch the raw edges.

2 With the zipper tab on the right-hand side, pin the pressed edge of the large panel along the bottom of the zipper teeth, then tack (baste) and machine stitch in place.

3 Pin the small panel over the zipper so that it overlaps the other panel by 3mm/⅛in. Working from the right side, tack the other side of the zipper. Using a zipper foot attachment, stitch the zipper.

4 Pin a tassel to each corner of the front cover before stitching the front and back together. Alternatively, thread the tassel cord into a large-eyed needle and insert it into the finished cover from the right side.

basic cushion with a semi-concealed zipper

This method of inserting a zipper is used when the cushion is circular or an unusual shape. The zipper is inserted, either horizontally or vertically, across the widest part of the cushion back, depending upon the cushion shape, and in a place where it will be less conspicuous.

you will need

- paper and pencil for template
- round cushion pad
- fabric, for the cushion front and back
- dressweight zipper
- fringing
- sewing kit

tips for basic cushion with a semi-concealed zipper

- To calculate the length of fringing on a circular cushion multiply the diameter by 3.14.
- Zigzag-stitch close to the stitching to finish raw edges and trim the excess fabric.

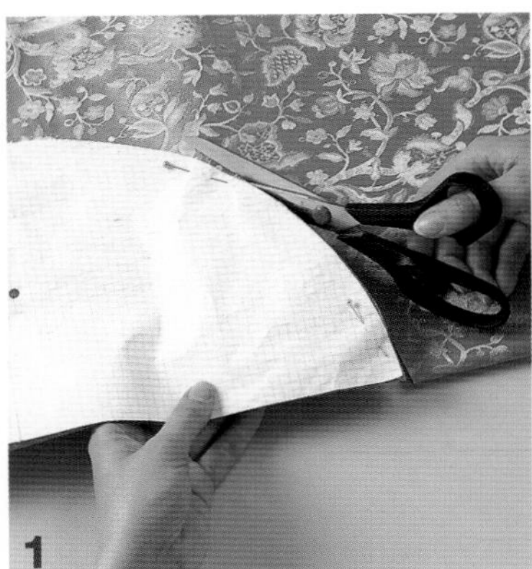
1

2

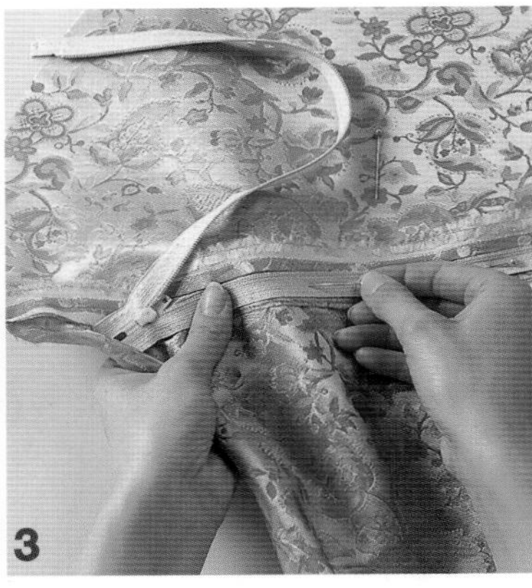
3

1 Draw a paper template the same size as the cushion pad adding 1.5cm/⅝in all round. Cut one cushion front. Fold and cut the template in half across the centre line. Use one piece to cut out two back panels, adding 1.5cm/⅝in seam allowance to the straight edge.

2 Centre the zipper along the straight edge of one back panel and mark its position. Remove the zipper. Place the two halves of the cushion back right sides together.

3 Stitch the seam at each end up to the marks. Tack (baste) the section of seam inbetween the stitching and then press the seam open. With the zipper open and right side down, align the teeth with the seam, and pin in place. Tack along one side of the zipper, 3mm/⅛in from the teeth. Close the zipper, then pin and tack the other side, again 3mm/⅛in from the teeth.

4

5

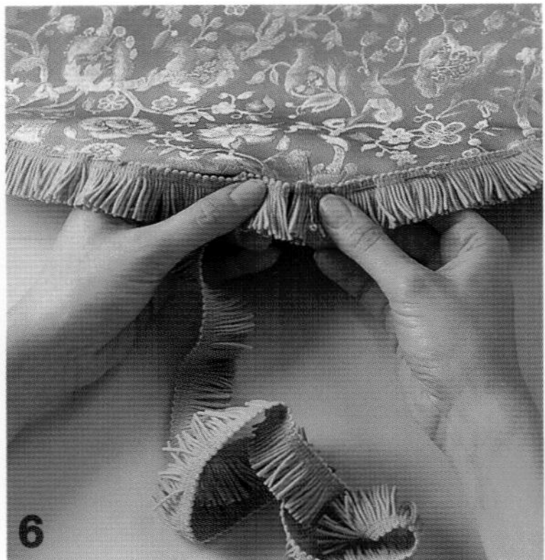
6

7

4 Stitch the zipper from the right side. At the corner, count the number of stitches into the centre and stitch the same number on both sides to make sure they are equal. Pin and stitch the front cover to the back.

5 Beginning in the middle of the bottom edge, pin the fringe or braid around the cushion cover. Tack (baste) in place.

6 Trim the ends so that they overlap slightly, then neatly fold under the ends so that they meet, and slip-stitch the join.

7 Oversew or back stitch the braid to the front of the cover, without catching the underside in the stitching. Match the thread to the braid and use the least conspicuous stitch.

piping a cushion

Piping adds a professional finish to a cushion and emphasizes its shape, particularly if the piping is in a contrasting colour to the main body of the cushion. Piping cord is available in a range of thicknesses and the piping fabric can be in a contrasting or matching fabric type to the cushion. Choose the thickness of cord according to the size of the cushion and the effect required.

you will need

- cushion pad
- one cushion front
- one made-up cushion back
- 5mm/¼ in wide piping cord
- dressweight zipper (optional)
- bias strips (see basic techniques)
- sewing kit

tip for piping a cushion

Join the ends of the piping in the centre of the bottom edge of the cushion using one of the methods described in the basic techniques chapter.

1 Cut a cushion front and make a cushion back, adding a zipper if desired. Cut bias strips wide enough to fold over the piping cord leaving a 1.5cm/⅝in seam allowance. Pin the bias strips around the cord and stitch close to the cord, using a zipper foot attachment.

2 Pin and tack (baste) the piping around the edge of the cushion front with raw edges facing outwards. Snip into the seam allowance to allow the piping to bend around the corners.

3 If using a zipper, open it slightly. With right sides together, pin the front and back covers together. If the fabric is slippery, such as velvet, tack them together first. Stitch as close as possible to the piping cord, using a zipper foot attachment. Trim the corners and turn through.

1

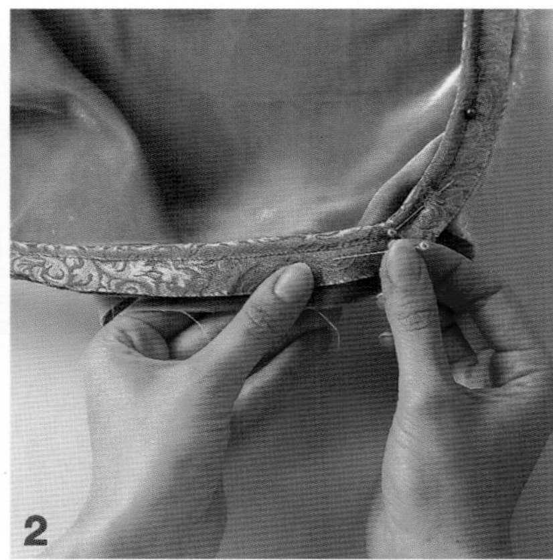

2

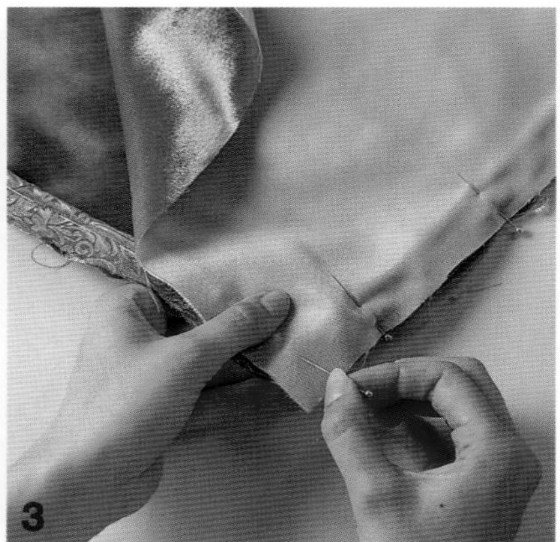

3

frilled cushion

A frill gives a cushion a pretty, feminine look. It can be made from matching fabric or a contrast such as lace or ribbon. To find the length of frill required for a circular cushion, measure around the outside edge of the cushion pad and then double the length. For a square or rectangular cushion, allow four times the length plus four times the depth.

you will need

- cushion pad
- one cushion front
- one made-up cushion back
- fabric, for the frill
- sewing kit

tip for frilled cushion

Add piping around the edge of the front panel before pinning the frill in place.

1

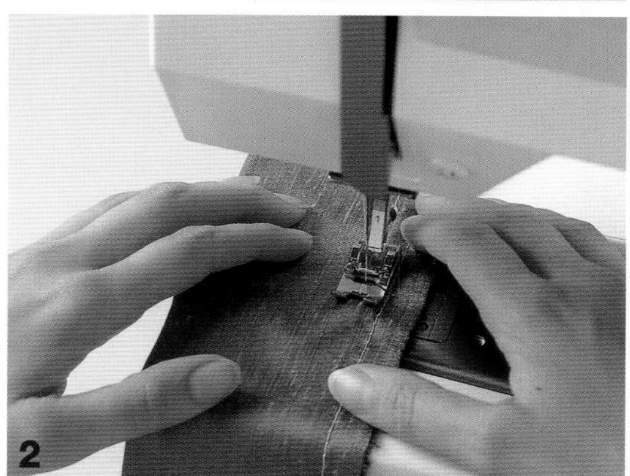

2

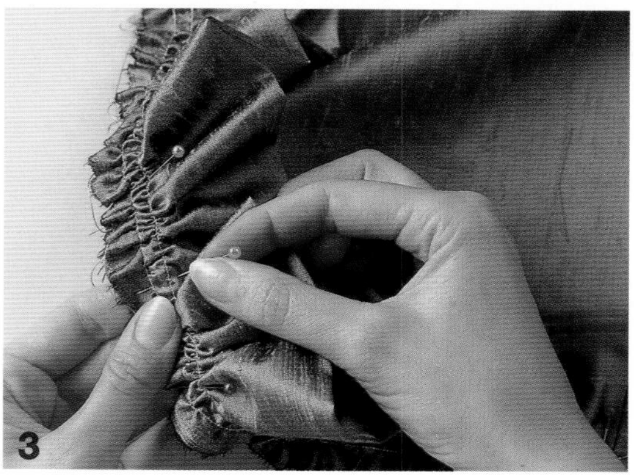

3

1 Cut a cushion front and make a cushion back, adding a zipper or envelope opening as desired. Decide on the width of the frill, usually about 8cm/3in. Cut sufficient strips of fabric to fit around the cushion, twice this width, plus 3cm/1¼in seam allowance. Join the strips together at the short ends into a continuous loop with plain seams. Press the seams open and trim to 5mm/¼ in.

2 Fold the frill in half widthways, right side out and raw edges aligned. Sew a row of gathering stitches at each side of the seamline, using a long machine stitch. Start a new thread at each join rather than stitching all the way around.

3 Fold the frill into four. Mark the cushion cover into quarters. Pin the frill to the cover, aligning the folds and marks, then pull up the gathers evenly. Adjust, allowing slightly more fullness at the corners. Tack (baste) in position and stitch.

basic cushion with a back envelope opening

An envelope opening is a good alternative to a zipper. If the two hems overlap by less than 10cm/4in, a fastening such as buttons or poppers (snaps) will be needed to hold the edges together.

you will need

- paper and pencil for the template
- cushion pad
- fabric, for the cushion front and back
- sewing kit

tip for basic cushion with a back envelope opening

Reverse stitch along the side seams where the hems overlap for extra strength.

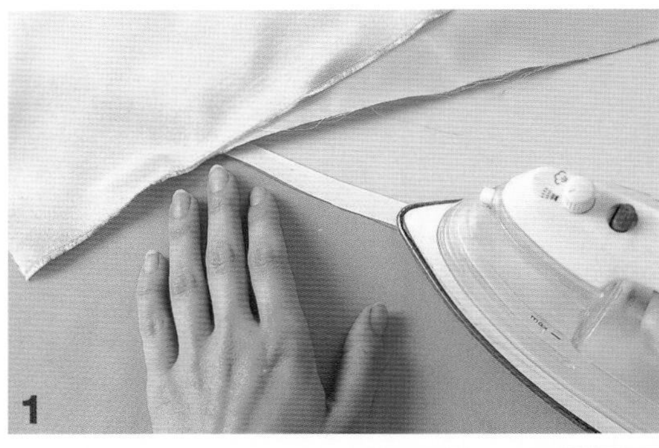

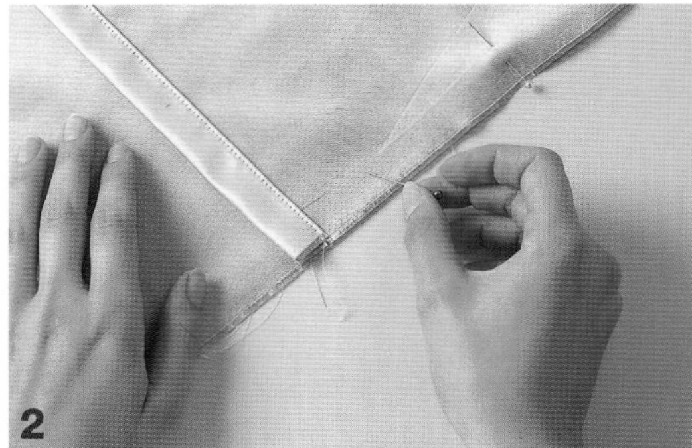

1 Draw a paper template the same size as the cushion pad and cut it in half widthways. For the cushion back, cut out one panel this size and a second panel about 15cm/6in longer, adding 1.5cm/⅝in seam allowance all around each side. Press under a 2cm/¾in hem on each panel where they will overlap and stitch. Cut out a full-size piece of fabric for the front cover, adding 1.5cm/⅝in seam allowance all around.

2 Place the front cover right side up. Pin the back panels to the front along the top and bottom edges with right sides together. Overlap the hems, keeping the larger panel on top and pin in place.

3 Stitch the front and back together using a 1.5cm/⅝in seam allowance. Trim across the corners and turn through.

above *Envelope openings are an easy alternative to inserting zippers and a good first project.*

basic cushion with a front envelope opening

An overlap makes an attractive feature on the front of a cushion. It can be horizontal or vertical. For a centre opening, plan the overlap so that the buttons are positioned in the centre of the cushion.

you will need

- fabric, for the buttons
- button kit
- cushion pad
- fabric, for the cushion front and back
- sewing kit

tip for basic cushion with a front envelope opening

If the overlap is off-centre make sure the size of the panels are in proportion to the finished cushion.

1

2

3

1 Decide what size buttons you wish to use and how many are needed to fit across the cushion pad. Cover the buttons with a contrast fabric, using a button kit (see basic techniques).

2 For the two halves of the cushion front, cut a piece of fabric 30cm/12in wider than the cushion pad, adding 3cm/1¼in seam allowance to the width. Cut the fabric in half widthways, then measure an 8cm/3in turning on each cut edge and fold under to the wrong side. Cut the fabric for the back cover, allowing 1.5cm/⅝in seam allowance all around.

3 Allowing for the seams, space the buttons right side down along the folded edge of one panel. Position the buttons at least half the width of the button away from the fold and insert pins to mark the length of the buttonholes, allowing an extra 3mm/⅛in ease. Stitch the buttonholes and cut between the stitching.

4 Overlap the two front panels so that the buttonhole side is on top. With right sides together, pin the back cover on top and trim any excess fabric from each end. Stitch, reverse stitching where the panels overlap for extra strength. Turn through to the right side. Mark the position of the buttons and sew in place.

Oxford cushion

A classic Oxford cushion has a plain flat flange around the edge of the cushion pad. The flange is a flat fabric border created by cutting the cushion cover extra large and stitching a line around the edge before inserting the cushion pad.

you will need

- paper and pencil for the template
- cushion pad
- fabric, for the cushion front and back
- sewing kit

tips for Oxford cushion

- Use a piece of masking tape to mark the width of the flange on the needle plate before beginning to stitch.
- The size of the flange should be in proportion to the size of the pad. A 5cm/2in flange is ideal for a 40cm/16in pad.
- A basic back envelope opening is the neatest method for this type of cushion.

1

2

3

4

1 Measure the cushion pad and add the flange width all around. Draw a paper template adding 1.5cm/⅝in seam allowance and cut out a piece of fabric to this size for the front cover. Cut the template in half widthways and cut out one back panel this size. Cut out another back panel 15cm/6in longer. Press under or pin a 2cm/¾in hem on each panel where they will overlap. Stitch.

2 With rights sides together, pin the back panels along the top and bottom edges to the cushion front. Overlap the hems, keeping the larger panel on top.

3 Stitch the front and back together with a 1cm/½in seam, reverse stitching along the side seams where the hems overlap for extra strength. Trim across the corners to reduce bulk.

4 Turn the cushion cover through to the right side, ease out the corners carefully and press. Pin and tack (baste) around the cover 5cm/2in from the stitched edge. Stitch just inside the tacked line. Remove the tacking threads and insert the cushion pad.

flap cushion

A flap is a simple way to make an opening in a cushion cover. It can be held in place with a sash or with a fastening such as buttons, ties or poppers (snaps). The depth of the flap depends on the shape of the cushion as it has to be sufficient to lie flat, but it is usually at least one-third of the depth of the front panel. On a narrow, rectangular cushion the flap can come halfway down the front of the cushion.

you will need

- **paper and pencil for the template**
- **one cushion pad**
- **fabric A, for the cushion front and facing**
- **fabric B, for the cushion back and flap**
- **fabric C, for the tie**
- **25g/1oz wadding (batting)**
- **sewing kit**

tip for flap cushion

Cut a strip of scrap fabric and tie around the cushion pad to find the length required for the sash.

1 Draw a paper template the same size as the cushion pad, adding the flap to the top edge. Cut out a back cover and a facing to the size of the template, adding 1.5cm/⅝in seam allowance all round. Pin the facing and back cover right sides together and mark the depth of the flap plus the seam allowance, at each side with tailor's chalk.

2 Stitch the two pieces together between the marks, reverse stitching at each end of the flap for strength. Snip into the seam allowance at each side, trim across the corners and turn through.

3 Cut out the front panel to the size of the template minus the flap, adding 10cm/4in for the facing. Turn under 5mm/¼in along the facing edge and stitch. With right sides together, pin the front panel to the back cover. Turn over the facing at the top of the front panel and pin in line with the flap as shown.

4 Stitch around the remaining three sides, reverse stitching at each end for strength. Zigzag-stitch the seam allowance and trim neatly.

5 Cut two pieces of fabric long enough to fit around the cushion and tie at the front. Cut the ends at 45°. Cut a piece of thin wadding (batting) the same size and pin to one side. Stitch, leaving a gap for turning.

6 Trim the wadding close to the stitching and trim across the corners to reduce bulk. Turn the sash through and press lightly. Slip-stitch the gap. Tie the sash around the finished cushion.

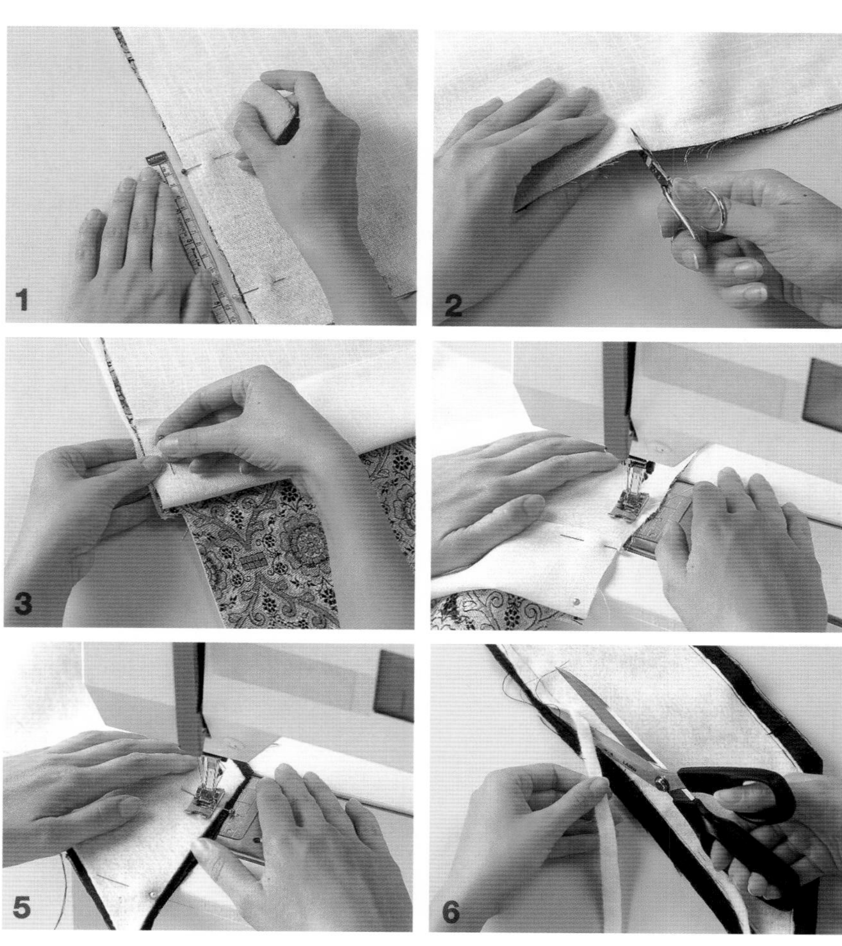

heart-shaped cushion pad

Small, shaped cushions add interest rather than comfort to a group of scatter (throw) cushions. If you make the pad yourself the cushion can be any simple shape that you like. Stuff the pad with feathers, polyester stuffing or foam chips.

you will need

- paper and pencil for the template
- calico
- stuffing
- sewing kit

tip for heart-shaped cushion pad

Use a "featherproof" weight of calico to prevent feathers escaping from the cushion pad.

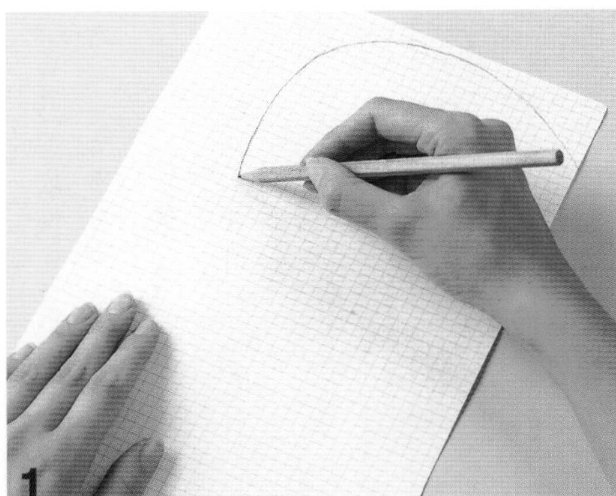

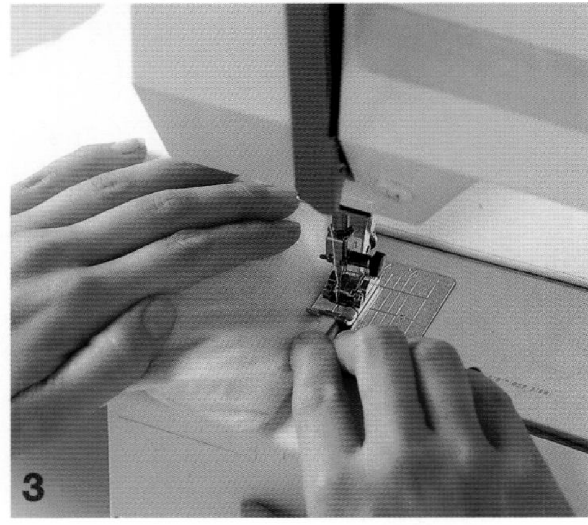

1 Draw the desired cushion shape on paper. Use this as a template to cut out two pieces of calico, including 1.5cm/⅝in seam allowance all round. Tack (baste) the two pieces together.

2 Stitch around the edge, leaving a gap along one of the straighter edges. If you are making a heart shape, snip into the "V" at the top and notch the curves. Turn through and stuff firmly with your chosen filling.

3 Pin the gap closed and stitch the edges together by machine, or slip-stitch the opening shut.

heart-shaped cushion cover

Making a shaped cushion cover is not difficult, especially if you have made the cushion pad yourself. It is actually very easy to make the pad, and that way you will be confident that the cover you make will be exactly the right shape and size.

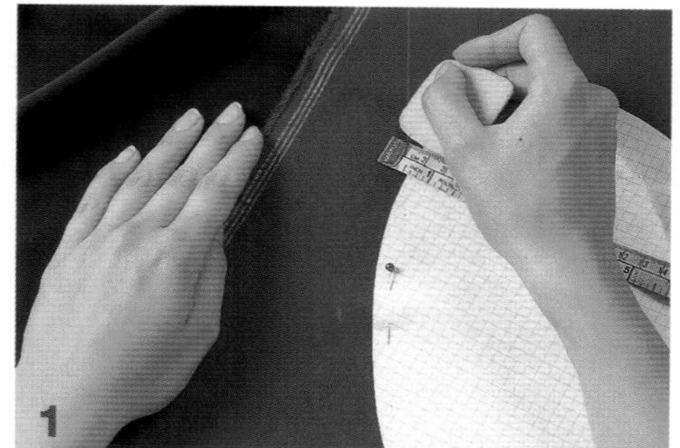
1

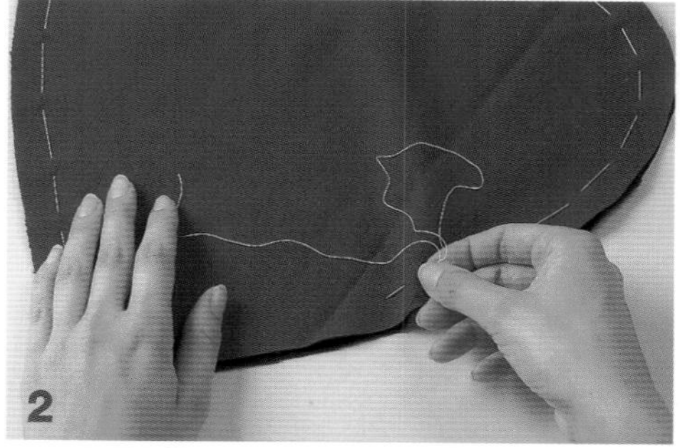
2

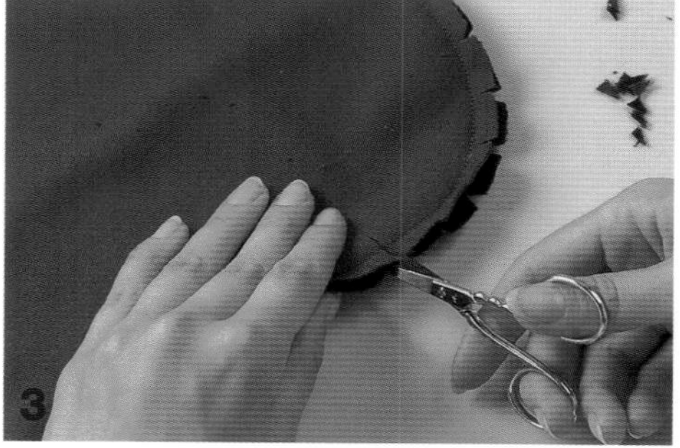
3

4

you will need

- **paper and pencil to make the template**
- **velvet**
- **sewing kit**

tip for heart-shaped cushion cover

If the cushion is quite large insert a zipper or make an envelope opening in the back across the widest part of the cover.

1 Draw round the cushion pad to make a paper template. Cut out two pieces to this size for the front and back covers, adding 1.5cm/⅝in seam allowance all round.

2 With right sides together, tack (baste) the two pieces together. Tacking is particularly important when using velvet as the fabric has a tendency to creep (move).

3 Stitch, leaving a large gap for inserting the cushion pad along one straighter side. Snip into the "V" at the top of the heart and along any inward-facing curves. Cut notches around the outward-facing curves, making the notches closer together on deeper curves. Trim across the point of the heart.

4 Turn the cushion cover through and insert the pad. Pin the gap closed and slip-stitch securely.

round box cushion

Box cushions have a gusset separating the front and back panel. The cushion pads, which can be bought in similar shapes and sizes to ordinary pads, also have a gusset. Box cushions usually have a zipper opening in the centre of the gusset along the back edge.

you will need

- paper and pencil to make a template
- round box cushion pad
- fabric
- dressweight zipper
- two covered buttons (see basic techniques)

tip for round box cushion

When adding the buttons, pull together firmly to make an indent on the flat sides of the cushion.

above *Tied buttons keep the cushion in a flat shape.*

1

2

1 Measure the cushion pad to make a paper template. Cut out the template, adding 1.5cm/⅝in seam allowance all round. Cut one front and one back cover using the template. Measure the depth of the cushion pad. Cut out one piece of fabric the depth of the pad plus 6cm/2½in for seam allowances, and the length of the zipper, plus seam allowances.

2 To make the zipper panel, cut the strip of fabric in half lengthways. Place the pieces right sides together and tack (baste) along one long edge. Open out. Mark the length of the zipper in the centre and stitch the seam allowance at each end. Press the seam open and centre the zipper teeth on the tacked line. Pin in place, then tack down each side 3mm/⅛in from the zipper teeth. Stitch just outside the tacking stitches from the right side.

3

4

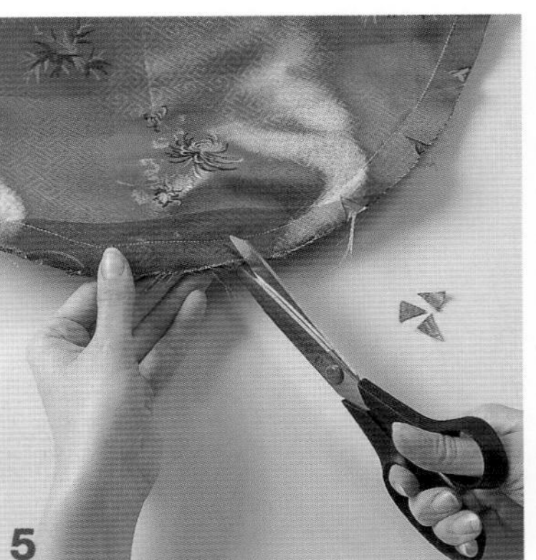

5

6

3 Cut out the rest of the gusset, adding 1.5cm/⅝in seam allowance all round. With right sides together, stitch one end of the gusset to the zipper panel and press the seams open. Pin in place around the front cover.

4 Pin the other end of the gusset to the zipper panel. Remove several pins and stitch the gusset ends together. Open the zipper. Pin the back cover in place.

5 Stitch the cushion back and front in place. Notch the curves. Turn the cushion cover through and insert the cushion pad.

6 Mark the centre front and back with pins. Using strong thread and a long needle, thread a button on to one side. Push the needle right through the pad. Thread on the other button on the other side. Fasten off the thread securely.

square box cushion with piped edge

Piping defines the edges of a box cushion and is particularly effective in a contrast colour. For an unusual effect, back muslin with a contrasting firm fabric.

above *Backing the lightweight muslin with calico stabilizes the finished project.*

1 Cut a back and front cover the size of the cushion pad plus 1.5cm/⅝in seam allowance all round. Cut the same from muslin. With wrong sides together, steam press each muslin piece to each backing piece. Tack (baste) the layers together around the edge.

2 Make up the required length of piping (see basic techniques). Pin the piping along the edge of the right side of the front and back covers. Snip into the raw edges of the piping at the corners. Join the ends and stitch in place using a zipper foot attachment.

3 Cut a gusset to fit around three sides of the pad. Fit a zipper into the remaining side and make the gusset into a continuous strip. With right sides together, tack the gusset in place between the front and back. Stitch close to the piping and turn through.

you will need

- square cushion pad
- backing fabric
- muslin
- contrast fabric for piping
- piping cord
- dressweight zipper
- sewing kit

tip for square box cushion with piped edge

Before fitting the back cover, snip into the gusset at each corner to ensure that it is absolutely square.

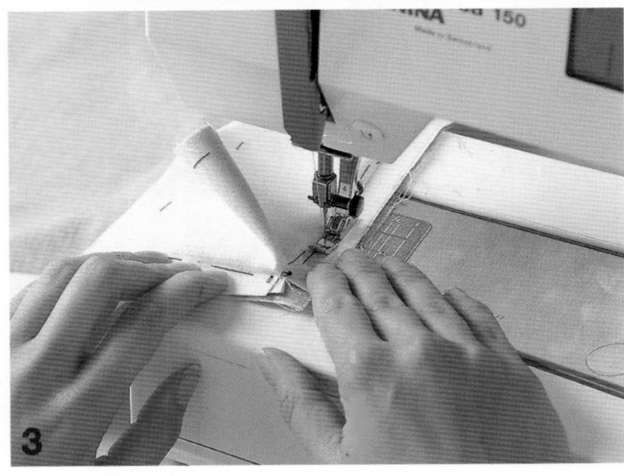

right *These box cushions have been made without piping.*

bolster cushion with gathered ends

Bolster cushions are an ideal armrest or headrest for a sofa or bed. Add a tassel or button at each end of the bolster to finish the ends.

To calculate the amount of fabric needed for a bolster, measure the length and circumference of the bolster pad. The length of fabric for the gathered ends is the circumference of the pad and the width is equal to the radius. The cover needs an opening wide enough for the bolster pad to be inserted along the side seam, so fit a zipper, or alternatively slip-stitch the gap once the pad is in place.

above *Buttons or tassels add a decorative finish.*

you will need

- **bolster cushion**
- **main fabric**
- **contrast fabric**
- **piping cord**
- **button kit**
- **zipper (optional)**
- **sewing kit**

tip for bolster cushion with gathered ends
Trim the piping cord flush with the seam to reduce bulk.

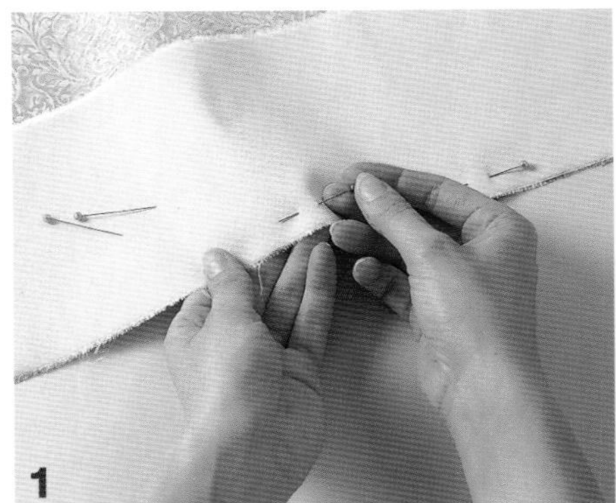

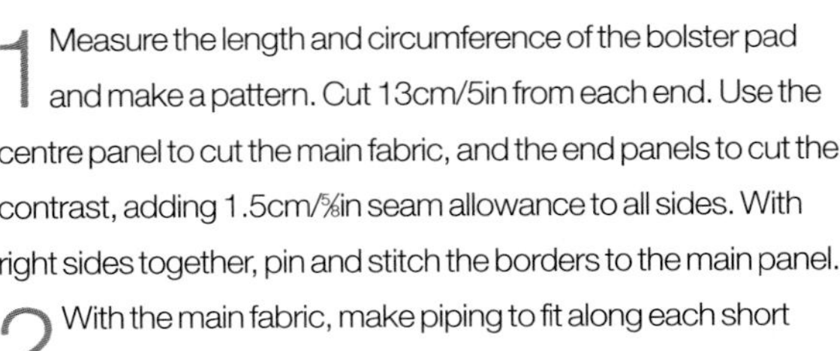

1 Measure the length and circumference of the bolster pad and make a pattern. Cut 13cm/5in from each end. Use the centre panel to cut the main fabric, and the end panels to cut the contrast, adding 1.5cm/⅝in seam allowance to all sides. With right sides together, pin and stitch the borders to the main panel.

2 With the main fabric, make piping to fit along each short end of the bolster (see basic techniques). Pin and tack (baste) in place with raw edges aligned.

3 For the gathered ends, cut out two lengths of contrast fabric, the length of the bolster's circumference and as wide as the radius, plus 1.5cm/⅝in seam allowance. Stitch in place, sandwiching the piping. Matching the seams, stitch the side seam, leaving a gap. Insert a zipper if desired. Press.

4 Stitch two rows of gathering threads around each end of the bolster. Pull up the threads tightly.

5 Holding each gathered end in turn, wrap a strong thread around just below the gathers. Fasten off securely. Turn the bolster cover through the side opening.

6 Cover two large buttons, using a button kit. Thread them into the centre of the gathers, one at each end of the bolster, then stitch the thread ends in securely. Insert the bolster pad and slip-stitch the gap if you do not have a zipper.

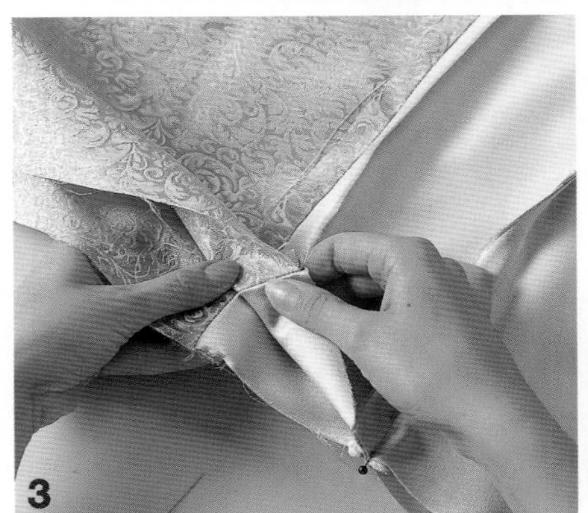

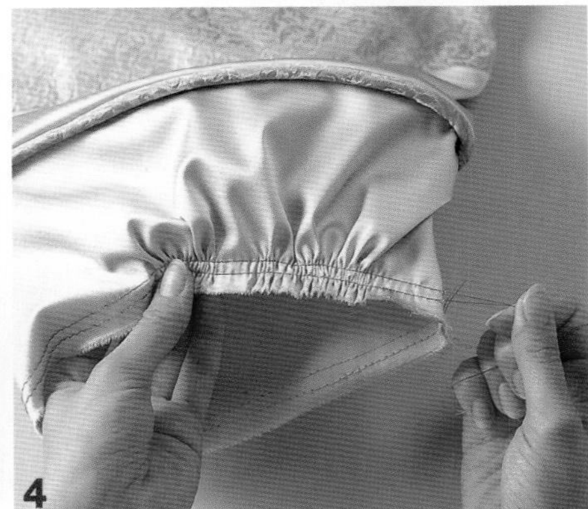

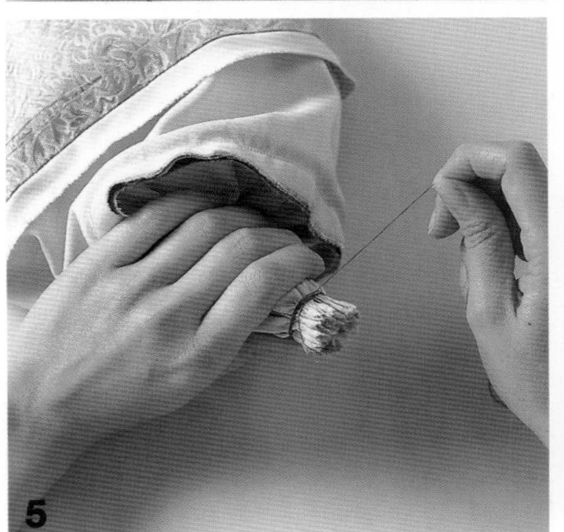

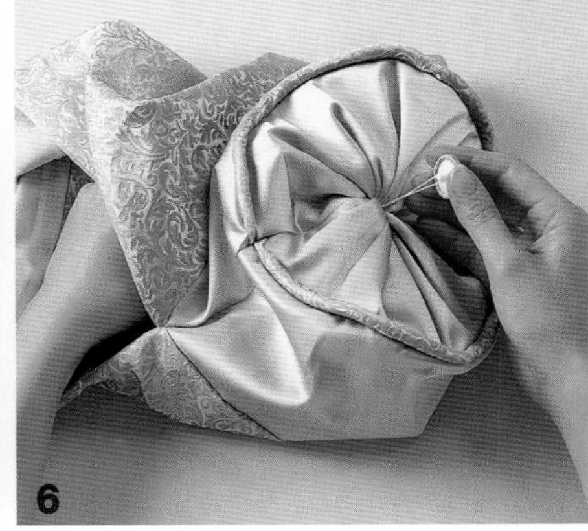

flat-end bolster cushion

This bolster cover has plain instead of gathered ends, with piping to define the shape. Using contrast fabric for the ends creates an elegant effect.

you will need

- **bolster cushion pad**
- **paper and pencil to make a template**
- **main fabric**
- **contrast fabric**
- **piping cord**
- **dressweight zipper (optional)**
- **sewing kit**

tips for flat-end bolster cushion

- **When stitching a circle, work at a slow speed and feed the fabric at a slight angle to create a smooth curve.**
- **Join the ends of the piping by stitching a seam and trimming the piping cord so that it runs right round the circle.**

1 Draw a paper template to fit the end of the bolster pad and add 1.5cm/⅝in seam allowance. Using contrast fabric cut out two circles.

2 Measure a length of piping cord to fit around the bolster ends. Cover in the main fabric (see basic techniques). With raw edges aligned, pin the piping around the edge of each contrast circle. Join the ends neatly and stitch using a zipper foot.

3 Cut out the main panel to fit the bolster pad, adding1.5cm/⅝in seam allowance all round. With right sides together, pin the long edges. Mark the position of the gap for inserting the pad or the zipper, and stitch from the marked point to the edge of the fabric. Add a zipper if required.

4 With right sides together, pin the circular ends to the main panel. Stitch in place close to the piping, using a zipper foot.

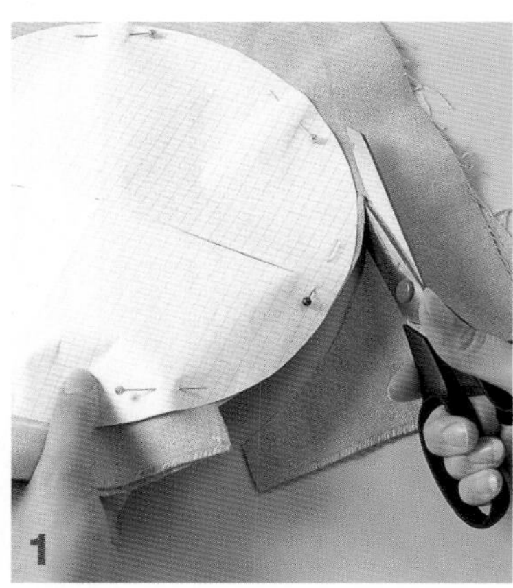
1

2

3

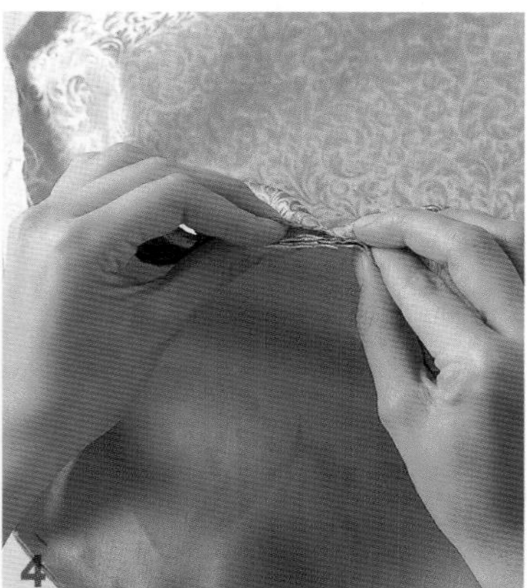
4

tied-end bolster cushion

This is the easiest style of bolster cover to make and is particularly effective as a pillow on a day bed or sofa. A rich fabric such as crushed metallic organza adds a touch of luxury to the simple design.

you will need

- bolster cushion pad
- metallic organza or lightweight fabric
- sewing kit

tip for tied-end bolster cushion

Because the seam may be visible inside the tie ends, a French seam is used to enclose the raw edges neatly.

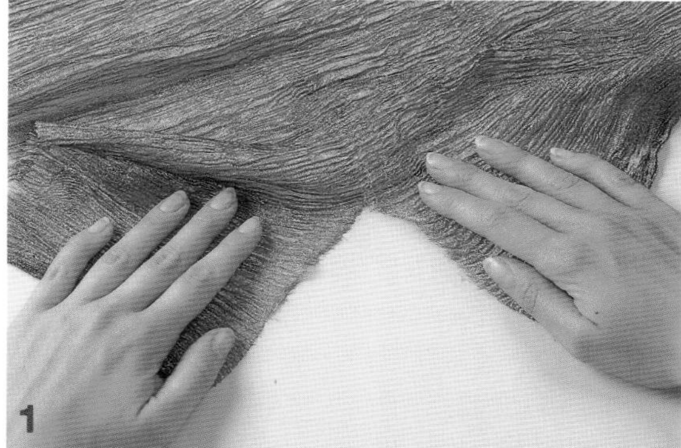

1

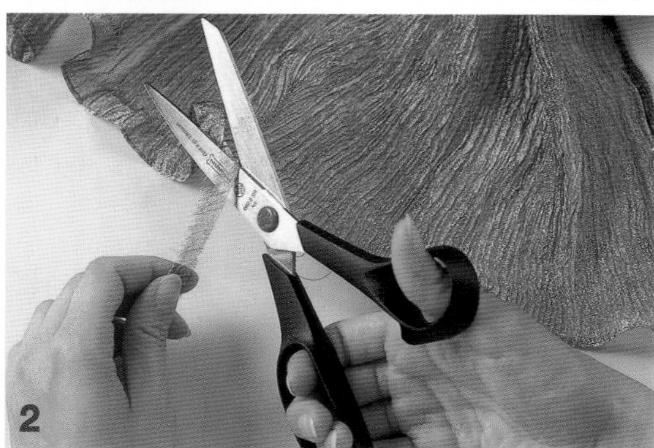

2

3

1 Measure the length and circumference of the bolster pad. Add 50cm/20in to each end for the ties and 1.5cm/$\frac{5}{8}$in seam allowance to the circumference. Pull a thread or tear carefully across the width of the fabric to straighten it before cutting, as shown.

2 Turn under 1cm/$\frac{1}{2}$in along the edge of the fabric at each short end and stitch, stretching the fabric slightly as you go. Trim the seam allowance close to the stitching. Fold the stitched edge over to make a narrow hem at each end and stitch again on top of the previous stitching. Fold the fabric in half lengthways, wrong sides together to make a tube, and stitch a 7mm/$\frac{3}{8}$in seam. Trim the seam to 5mm/$\frac{1}{4}$in and press open. Turn the tube through to enclose the raw edges and stitch a second 7mm/$\frac{3}{8}$in seam. Turn right side out.

3 Tie the fabric in a knot at one end. Insert the bolster pad and tie the other end.

flat cushion with ties

A beautifully tailored cushion will transform a hard wooden chair, making it more comfortable and much warmer to sit on. Use a fabric to match curtains or other cushions already in the room. Add fabric or ribbon ties to hold it securely in position.

you will need

- paper and pencil to make a template
- main fabric
- contrast fabric
- blunt tool
- wadding (batting)
- sewing kit

tip for flat cushion with ties

Cut a strip of fabric and tie around the chair back to find the exact length of tie required.

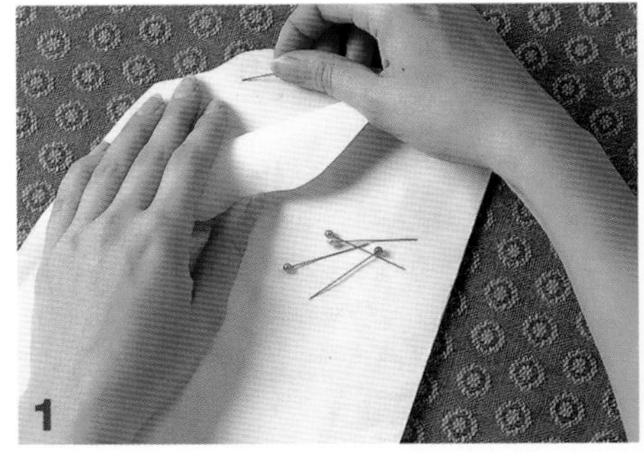

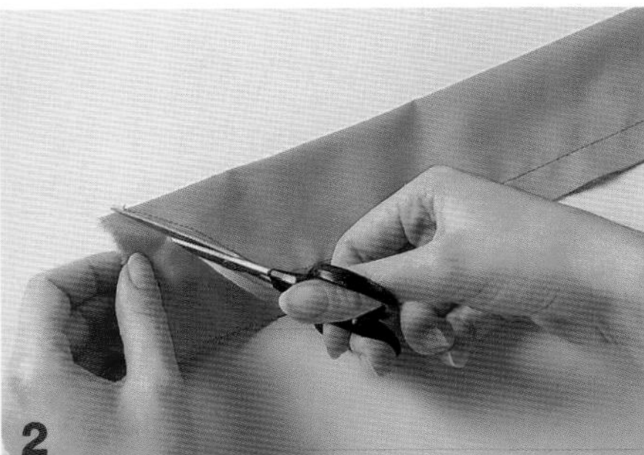

above *Ties can be as plain or flamboyant as you like.*

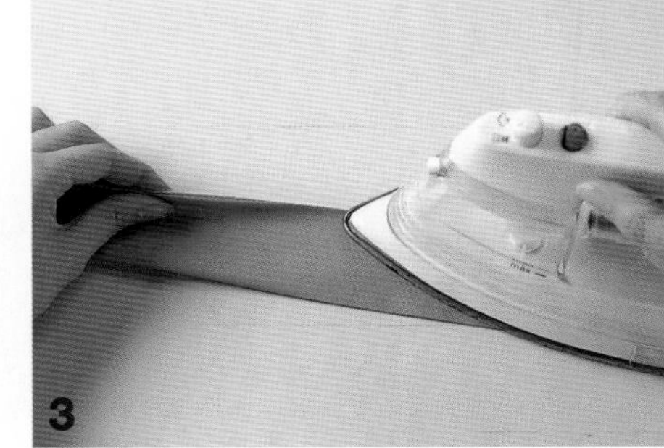

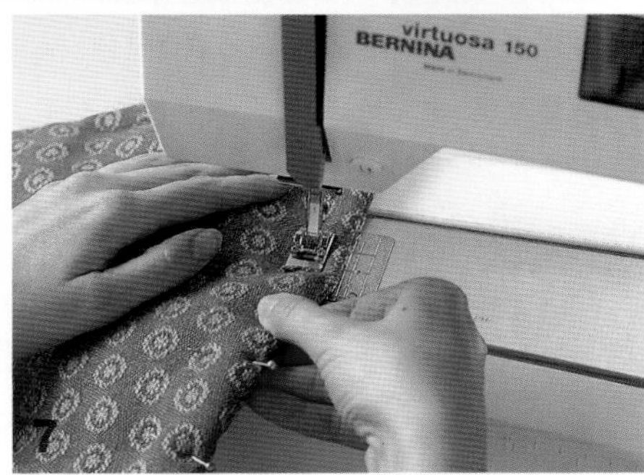

1 Make a paper template of the chair seat, carefully marking the position of the back of the seat for the ties. Fold in half. Place the fold along the centre of the fabric design, if any, and pin. Open out the template and cut out two full-size fabric pieces, adding 1.5cm/⅝in seam allowance all round.

2 Cut four strips of contrast fabric, each 8 x 50cm/3 x 20in. With right sides together, fold each in half lengthways. Stitch down the long side and diagonally across one short end to create a neat finish for the end of the tie. Trim the excess fabric from the pointed end to reduce bulk.

3 Turn the ties through and ease out the point with a blunt tool. Roll the seam between your thumb and finger, then press.

4 With raw edges aligned, pin two ties to each back corner of a cushion piece, on the right side. Bundle the tie ends in the centre.

5 Place a second cushion piece on top of the first, with right sides together, then add a piece of wadding (batting) cut to size on top. Pin the layers together then stitch around the edge, leaving a gap along the back for turning through.

6 Notch the outward-facing curves and turn through. Ease out the seams and pin all the way around. Slip-stitch the gap.

7 Using a slightly longer stitch, top-stitch around the cushion 1.5cm/⅝in from the stitched edge. Mark the lines with a fabric marker if you are unsure. Tie the pad in position on the chair back.

frilled stool or chair cushion

A frill is a very pretty way to finish a cushion. The main difference between a stool and a chair cushion is the positioning of the ties. On a stool, the ties are attached underneath the frill so that they can be tied around the legs. A chair cushion has no frill along the back and the back ties are attached to the end of the frill at both corners.

you will need

- paper and pencil for a template
- main fabric
- 100g/4oz wadding (batting)
- contrast fabric for frill and ties
- sewing kit

tip for frilled stool or chair cushion

Fold the frill on to the reverse side of the cushion and leave for a day or two to "set" the frill so that it will hang neatly.

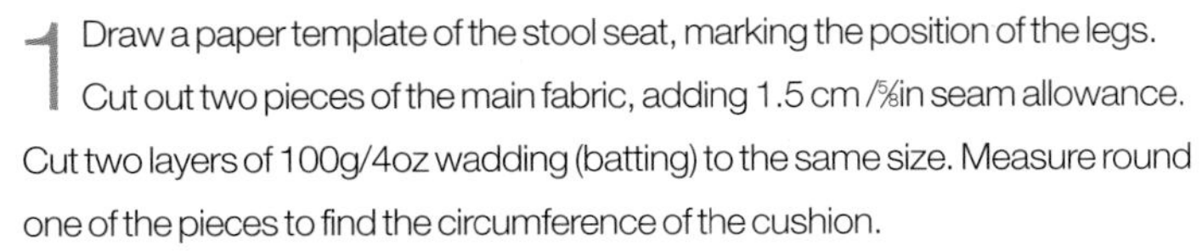

1 Draw a paper template of the stool seat, marking the position of the legs. Cut out two pieces of the main fabric, adding 1.5 cm/⅝in seam allowance. Cut two layers of 100g/4oz wadding (batting) to the same size. Measure round one of the pieces to find the circumference of the cushion.

2 Decide on the depth of the frill and cut strips twice this measurement, plus 3cm/1¼in seam allowance. The frill length is twice the circumference of the cushion. With right sides together, stitch the lengths together to make a circle. Fold in half lengthways, with wrong sides together. Fold the frill into four equal pieces and press the folds. Stitch two rows of gathering stitches between the folds.

3 Tie off one end of each set of gathering threads. Fold the top cover piece in four and mark the quarter sections. Pin the frill to each section matching the folds to the quarter sections, then gently pull the gathers up to fit. Distribute the gathers evenly then pin the frill and cover together. Tack (baste) the gathers and remove the pins. Stitch in place.

4 For each tie, cut one strip of fabric 8cm x 1m/3in x 1yd. Fold each in half lengthways, right sides together. Stitch around the raw edges, leaving a gap in the centre. Trim the seams and across the corners. Turn through and slip-stitch the gap. Fold in half and pin the fold to the cover in the position of each stool leg. Bundle the ends in the centre. Place the bottom cover on top with right sides together, then two layers of wadding, and pin. Stitch, leaving a gap for turning. Notch round the curved edge, turn through and slip-stitch the gap. Press the frill.

1

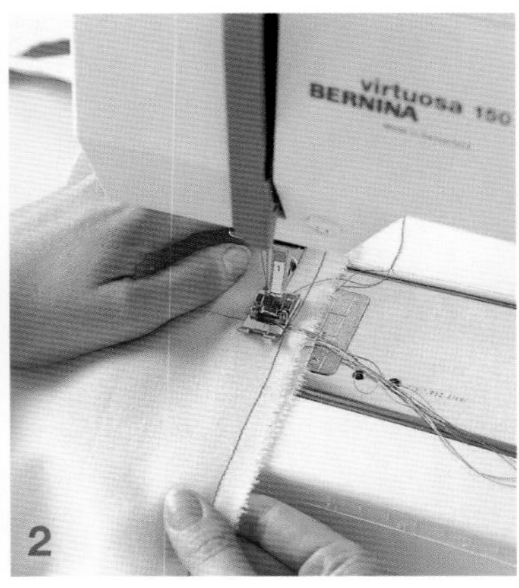

2

3

4

box-style shaped cushion

Some chairs are more comfortable with the addition of a thick, fitted cushion. Make a template of the shape required, then have the cushion pad cut to shape from foam. Stitch a layer of wadding (batting) to the foam.

you will need

- paper and pencil to make a template
- main fabric
- foam, cut to size, for the pad
- dressweight zipper
- piping cord
- foam pad cut to size
- sewing kit

tip for box-style shaped cushion

For added softness, cover the foam with a layer of wadding before covering.

1 To make a template, tuck a large sheet of paper into the chair, folding in the edges until it is the exact size, then trim to fit. Cut out two pieces of fabric to this size, adding 1.5cm/⅝in seam allowance all round. Measure the curved area to find the optimum zipper length.

2 Cut out the gusset for the straight side the depth of the cushion pad plus the seam allowance. Cut the gusset for the curved zipper edge 3cm/1¼in wider, then cut in half lengthways and tack (baste) together. Mark the length of the zipper and stitch the seam at each end. Tack, then stitch the zipper in place. Stitch the main gusset to the zipper gusset.

3 Make two lengths of piping to fit around the cushion pad (see basic techniques). Beginning at the centre back, pin the piping around the edge, snipping the piping at the corners. Overlap the ends and trim the cord back to the seamline. Tack in place.

4 With right sides together, pin the gusset around the cushion pad, with the zipper along the curved edge. Stitch in position. Open the zipper slightly. Pin the other side of the cover in place. Stitch and turn through. Fold the pad in half to insert it into the cover.

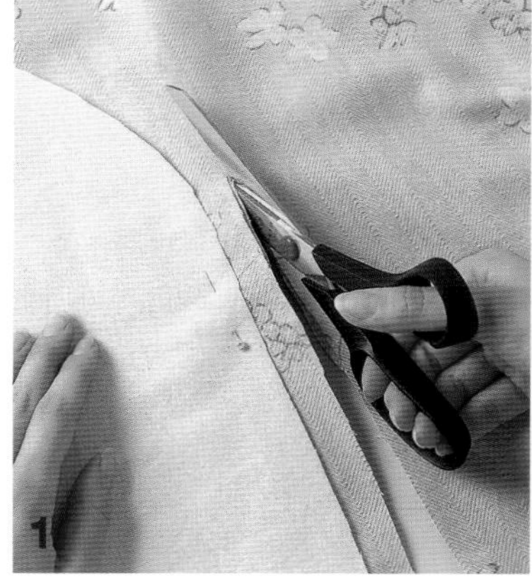
1

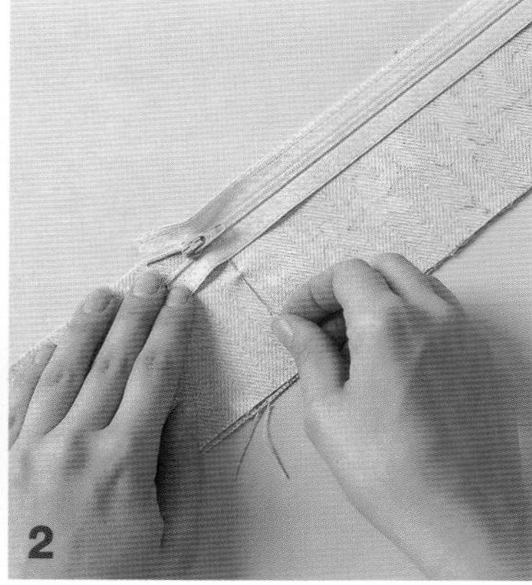
2

3

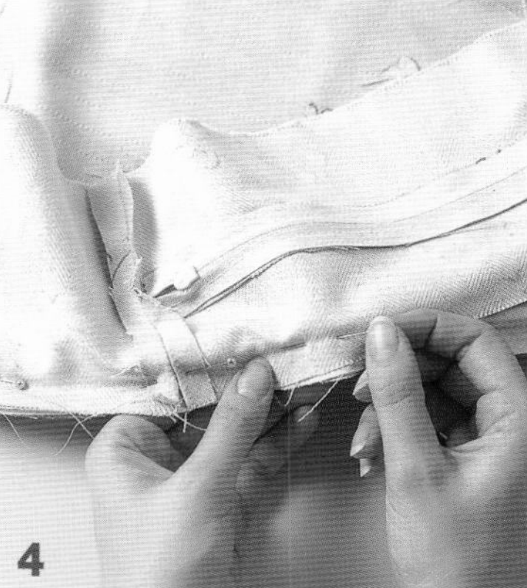
4

fleece pet bed

Fleece is the ideal fabric for a pet's bed as it doesn't crease and can be washed easily. The size of the bed will depend on the size of your pet. This bed is 70cm/28in diameter and 15cm/6in deep.

you will need

- paper and pencil to make a template
- calico for lining
- fleece fur fabric
- upholstery zipper
- washable polyester stuffing or polystyrene beads (styrofoam pellets)
- sewing kit

tips for fleece pet bed

- The zipper has to be as long as possible so that the liner can be inserted easily. Buy zipper tape by the metre, long enough to fit halfway round the gusset.
- See basic techniques for instructions to insert the zipper.

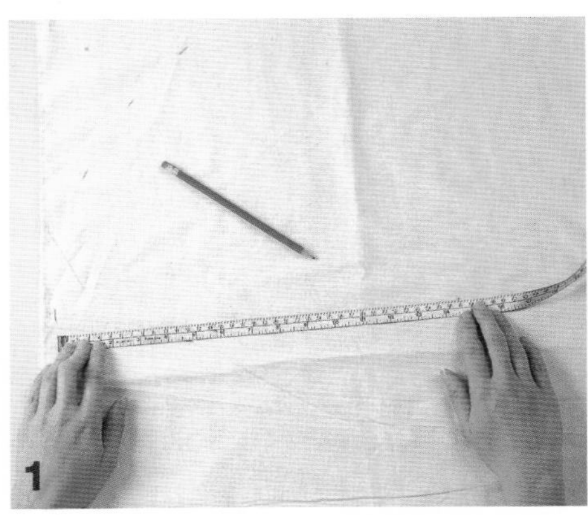

1

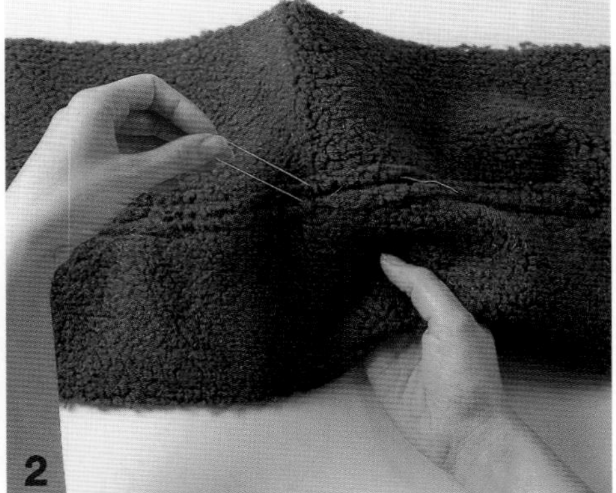

2

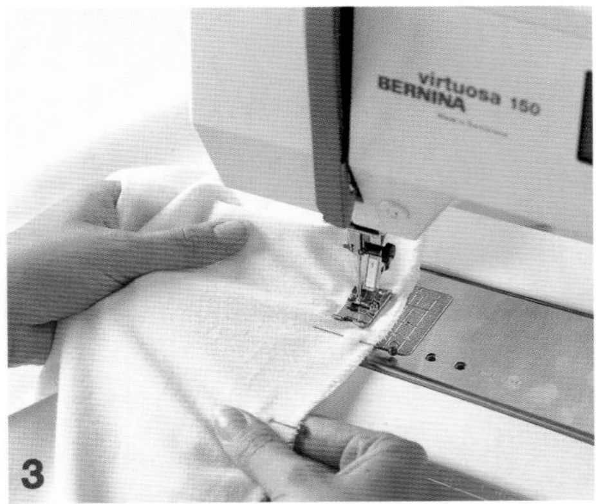

3

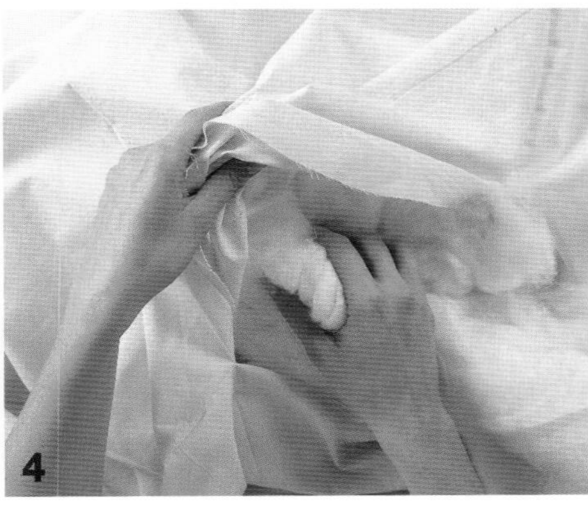

4

1 Draw a circle the required size of the base on to calico. Cut two pieces for the lining plus seam allowances. Cut the same from main fabric. Measure around the circle to find the length of the gusset and add seam allowances. Cut one piece from calico and one from the fabric 18cm/7in wide.

2 From the main fabric gusset piece, cut a length 5cm/2in longer than the zipper. Cut in half lengthways then tack (baste) along one long edge, with right sides together, 1.5cm/⅝in from the raw edge. Stitch in the zipper, then pull out the tacking threads.

3 Pin and stitch the zipper panel to the rest of the gusset. With right sides together, pin the gusset to the top circle of fabric, easing in the fabric to fit. Stitch in place with a 1.5cm/⅝in seam. Open the zipper slightly. Stitch the bottom circle in position in the same way then turn the bed through. Make up the calico liner in the same way, but leaving a large gap for stuffing instead of the zipper.

4 Stuff the liner with washable polyester stuffing or polystyrene beads (sytrofoam pellets) until it is fairly firm. Pin and stitch the gap, reverse stitching for extra security. Insert the liner into the cover.

shaped beanbag

Beanbags are fun for children and make ideal seating in their bedrooms. They are easy to move around as they are so light, and this one can be hung up out of the way using the handle at the top. These measurements will make a small beanbag for a toddler or young child, and could be scaled up to adult size. Make the liner from a soft, loose-weave calico that will stretch to take the shape of the body.

you will need

- **calico for lining**
- **paper and pencil to make a template**
- **fleece fabric**
- **polystyrene beads (styrofoam pellets)**
- **sewing kit**

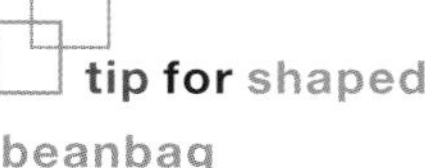

tip for shaped beanbag

Only fill the liner half full of polystyrene beads so that they have plenty of room to move about when you sit down.

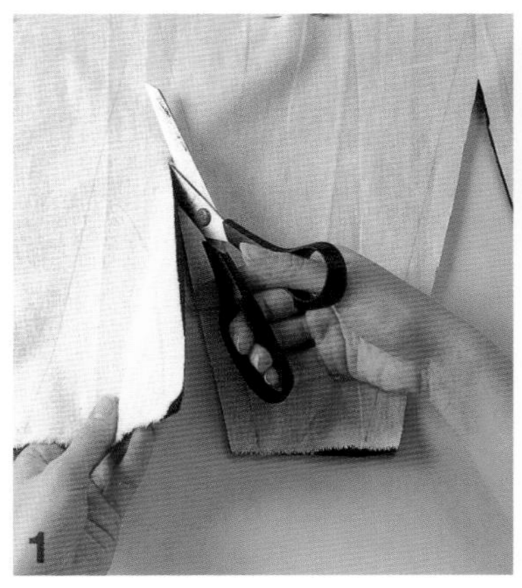

1

2

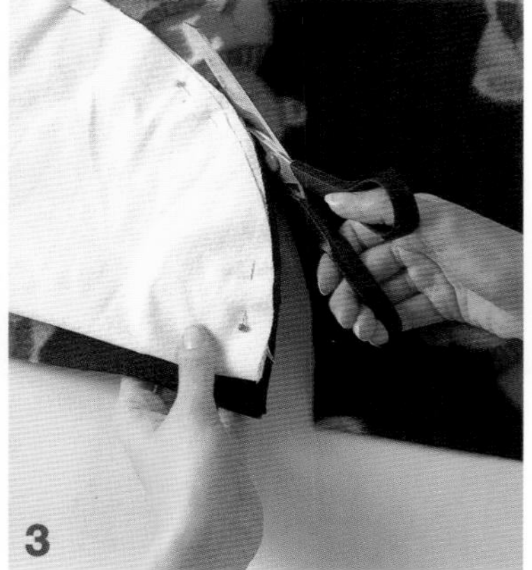

3

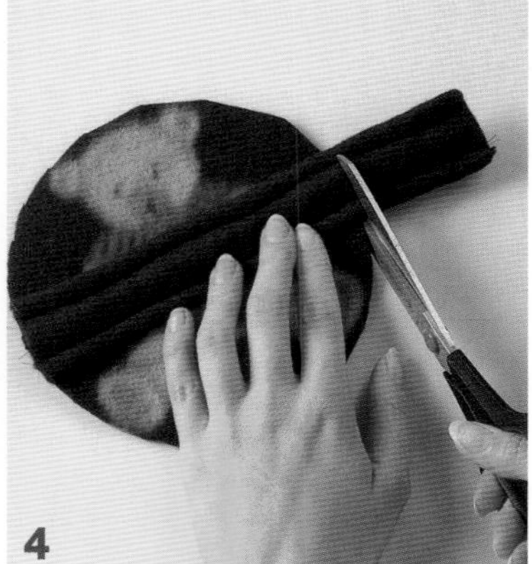

4

1 For the side lining, cut a piece of calico, 70 x 150cm/28 x 59in. Draw a line across the width 30cm/12in from one long end. The bag top shaping begins at this point. Use the pattern at the back of the book as a guide to shape the sides . Place the marked calico on top of the fleece and cut out both together, adding 1.5cm/⅝in seam allowance on the shaped sections. Separate the lining from the fleece.

2 With right sides together, stitch the straight back seam. Pin adjacent diagonal edges together and stitch. At the point, take the last few stitches along the edge of the fold and tie off the threads securely. Repeat for the calico lining.

3 For the base, cut a 50cm/20in diameter circle from calico and fold in half. Using the half circle as a template, cut two half pieces from fleece, adding a seam allowance to the straight side. Insert a zipper between the straight edges.

4 To make a handle, cut one piece of fleece 20 x 6cm/8 x 2½in. Fold in half lengthways, with right sides together and stitch the long edge. Turn right side out and centre the seam in the middle back and top stitch. To make the bag top, cut an 18cm/7in diameter circle from fleece and calico. Position the handle on the right side, trim the raw edges and pin in place. With right sides together, pin the bag top and bottom to the sides of the beanbag. Open the zipper slightly before stitching each in place all the way round. Turn the bag right side out. Make up the liner in the same way, but instead of adding a zipper to the base, use the calico base template whole and leave a large gap in the seam joining it to the bag sides. Half-fill the liner with polystyrene beads (styrofoam pellets), then stitch the gap securely. Insert the liner into the cover.

chair covers

Slipcovers are made to protect favourite upholstery, to hide faded or damaged furniture, or to completely alter its appearance. When you put a slipcover on a chair or footstool, you have the opportunity to transform a piece of furniture, adding ties, tabs and buttons as desired. Choose colours that complement your room scheme either by introducing new accent colours as a contrast or choosing solid colours that enhance existing furnishings. Slipcovers are the ideal way to freshen up a dull or dated interior scheme and can be used to ring the changes, so that the appearance of a room changes with the seasons – cool, crisp linen for summer and warm, rich colours for winter.

Slipcovers are literally clothes for furniture and as such can change the appearance of chairs, footstools or ottomans dramatically. Just like clothes, a slipcover can be casual or classic, plain or exotic depending on the style and fabric chosen. Unlike the majority of clothes, slipcovers cannot be bought off the shelf or even made to a pattern because there are so many different shapes. Each cover has to be designed individually and fitted to the particular piece of furniture. Obviously some styles of furniture are easier to cover than others but, as a general rule, a tight-fitting cover is more difficult to cut and fit than a looser style.

Don't be too adventurous to begin with – choose a footstool or an odd chair as a first project that you would like to match to other furniture in a room. Look at magazines and catalogues for inspiration and pick out features that you like, such as hemlines, trimmings or fabric, bearing in mind that the new cover should blend into its new surroundings.

There are lots of different fabrics that you can use for soft furnishings, but slipcovers should be made from a proper furnishing fabric. These fabrics are sold in wider widths than dress fabrics and are harder-wearing. They are often fire-retardant to set standards and can be washed or dry-cleaned. It is essential to pre-shrink fabric before making it up into slip covers, otherwise you may not get it back on after cleaning.

This chapter has design ideas for covering a variety of different chairs and footstools. It is unlikely that your furniture will look the same, but by reading and understanding the step-by-step instructions on pin-fitting and cutting fabrics you should be able to make a tailor-made cover for your piece of furniture.

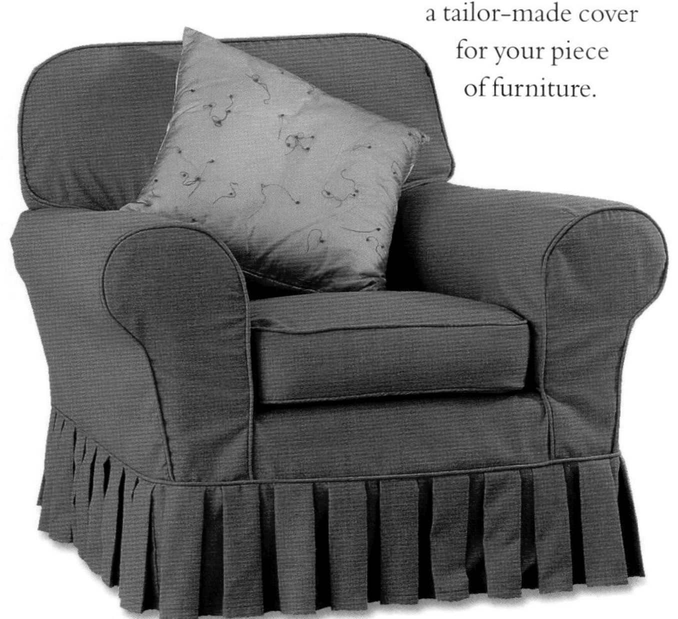

above left Simple tabs and covered buttons make an effective and attractive fastening down the back of this dining chair cover.

above Square-shaped chairs suit slip covers with flat valances and neat inverted box pleats at each corner.

right Pretty self-coloured fabric bows soften the lines of this fully fitted dining chair cover and give it a less formal look.

left Spaced box pleats use much less fabric than traditional full pleats, and add a more textural finish to the bottom edge of an armchair or sofa cover.

far left Careful use of piping makes the matching of stripes or checks on a slipcover less of a problem.

making a pattern for a dining chair

Dining chairs come in all shapes and sizes, but any of them can be fitted with a slipcover. The cover may be to protect the chair, to hide a chair that has seen better days or to make your dining room look more formal. The first thing is to create a pattern, and the easiest way to do this is by "pin-fitting" a cheap fabric such as calico or curtain lining, which will follow the shape of the chair. The pattern can then be used to cut out and make one or several slipcovers.

Each chair is different, so you need to decide the style you want to create. Is the opening to be a zipper hidden in one of the seams, or do you want a more decorative opening down the back? Do you want to cover the legs, or does the chair have elegant Queen Anne feet that you wish to show? As you begin to pin-fit, it will become obvious how the fabric is going to lie and whether darts are needed for shaping. If the chair has a shaped back, a gusset will almost certainly be required to follow the curve. The advantage of using a cheap fabric for pin-fitting is that mistakes can be made and rectified before you cut the main fabric.

right *If you are making just one slipcover, the pattern could be used as a lining for the main fabric.*

you will need

- **calico**
- **pencil**
- **sewing kit**

1 Begin with a piece of calico at least 8cm/3in larger all round than the area you want to cover. Fit the front of the chair back first, aligning the straight grain of the fabric with the centre line of the chair. Work out from the centre to the outside edges, inserting pins every 5–8cm/2–3in, and pulling the fabric to fit snugly.

2 Once you are satisfied with the fit of the calico, trim the excess fabric, leaving approximately 2.5cm/1in seam allowance along the side edges, and the bottom edge, if you have chosen to fit the seat and chair back as two separate pieces.

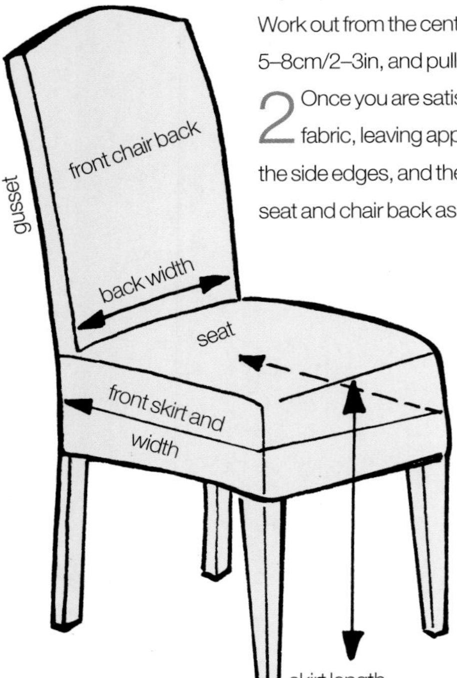

left *Each dining chair is slightly different, but the terminology used is the same. The skirt length doesn't necessarily reach the floor.*

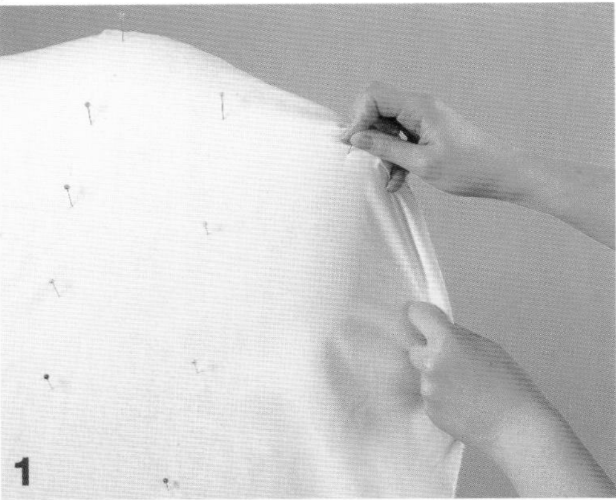

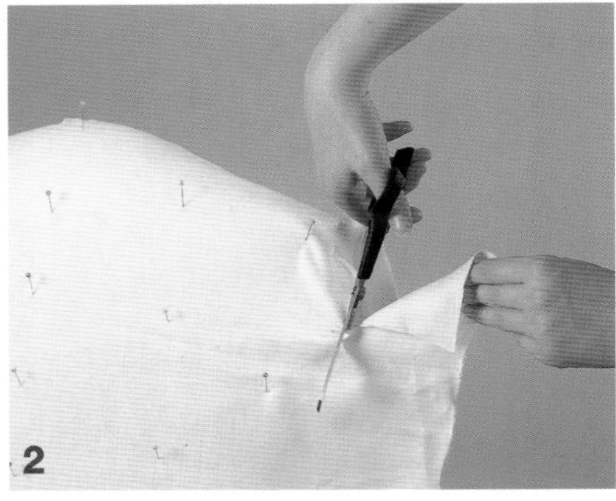

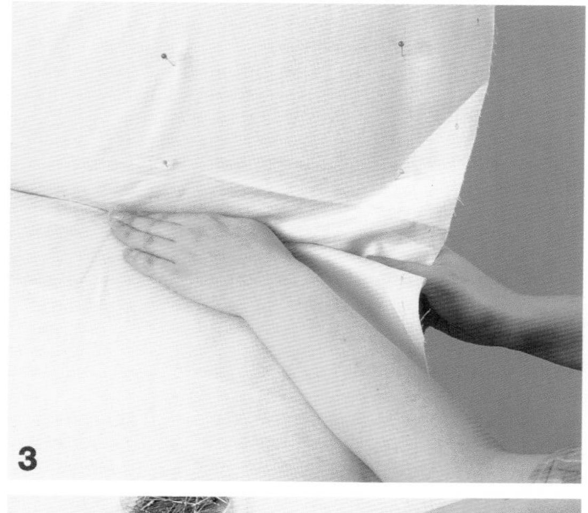
3

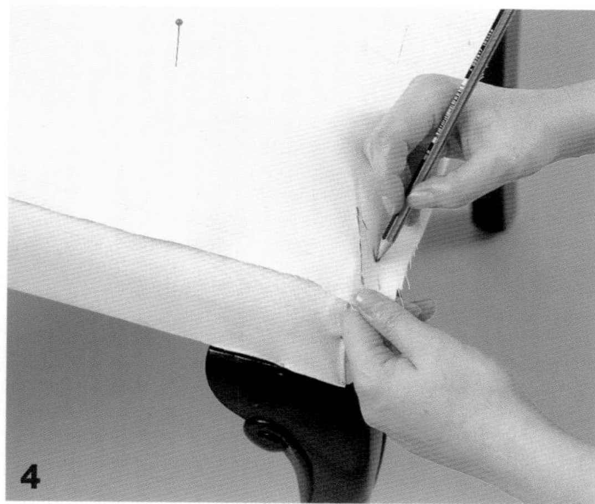
4

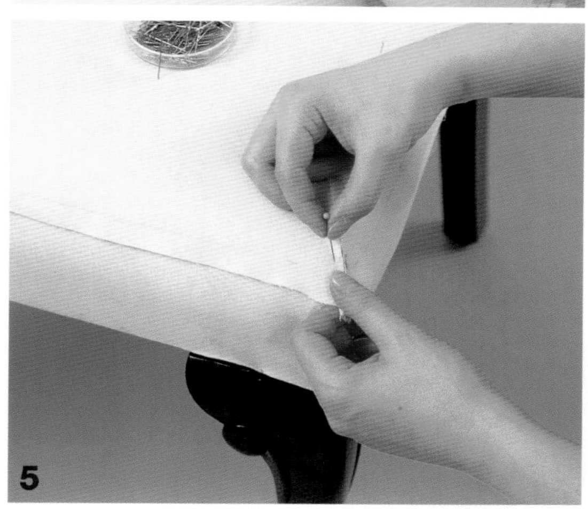
5

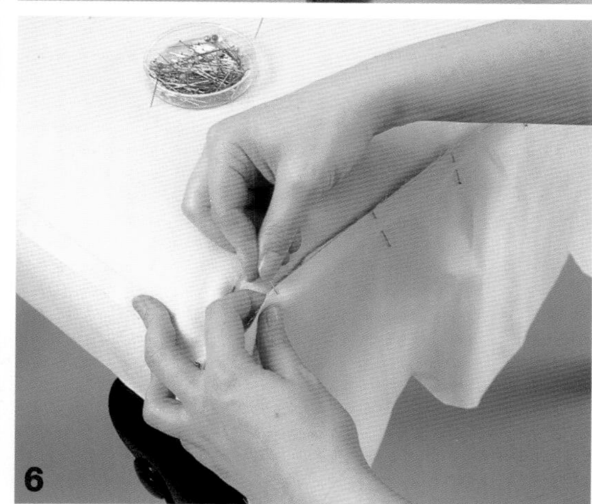
6

3 If there is a gap at the back of the chair, tuck the calico in. Otherwise, at the base of the front chair back pin-fit the panel to the seat piece.

4 If the front edge of the chair seat is curved, make a small dart on each corner to remove excess fabric. Mark the position lightly with a pencil.

5 Pin the darts and check the fit. You should check that the darts are equally spaced and exactly the same size before stitching the main fabric.

6 To make the skirt pattern, measure along the sides and front of the chair seat. Decide on the length of the skirt, and cut and piece lengths of calico the required width and long enough to accommodate any features. Ensure any seams will be placed at the back on a leg or will be hidden in a pleat. If you wish to have a decorative edge such as the scallop-edge illustrated, plan it carefully so that the design will finish neatly at each corner. You can use a small plate or saucer to create the curves. Pin the skirt to the seat.

7 If the chair back is quite thick, you will need a gusset panel to join the inside and outside chair back panels together. Measure the width of the gusset (the thickness of the chair back) and add 2.5cm/1in seam allowance. The gusset may be narrower at the top. Cut a strip of calico this width and pin to the chair front. Pin the seams, attaching the gusset to the top edge of the skirt. Repeat at the other side of the chair.

8 Fit another strip along the top edge of the chair (it may be possible to make the entire gusset from one piece of fabric). Finally, cut and fit the back chair back panel, which should be as long as the skirt. Ensure all seam allowances are trimmed to 2.5cm/1in before unpinning the calico. Use the pattern pieces to cut the main fabric.

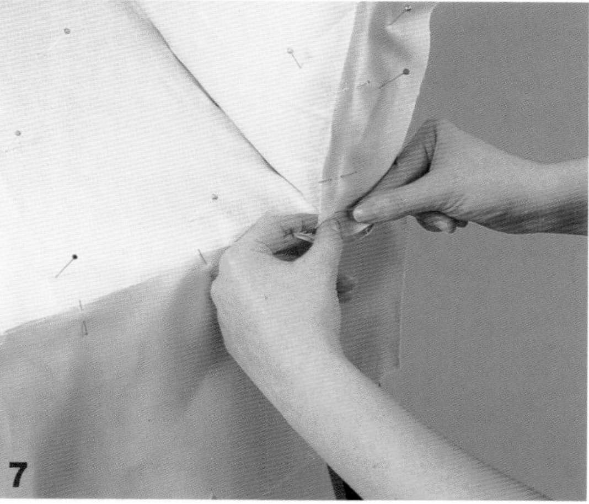
7

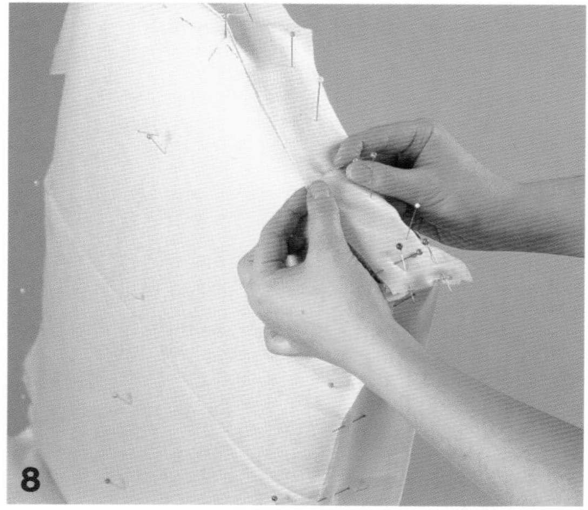
8

pleated chair back panel

Fastened with buttons and tabs, this is a distinctive, modern finish for the back of a chair cover. Quick and easy to remove for washing, it is an ideal choice for a family home. Use toning buttons or cover them in the same fabric as the chair.

you will need

- calico pattern
- washable fabric
- small, sharp scissors
- 3 buttons or self-cover button kit
- sewing kit

tips for pleated chair back panel

- Make a calico pattern first to ensure you understand the instructions before cutting into your fabric.
- For a different effect, attach a tie to each side of the pleat and tie into a bow.

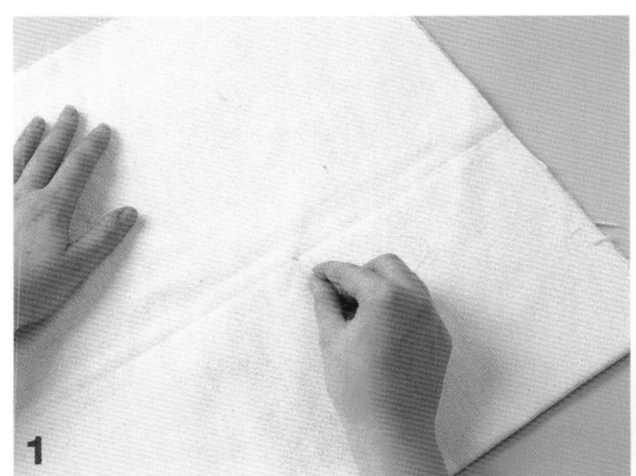

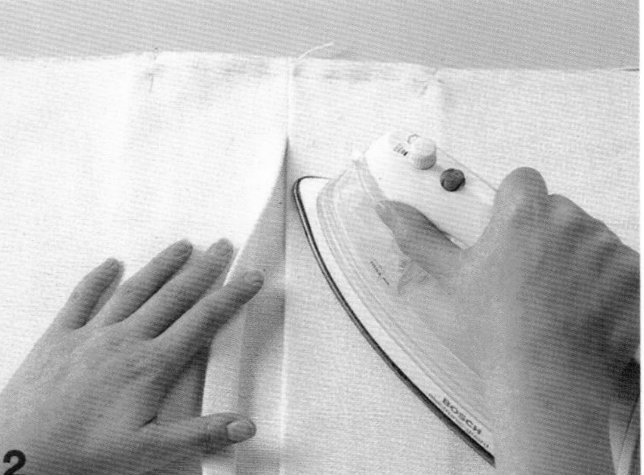

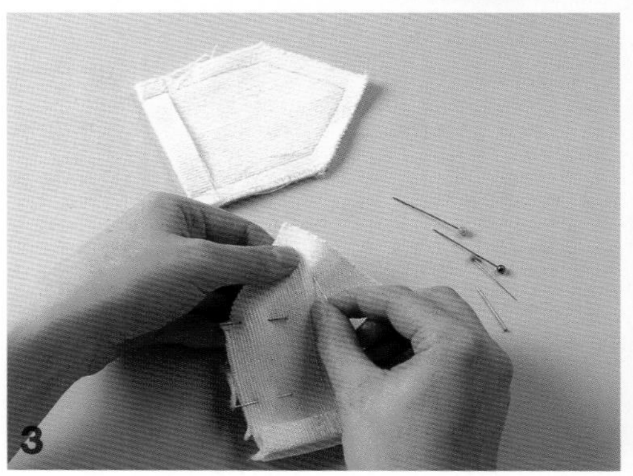

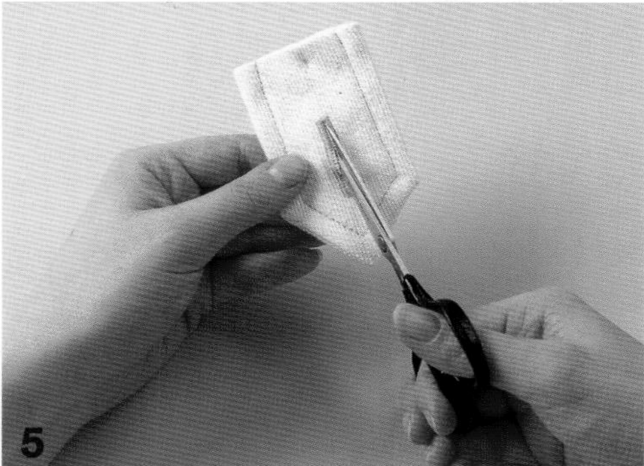

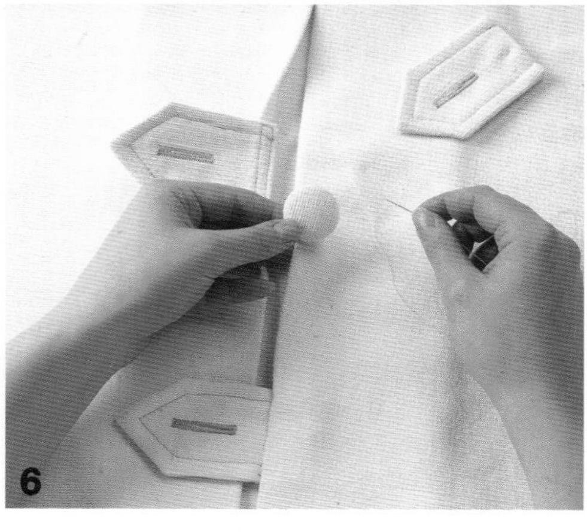

1 To make the pleat in the back panel, cut one piece of fabric 36cm/14in wider than the chair back and the same length, adding seam allowances all round. With right sides together, fold the back panel in half widthways and press. Measure 18cm/7in from the fold and tack (baste) along the 18cm/7in line. Stitch 2.5cm/1in down from the top edge, reinforcing the stitches at each end.

2 Open the pleat out so that the pressed foldline is centred behind the tacked seam. Press the pleat, then tack it in place across the top edge. Press again. Try the panel on the back of the chair and adjust to fit. Remove the tacking threads from the front of the pleat and press again.

3 Cut six tabs, each 8 x 12cm/3 x 4¾in. Cut a right-angled point at one end. Press under 1cm/½in along the short straight end of each tab. With right sides together, pin three sets of two tabs. Stitch a 1cm/½in seam around the raw edges. Trim the tab seams and cut across the corners.

4 Turn the tabs through and ease out the points. Top-stitch 5mm/¼in from the stitched edge, leaving the pressed-under edge free of stitching.

5 Mark the length of the buttonhole on each tab and stitch by machine. Cut along the centre of each buttonhole with a small pair of sharp scissors.

6 Pin the three tabs on the inside edge of the pleat, alternating them from side to side. Stitch the end of each tab securely to the inside edge only. Cover three buttons with fabric. Mark the position of each on the opposite edge to correspond with the buttonholes and stitch in place.

adding corner pleats

Corner pleats add fullness to the skirt of a slip cover and allow the person sitting in the chair to tuck their legs underneath without straining the seams. The calico pattern is extended to include the extra fabric required for the pleats before cutting the main fabric. If the fabric needs to be joined, make the seam down one of the inside edges of the pleat. Insert a zipper down one back corner seam.

above *Piping defines the chair seat, providing a clearer "fit".*

you will need

- **calico pattern**
- **fabric**
- **sewing kit**
- **piping cord (optional)**

tip for adding corner pleats

Cut the back skirt and back chair back as one continuous length for a professional finish.

1 To make the skirt pattern, measure from one back leg around the front of the chair to the other back leg. Add 60cm/24in to the total length for the pleats, and use to cut out the main fabric. Fold into three equal lengths, then press. Measure 15cm/6in in from each pressed fold and tack (baste) along the 15cm/6in line, through the two layers nearest the fold. Stitch 5cm/2in from the top edge, along the tacking line.

2 Open out the pleat so that the pressed line lies behind the stitch line. Tack along the top edge then stitch above the seamline to hold the fabric pleat. Press the pleat folds.

3 Add piping to the edge of the seat panel, if required. Pin the seat panel to the skirt, matching the centre line of each pleat to the front corners. Stitch the seam carefully, folding the skirt to the opposite side when you get to the centre seam of the pleat.

4 Attach the front of the chair back to the back edge of the seat and stitch the darts to shape the top corners or attach a gusset if required. Finally attach the back of the chair back, sandwiching piping between the two layers.

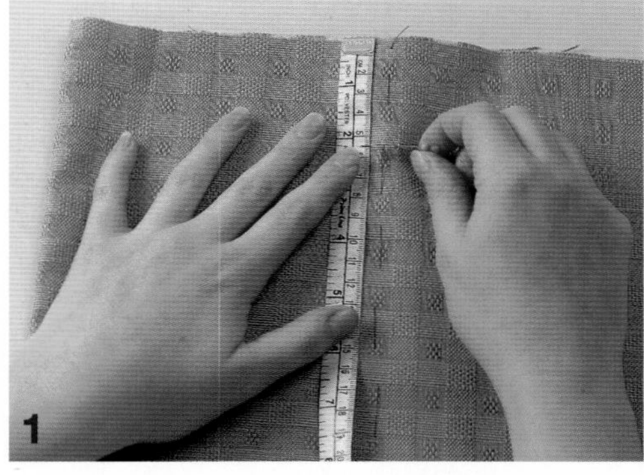

1

2

3

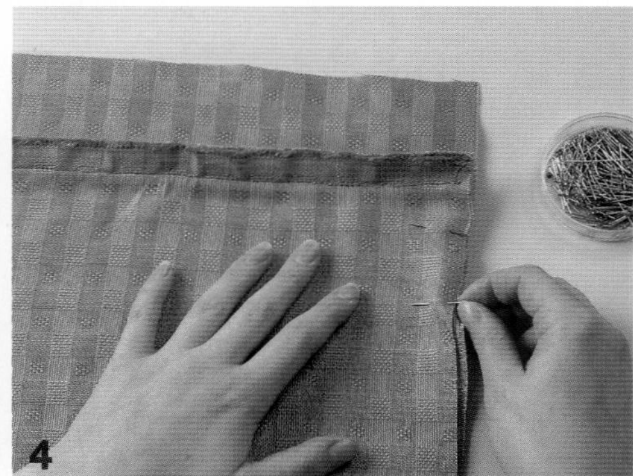

4

simple chair cover

This simple slipcover has darts at the top of the chair back instead of a gusset. Pin-fit calico to make a pattern, creating a seam between the seat and back. This seam continues round the edge of the chair, and is used to attach the front chair back to the back edge of the skirt. Fit a concealed zipper down one of the back seams. To fit a cover over a chair back that is wider at the top than the bottom, fit a zipper the full length of one of the back seams.

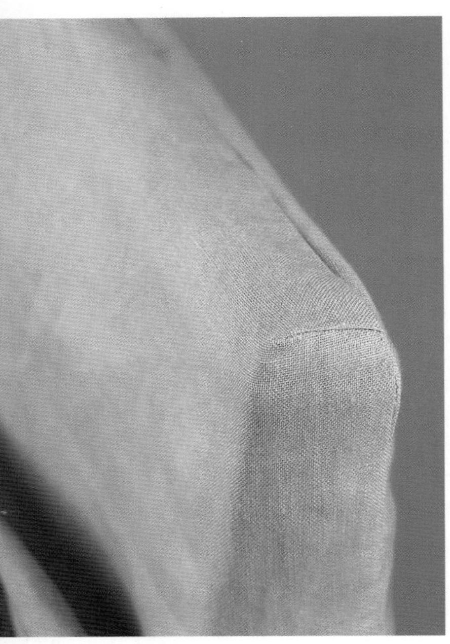

above *Darts make neat seams.*

you will need

- **calico pattern**
- **fabric**
- **invisible zipper**
- **sewing kit**

tip for simple chair cover

The skirt of this chair design is made in three pieces which have been stitched together. The back of the chair back extends down to complete the back of the skirt.

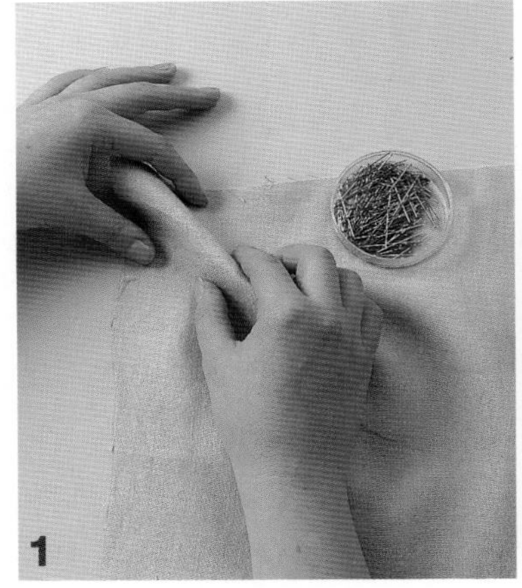

1 Cut out the fabric pieces, using the calico pattern. On the wrong side, fold and pin darts at the top corner of the front chair back. Tack (baste) in place, then check the fit on the chair.

2 Adjust the fit to ensure the fabric fits snugly over the thickness of the top of the chair. Stitch the darts in place and remove any pins or tacking stitches.

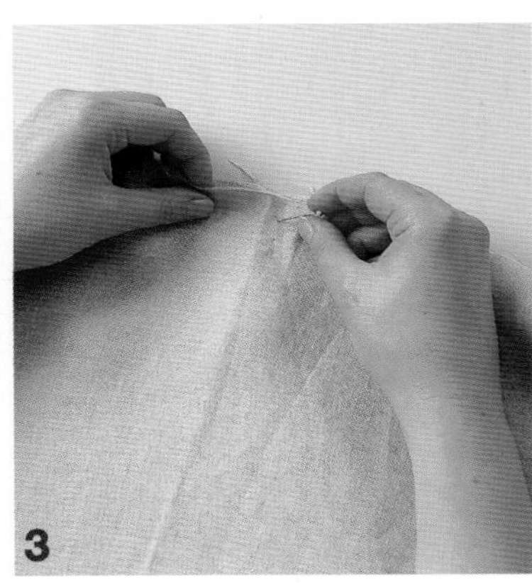

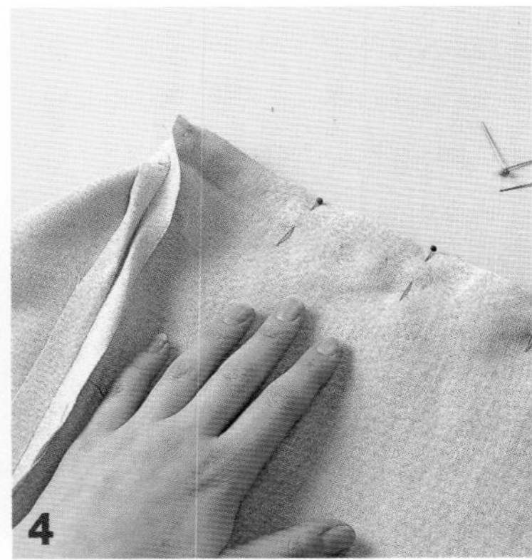

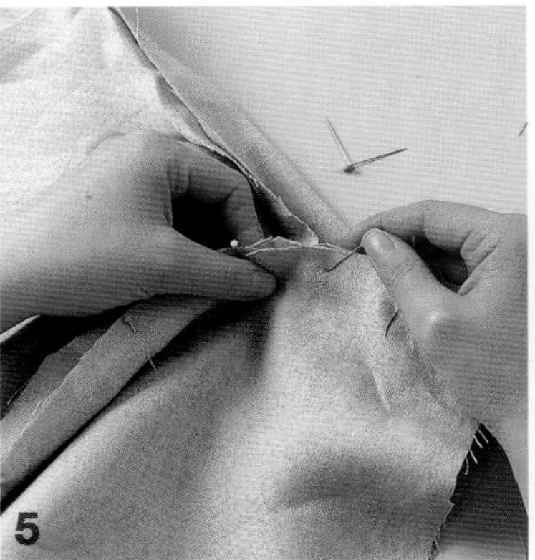

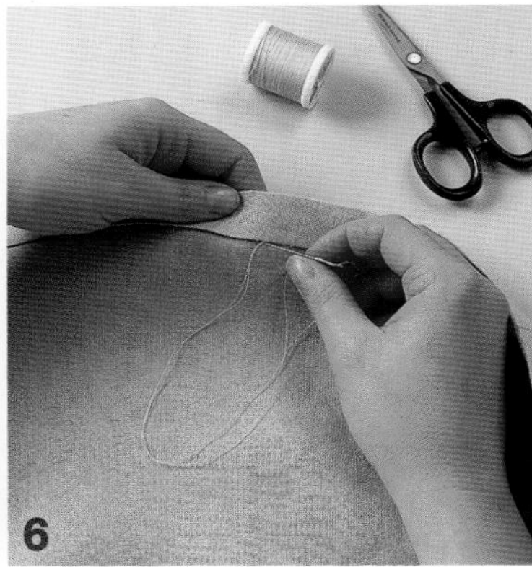

3 Pin the skirt panels together down the front seams. Stitch the seams and press open.

4 Pin the skirt around the two sides and along the front edge of the seat panel, making sure the front skirt seams are exactly on the corners. The skirt fabric will overhang the back edge of the seat panel at this stage. Stitch the seam, leaving the seam allowance free at the back edge.

5 Pin the front chair back panel to the seat panel, then on to the back edge of the skirt. This join needs to be pinned and stitched accurately, so that the three seams meet at a single point. Attach the back of the chair cover, inserting a zipper down one of the seams.

6 Fit the cover on the chair and mark the hem length. Turn up a double 2cm/¾in hem and slip-stitch.

adding a scallop edge and gusset

A gusset is the neatest way to fit a slipcover if the top edge of the chair back is shaped or curved. It is cut on the straight grain of the fabric and should be exactly the same thickness as the chair back plus seam allowances. Join the gusset at the corners of the chair back or in the centre of a curved edge, so that any pattern or nap doesn't end up upside down. Drawing round a small plate or saucer is a simple way to create an evenly scalloped edge. Plan the design so that it finishes neatly at the corners of the chair.

you will need

- **calico pattern**
- **main fabric**
- **lining fabric**
- **small plate**
- **pencil**
- **blunt tool**
- **sewing kit**

tip for adding a scallop edge and gusset

Continue the back of the chair back down to the same length as the chair skirt and cut matching scallops along the bottom edge.

1 Using the calico pattern, cut the gusset pattern pieces out of fabric so that the joins are in the least conspicuous position, and so that each gusset pattern piece matches the direction of the grain or pattern of the piece it will be joined to.

2 If the gusset panels are separate for the top and chair sides, stitch them together, beginning and finishing stitching a seam allowance' width from the raw edge of the fabric. Press the seams open.

3 Pin the gusset to the front of the chair back, matching the seams to the corners. Stitch up to the corner seam then, keeping the needle in the fabric, rotate the fabric until the next seam is lined up.

4 Attach the gusset panel to the chair back panel in the same way. Add the seat panel to the bottom of the front chair back.

5 Mark the length and width of each panel of the slipcover skirt, including the chair back, on a piece of lining. Divide the panel by the number of scallops and find a small plate to fit. Mark the shape of the scallops along the bottom edge.

6 With right sides together, stitch the skirt fabric to the lining along the pencil line. Add a lining to the skirt section of the chair back in the same way. Leave the sides and top edge open.

7 Trim the curved seam to 5mm/¼in. Notch the curved edge every 1–2cm/½–¾in. Snip into the point between each scallop.

8 Turn the skirt through and ease out the scallops with a blunt tool. Press the scalloped edge. Tack (baste), pin and stitch the skirt panels right sides together. Stitch the top edge of the skirt to the seat of the slipcover and the side edges to the chair back. Zigzag-stitch any raw edges.

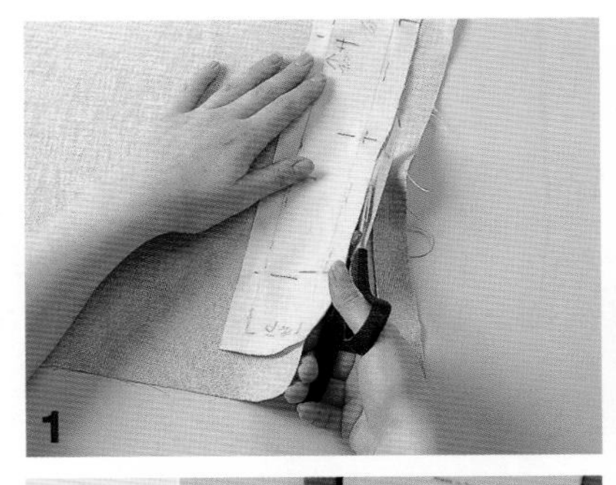
1

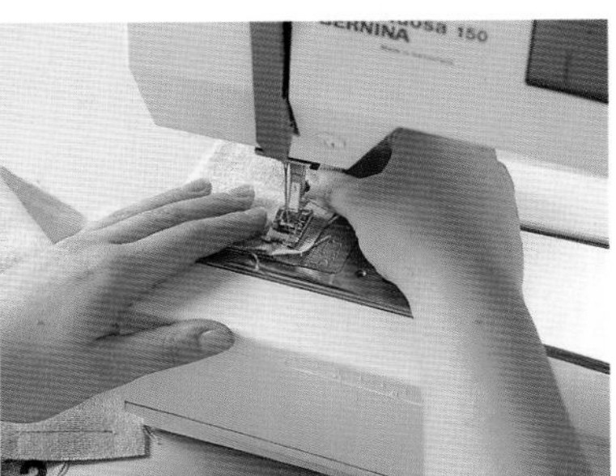

2

3

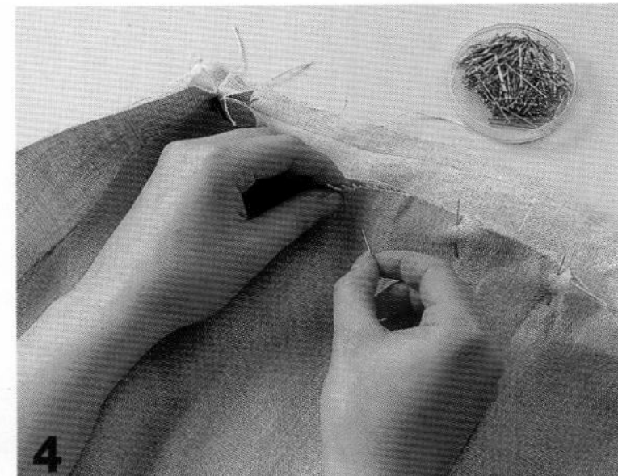
4

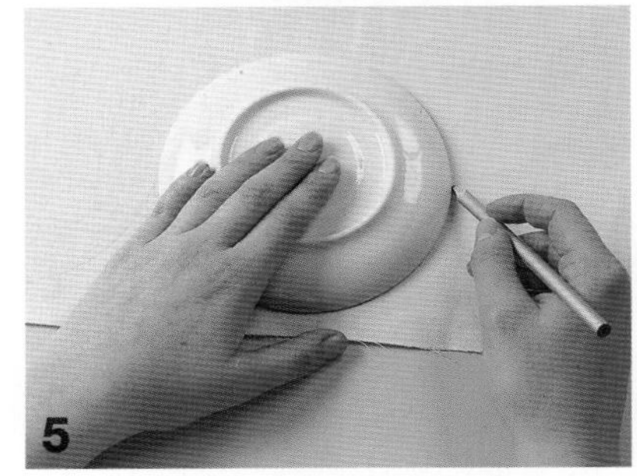
5

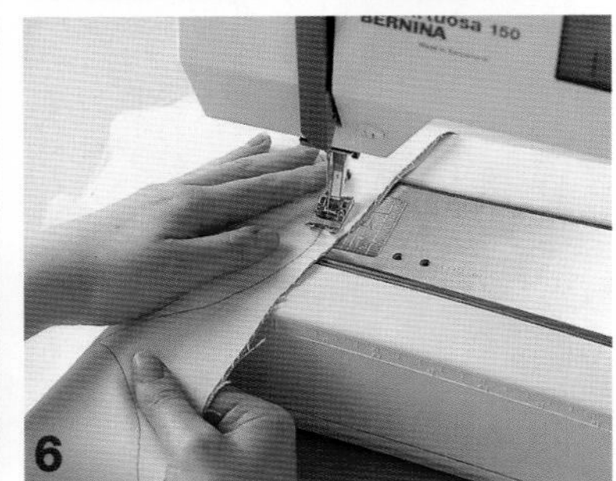

6

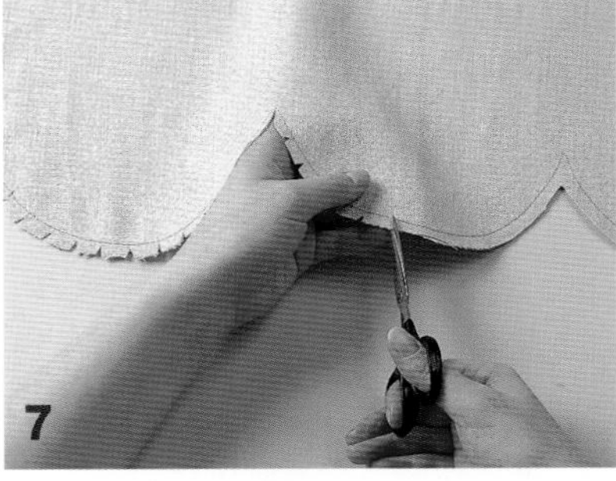
7

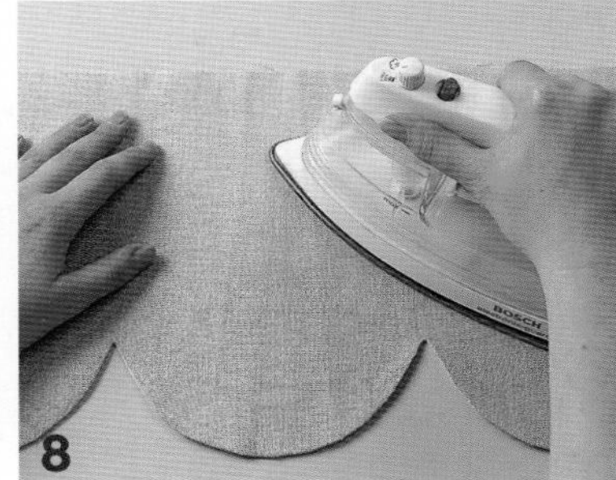

8

making a loose armchair cover

The cover is made in the same order as the calico pattern was pin-fitted. Add a generous 15cm/6in tuck-in allowance around the edge of the seat if there wasn't sufficient to cut from the calico. Before stitching, it is a good idea to tack (baste) the main fabric pattern pieces together, and to fit them on to the chair the right way out so that you can check that the design (if any) matches and that no mistakes have been made. Mark the valance line at this point.

you will need

- calico pattern
- fabric
- piping cord
- dressweight zipper
- sewing kit

tip for making a loose armchair cover

Covering an armchair is a major undertaking but well within the scope of the competent sewer. If this is your first slipcover project, use a plain, self-coloured fabric to avoid potential problems with matching a pattern.

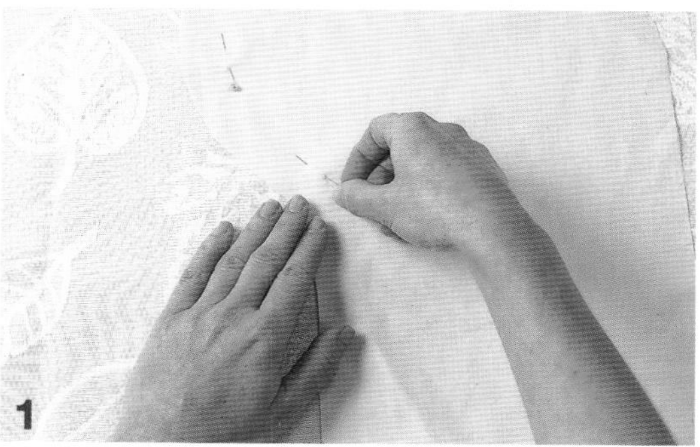
1

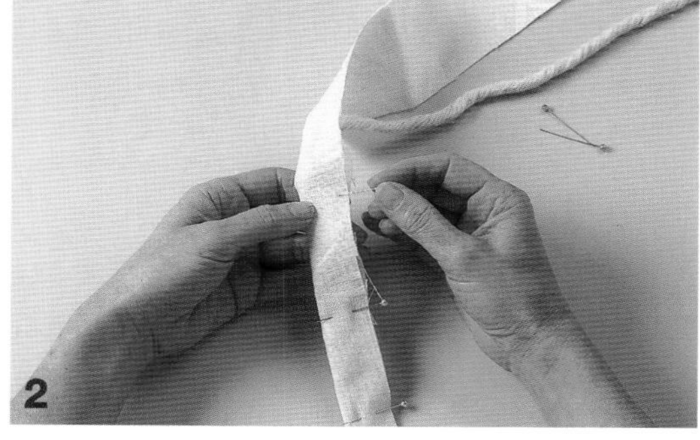
2

3

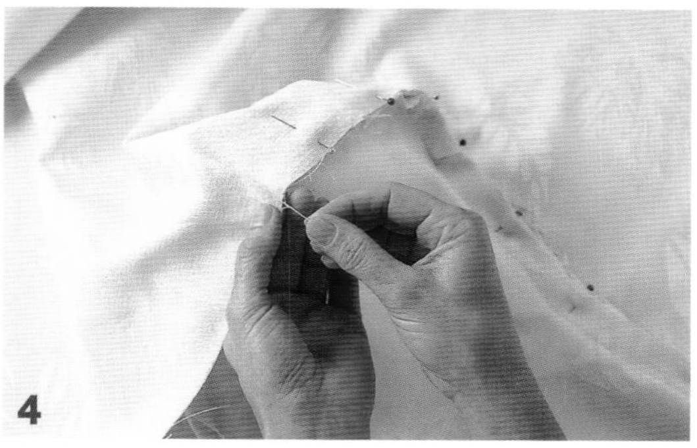
4

cutting out the pieces

To be on the safe side, cut the main fabric with the pattern pieces all facing the same way. This avoids potential problems with a pattern, or the pile of a nap fabric such as velvet, ending upside down.

1 Pin all the calico pattern pieces on to the fabric, centring any design on the inside chair back and seat cushion. Use the pattern as a guide to match the design on the seat and arm fronts.

2 If any seams are to be piped, join strips to make a continuous length of fabric, wide enough to fit over the piping cord plus 2.5cm/1in seam allowance. Piping for slipcovers is usually cut on the bias, but it is better to cut it on the straight grain if the fabric is checked or has a distinct design.

3 Stitch the strips of fabric over the piping cord, using a zipper foot attachment. Pin the piping around the edge of each piece to be piped, with raw edges aligned, and stitch in place.

4 Stitch the fabric pieces together in the same way that the pattern was assembled. Stitch the inside back to the gusset panel, then add the outside back. Add the arms, leaving the left-hand seam between the back of the arm and the outside back open for a zipper. Stitch the tuck-in seams before attaching the seat front.

▷

adding a gathered valance

This is the simplest way to finish the bottom of an armchair or sofa, giving a soft, casual appearance.

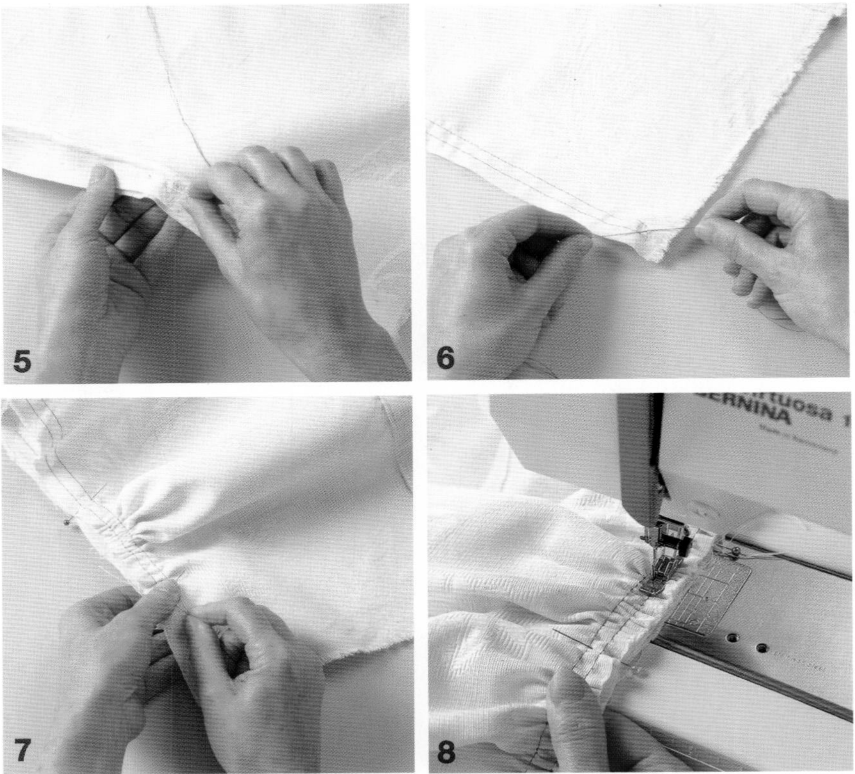

5 Trim the lower edge of the slipcover, leaving 2.5cm/1in seam allowance below the valance line mark. Mark the edges of the back opening for the zipper. Pin and tack (baste) piping along this edge, between the marks, around the bottom of the slipcover.

6 Measure the depth of valance required and add 5cm/2in seam and hem allowance. Cut and join strips of fabric to make a strip twice as long as the bottom edge. Turn up and stitch a 2cm/¾in hem. Measure and mark the valance into separate metres (yards) with pins and stitch two rows of gathering stitches between the metre (yard) marks. Tie the gathering thread off at one end of each section.

7 Measure every 50cm/20in around the bottom of the slipcover. Pin the valance to the slipcover, matching the metre (yard) marks with the 50cm/20in marks. Pull up the gathering threads.

8 Adjust the gathers evenly. Stitch the valance in place, using a zipper foot attachment so that you can stitch as close as possible to the piping cord. Remove the gathering threads and zigzag-stitch the raw edge.

adding a zipper

A zipper on the back of an armchair or sofa should be as inconspicuous as possible. Fit the zipper using the concealed method, down the left back seam. On a sofa, where the back panel has been joined, fit the zipper down the left seam on the back, using the semi-concealed method (see basic techniques).

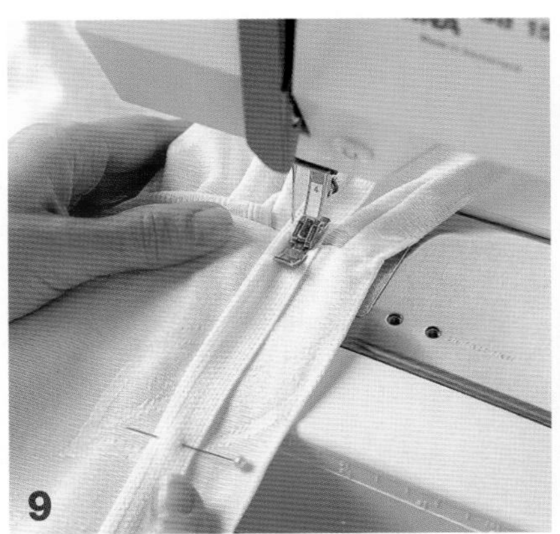

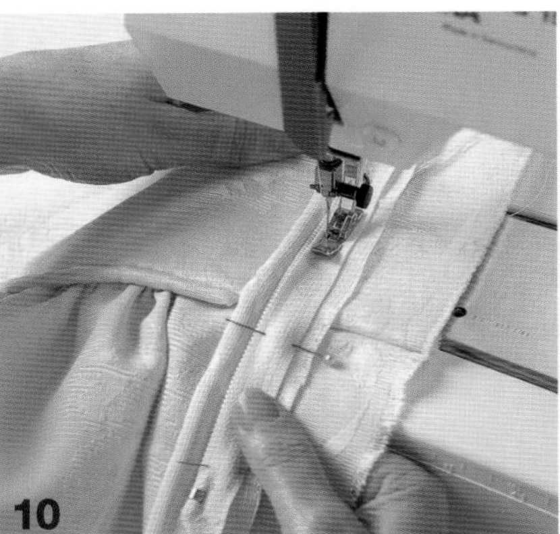

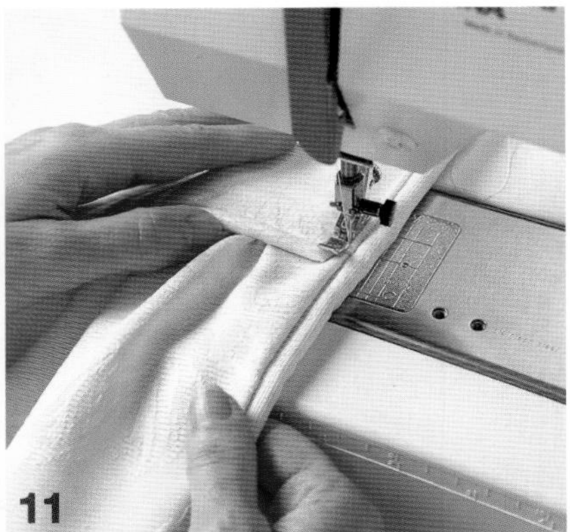

9 Fit the zipper into the gap left open down the back left-hand seam. Open the zipper and pin, face down, along the seamline on the back panel. Stitch, using a zipper foot.

10 Pin and stitch piping down the seamline on the outside arm section of the gap. Stitch the other half of the zipper in place over the piping.

11 Fold the zipper and seam allowance to the wrong side. Top-stitch close to the piping to hold the zipper in position. Fold and stitch the other side of the zipper in the same way.

right *A deep frilled valance adds a feminine and luxurious touch to a classic armchair cover.*

making a box-pleated valance

Box pleating is a more formal finish than a gathered valance. The box pleats can be full, so that the folds of the pleats meet at the front and the back, or they can be half-pleats with a gap in-between. Full pleats are more formal and use three times the finished length. Half-pleats need approximately twice the finished length.

To check the length and spacing required, cut a strip of calico and fold it to form whichever pleats you have chosen. Press the pleats and pin. Pin around the armchair and adjust to fit.

you will need

- **main fabric**
- **calico strip**
- **piping cord**
- **sewing kit**

tip for making a box-pleated valance

The spacing of the pleats can be adjusted slightly so that the edge of the pleat finishes at each corner.

1 Cut the valance fabric the required length and depth, adding 5cm/2in seam and hem allowance. Turn under 1cm/½in along the lower edge and then fold up another 1.5cm/⅝in. Stitch the double hem in place.

2 Open the calico strip to it's full length and use it as a pattern for spacing the pleats. Insert pins along both edges of the main fabric to mark the foldlines of the pleats. Arrange the pleats so that the edge of one pleat will finish at each end of the front of the armchair or sofa.

3 Fold the valance at each of the pins to make the box pleats. Press the edges of each batch of pleats with a steam iron and leave to cool before moving them. Tack (baste) the bottom of the pleats temporarily.

4 Cover a length of piping with fabric and pin it along the top edge of the valance. Fold the end of the piping over at the left-hand seamline where the zipper is to be inserted. Pin the valance along the valance line on the slipcover and stitch securely in place. Zigzag-stitch any raw edge and press upwards.

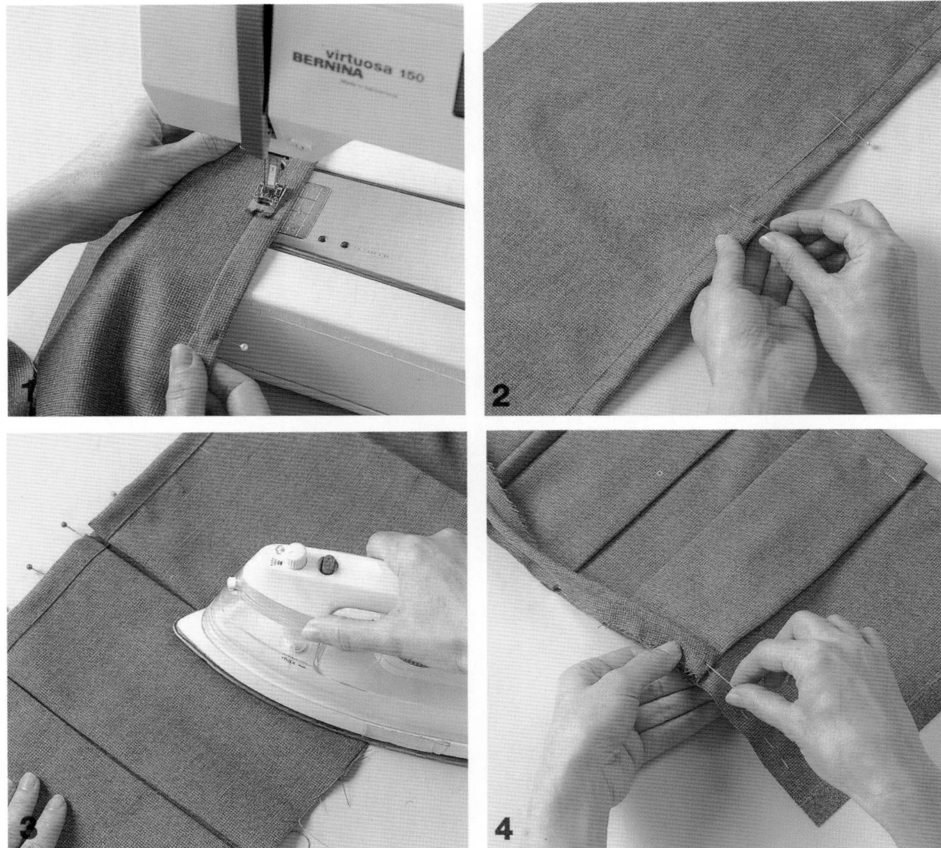

semi-fitted cover for a tub chair

Modern tub chairs look much better with a semi-fitted cover that is halfway between a loose cover and an upholstered cover. The pieces for the cover are assembled in the same way as for a traditional armchair, but the cover is held in place underneath the chair with a cord that runs through a casing.

Pin-fit calico to create a pattern, then cut out the fabric panels. Allow 10–12.5cm/4–5in along the bottom edge for the casing. Fitting is easier on a tub chair if two seams are added on the inside and outside chair back panels. Insert a zipper behind the piping on the back left-hand seam.

you will need

- **fabric**
- **piping cord**
- **thin cord**
- **upholstery zipper**
- **sewing kit**

tip for semi-fitted cover for a tub chair

Use a loose weave or stretch fabric for this style of chair so that the fabric can stretch slightly to fit the curved back edge.

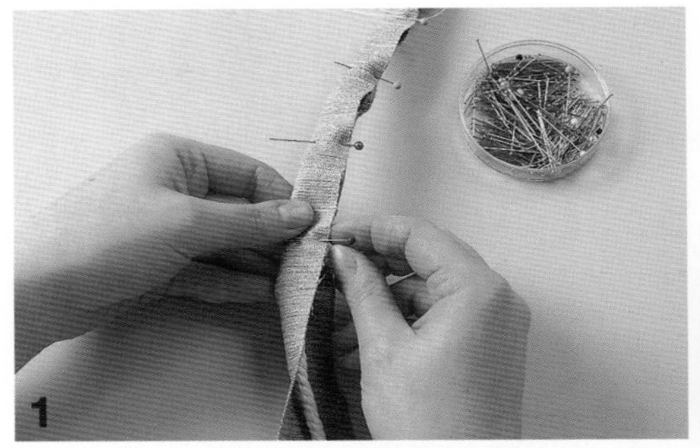

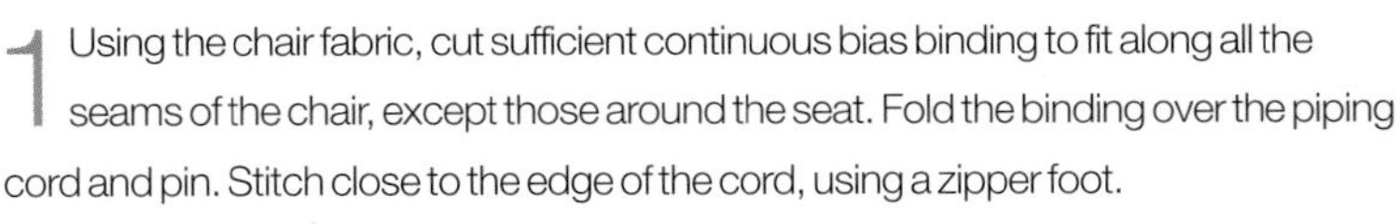

1 Using the chair fabric, cut sufficient continuous bias binding to fit along all the seams of the chair, except those around the seat. Fold the binding over the piping cord and pin. Stitch close to the edge of the cord, using a zipper foot.

2 Pin the piping on the right side of all the relevant cover pieces. Snip into the piping seam allowance if necessary to ease the piping around any tight curves, such as at the top of the arm fronts.

3 Stitch the cover pieces together. The seat seam is stitched without piping, instead of being tucked in like a traditional armchair. Fit the cover and mark the position of the legs with pins. Lift the cover off and draw a smooth curve with tailor's chalk. Cut along the chalk line.

4 Zigzag-stitch or overcast the raw edge of the curve and turn to the reverse side. Top-stitch the curve to secure. Turn up and stitch a 1.5cm/⅝in hem along the bottom edge to make a casing. Thread the cord through the casing, leaving loops in the gaps to fit over the legs of the chair.

5 Insert a zipper behind a piped edge in the left-hand back seam. Leave the other side plain. Fit the cover over the chair and pull the cord tight. Tie the cord in a double bow to secure and tuck up inside the cover.

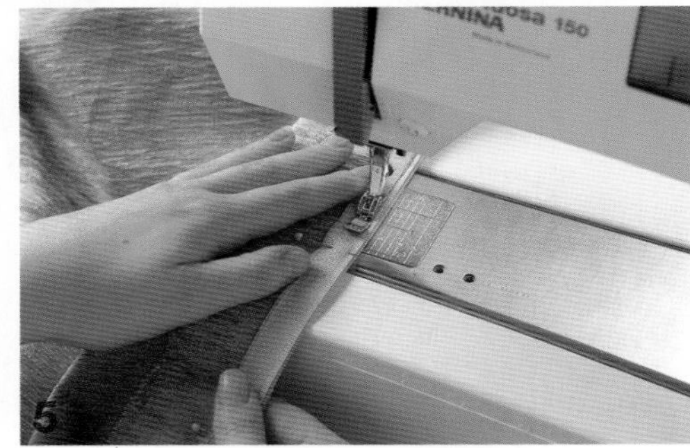

covering a square or rectangular footstool

The method of covering a footstool depends very much on the design and the way the stool is constructed. This footstool is covered with a simple drawstring covering for the cushion and a semi-fitted base. Its success relies on accurate cutting and perfect fitting.

you will need

- calico pattern
- heavyweight furnishing fabric
- thin cord
- strong thread or Velcro
- sewing kit

tip for covering a square or rectangular footstool

Pre-shrink fabric before making a close-fitting cover like this, as you may find it will not fit after cleaning.

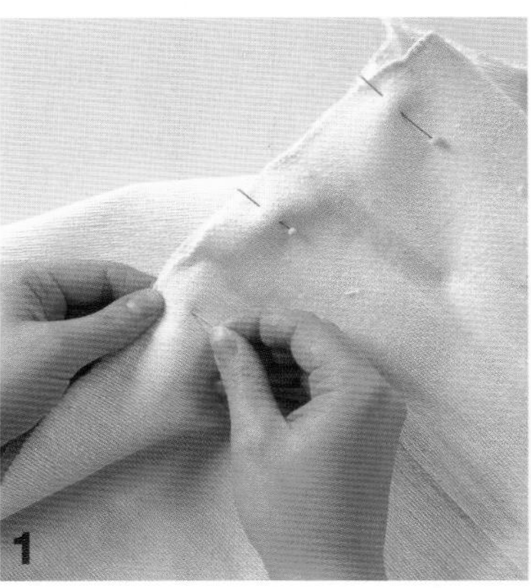

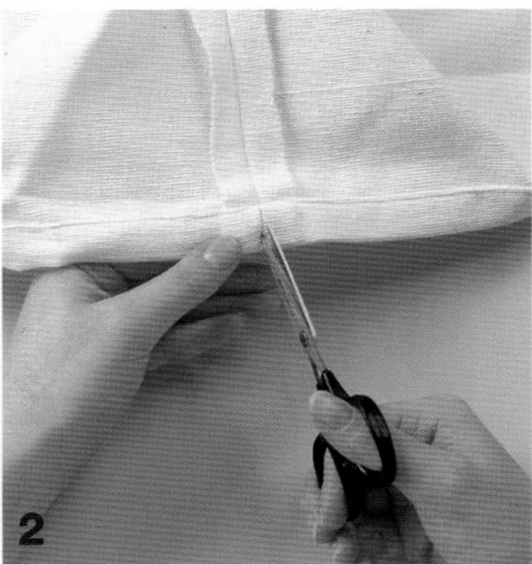

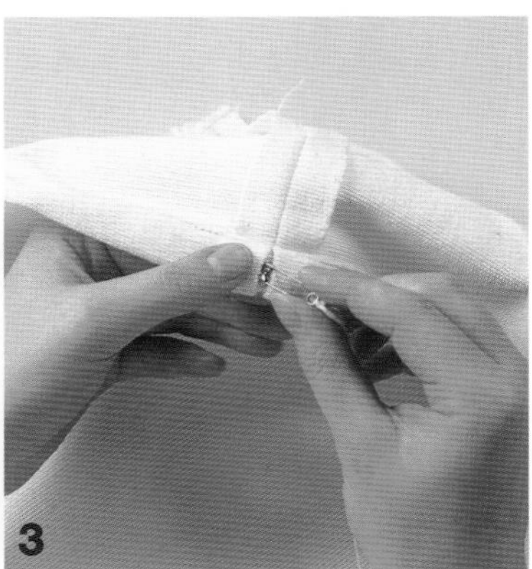

1 Cut the fabric for the cushion top, adding 1.5cm/⅝in seam allowances all around. Measure the cushion sides and cut four strips the same length plus seam allowances plus 5cm/2in deeper. Stitch the side seams into one piece, starting and finishing a seam allowance' width from each raw edge. Pin the sides to the top and stitch in place.

2 Turn up a 2cm/¾in double hem around the bottom edge and stitch in place. Snip into the casing at one of the corner seams.

3 Cut a length of cord to fit around the footstool and thread it through the gap in the hem. Fit the cover over the cushion. Pull up the cord tightly and tie on the underside.

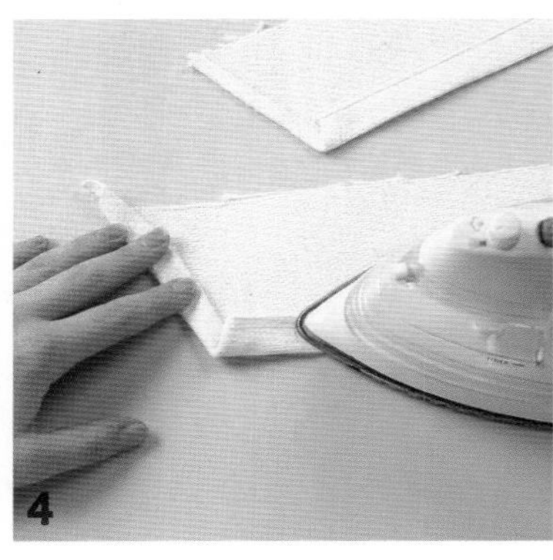

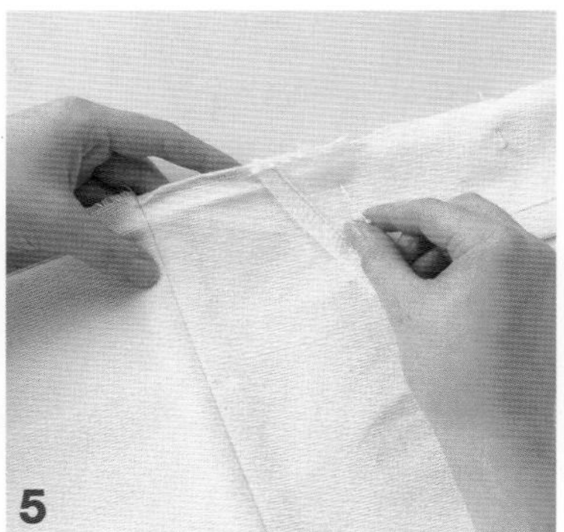

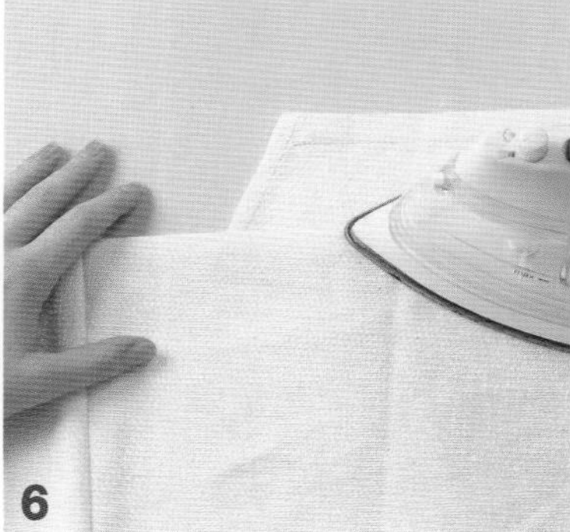

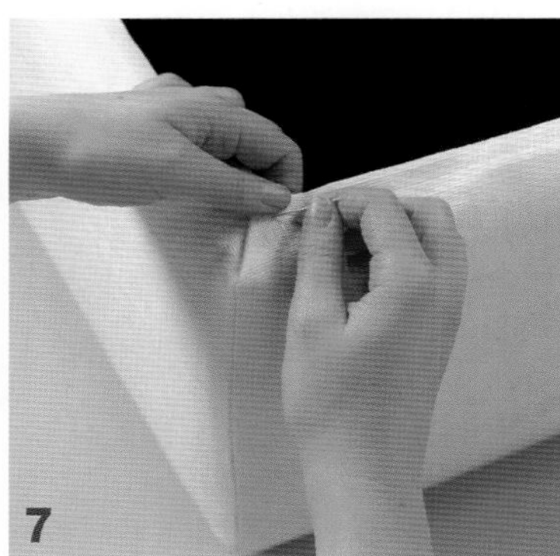

4 Cut four panels of fabric to fit each side of the base, adding 1.5cm/⅝in seam allowance to the sides and bottom edge and 5cm/2in along the top. With right sides together, stitch the short sides and press the seams open. Cut four strips, each 10cm/4in wide, to fit as flaps between the legs of the footstool. Trim the ends of each strip at an angle and press under 1cm/½in along the sides and bottom edge. Turn up another 1.5cm/⅝in on the bottom edge to form a casing to thread a cord through and stitch. Top-stitch the flaps.

5 Pin the flaps along the bottom edge, leaving a gap to each side of the side seams for the legs of the footstool. Stitch each in place.

6 Neaten the seam allowances with zigzag stitch and press the flaps outwards. At the top raw edge of the base cover, turn under 1.5cm/⅝in, press and top-stitch. Fit the cover on to the base. Thread a thin cord through the casing of the flaps and pull tightly under the base to secure a snug fit.

7 Pin the top edge of the base cover, mitring the corners neatly. Oversew the corner seams by hand, using a strong thread. Alternatively, secure the top edge with Velcro. To do this stitch strips of loop Velcro along the top edge of the footstool cover. Hand stitch or staple hook Velcro around the top outside edge of the footstool.

loose cover with pockets for a round footstool

A footstool without a cushion is firm enough to double as an occasional table. It can easily be transformed into a mini-workstation with ample storage space for scissors, tape measure and other sewing equipment.

you will need

- **calico pattern**
- **mediumweight furnishing fabric**
- **lining if necessary**
- **large buttons**
- **small, sharp scissors**
- **thin cord**
- **sewing kit**

tip for loose cover with pockets for a round footstool

A wicker footstool can be covered with wadding (batting) to soften the surface before covering with fabric. Alternatively, cut a circle of firm crumble foam to make a more comfortable seat.

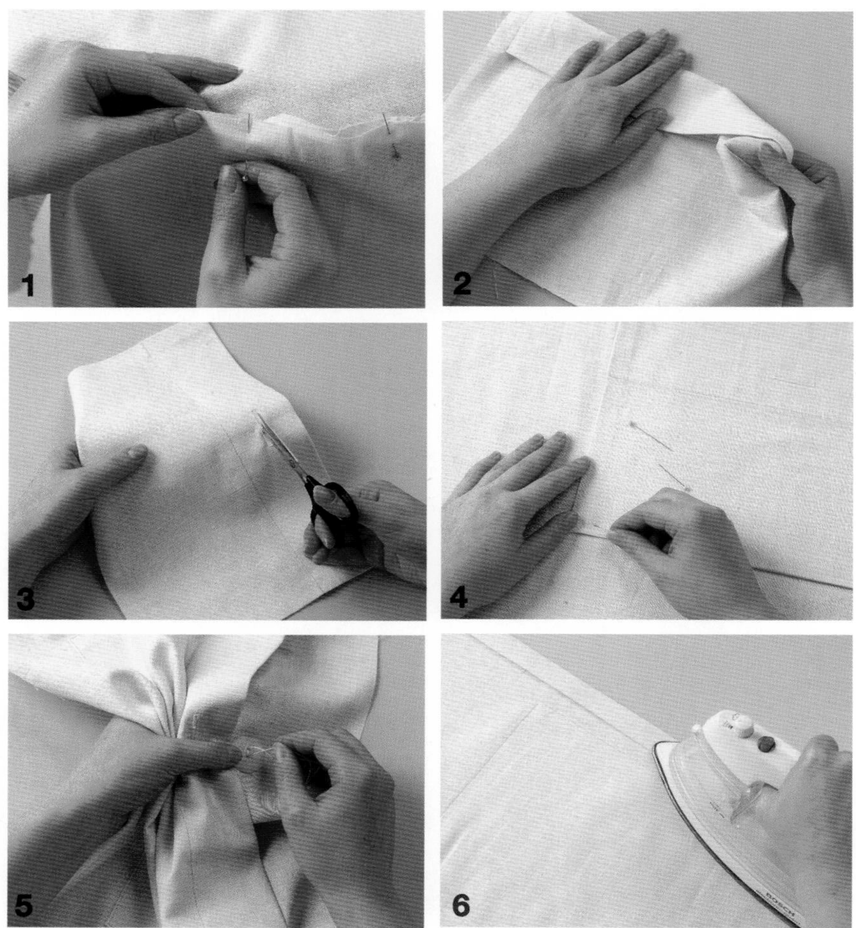

1 Measure the footstool. Cut a circle of fabric for the top and a strip of fabric to fit around the footstool, adding 2.5cm/1in seam allowance on all edges. Pin-fit the cover to check the size.

2 Decide on the finished size of the pockets, adding 1.5cm/⅝in seam allowance to the sides and bottom and 12cm/4¾in for the hem. Turn under a small seam allowance along the top edge. Press and stitch. With right sides together turn the folded edge down by 10cm/4in. Press, stitch each side and turn through.

3 Top-stitch the hem, then turn in the seam allowance and press. Mark the position of the buttonhole on the top edge of each pocket and stitch. Cut along the centre of each buttonhole with a pair of sharp scissors.

4 Lay the side fabric flat and space the pockets evenly along the length. Position so that the bottom edge of the pocket lies along the lower edge of the footstool. Pin and stitch the pockets in place.

5 Sew a button behind each buttonhole. Stitch the side seam and press open. Pin the circle of fabric for the footstool top in place with right sides together and stitch. Zigzag-stitch the raw edges to neaten them.

6 Turn up a 5mm/¼in hem at the bottom edge. Press, then turn up another 2cm/¾in hem. Stitch in place. At the seam unpick a few stitches to make a gap to thread a length of thin cord through. Fit the cover and pull the cord tight underneath.

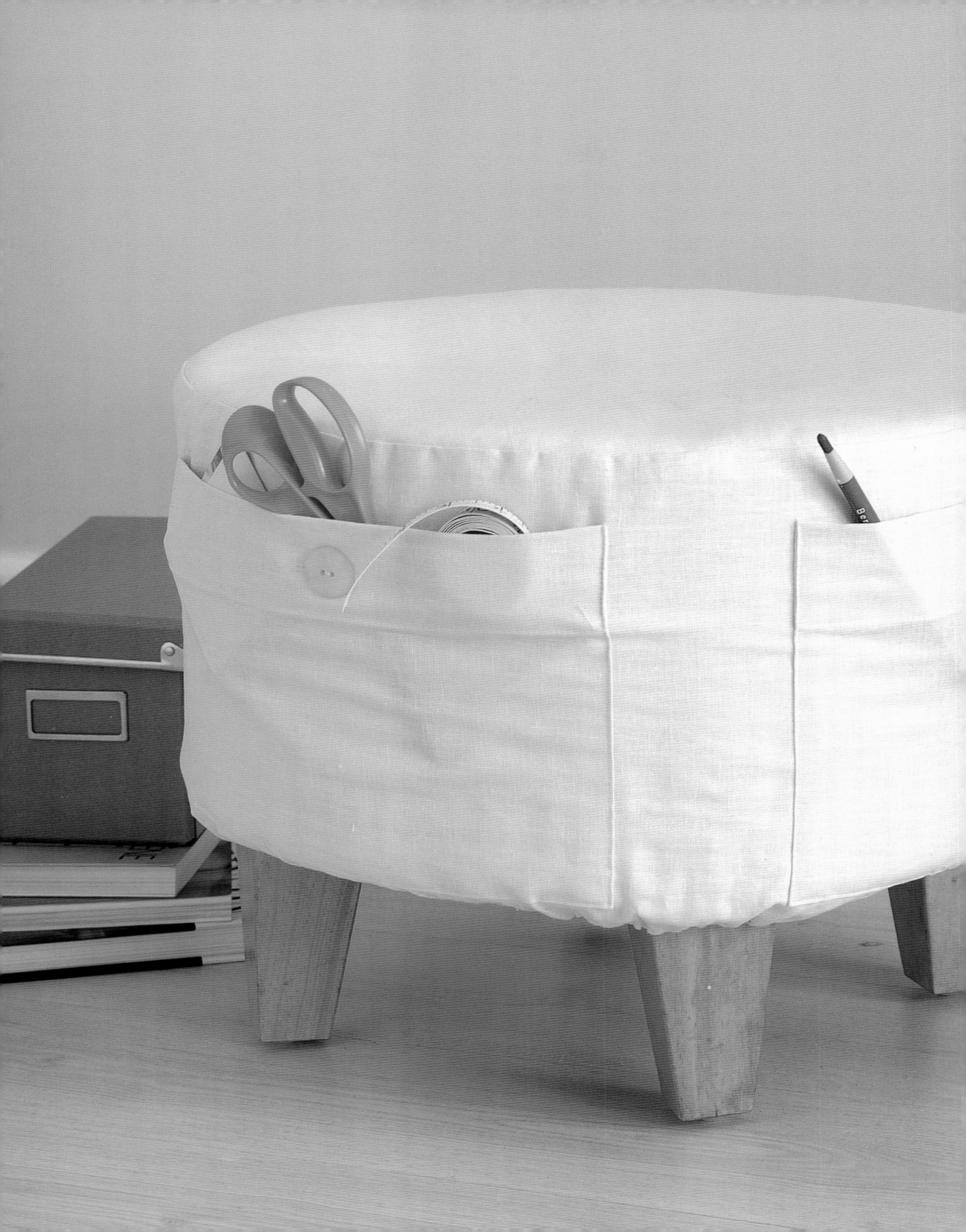

covering a deckchair

Deckchair canvas often begins to perish after a few years, long before the frame is showing signs of wear. This method of attaching a new cover using eyelets to fasten the turning is quick and easy. The eyelets can be threaded with a colourful cord.

you will need

- **deckchair canvas**
- **pencil and ruler**
- **eyelet tool**
- **bodkin (optional)**
- **5mm/¼in eyelets**
- **hammer**
- **thick, coloured cord**
- **sewing kit**

tip for covering a deckchair

Canvas can be bought in a standard width for deckchairs. If you want to use an alternative fabric, fold and stitch a narrow double hem down each side before fitting.

1

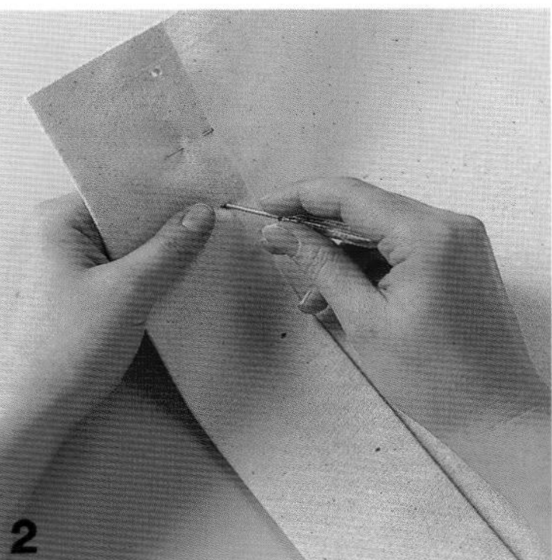

2

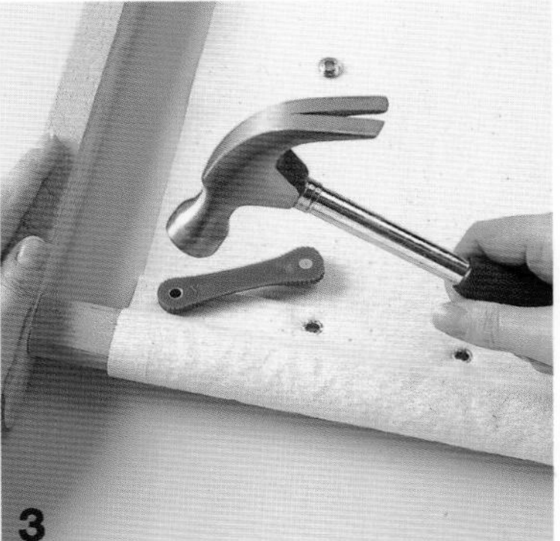

3

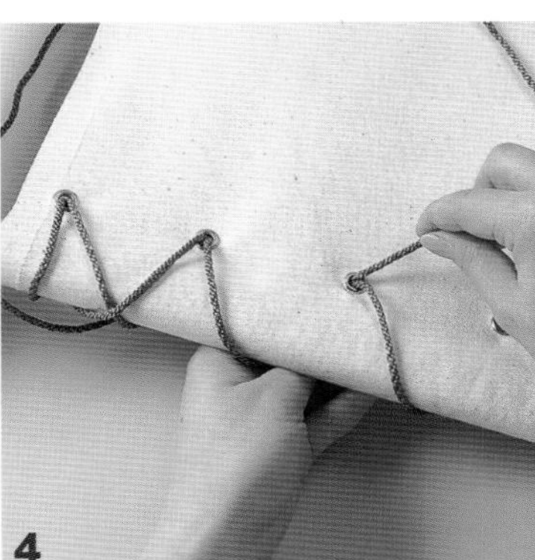

4

1 Measure the length between the outside edge of the bars when the deckchair is flat and add 32cm/12¾in hem allowance to the length. Turn under a double 8cm/3in hem at each short end of the fabric and press.

2 Mark the position of the eyelets approximately 6cm/2½in apart. Cut holes for the eyelets, using an eyelet tool or the point of a pair of sharp scissors. If the canvas is too thick, use a bodkin to make a hole.

3 Place the chair face down and fold the hem over the bar. Insert the tube section of the eyelet from the right side and fit the ring on top. Hammer into position through all the layers, following the manufacturer's instructions.

4 Thread the cord through the eyelets, either working a row of back stitch or crossing the cord over the top of the bar to make a decorative pattern. Knot the ends at one edge on the back of the chair.

covering a director's chair

As with deckchairs, the covers on wooden chairs often wear out long before the chair itself needs replacing. If you use the old cover as a pattern, remember to make some allowance if the fabric has stretched out of shape. If you are not using striped fabric for the new cover, draw parallel lines on the fabric with a ruler as a guide for stitching the quilting lines.

you will need

- **calico pattern**
- **mediumweight furnishing fabric**
- **wadding (batting)**
- **sewing kit**

tip for covering a director's chair
Use the old cover as a guide for sewing and fitting the new seat cover.

1 Make a calico pattern, then measure the depth needed for the chair back and the length from one strut to the other, around the strut and back again. Cut the chair back from fabric, adding 1.5cm/⅝in seam allowance all round. Fold the fabric in half, right sides together, and stitch the short ends together. Press the seam open, then rotate the seam so that it is 6cm/2½in from the right-hand side. Press under 1.5cm/⅝in along the long edges.

2 Top-stitch through all layers 5cm/2in from both side edges to make channels for the chair back struts. Stitch another line 5mm/¼in from the first.

3 Cut a piece of wadding (batting) to fit inside the back panel. Tuck the wadding under the seam allowances on the front of the panel and pin. Tack (baste) the layers together with lines radiating out from the centre.

4 Using a quilting or clear-view foot on the sewing machine, stitch down the stripes to quilt the panel and to close the top and bottom seams. Stitch all the lines in the same direction. Alternatively mark parallel lines 3cm/1¼in apart. Make the seat panel in the same way. Remove the tacking stitches.

1

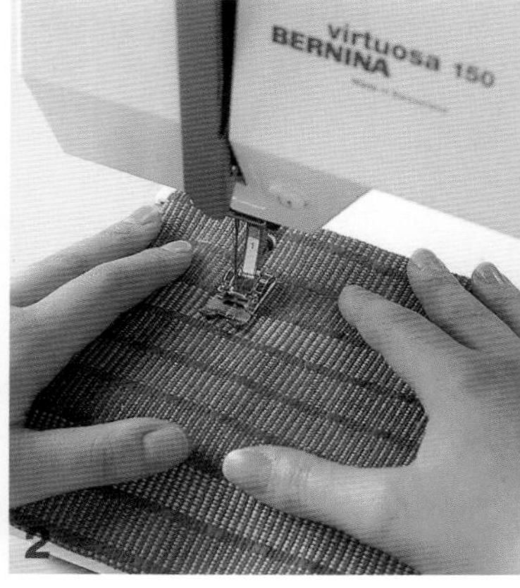

2

3

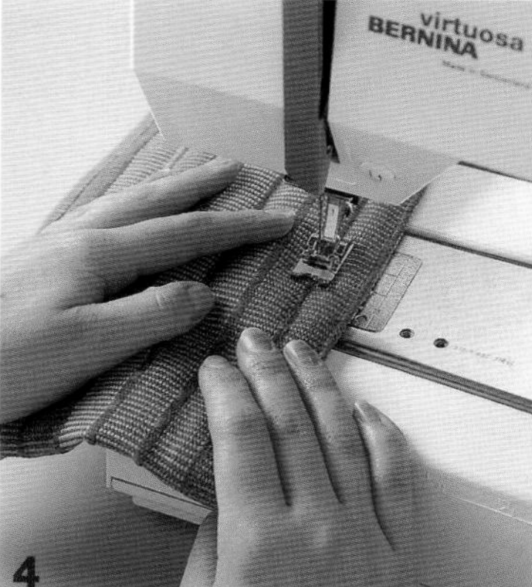

4

covering a plastic garden chair

Plastic chairs make cheap and hard-wearing seating but they do not always look attractive, especially if used as additional seating beside a wooden or wrought iron table. Transform them with simple fitted covers and co-ordinated seat pads, which can easily be removed and taken indoors at night. The size of the cover pieces is worked out using the pin-fitting method for dining chairs. Because you cannot insert pins into the plastic, use tape to hold the first panels in position.

you will need

- light- or mediumweight cotton fabric
- adhesive tape
- self-cover button kit
- sewing kit
- paper and pencil to make a pattern
- calico and stuffing or thick foam

tip for covering a plastic garden chair

Use a contrast piping around the seat cushion to give a professional finish.

1

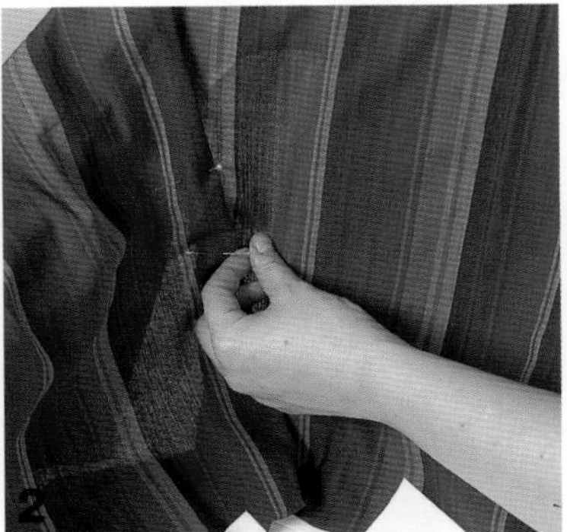

2

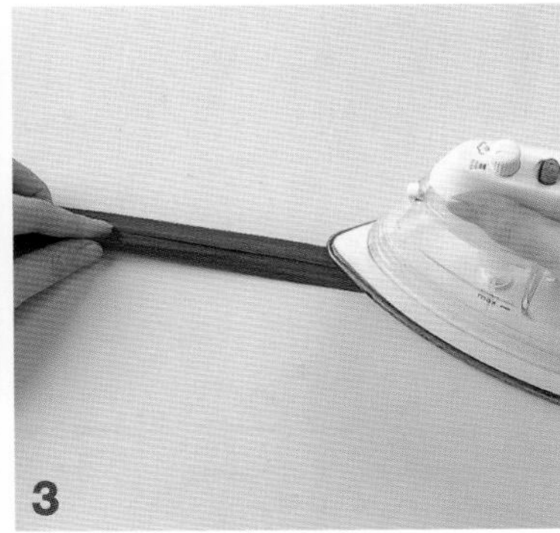

3

1 Cut the fabric panels for the cover oversize and fit them to the chair, using tape to hold them in position. Cut the outside back and sides in one piece of fabric. Also cut the seat and front panels in one piece so that there is no seam at the front edge.

2 Pin-fit the inside back seams, making sure that any design is balanced on both sides. When you are satisfied with the fit, trim the seam allowance to exactly 2.5cm/1in along all seams. Stitch the sections together with a 2.5cm/1in seam allowance, leaving a gap down both front seams from the seat to the floor.

3 Cut a 4 x 30cm/1½ x 12in strip of fabric for the button tabs. With wrong sides together, press the long edges of the strip into the centre then fold it in half again.

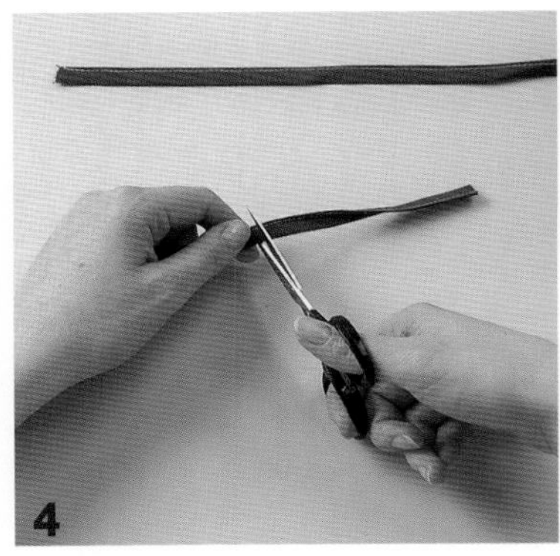

4

5

6

7

4 Stitch the strip close to the folded edge. Cut it to make two lengths, each 14cm/5½in. Fold each tab in half and press into shape.

5 Fold over and press a 1cm/½in hem along each edge of the gaps in the skirt front seams. Mark the position of the tabs on the front edges of the side piece, 20cm/8in from the seat edge. Tuck the ends of each tab under the hem and pin. Check that the buttons fit the tabs. Stitch the hem.

6 Fold each tab out over the edge. Top-stitch a decorative triangle to secure and strengthen it. Turn up and pin the bottom hem of the cover, then stitch. Sew buttons on the opposite side of each skirt gap to match the position of the tabs.

7 Draw a paper pattern for the seat cushion. Make a box cushion pad or have a piece of thick foam cut to size. Make a cover for the cushion, following the instructions for the box-style shaped cushion.

SENSATION
FROM THE SAATCHI COLLECTION
PHOTOGRAPHS 1935-1990

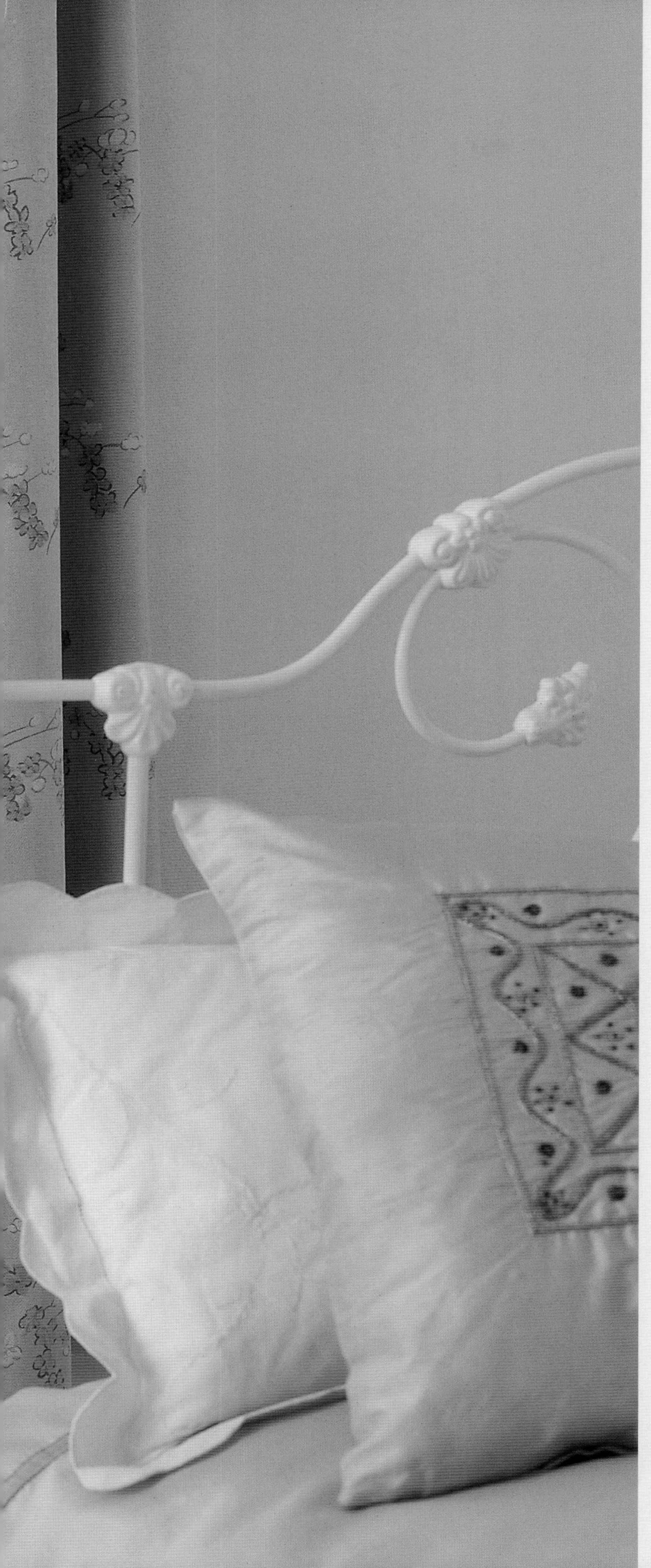

3 curtains & blinds

Curtains and blinds are effective ways to provide privacy and to screen light and noise, but as windows are one of the most prominent features in a room they also need to look as beautiful as possible. Windows can be made into a focal point, no matter how small they are or how they are situated in a room.

window treatments

Regardless of size, a window is more often than not the focal point of a room and the way it is covered is an important element in interior decoration. Curtains or blinds immediately give a room a "lived-in" look, and different styles can change the appearance and mood of a room dramatically. It is essential to take into consideration the proportions of the window and to choose a treatment that not only suits your personal taste but also the proportions of the window and its shape in relation to the room. Choose fabric for curtains and blinds carefully; not only will you live with them for a long time, they also need to be the correct weight, and the style needs to suit the purpose of the room they are in.

right Luxurious interlined silk curtains have been made extra long to pool on to the floor. They are not designed to be closed except on cold, winter nights as the blind can be lowered to screen the light.
above left Sheer unlined curtains in a pretty striped floral pattern give a lovely summery feel to this light, airy room. The pelmet board has been covered in a strip of fabric, softened with deep, inverted box pleats at each end.
below left Unusual fabrics with bold patterns can be used successfully on simple blinds.

Professionally made curtains and blinds can be prohibitively expensive but much of this cost is in labour charges so it is well worth making them yourself. Some of the skills required are similar to dressmaking, but it is easier to make curtains and blinds as the seams are usually straight. This chapter starts with simple, unlined curtains, describes how to line and interline curtains, and progresses to impressive swags and tails. It finishes with a selection of blinds that are easy to make.

As well as the immense satisfaction of creating beautiful, practical window treatments, there is tremendous pleasure to be gained from choosing the best style of curtains or blinds and finding the ideal colour and pattern of fabric. There is so much choice available today that it may seem daunting even before you start but, by selecting the reasons for covering a window, you can begin to narrow the choice. Curtains and blinds have several purposes: they can provide privacy, screen an unattractive view, block out the light or provide insulation from noise and cold. The curtain or blind on a bedroom window, for example, needs to provide privacy and block out the light in the early morning – other rooms in the house will have quite different needs.

As each room in the house has a specific function it should be approached separately. Unless you are starting completely from scratch in a new house, the existing furnishings should be taken into

consideration. The first decision you have to make is the kind of atmosphere or visual impact you want to achieve. Looking through books and magazines will give you ideas and browsing through furnishing fabric departments will bring you up to date with current trends and colours. Even if you are aiming for a contemporary look, there is a wide variety of styles, such as Oriental, folk art, minimalist or ethnic to choose from.

The style you choose will depend on the size and shape of the window or windows in relation to the room, and should reflect the style of your furnishings and the period the house was built. The window treatment for a Georgian town house with high ceilings and very tall windows will be quite different from a modern house with low ceilings and short windows. Most windows look best if the curtains reach the floor, but proportion is very important and the scale of the window treatment should match the room. Tall

right Heavy striped ticking curtains are used as a room divider to hide the kitchen area in this holiday home.
below A white sheer curtain screens the window, and a coloured voile allows the light to filter through gently.
below left Floral prints look equally good in the town or country. They frame the view from these room-length windows beautifully.
above left The warm-coloured fabric behind this panel of cupboards softens the look of the bathroom and makes it look less clinical.

windows look more in proportion with elegant swags and tails or a deep valance with tie-backs to balance their height. In small country cottages, swags and tails would completely overwhelm the room. Traditional cottages often have bays or deeply recessed windows, which suit a window treatment that reaches the windowsill or at most the radiator.

Curtains and blinds are not only restricted to windows. They can also be used for screens and partitions in certain situations. Perhaps it is difficult to fit a door, or you may want to hang a large curtain across a room to hide the cooking area in a kitchen/diner for a dinner party or special occasion.

Curtains and blinds also make excellent "doors" for wardrobes (closets) or shelf units. The fabric softens the harsh lines of woodwork, hides any clutter and keeps the dust away. Lightweight, softly gathered sheer fabrics can be fitted behind clear panels in wardrobe doors. The fabric screens the contents and gives a warmer look especially if there are several doors in the room.

Whatever you decide to make, there will be a similar project in this book. Read through the technical section before you begin and make sure you have all the equipment to help you complete the project as easily as possible.

curtain fittings

Curtains can be hung from a wide range of tracks and poles and the type that you choose will depend on the style of the room, the weight of the fabric used to make the curtain and the finished appearance you want to achieve. Most curtains can be fitted from either a curtain track or a pole. If there is no valance or pelmet, a pole is the more attractive option, since poles are frequently decorative features in their own right. Curtain tracks can be fitted with a valance rail or attached to the underside of a pelmet board. Always ensure that you use the correct type of hook to suit the curtain fitting and heading tape chosen.

Brass track
This high-quality traditional rail is ideal for conservatories because it can withstand high temperatures without distorting. It has a certain unique design appeal in ultra-modern houses and the metal rollers run very smoothly.

Brass café rod
This beautiful brass rod is too elegant to cover. It can be used with a self-heading curtain but looks particularly elegant when the curtain is hung from brass rings.

Contemporary curtain pole
The finials on this retro-look curtain pole are available in a range of shapes and colours to suit your decor. You can choose from many different poles and fit matching tie-backs to create a distinctive and individual look for your room.

Wrought iron pole
Wrought iron poles make a distinct design statement in the home. These poles are less heavy than traditional wrought iron and are suitable for light- to medium-weight fabrics. Several different finials are available to suit your particular decor.

Wooden pole
Wooden poles are normally supplied with matching curtain rings. They are available in a variety of different wood and decorative paint finishes, and with a choice of carved finials.

Brass curtain clips
Curtain clips are a modern alternative to traditional curtain hooks. They do away with curtain tapes and are ideal for simple curtains. Curtain clips are spaced evenly along the top of the curtain (in the same way as bulldog clips grip paper), and the hoop at the top of the grip slides on to the pole.

Hold-backs
Hold-backs are used to hold the curtain away from the window. With some, the curtain is simply draped over the pole and held in place by the decorative disc, and with others a tie-back is used.

Net wire
This steel wire with a plastic coating can be cut to length and fitted using hooks and eyes. It is suitable for sheer or lightweight fabrics with a simple self-heading.

Net track
This lightweight, extendible track is suitable for sheer and lightweight fabrics. Some types can be fitted to the window with hooks or fittings. Others have adhesive pads for use with plastic frame windows.

Valance track
This standard valance track is fitted behind the curtain rail fittings and can be bent to fit a bay window. It is strong enough to be used for all weights of valance.

Cord track
Cord tracks are pre-corded to allow easy access for opening and closing curtains without touching them. This type is suitable for straight runs with medium-weight curtains.

PVC curtain track
This is a basic, general-purpose curtain track, which is easy to fit and to remove if you are decorating the room. It is suitable for mediumweight curtains and can be bent into shape.

Curtain hooks
Curtain hooks are made to fit particular curtain tracks. The end hooks have a screw to keep them in position. Smaller hooks are used for attaching linings to curtain tape.

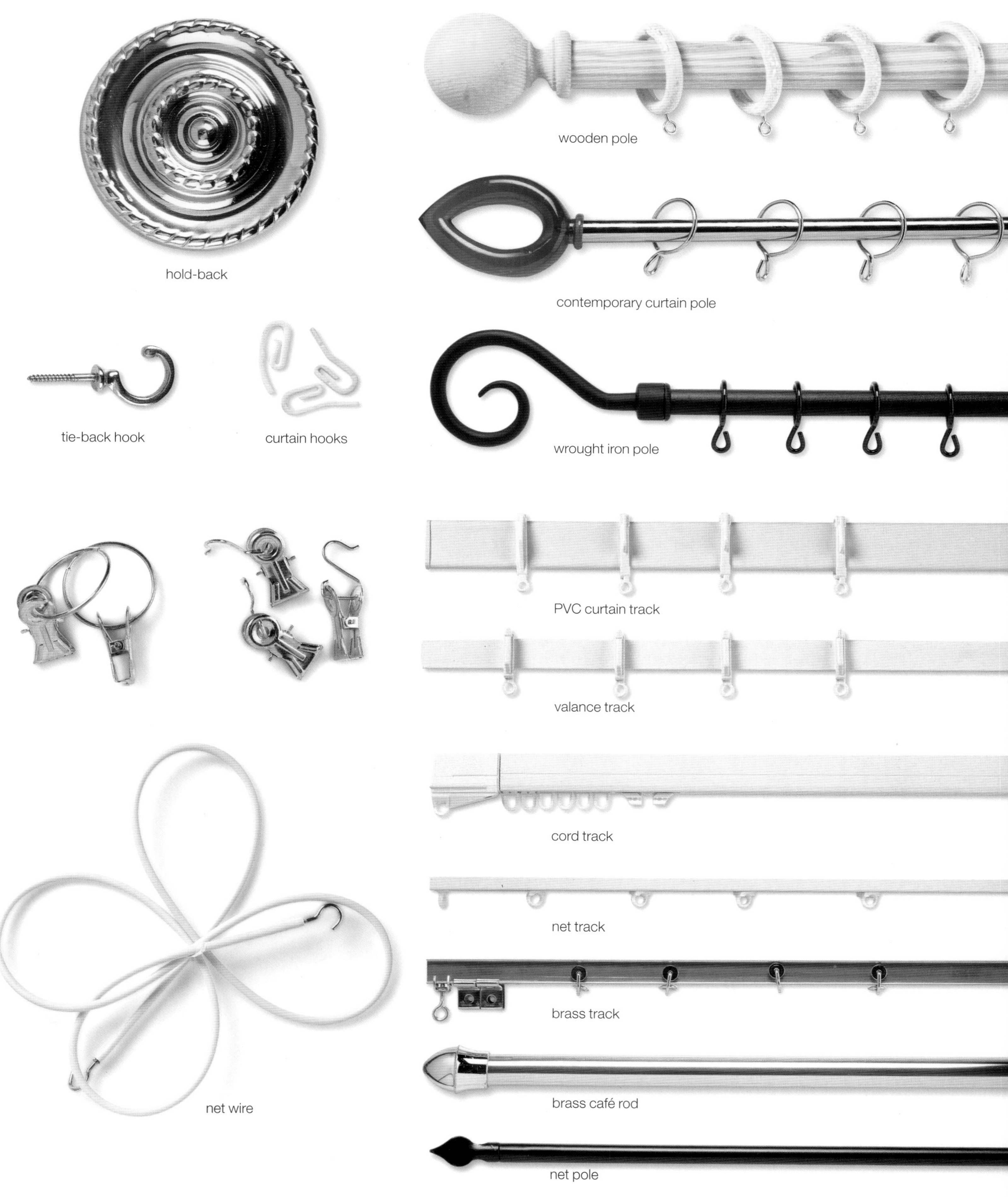
hold-back
wooden pole
contemporary curtain pole
tie-back hook
curtain hooks
wrought iron pole
PVC curtain track
valance track
cord track
net track
brass track
net wire
brass café rod
net pole

tailor-made curtains

Making curtains and blinds is an exciting and creative process that combines both artistic and practical skills. In addition to sewing, you will need to use some simple woodwork to complete some of the blinds and to make pelmet boards for hanging pelmets, valances, swags and tails. In general, this is simply a case of cutting a particular piece of wood to length. The wood used is all standard size and readily available in a DIY store or timber yard. Indeed, if you figure out the exact length required, the timber yard will cut it for you.

On the other hand, attaching the pelmet board to the wall is a job for the professionals. Every wall is different and there are special fittings designed for particular types of wall. In some cases there is only a certain area that can be drilled into because of a metal lintel or soft plaster and this will affect your measurements. Whatever fitting you choose, it will need to be strong enough to take the weight of the curtains and the pelmet board. It is important to get this right as an inadequate choice could damage the wall considerably.

left *These curtains are not designed to be drawn, but to frame the view through the window and to allow light to fall on to the desk.*

DECIDING ON A STYLE

Proportion is one of the most important aspects of curtain and blind making. The finished window treatment should blend in with all the other furnishings in a room and be of similar style. Dramatic swags and tails are ideal in a main reception area if there is sufficient height, but would be overpowering fitted over smaller kitchen or bathroom windows. Simple curtains and blinds in pretty colours soften the harsh lines and clinical appearance of these rooms and make them look more inviting.

The shape and position of the window need not limit your furnishing options as there are many ways to alter the window's appearance. Windows that are too wide or narrow can be disguised by keeping the curtains partly drawn on a short track, or fitted on track that extends more than 15 per cent on each side respectively. Curtains that need to have as much height as possible can be fitted to a pelmet board that is attached to the ceiling for maximum length.

LIGHT AND VIEW

Whatever style of window treatment you would like, take into consideration the view from the window and the amount of light that you want to come through. If the view is unattractive or the window looks out on to the street, sheer curtains or a flat blind can be hung inside the recess to provide screening or privacy. A dramatic view through a large window, on the other hand, will influence the colour choice of any fabric in the same way as a frame or mount can change the appearance of a picture.

Once you have chosen a particular style of curtain or blind, decide how and at what height it is going to be hung and if possible arrange to fit the curtain rail, pole or pelmet board before you begin to measure.

Further instructions for measuring and fitting blinds in particular are included at the end of this section.

MEASURING THE WINDOW

Measuring is the most important part of curtain-making. The best advice is to use a steel or wooden ruler and to double-check every measurement before

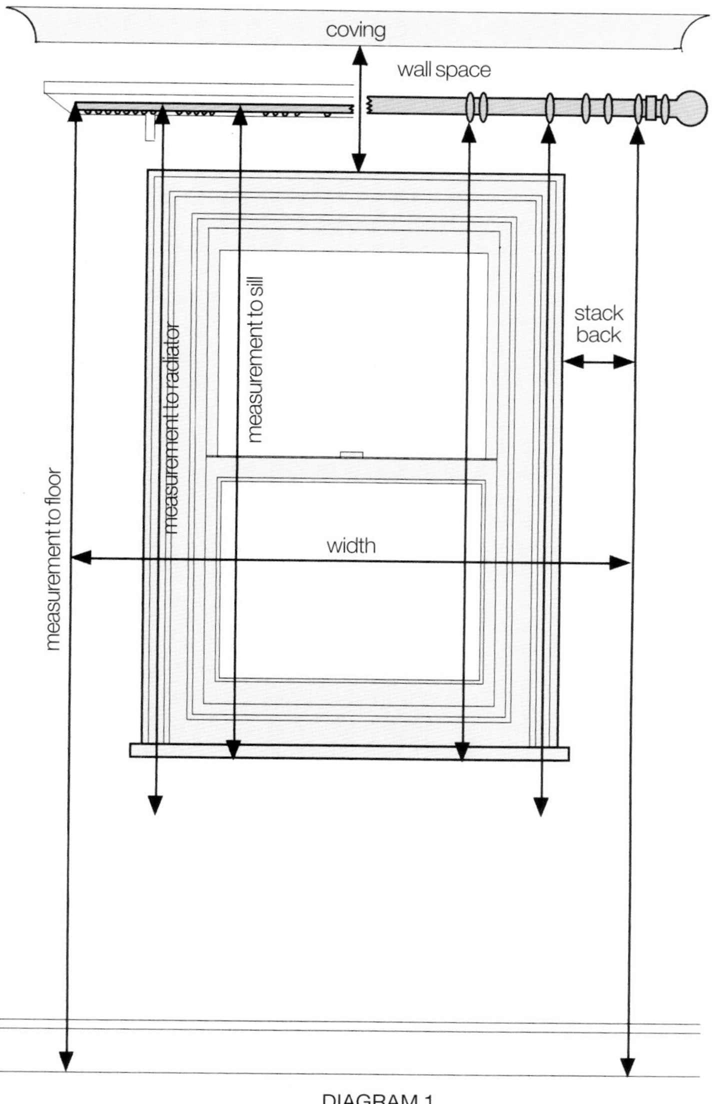

DIAGRAM 1

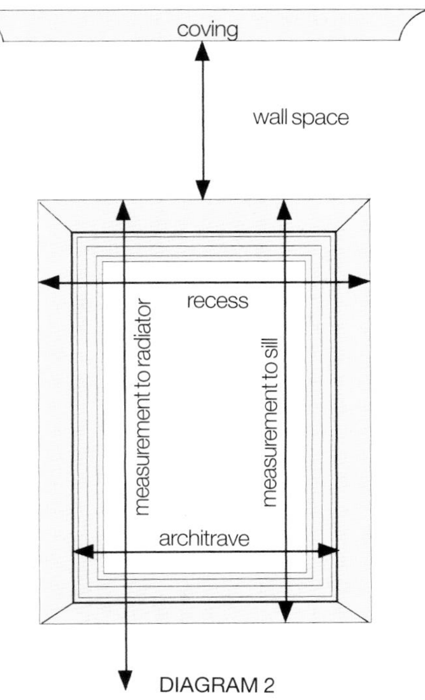

DIAGRAM 2

cutting out the fabric. Measurements are also required for working out the length of hardware (such as a curtain pole) and estimating the amount of fabric and trimmings you will need.

It is better to take every possible measurement at one time, rather than just those you think you will need. If your plans change, there will then be no need to re-measure. Measure each window individually, even if they appear to be the same size. If there is more than one window on a wall, measure the space between them so that you can plan for a picture or other decoration.

MEASURING EXISTING FITTINGS

If you are using existing tracks and fittings, the measuring is fairly straightforward but it is still essential to keep a record.

Curtain track or pole

- Measure the length of the track or pole and the distance away from the wall (the return).
- Measure the curtain length from the bottom of the curtain hooks to the windowsill, top of the radiator or the floor.

Pelmet board

In addition to the above, measure the length of the pelmet board and the return (from the front edge of the pelmet board to the wall). Consider whether you would like a decorative finish, such as box pleats at the corners, as this will affect the required fabric quantity.

Measuring bare windows

When measuring windows for the first time, take measurements in the middle and at each side in case the floor or ceiling is uneven.

- Measure from the ceiling or from the bottom of the coving to the floor.
- Measure the wall space from the ceiling or from the bottom of the coving to the top of the window or recess.
- Measure the length and width of the window, including the frame or the inside of the recess.
- Measure from the windowsill to the floor.
- Measure the space available on each side of the window for an extended curtain track. The curtain pole or track is usually 30 per cent longer than the width of the window.

curtain choices

With a curtain style in mind, the next stage is purely practical – how much fabric will be required?

DECIDING ON THE CURTAIN LENGTH

Curtains look very elegant if they are full-length, touching the floor or even draping on to the carpet. However, curtains that drape on to the floor have their disadvantages. They need to be re-arranged every time they are opened or closed, and they make vacuuming difficult. Pets love to use the comfortable "pools" of fabric as a bed!

below *Tab curtains should be hung above a door frame so that no light is visible between the tabs.*

Suitable lengths for short curtains are windowsill-length if they fit inside the recess, or radiator-length when they hang 10–15cm/4–6in below the sill. If the curtain is to be held back with tie-backs, add an extra 2.5–5cm/1–2in allowance.

THE CURTAIN TRACK OR POLE

Tracks for sheer and lightweight curtain fabrics can be fitted to the ceiling, or to the window frame inside a recess for a windowsill-length curtain. The track is therefore the width of the recess less 2–3cm/¾–1¼in to allow for fitting the hooks and curtains.

Curtain poles and tracks that are fitted outside the window recess are 30 per cent wider than the window.

This allowance, known as the "stack-back", enables the curtains to be pulled back to the edge of the window, allowing the maximum of light in during the day. Full or very bulky interlined curtains need slightly more stack-back, as do corded tracks and poles.

Solid metal lintels above a window can sometimes determine the position of the curtain pole. In general, the pole should be high enough to allow the top of the curtains to cover the top edge of the window. You need to decide on the style of the curtain at this stage as the curtains will hang at different heights if they have ties or tabs, or hang from curtain rings.

FITTING A PELMET BOARD

A bare curtain track is not very attractive and should, if possible, be fitted with a separate valance track, or secured to a pelmet board. The pelmet board is fitted to the wall space above the window and hangs down to cover the track. The height of the board depends on the proportions of the window – a pelmet or valance is usually one-fifth to one-sixth the length of the finished curtain. The pelmet board can be moved within the wall area above the window, but should ideally be fitted directly underneath the cornice or coving.

MAKING A PELMET BOARD

A pelmet board is simply a wooden plank 2cm/¾in thick and 15cm/6in wide. It should be the length of the curtain track, plus an average 10cm/4in curtain housing allowance on either side. If the curtains are extremely full, this allowance can increase to as much as 30cm/12in.

Brackets (which must be strong enough to hold the weight of the curtains and valance) are fitted flush with the back edge of the pelmet board. The curtain track is fitted 8cm/3in from the front edge. To allow the curtains to turn at right angles at the end to touch the wall, insert a large screw-eye to each back corner of the pelmet board and insert the last hook of the curtains at each end.

The front edge and sides of the pelmet board are covered in hook Velcro. Even if this is the self-adhesive kind, it should also be stapled to make it secure.

above *Make sure the wall will support the weight of heavy curtain fabric as well as the pelmet board and always use suitable materials.*

WORKING OUT FABRIC QUANTITIES

Once the pelmet board, curtain track or pole is in place, you can work (figure) out the amount of fabric required.

Calculating the drop

Use a wooden or steel ruler to measure the drop. Begin from the floor, radiator or windowsill, and measure up to the bottom of the hook on the curtain track or pole. This is the finished length of the curtain, to which you will have to add the hem and turn-down allowances. Both of these two measurements vary depending on the style of curtain and heading used, and you should refer to the individual instructions for each project. As a general guide, for the majority of curtains using a heading tape, add 15cm/6in hem allowance and 10cm/4in for the turn-down at the top.

Calculating the width

The length of the curtain pole and the fullness of the curtain determine the curtain width. Add extra allowances for an overlap arm and the return if you are using a pelmet board.

- For curtains on a pelmet board, add 10cm/4in for the return and overlap arm to each curtain.
- For a valance fitted to a pelmet board, measure along the front edge and down both sides.

CURTAIN WIDTHS

Different heading types use varying amounts of fabric, but these can be estimated fairly accurately. Work (figure) out the finished curtain width using the chart below, then add 10cm/4in side hem allowance.

Types of heading	Required width
Tie top or flat with clips	1½–2 times the width
Tab top	1–1½ times the width
Pencil pleats	2–2½ times the width
Pinch pleats or goblet tape	2 times the width
Box pleats	3 times the width
Hand-sewn headings	2– 2½ times the width

getting started

Curtain fabric is normally 137cm/54in wide, and curtains are made with several lengths joined together. Divide the width of the fabric into the curtain width plus allowances to find the number of drops required. Multiply this number by two if there are two curtains. It is always better to round measurements up rather than down, and any length or drop should not be under half a width. If there are half-widths, join one half to the outside of each curtain.

Working with patterned fabric

The usable fabric width for curtain making may be slightly narrower if a design, check or stripe has to be matched. Match the fabric and measure the usable width before calculating the number of drops.

Buying the fabric

Once you have calculated the amount of fabric required, remembering to add the hem and turn-down allowances to each drop, take the measurements to the fabric shop. Choose your fabric and ask the sales assistant to double-check your measurements. Extra allowance will have to be made for a patterned fabric, but the sales assistant will be able to calculate the extra fabric required to match a design. As a general guide, add one design repeat for each drop. This additional fabric can add considerably to the cost of the curtains, particularly if the fabric has a large pattern repeat.

Before you begin

Check against your original sample that you have the right fabric and unroll it completely on a flat surface, to look for any flaws. Check the front and back of the fabric carefully.

Curtains hang better if the fabric is cut on the straight grain. On coarsely woven fabrics you can cut straight along a thread and some plain fabrics can be torn across, but there is always a risk that this will damage the fabric.

Snip into the selvage and pull one of the threads carefully so that the fabric gathers. Ease the gathers as far as you can and cut along the line. Work all the way across the fabric.

Fold the fabric in half and check that the corners meet. If not, match the corners and side seams and pin. Steam-press the fabric to straighten.

If the fabric is very off-grain, pull the adjacent sides apart either side of the corner, then press as before.

CUTTING THE FABRIC

Check the cutting length of each drop one last time, then measure up the selvage. Line the selvage up along the edge of the cutting table, and use a set square and metre (yard) stick to make a line at right angles across the fabric. A rotary cutter and quilter's ruler is a worthwhile investment for this as the fabric can be cut without marking a line.

Cutting patterned fabrics

Always cut complete pattern repeats so that they will lie across the hemline of the curtain. A part-repeat will be less noticeable hidden in the gathers or folds of a heading.

Remember to add the hem allowance below the pattern repeat before cutting out the fabric.

above *Fold the first length lengthways along the side seamline and lie it along the fabric, moving it until the design matches. Mark the length at both ends and cut as before.*

curtain construction

With the fabric in hand and your measurements carefully checked, you are ready to begin.

MAKING THE CURTAINS

Curtains are always made from the hem up. The side seams and hem are completed and any lining inserted, before the heading is attached. Complete the curtains according to the individual project instructions. The following is a rough guide to the order of stitching but should be read in conjunction with the project instructions.

Stitch the widths of fabric together with plain seams. Press the seams open. If the fabric has a design, slip-tack (baste) the seams before sewing. Fold under and then accurately measure and press the side seam and hem allowances.

Trim the lining to exactly the same width as the curtain at this stage. Fold up and press a double 5cm/2in hem along the bottom. Stitch the hem. Press under 2.5cm/1in down each side seam. With right sides together, pin the lining and curtain raw edges together. Stitch along the pressed line or slip-stitch along the fold.

Adding weights

Curtain weights are used to add extra weight to the hem of curtains, or in the corners of swags and tails. They prevent a curtain from blowing about if the window or a door is open, and help the fabric to drape well.

1 Stitch the lead weight just above the fold in the corner of the hem. Take care not to stitch through to the front of the curtain.

2 Lengths of lead chain can be stitched along the fold of the hem. Oversew the hem, catching only a thread on the hemline.

Cutting the curtain to length

Once the curtain is complete, except for the top edge, it can be trimmed to the required length, ready for the heading. Work on a long table or on the floor.

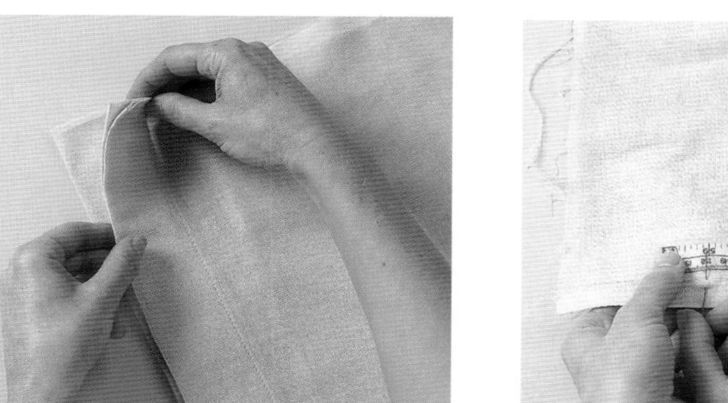

1 Fold the curtain in four, matching the corners, hem and side seams exactly.

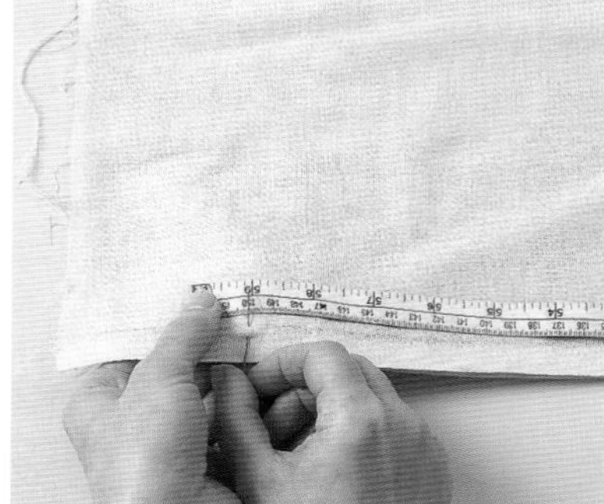

2 Measure the length of the curtain drop, add the turn-over allowance for the particular heading you are using and mark the length with a pin.

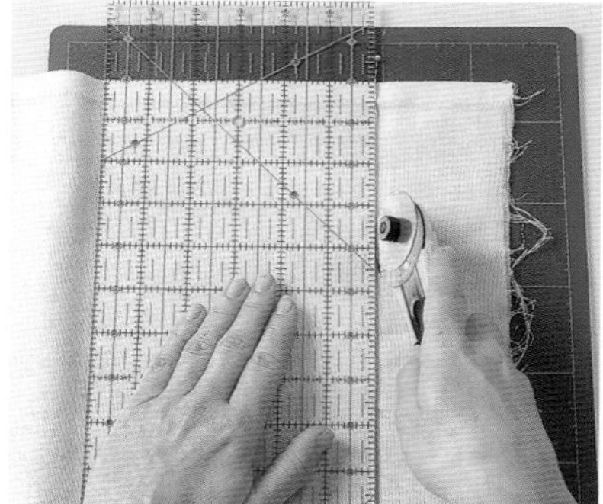

3 Ideally use a quilter's ruler and rotary cutter to trim the curtain to length. Alternatively, mark a line at right angles with a set square and ruler.

Completing the heading

Curtains with heading tapes have long cords that are pulled up to gather the heading. These cords can be quite bulky and need to be stored neatly on the back of the curtain at the outside edge. Use either of these methods.

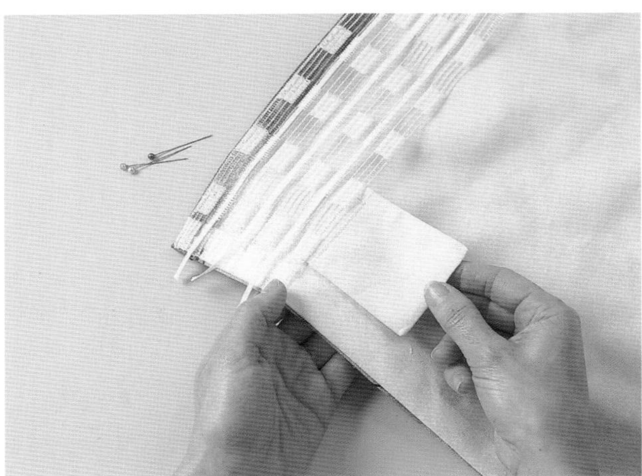

1 Cut an 8 x 15cm/3 x 6in piece of lining and stitch a narrow hem at one short end. Fold the lining in half widthways, right sides together, so that there is a 2cm/¾ in seam allowance above the hem. Stitch the side seams and turn through. Tuck the seam allowance under the tape and stitch in place.

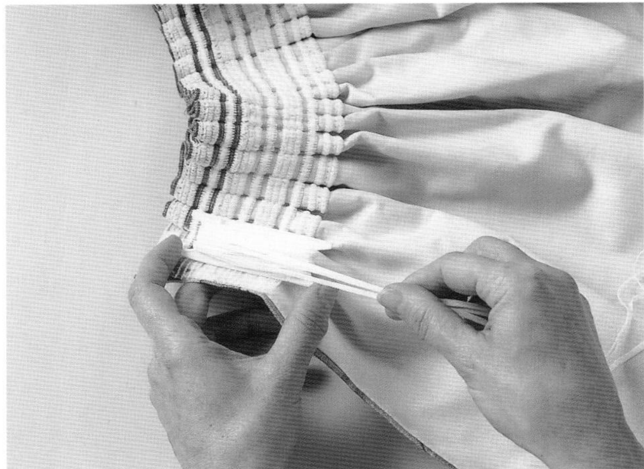

2 Alternatively, you can buy a cord tidy to wrap the cords around. Hold the tidy against the heading tape and wrap the ends neatly around it.

Inserting the curtain hooks

Gather the heading tape up fully – it can be let out slightly later to fit the window. Insert a curtain hook in every fourth pleat along a pencil-pleated tape. Fancy heading tapes and hand-stitched headings have their own style of hook. Ask for the correct hooks at your furnishing fabric department.

above *Curtains with a contrast lining always look striking. Choose a colour that appears in the main fabric for best effect.*
left *Combining plain and pattern fabrics is a good way of making costly fabric that you like go further.*

MAKING A PATTERN FOR A VALANCE

Draw a paper template of the shape required. Pin the template over the top of the window to check how it looks. The centre depth should be approximately one-sixth of the finished length of the curtains, and the outside edges about 30–45cm/12–18in longer. Adjust the shape until you are satisfied.

Measure the length of the pelmet board and add twice the return (the side edge). Join the widths of fabric and lining together to make panels three times this width plus 3cm/1¼in seam allowance. Cut the panels to the required width.

Multiply the length of the return by three and add 1.5cm/⅝in hem allowance. Fold the lining panel in half and mark this point with pins in from the raw edges. Measure down from the top edge and mark the longest valance measurement.

Measure the midway depth on the original template, one quarter of the way across. Mark this length on the lining halfway between the other measurements. Join the marks in a gentle, smooth curve, keeping the line perpendicular to the fold and selvage at each end. Ensure the design is symmetrical and there are no awkward lines. When you are satisfied with the shape cut along the line.

above *Valances look attractive at tall windows, but use a lot of additional fabric.*

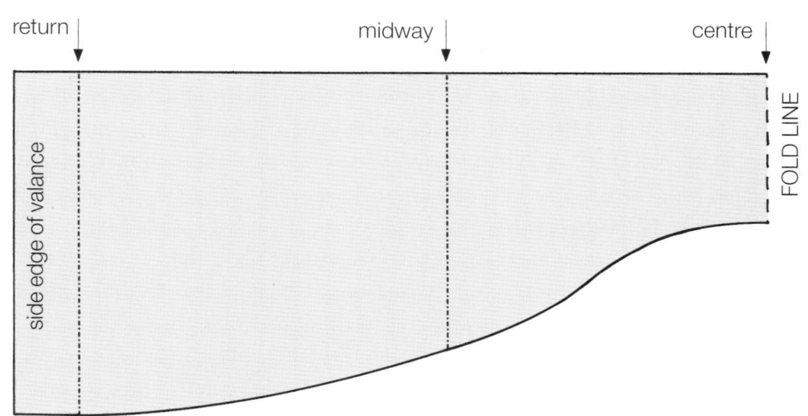

MAKING A PATTERN FOR A DRAPED SWAG

The centre of the swag should hang down to one-fifth of the length of the curtains. This is also the measurement for the short side of each tail. The long side of the tails should hang down one-third of the curtain length. Cut a wooden batten or put pins into your work surface to mark the length of the pelmet board. Pin a curtain weight chain to one mark and drape it around to the other mark so that the chain hangs down to one-fifth of the length of the curtains in the middle. Measure the length of the chain between the marks.

Cut out the lining fabric twice the depth of the finished swag (i.e. two-fifths of the curtain length). The width should be twice the long side of the tail (i.e. two-thirds the curtain length) plus the length of the pelmet board. Transfer the measurements to the lining fabric as shown in the diagram. Join the outside marks with a straight line and the inside marks with a dotted line.

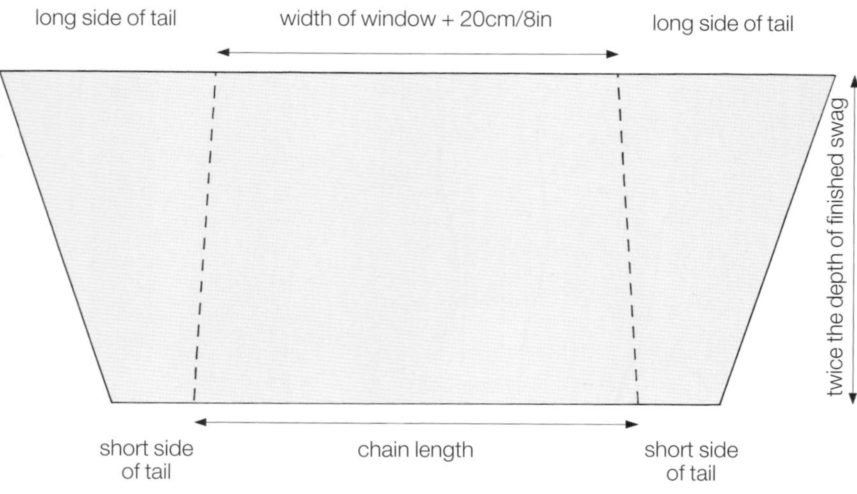

left *Draped swags use less fabric than valances and frame tall windows well.*

hanging curtains

Once you have completed the curtains, hang them as soon as possible to prevent them being creased. Never hang curtains alone as it is all too easy to lose your balance and fall from a step ladder. If there is a delay, place the completed curtains on the bed or over the banister, using a sheet to keep off the dust.

Count the number of hooks across the curtain and check there are a corresponding number of runners on the rail. Allow a hook for each screw-eye on a pelmet board. Find a step ladder that is tall enough for you to reach the top of the window easily.

below *These neatly dressed curtains are swept back in low tie-backs for a dramatic effect.*

Drape the curtain over your shoulder, with the heading tape in front. Hook the curtain to the rail, beginning at the outside edge. Don't begin in the centre as the entire weight of the curtain may cause the rail to buckle.

Hang a second curtain in the same way. Close the curtains and adjust the gathers on the tape until they are exactly the right length. Tie the cords together in a bow and secure them in a pocket or cord tidy.

DRESSING THE CURTAINS

All curtains hang much better if they are "dressed", or arranged, before use. This encourages them to fall in neat folds and helps the lining, interlining and main fabric to work as one fabric.

Open the curtains fully and begin in the middle of the right-hand leading edge. Tuck the outstretched fingers of your left hand behind the curtain and fold the curtain back over your fingers with your right hand to form a soft pleat. Keep working across the curtain, making finger-length folds of about 12cm/5in. Hold the pleats in place against your body. The outside edge of the curtain should end up facing the wall; if it doesn't, re-pleat, making the pleats slightly smaller or larger. Tie the pleated curtain loosely with a piece of seam tape. Repeat the process at the top and bottom of the curtain. If possible, leave the curtains for two or three days to "set" the pleats.

Fitting a tie-back hook

Be careful when fitting tie-back hooks to preserve the proportions of the curtains. On full-length curtains the hook is usually fitted about 95–100cm/37–39in from the floor. Ask a friend to hold the tie-back in position, blousing the fabric over the top. Stand back and decide if it looks right, adjusting it up or down until you are satisfied with the result.

right *Screw the tie-back hook into the wall, level with the outer edge of the curtain. Both ends of the tie-back can be fitted to the same hook, or a second hook can be attached 5cm/2in further in.*

making blinds

There are many different blinds you can choose, in all shapes and sizes to suit a wide variety of rooms and decorative styles. Some blinds such as roller blinds and Roman blinds are plain and are positioned flat to a window, whereas Austrian and London blinds are fuller and may have gathered headings.

MEASURING FOR A BLIND

Blinds can be fitted inside the recess of a window or on the outside. The instructions given earlier for measuring a window for curtains apply to blinds as well.

Inside the recess

If the blind will hang inside the recess, subtract 3cm/1¼in from the width to allow for the blind mechanism or cord. You do not need to allow for side hems on a roller blind, but check the individual project instructions for all other styles before cutting the fabric.

On the length, allow extra fabric for fitting a roller blind to the roller. Allow a hem allowance on other kinds of blind.

Outside the recess

Blinds that fit outside the recess should overlap on to the wall by at least 5cm/2in on either side. The blind can end at the windowsill, or can drop 10–15cm/4–6in below. This extra length can be particularly effective on an Austrian blind, cut slightly long so that the hem will still fall in scallops. The blind can be fitted at ceiling height or just above the window.

FITTING A BLIND

Blinds can be fitted to a blind track or to a specially prepared wooden batten. Most blinds can be fitted to a batten, but it is easier to use a ready-made track for Austrian or festoon blinds. The batten method is ideal for all other blinds and is simple to make without any specialist woodworking skills. The size of the battening will depend on the space available at the top of the window. Use 5 x 2.5cm/2 x 1in if possible, otherwise 2.5 x 2.5cm/1 x 1in, and cut the wood to the exact width of the finished blind. The wood can be painted to match the window frame or covered in the blind fabric, with the raw edges hidden on the back edge. Fold the fabric over the wood and staple it in position.

1 Velcro is indispensable for fitting blinds. It is a secure method for fitting and allows the blind to be removed for cleaning. Stick a strip of Velcro along the front edge of the batten and secure it with staples.

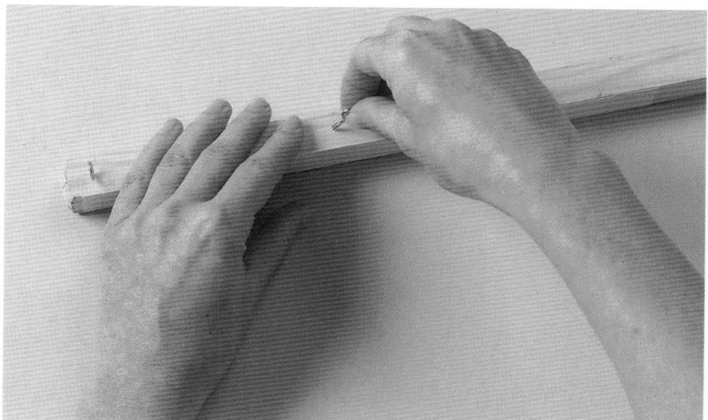

2 Lay the batten along the top edge of the blind and mark the position of the cords. Insert a large screw-eye at each mark along the bottom of the batten. Fit a screw-eye at the end of the batten where the cord will hang. Screw the batten to the top edge of the window frame inside the recess, or fit it with brackets in the wall space above the window. The blind can hang from just below the coving, at ceiling height or about 10cm/4in above the window.

Fitting a cleat

The cleat for securing the blind cord is usually fitted on the right-hand side of the window. It can be quite high up the wall, where it will be hidden in the fullness of a London or Austrian blind, or at windowsill height for a flat blind such as a Roman or roller blind.

choosing a heading tape

Heading tapes for curtains are now available in a wide range of styles to suit every possible situation. There are different widths for short and long curtains, and different tapes for attaching with curtains hooks or Velcro. Standard curtain tapes can be used with either curtain tracks or poles, and can be fixed or drawn. The more decorative styles of tape have special hooks to allow the curtains to hang as elegantly as possible.

Check when you buy the tape that you purchase the correct hooks. Velcro tapes are used for fixed curtains or valances. The Velcro can be attached to the edge of a pelmet board, on to a baton or even directly on a painted wall. With these tapes, the width of the curtain has to be pulled up to exactly the same width as the Velcro. Velcro tapes are ideal for unusual-shaped windows where it isn't possible to fit a curtain track.

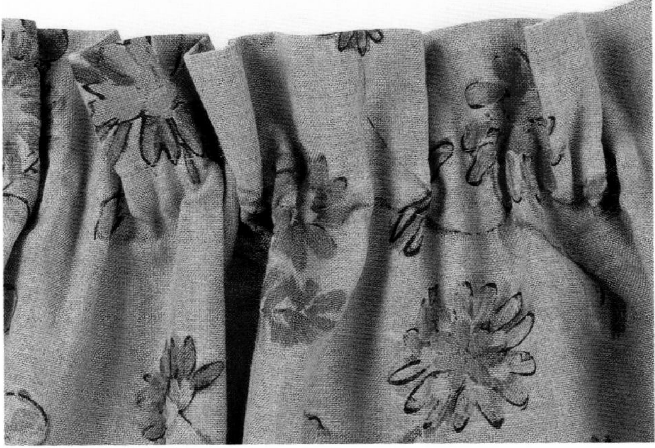

Standard tape

This is the original heading tape. It is 2.5cm/1in wide and is usually attached 2.5–5cm/1–2in below the top of the curtain to create a soft frill that partly covers the pole or track. The curtain needs to be 1½–2 times the length of the track for a softly gathered heading. To attach, fold the tape over at the first pocket. Standard heading tape can be hung with standard curtain hooks.

Pencil pleats

The standard 8cm/3in pencil pleat tape is without doubt the most popular heading tape used today. Its neat pencil-width pleats are held firmly upright because of a special plastic weft thread woven into the tape. Use standard hooks in one of two rows of pockets for fitting to a curtain track or pole. The tape is also available as a Velcro tape for valances and fixed curtains.

Deep pencil pleats

Full-length curtains without a valance look much more elegant with a deeper heading tape because the longer pencil pleats are in better proportion to the length of the curtains. Both the 8cm/3in tape and this 14cm/5½in tape require 2–2½ times the length of the track for optimum fullness, allowing the pleats to lie neatly side by side. The deeper tape has three rows of pockets.

Triple pleat

Triple pleat tape creates one of the most elegant curtain headings and looks equally good whether the curtain is open or closed. There are several widths of triple pleat tape for all lengths of curtain. When attaching the tape, cut the tape in the centre of a group of pleats and pull the cords out to where they emerge. Triple-pleated curtains require special hooks for hanging.

Box pleat

This heading tape is one of the most formal and is used primarily for valances as it is not recommended for curtains that can be drawn. Box pleating tape comes in a standard 8cm/3in width and requires three times the length of the track. Cut the tape in the centre of a group of pleats and pull the cords out to where they emerge from the tape. Special hooks are used for hanging.

Trellis tape

Trellis tape is an attractive variation of the standard pencil pleat. It has half-length pleats that lock together just like clasped fingers. It is available in both 2.5cm/1in and 8cm/3in widths and each requires 1½–2 times the track length. Trellis tape uses standard curtain hooks for hanging. The wider tape has two rows of pockets to allow the curtain track or pole to be partly hidden if required.

Smocking

This decorative heading tape creates a soft, smocked effect across the top of the curtain. It uses standard curtain hooks and track, and has two rows of pockets for using with a curtain pole or track. Smocked headings require 2½ times the length of the track but are only suitable for valances or fixed curtains. The tape should not be pulled up too tightly or the smocked effect will be lost.

basic curtain

The simplest and quickest way to make a curtain is to create a flat rectangle, with machine-stitched hems. The finished curtain can be decorated with simple embroidery patterns such as the running stitch spirals shown here (see basic techniques). It is designed to be hung with curtain clips.

calculating the fabric

Flat curtains only need 1½ times the width for fullness. Remember to divide the finished width by half if there are two curtains. Add 8cm/3in to the width and 26cm/10in to the length for hems.

you will need

- fabric
- sewing kit

tips for basic curtain

- Space the clips every 10–15cm/4–6in.
- After making the curtains, mark any embroidery design with a vanishing marker and stitch with a tapestry needle and crochet cotton or coton à broder.

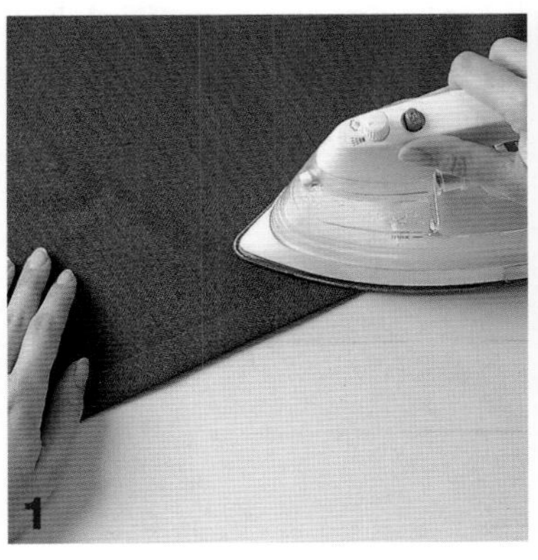

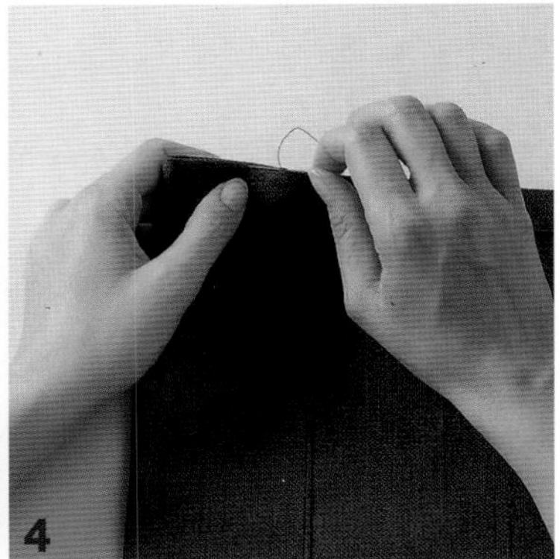

1 Turn under and press a 2cm/¾in hem down each side of the curtain fabric. Fold the hem under again to make a double hem and press.

2 Check the curtains for length, and turn under and press a double 8cm/3in hem along the bottom edge.

3 Stitch the side seams, stitching close to the inside fold. Textured fabrics such as velvet or satin can be slip-hemmed by hand.

4 Stitch the bottom hem then slip-stitch the sides by hand. Mark the length of the curtain and stitch a 5cm/2in double hem along the top edge.

tie-top curtain

An alternative way to hang a flat curtain is with decorative ties along the top edge. Make up the curtain in the same way as the basic curtain, but mark the required length up from the bottom hem and cut 1.5cm/⅝in above this mark. The ties can be attached into a lining or using a facing. The length of the ties depends on how far the top of the curtain will hang below the curtain rail and whether they are tied in a knot or a bow.

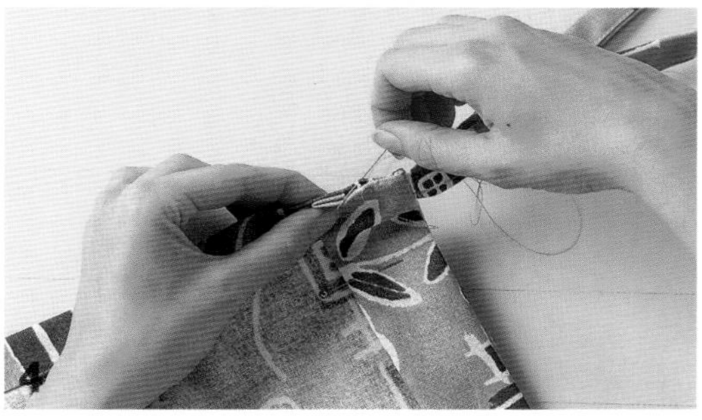

calculating the fabric

Tie-top curtains require 1½–2 times the window width for fullness. Add hem allowances as for the basic curtain. Check the length of the tie, usually about 60cm/24in and add this to the length of fabric required. The ties are cut vertically across the fabric so that the pattern matches.

you will need

- fabric
- sewing kit

tip for

If the centre of each tie is offset when attached to the curtain, the bow will lie at the top of the curtain pole.

1 To make the ties, cut 5cm/2in-wide strips of fabric, double the required length of the ties plus 2cm/¾in seam allowance. Press under 1cm/½in along each edge. Fold the ties in half lengthways and stitch close to the edge.

2 Make sufficient ties for one to be spaced every 15–20cm/6–8in along the top of the curtain. Fold each tie in half and pin in position on the right side of the curtain, along the top edge.

3 For the facing, cut an 8cm/3in-wide strip of fabric to fit across the width of the curtain plus 3cm/1¼in seam allowance. Pin it right side down over the ties and stitch along the top edge. Fold the facing over to the inside of the curtain.

4 Press 1.5cm/⅝in along the sides of the facing to the wrong side. Slip-stitch the sides of the facing, and hem or stitch the bottom edge.

tab-top curtain

A deep border and facing make it much easier to attach tabs, which are particularly suitable for heavier-weight curtains. The depth of the border depends on personal taste but should be in proportion to the length of the curtain. Stitch the hem and side seams of the main body of the curtain before adding the border and add a lining at this stage, if required.

calculating the fabric

Plan the depth of the border and the length of the curtain. Allow 10cm/4in on the width and 16.5cm/6½in lengthwise for the hem and seam allowances. Cut two contrast border panels, adding 1.5cm/⅝in seam allowance all round. The average tab is 40cm/16in long. Allow an extra ½m/½yd to cut the tabs.

you will need

- **fabric A**
- **fabric B**
- **sewing kit**

tip for tab-top curtain

Space the tabs approximately every 15–20cm/6–8in.

1 Using contrast fabric, cut tabs twice the required finished width and length plus 3cm/1¼in seam allowance. Fold each tab in half lengthways, right sides together, and stitch along the long edge . Trim the seams and press open. Turn the tabs right side out and press, with the seam down the centre back.

2 Using contrast fabric, cut a border panel the required depth and the same width as each curtain, adding 3cm/1¼in seam allowance to both measurements. With right sides together, stitch the panel to the top of each curtain piece. Open out and press. With the seams to the inside, space the folded tabs along the top of the border on the right side. Align the raw edges.

3 For the facing, cut a second panel the same size as the border from contrast fabric. With right sides together and raw edges aligned, pin in position on top of the border, and stitch along the top edge. Press the seam flat. Turn the facing over to the wrong side of the curtain. Turn the side edges in to match the width of the curtain. Press.

4 Turn under the lower edge of the facing in line with the stitching and pin. Slip-stitch the side edges of the border and hem the facing to the stitches.

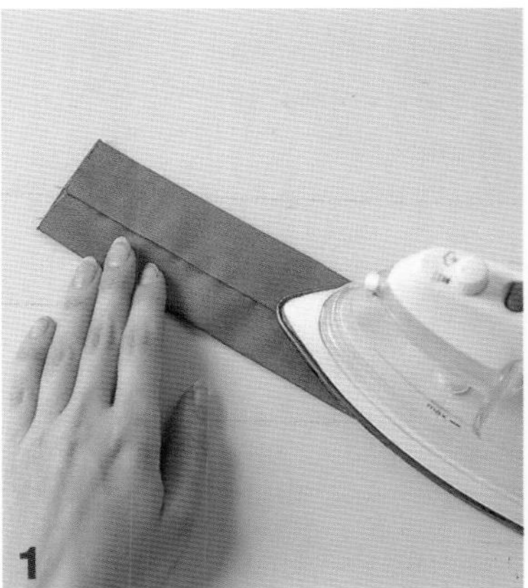

1

2

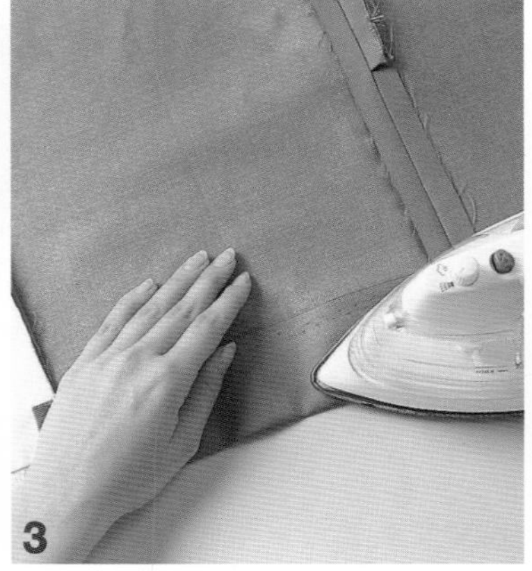

3

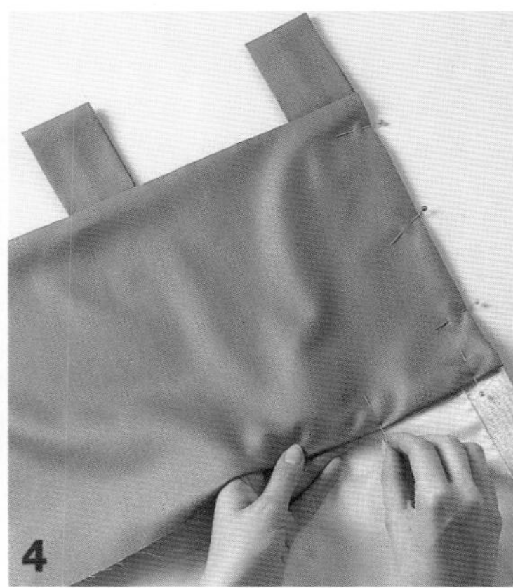

4

mitred corner curtain

Fabrics that are equally attractive on both sides are ideal for making this flat curtain. The wrong side will show on the mitred hems and where the curtain is folded over to create a mock valance. The finished curtain is hung from clips.

calculating the fabric

The depth of the mock valance is entirely personal, but a good guide is ⅙–⅕ the finished length. Allow 1½ times the track length for fullness. Add the valance depth to the finished length of the curtains and allow 15cm/6in on each edge for the hems.

you will need

- **reversible fabric**
- **sewing kit**

tip for mitred corner curtain

The length of the curtain can be adjusted by changing the depth of the valance.

1 If you are using a patterned fabric, the width of the hem all round the curtain will depend on the depth of the pattern. Fold the fabric along a line in the pattern and mark the hem width, approximately 8cm/3in depending on the pattern repeat. Trim 1.5cm/⅝in away from this mark.

2 Decide which side of the fabric you wish to be the right side and place it facing outwards. Turn over a double hem on each side and the top and bottom edge and press.

3 Open out the hems and fold diagonally across the corner at the first crease marks. Trim 1cm/½in in from the fold to reduce bulk.

4 Refold the double hems and press. Pin and tack (baste) the hems then stitch close to the inside fold. Slip-stitch the mitred corners.

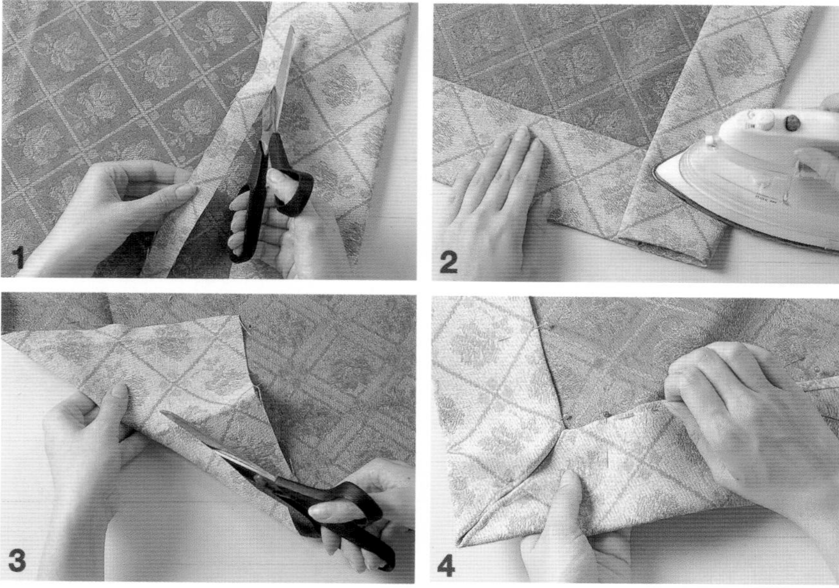

lined flat curtain

A fitted lining will improve the look of a basic curtain, making it hang better and will protect the body of the fabric from fading. Linings help prolong the life of the curtain and when worn can be replaced more economically than replacing an entire set of curtains.

calculating the fabric

Allow 1½–2 times the finished track length depending on the amount of fullness required. Add 10cm/4in to the width and 20cm/8in to the length for hems. The lining is the same width as the finished curtain and 13cm/5in longer.

you will need

- **fabric**
- **lining**
- **sewing kit**

tip for lined flat curtain

Insert a weight into the bottom corners of each curtain.

above *Attach clips every 10–15cm/4–6in.*

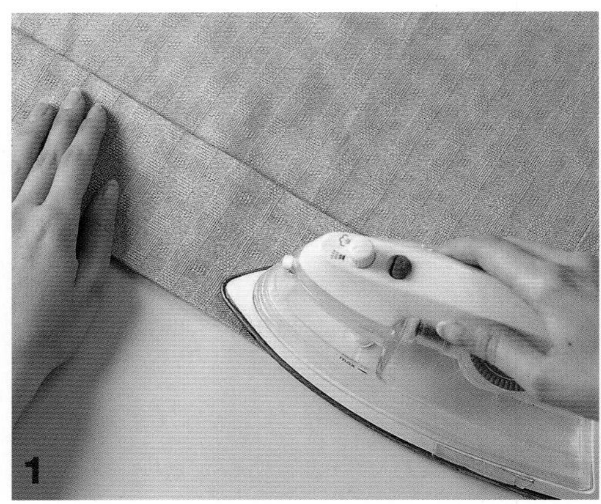

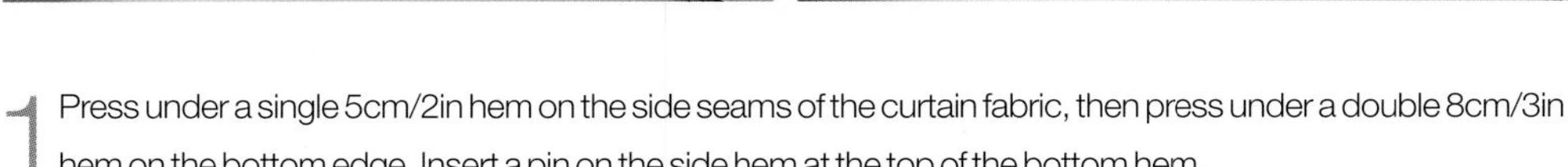

1 Press under a single 5cm/2in hem on the side seams of the curtain fabric, then press under a double 8cm/3in hem on the bottom edge. Insert a pin on the side hem at the top of the bottom hem.

2 Open out the hems and fold the fabric diagonally, with the marker pin at the top of the new fold, and the bottom of the side fold meeting the lower new fold. Press and refold, then blind-hem the bottom (see basic techniques).

3 Cut out the lining the same width as the finished curtain and 13cm/5in longer. Press under a 5cm/2in double hem along the bottom and stitch.

4 Open out the side hem. With right sides together, pin one side of the lining down one side hem of the curtain so that the top of the lining hem is level with the curtain hem.

5 Repeat with the other side of the curtain and lining, and stitch 2.5cm/1in from the raw edge of the lining on both sides. Press the seams towards the lining. Turn the curtain through to the right side. Turn under 5cm/2in along the top edge of the lining and press so that the raw edges are between the layers. Pin the lining just below the curtain fabric and slip-hem in place.

lined tab-top curtain

This method of adding tabs is ideal if you do not want stitching showing on the right side. It is particularly suitable for fabrics such as velvet or satin.

calculating the fabric

Allow 1½–2 times the finished track length depending on the amount of fullness required. Add 10cm/4in to the width and 20cm/8in to the length for hem and seam allowances. Cut the lining the same width as the finished curtain and 7cm/2¾in longer. Allow 0.5m/½yd fabric for the tabs.

you will need

- **fabric**
- **lining**
- **sewing kit**

1

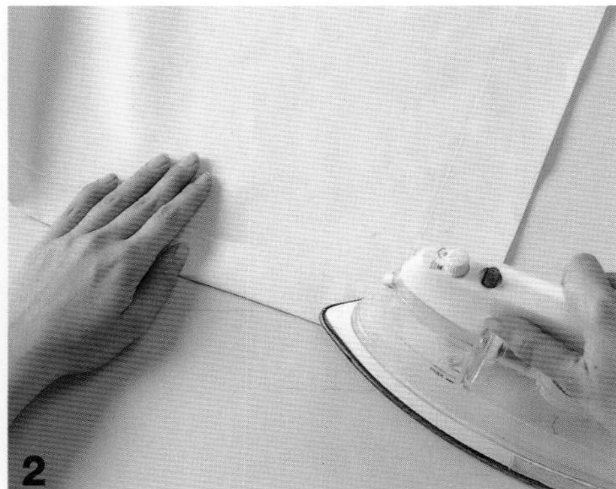

2

3

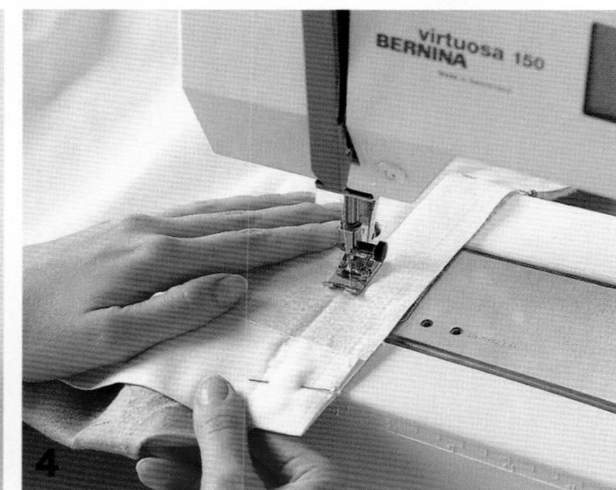

4

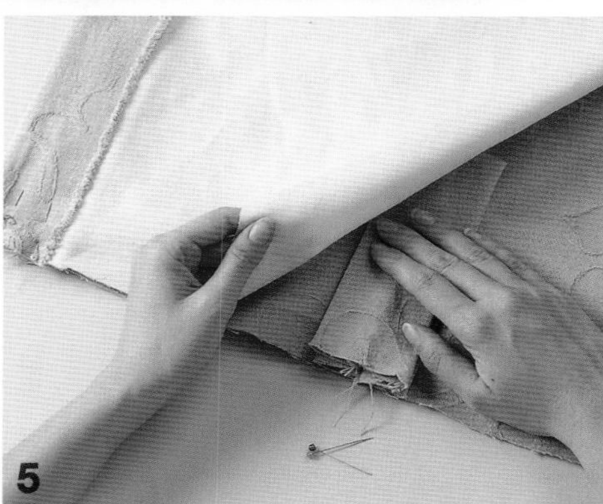

5

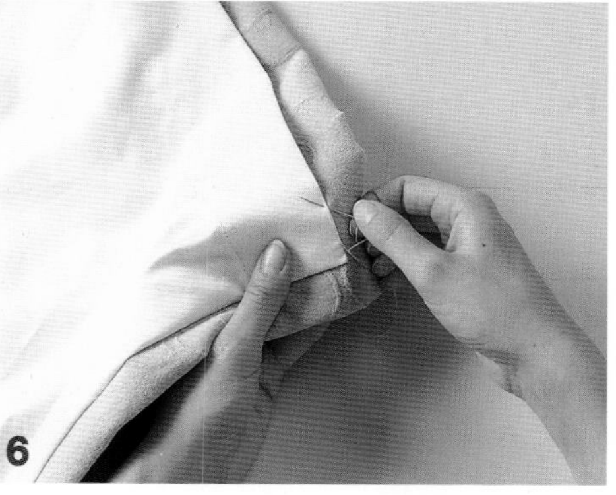

6

1 Press under a single 5cm/2in hem on the side seams of the curtain fabric, then press under a double 8cm/3in hem on the bottom edge. Fold and press the mitred corner. Blind-hem the bottom hem (see basic techniques).

2 Cut out the lining the same width as the finished curtain and 13cm/5in longer. Press under a 5cm/2in double hem along the bottom and stitch. Turn under 2.5cm/1in down the sides.

3 Pin the lining to the side seams with raw edges together, and so that the top of the hems are in line.

4 Turn the curtain through and stitch the side seams along the pressed fold line.

5 Make the required number of tabs (see tab-top curtain). Pin the first tab level with the pressed fold at the side of the curtain. Space the other tabs equally across the top of the curtain. Stitch along 2cm/¾in from the top edge.

6 Turn the curtain through and press the top edge. Stitch 2.5cm/1in from the top of the curtain for extra strength, if desired. Slip-stitch the mitre and hem along the bottom edge of the lining for 2.5cm/1in to hold it in place.

café curtain

A café curtain forms an attractive screen across the bottom half of a window. To find the length, secure a curtain pole halfway up the window. Measure from the top of the curtain pole to the windowsill.

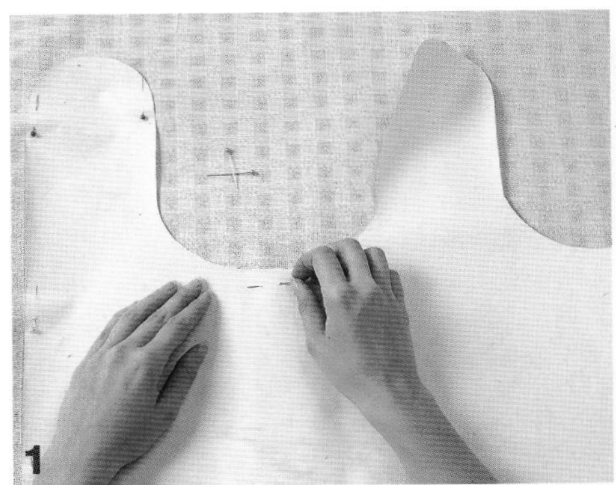

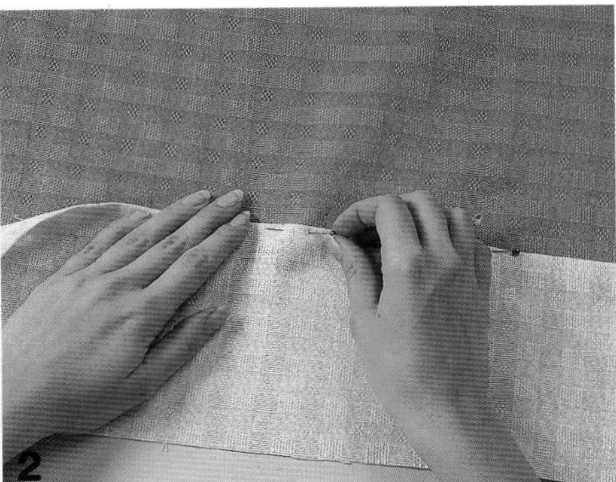

to make the pattern

Enlarge the template at the back of the book, adding as many tabs as necessary to achieve the required width. Fold the tabs over level with the bottom of the curved edges. Measure the finished length of the curtain from the top fold and cut off the excess paper.

you will need

- **paper and pencil to make a pattern**
- **fabric**
- **contrast lining fabric**
- **lightweight iron-on interfacing**
- **iron-on fusible bonding web**
- **self-cover button kit**
- **sewing kit**

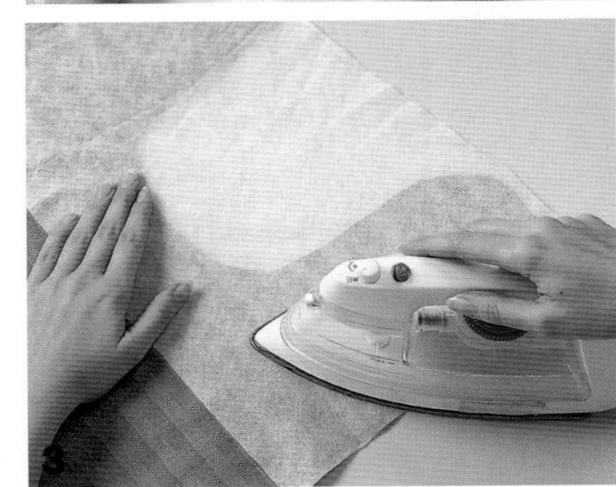

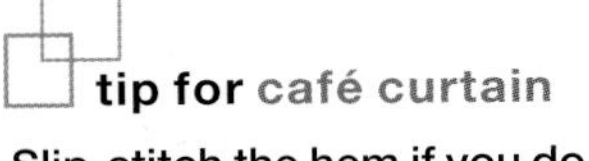

tip for café curtain

Slip-stitch the hem if you do not have any fusible bonding web.

1 Measure the size of the template and add 5cm/2in to the width and length. Cut a piece of main and contrast lining fabric this size and another 18cm/7in strip the same width in contrast fabric. Pin the template to the two large pieces and cut out adding 1.5cm/⅝in seam allowances all round.

2 Cut 13.5cm/5¼in from the bottom of the main curtain panel. Press under a 1.5cm/⅝in seam along the top edge of the contrast border and pin then slip-tack to the main curtain fabric. Stitch and press the seam towards the border.

3 Cut a band of lightweight interfacing 30cm/12in wide and iron to the wrong side of the main fabric. Trim the excess around the curved edges.

4 Pin the lining and main fabric panels with right sides together, and stitch around the curved edges and down the side seams. Notch the outward facing curves and snip into the inward facing curves.

5 Turn through and ease out the curves carefully before pressing. Turn under 1.5cm/⅝in along the lower edge of the curtain and the lining and press the two hems together using iron-on fusible bonding web.

6 Cover the required number of buttons following the instructions on the packet. Mark the position of the buttonholes on the end of each tab. Stitch the buttonholes. Fold the tabs over level with the bottom of the curves and stitch a button in line with the buttonhole. Fold over the curtain pole and button the tabs.

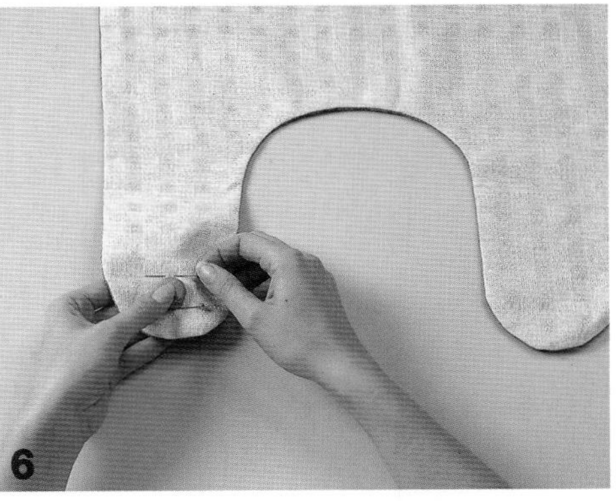

curtain to hang from a rod or wires

A softly gathered curtain is often used as screening behind kitchen cupboards, glass-fronted wardrobes (closets) or French windows. The curtain is stretched between two wires or rods that are screwed into the reverse side of the door 5cm/2in above and below the panels.

calculating the fabric

The width of fabric required depends on the weight of the fabric and the effect you want to create. In general, allow twice the width for a lightweight fabric and 1½ times for medium curtain weight. The length of the fabric is the distance between the curtain rods or wires at the top and bottom plus 20cm/8in hem allowance.

you will need

- **fabric**
- **curtain rods or curtain wires**
- **sewing kit**

tip for curtain to hang from a rod or wires

If the fabric is the correct width, use the selvage rather than make a hem.

1 Measure between the curtain rods and cut the fabric to this length plus 20cm/8in for hems to encase the wire. At each side, press under and stitch 1cm/½in double hems. Press under a double 5cm/2in hem along the top and bottom edges.

2 Stitch the top and bottom hems close to the inside folded edge, reverse-stitching at each end to reinforce the stitching.

3 To make the casing for the wire, stitch 1cm/½in away from the first row of stitches. If you are using a curtain rod, adjust the size of the casing to fit.

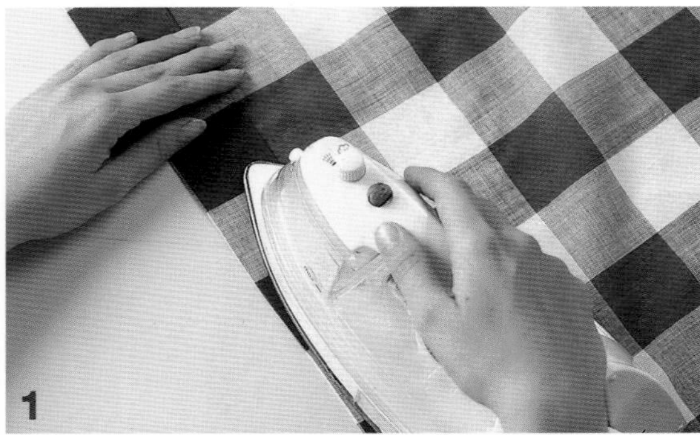

1

2

3

separate lining

above *Separate linings can be added to any type of curtain to help prolong the life of the fabric.*

Curtains last much longer if they are lined as the lining protects the fabric from sunlight and damp. Many curtains have a fitted lining but you can make a separate lining to attach to curtains with a heading tape. Usually the lining is attached to the bottom row of pockets on the curtain heading tape with separate hooks.

calculating the fabric

A separate lining doesn't need to be as full as the body of the curtain. One-and-half times the width is sufficient. Cut the lining 5cm/2in longer than the finished curtain. If you need to join two or more lengths of lining fabric to fit a large window, stitch flat seams and press them open.

you will need

- **lining**
- **heading tape**
- **sewing kit**

1 Press under a 5cm/2in double hem along the bottom edge and a 1cm/½in double hem down both sides of the lining. Stitch in place and press.

2 Pull out 4cm/1½in of the cords at one end of the heading tape and knot the ends. Trim the cord ends.

3 Tuck the top edge of the lining between the two flaps along the lower edge of the tape and pin. Fold under the knotted ends of the tape and stitch across the tape to secure the cords.

4 Stitch along the lower edge of the tape from the right side. The underside of the tape is slightly longer so that it will be caught in the stitching. Gather the lining in as far as it will go, then loosen the gathers until it fits across the curtain. Insert curtain hooks through the loops and attach to the tape on the curtain.

1

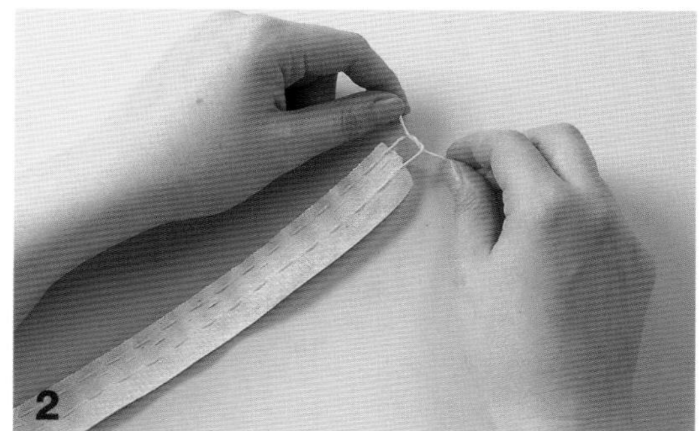

2

3

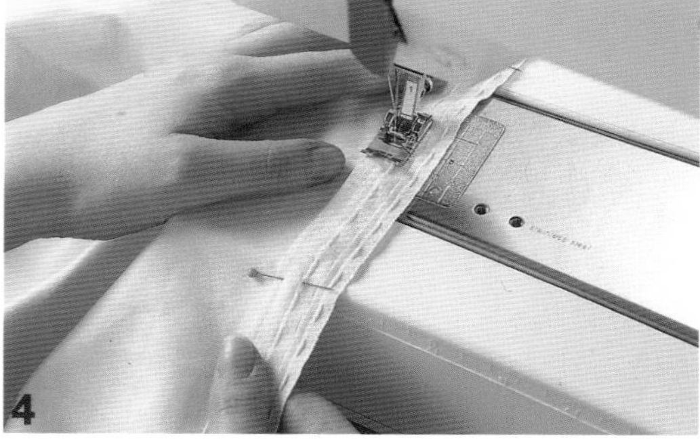

4

unlined curtain using heading tape

Heading or curtain tape is a popular way to hang curtains and is available in various styles to create different effects. Where you cut the tape depends on the type of tape. The pinch pleat tape shown here should be cut in the centre of a group of pleats at the edge of the curtain that will come to the centre of the window. The second curtain should have the loose cords of the tape at the other side. Be sure to purchase the correct curtain hooks for the tape you are using.

calculating the fabric

Measure the required curtain length and add 20cm/8in hem and heading allowance. Check the fullness ratio for your heading tape and add 8cm/3in for hems and 3cm/1¼in for any seam.

you will need

- **fabric**
- **heading tape**
- **curtain weights**
- **cord tidy or cord pocket**
- **sewing kit**

tip for unlined curtain using heading tape

Use pencil pleat or standard heading tape for an alternative look.

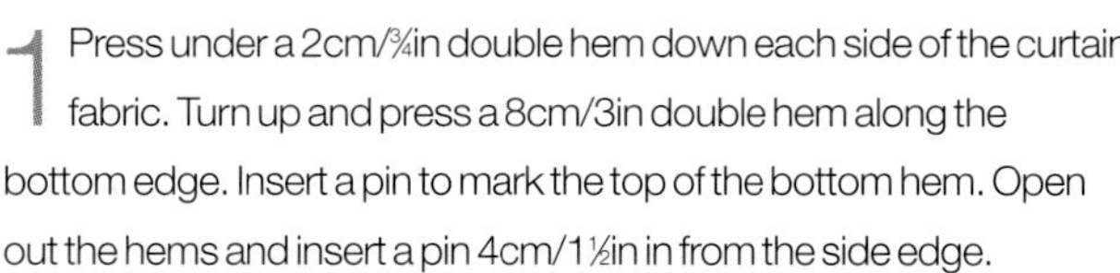

1 Press under a 2cm/¾in double hem down each side of the curtain fabric. Turn up and press a 8cm/3in double hem along the bottom edge. Insert a pin to mark the top of the bottom hem. Open out the hems and insert a pin 4cm/1½in in from the side edge.

2 Fold over the bottom hem diagonally between the pins and press flat.

3 Refold the side, then the bottom hems to make an uneven mitre corner, as shown, and press.

4 Slip-hem both side hems, catching only one or two threads of the main curtain fabric so that the stitching is almost invisible on the right side.

1

2

3

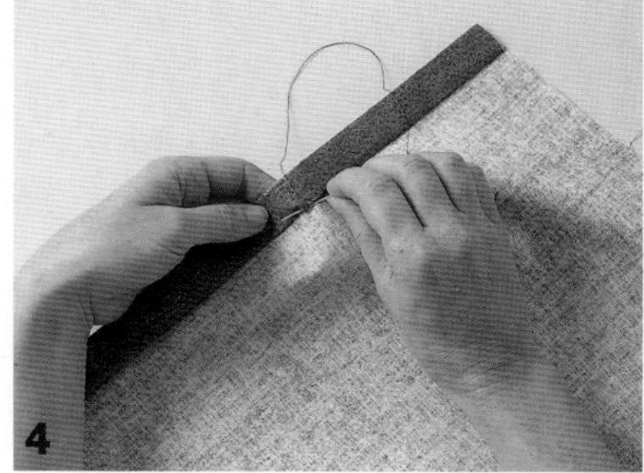

4

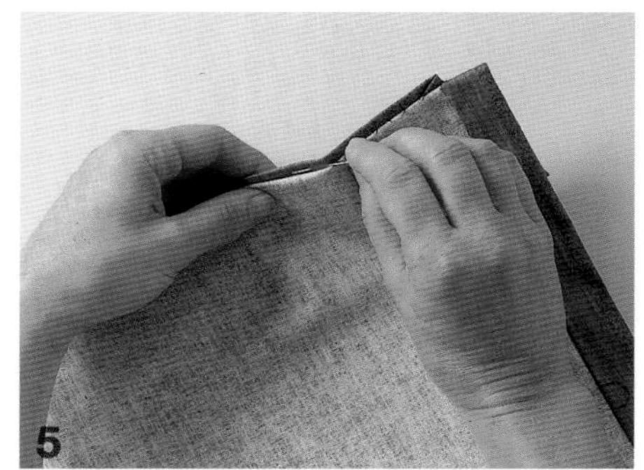

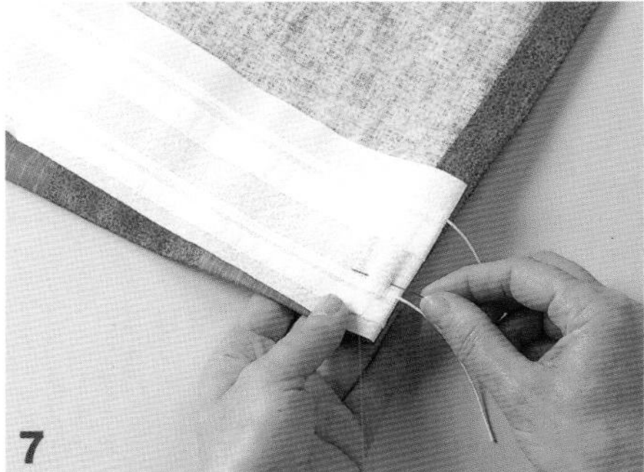

5 Fold the bottom hem back on itself so that 5mm/¼ in shows above the curtain fabric. Blind-hem, taking tiny stitches into the main curtain fabric and a longer stitch through the hem.

6 Tuck a weight into the hem at each bottom corner and stitch in place. Slip-stitch the mitred corners closed with invisible stitches.

7 Cut the curtain to the required length plus 1.5cm/⅝ in seam allowance at the top. Fold over the top seam allowance and press. Turn the curtain tape over at one side, leaving the cords free, and pin to the edge of the curtain. Make sure the tape is the right way up. Pin the tape 3mm/⅛ in from the top of the curtain. When you reach the other end of the curtain, trim the tape, allowing a little to turn under. Pull out the cords and tie together in a knot. Turn the end of the tape under and pin.

8 Stitch along the long sides of the tape, stitching both lines in the same direction. Stitch across both ends, but keep the cords free on the outside edge of each curtain.

to finish

Carefully pull up the pleats, using your thumb and fingers to support the tape. Hold the loose cords in one hand or tie them around a door handle. Keep working the pleats along the cords until the whole curtain is evenly pleated. Tie the cords in a slip knot, then tie the ends around a cord tidy or tuck them in a cord pocket. Insert a curtain hook into two adjacent loops at the back of each set of pleats.

attaching a permanent lining

Hand stitching a lining into a curtain gives a more professional finish. The lining is attached to the curtain with a series of parallel lines of lock stitch, which prevent the two layers from separating. Here standard curtain tape makes the curtain hang in soft, casual folds.

you will need

- fabric
- lining
- sewing kit

tips for attaching a permanent lining

- Contrasting colour linings work well and can be used on flamboyant curtains where the lining may show, for example, where the curtain is held part way down over a hold-back.
- Cut the lining to the same width as the finished curtain and 13cm/5in longer.

1

2

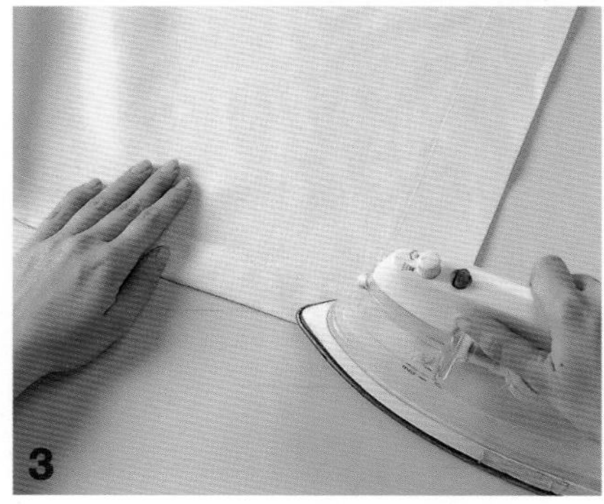

3

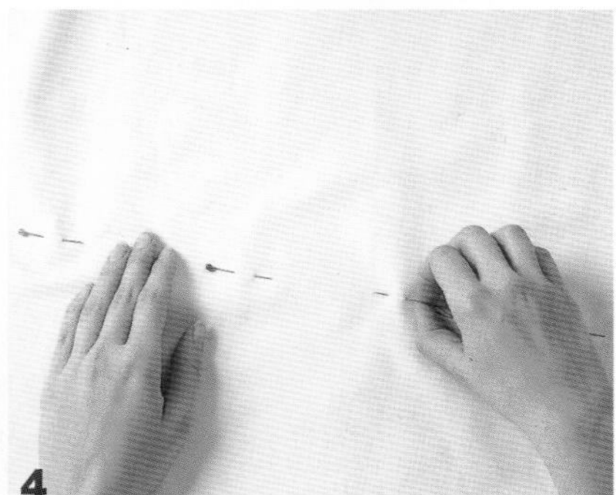

4

1 Press under a 5cm/2in single hem along both sides of the curtain. Turn up and press an 8cm/3in double hem along the bottom edge and mitre the corner (see basic techniques). Secure the edges of the side hems with herringbone stitch, catching just one or two threads on the main curtain so that the stitching is invisible on the right side.

2 Insert a weight into each corner and secure the bottom hem in place using blind hem stitch. On the wrong side, mark parallel lines with tailor's chalk down the curtain, midway across every width of fabric.

3 Cut out the lining to the same width as the curtains. Turn up and stitch a 5cm/2in double hem along the bottom edge. Turn in and press 2.5cm/1in down each side.

4 With wrong sides together, pin the lining to one folded edge of the curtain, then fold it back as far as the chalk line. Pin the lining and curtain fabric together along the chalk line, then tack (baste) along the line of pins, removing the pins as you go.

5 Work lock stitch down the fold to attach the lining to the curtain. Repeat the process for each chalk mark or seam until the lining is lock-stitched in place.

6 Slip-stitch each side of the lining to the curtain. Hem along the bottom for 2.5cm/1in so that the lining will not billow out if the window is open.

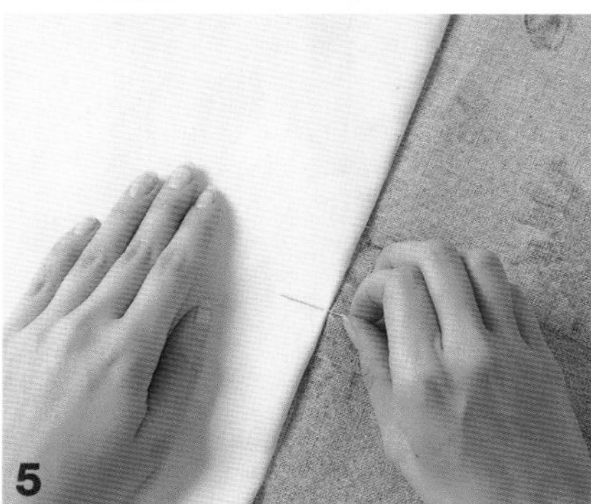

5

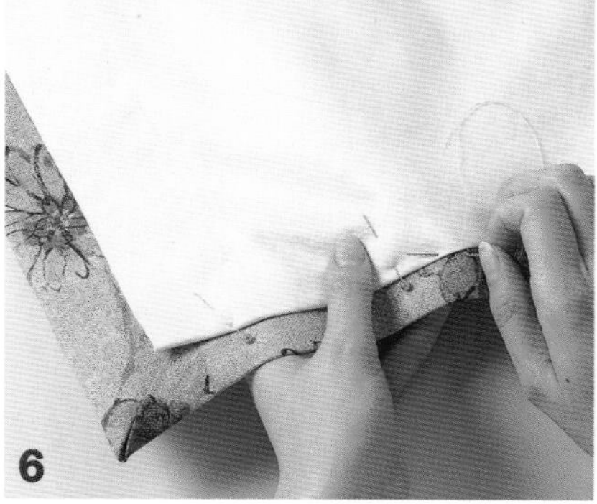

6

interlined curtain

Interlined curtains look substantial and luxurious, even if the curtains are made from lightweight fabric. Interlining or "bump" is a special cotton or mixed fibre wadding (batting) that is often added to door curtains, to insulate a room against draughts (drafts) and to absorb noise. It is available in a range of thicknesses, so hold the curtain fabric against the interlining to see how it affects the drape and appearance before deciding which to buy.

calculating the fabric

Interlined curtains do not need to be as full as ordinary curtains because of the bulk of the interlining. This heavyweight curtain is completed with a pencil pleat tape and requires only 1½ times the track length. Add 20cm/8in to the length for hems and turn-in allowance. Cut the borders twice the finished width, adding 20cm/8in to the length. Cut the interlining the same length, adding twice the border width to the width of the main curtain fabric.

you will need

- **fabric**
- **contrasting fabric**
- **interlining**
- **lining**
- **curtain weight**
- **sewing kit**

tip for interlined curtain

To join widths of interlining overlap the edges and secure with herringbone stitch.

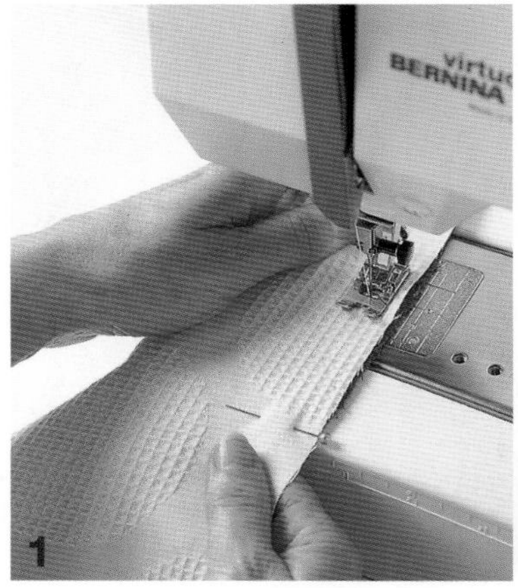

1

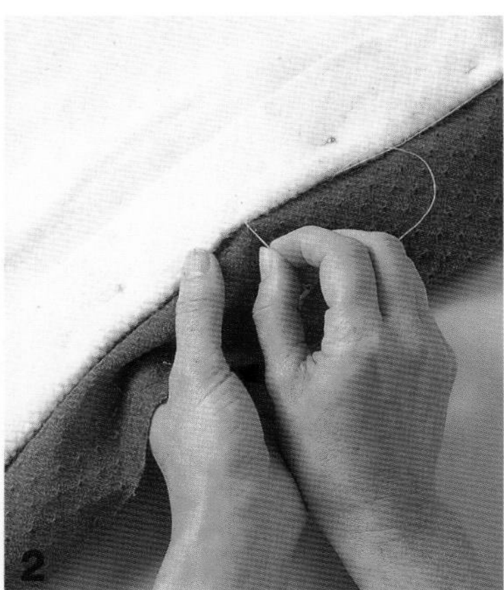

2

1 Using contrast fabric, cut out a border panel twice the required finished width for each curtain. With right sides together and raw edges aligned, pin the border down the inside edge of the curtain fabric. Stitch in place with a 1.5cm/⅝in seam allowance. Press the seam open.

2 Cut out a piece of interlining to fit the size of the opened-out curtain fabric and place it on top. Turn under a 5cm/2in turning on the interlining down the border edge of the curtain. Lock-stitch along the fold to secure the interlining.

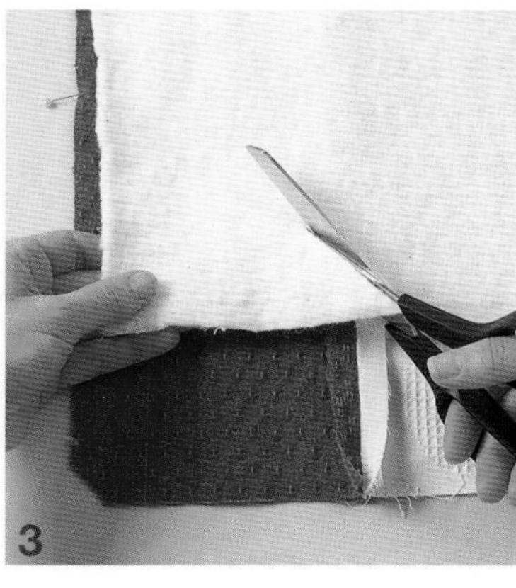

3

4

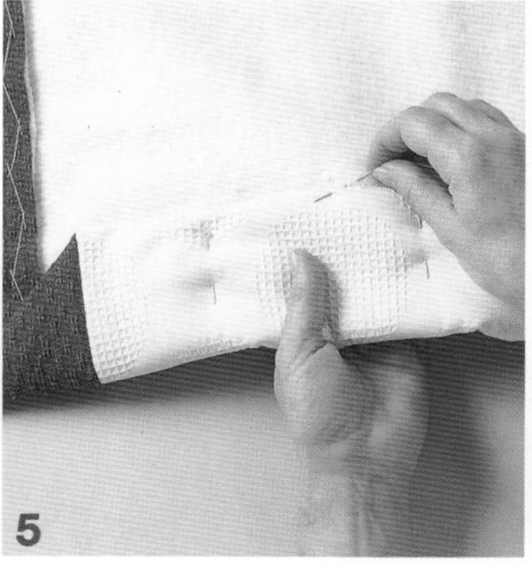

5

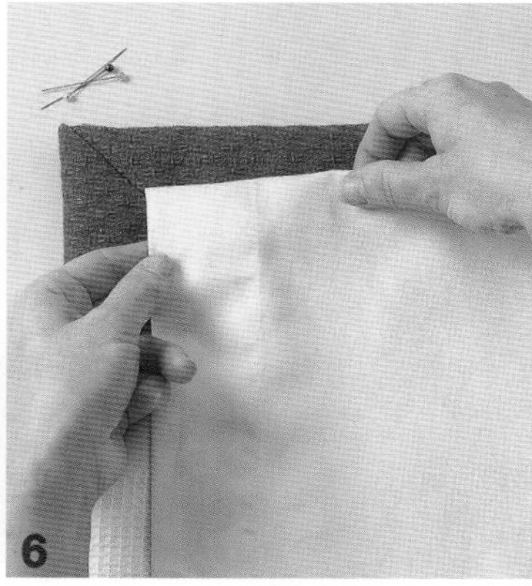

6

3 Fold the interlining back and lock-stitch the interlining in the centre of every width of fabric and down each seam. Cut off the interlining 8cm/3in from the bottom of the curtain and trim the corner, as shown, to reduce bulk.

4 Turn in the inside edge of the curtain and work a row of herringbone stitch into the interlining, close to the raw edge.

5 Turn up the bottom hem and pin, folding the corner into a neat mitre. Stitch a weight into the corner then hem the curtain fabric to the interlining.

6 Prepare the lining and pin the side seams. Mark, pin and lock-stitch every 30–50cm/12–20in across the lining (see attaching a permanent lining). Slip-hem the side seams. Hem along the bottom for 2.5cm/1in to secure. Trim the curtain to length and attach the curtain tape.

gathered valance with a shaped edge

A gathered valance is a soft, attractive way to finish curtains. It can be a short version of a curtain, or it can have a shaped lower edge. The valance can be decorated with binding, braid or another trimming to emphasize the curved shape of the bottom of the valance.

calculating the fabric

A valance is usually fuller than the curtain – normally three times the length of the track or pelmet board. Measure the length of the pelmet board and add twice the return (the distance to the wall) and multiply by three to calculate the width. The length of a straight valance is one-sixth of the curtain length. Make the pattern before calculating the fabric for a shaped valance. Buy 1m/1yd contrast fabric for the binding.

you will need

- paper pattern
- fabric
- contrast or toning fabric
- 8cm/3in heading tape
- lining
- sewing kit

tip for gathered valance with a shaped edge

For speed, make a length of continuous binding (see basic techniques).

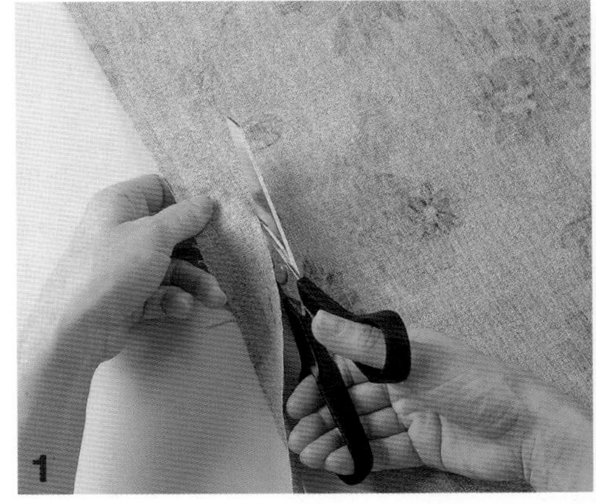

1

2

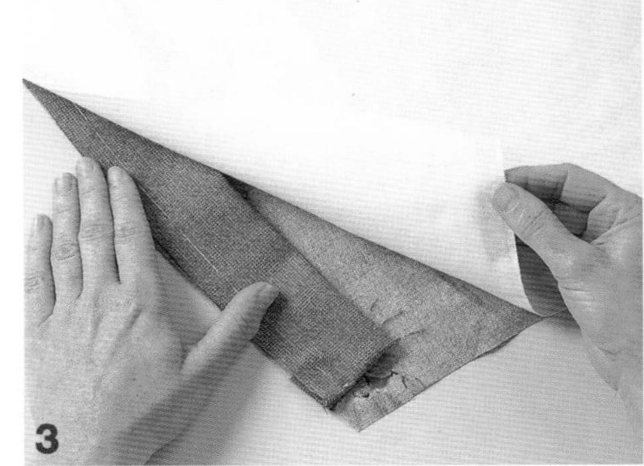

3

4

making the valance

You can make a valance with any style of Velcro curtain heading tape and make the lower edge straight or curved. To make a pattern for a shaped valance follow the instructions at the start of the chapter.

1 Join sufficient widths of fabric together to make a strip three times the width of the window. Adjust the depth of the pattern, taking the depth of the finished lower binding from the top edge. With right sides together fold the fabric in half. Draw around the pattern. Cut along the marked line.

2 Cut and join sufficient 13cm/5in-wide bias strips to fit along the curved edge of the valance. Press in the short ends. Fold the strip in half lengthways, wrong sides together and pin along the lower edge of the valance, raw edges aligned, beginning and ending 1.5cm/⅝in from both ends. Tack (baste) the binding to the valance.

3 Cut the lining using the valance pattern and place it on top of the binding, right sides together. Stitch the side seams and along the lower edge, leaving 1.5cm/⅝in seam allowance. Trim across the corners and turn through. Press the side seams and bottom edge.

4 Pin a 5cm/2in-wide strip of straight binding along the top edge of the valance and stitch, leaving 1.5cm/⅝in seam allowance. Press the binding away from the valance. Fold in the ends, then turn the binding over to the reverse side.

5 Stitch Velcro heading tape to the top edge of the valance on the wrong side. Knot the tape cords at one end, then pull up the tape as far as possible. Ease out the gathers to fit the window.

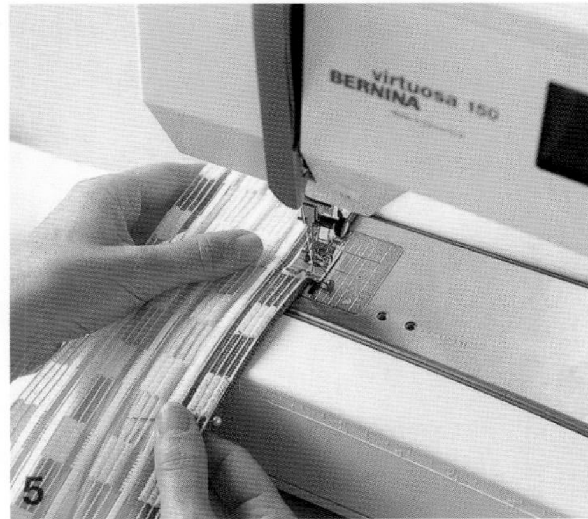

5

hand-pleated valance

Hand pleating is a simple way to create elegant triple or French pleats for the top of a valance or curtain. As there is no bulky heading tape, curtains with a hand-pleated heading will pull back into a smaller space. The effect is similar to a triple-pleat heading tape, but with this professional method there is no stitching on the right side and the pleats can be spaced to line up with stripes or patterns in the fabric. You can use any deep heading tape as an alternative.

calculating the fabric

For perfect proportions, a valance is usually one-sixth of the length of the finished curtains. The width required for a hand-pleated finish is 2–3 times the finished width, but will depend on the fabric pattern. Plan the pleats to make the best use of any stripes or pattern in the fabric. The pleats normally use 15cm/6in of fabric, with a 13cm/5in gap between them. Leave approximately 8cm/3in before the end pleats on a straight valance, and 23cm/9in if the valance is to be fitted to a pelmet board.

you will need

- **fabric**
- **lining fabric**
- **8cm/3in wide iron-on buckram**
- **self-cover button kit**
- **sewing kit**

tip for hand-pleated valance

Make the curtains with a pencil tape heading so that they hang elegantly below the valance.

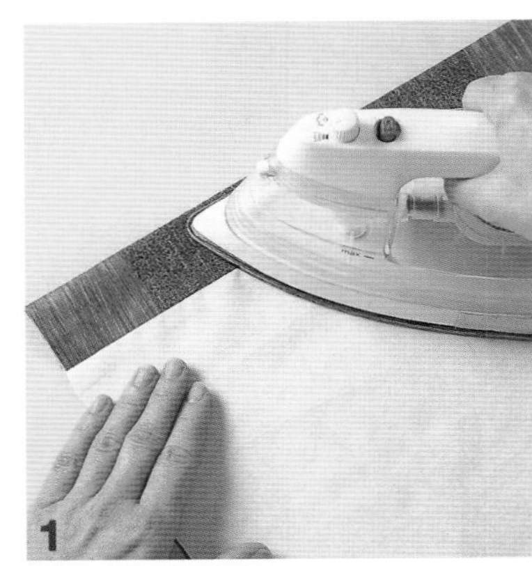

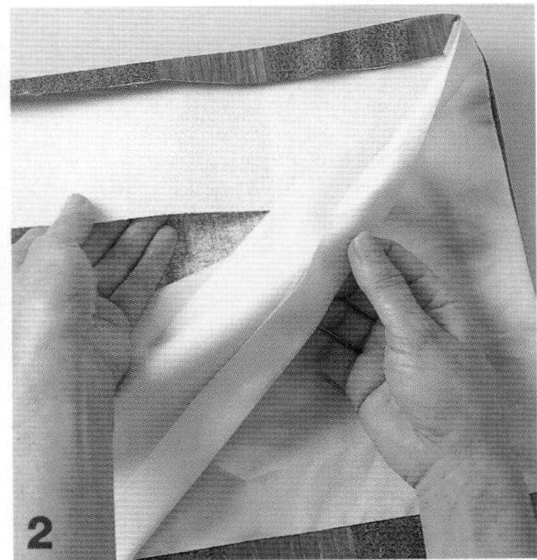

1 Cut the fabric 8cm/3in deeper than the finished valance, and the required width plus 1.5cm/⅝in seam allowance. Cut the lining the same width but 5cm/2in shorter. Stitch the lining to the bottom edge of the valance and press the seam open. Fold the fabrics wrong sides together so that all edges align and press the bottom edge.

2 With right sides together, stitch the side seams. Turn through, then press under 1.5cm/⅝in on the top edge of both the fabric and lining. Cut a piece of iron-on buckram to fit the length of the fabric and tuck it under the pressed turning, with the adhesive side facing the lining.

3 Smooth out the fabric and roll the seams so that they are directly on the edge. Press the lining to fuse it to the buckram.

4 Mark the return (the distance from the front of the pelmet board to the wall), the gaps and the pleat widths across the fabric. Fold the valance, matching the first two pleat marks, and stitch the pleat to the depth of the buckram only. Reverse stitch at each end.

5 Hold the centre of the fold and push down to form three equal pleats. Catch the top of the pleats in the centre with invisible hand stitches.

6 On the right side, oversew the pleats together at the bottom of the buckram. Cover buttons with matching or contrast fabric, using a button kit, and stitch on to the pleats to hide the oversewing stitches. On the wrong side, hand stitch loop Velcro along the top edge for hanging.

hard pelmet

A hard pelmet looks very impressive in a formal room. It can be any shape, but simple lines such as a soft curve or plain, straight edge are more modern. The most suitable backing board is 3mm/⅛in thick hardboard or plywood; you can use heavyweight buckram, but it is sensitive to atmospheric changes and may buckle if placed above a radiator. As a general rule, the depth of the pelmet is approximately one-sixth of the length of the curtains. Draw a paper template of the proposed shape and pin it over the top of the window to see how it will look. Adjust the shape until you are satisfied.

calculating the fabric

Decide on the finished depth of the contrast borders at the top and bottom. Measure the depth of the pelmet board and add 3cm/1¼in seam allowance, then subtract the depth of both borders. Cut out the main fabric to this measurement and add the length of the pelmet board plus twice the return, plus 30cm/12in. If the fabric needs to be joined, stitch half-widths at each side of one full width and press the seams flat.

you will need

- **pencil and paper**
- **3mm/⅛in hardboard or plywood**
- **jigsaw**
- **carpet tape**
- **interlining**
- **multi-purpose adhesive**
- **contrast fabric**
- **fabric**
- **lining**
- **staple gun**
- **curved upholstery needle**
- **Velcro**
- **sewing kit**

tip for making a hard pelmet

Interlining is not absolutely essential but gives a much better finish.

1 Using a jigsaw, cut a piece of hardboard or plywood the required shape for the main front piece of the pelmet. Cut two side panels the same depth as the outside edge and the length of the return, i.e. the distance the pelmet is away from the wall, (usually 15cm/6in). Attach the side panels to the board, using carpet tape down both inside edges.

2 Cut out a piece of interlining slightly larger than the pelmet board. Stick it to the front, using multi-purpose adhesive. Allow to dry, then trim the interlining flush with the sides.

3 Cut two strips of contrast fabric twice the depth of each finished border and 30cm/12in longer than the length of the board. With right sides together, pin and stitch the borders to the top and bottom of the main fabric, using 1.5cm/⅝in seam allowances.

4 Cut out the lining fabric the same size as the front of the board plus1.5cm/⅝in seam allowance on all sides. Trim the lower border to the finished size plus 1.5cm/⅝in seam allowance. Pin the lining centrally along this edge and stitch.

1

2

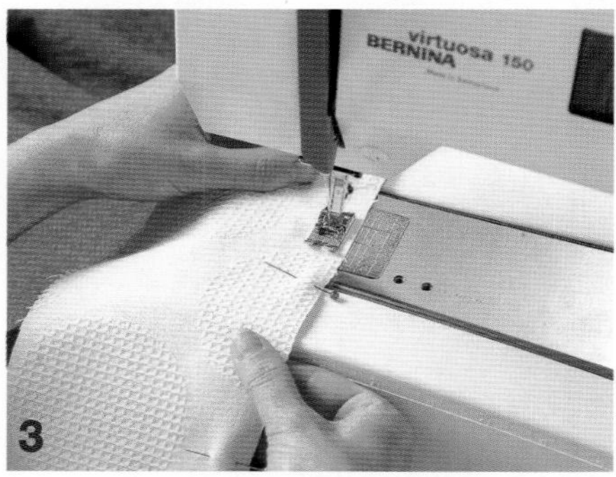

3

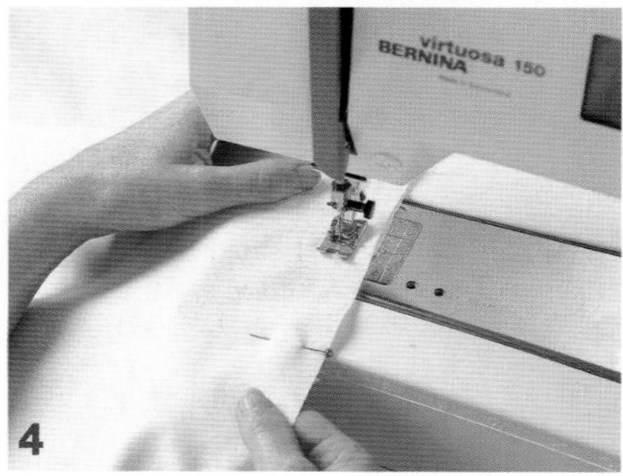

4

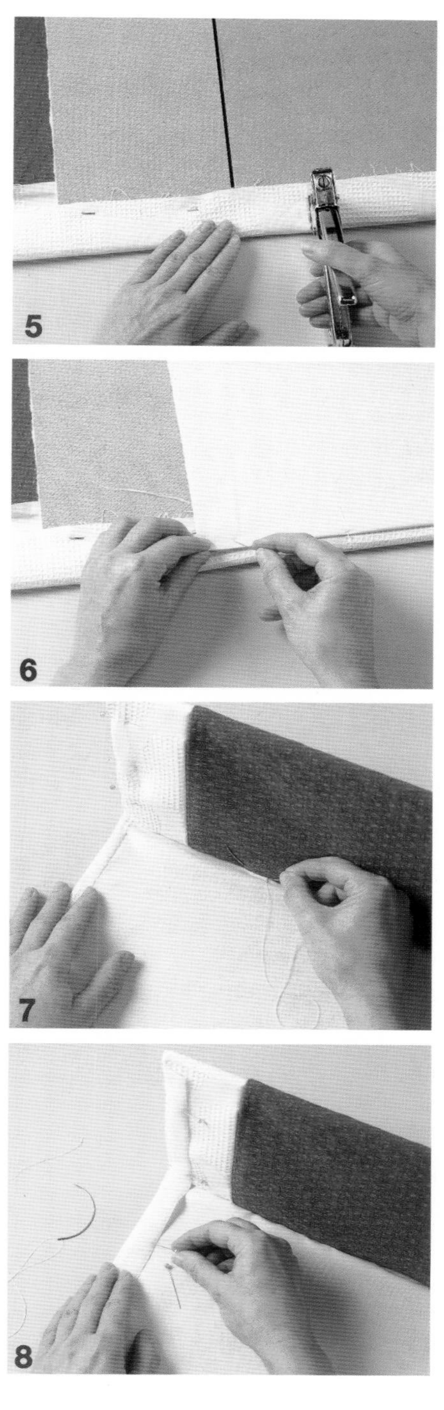

5 Place the pelmet fabric right side down on a flat surface. Place the board on top, with the bottom edge along the lining seam. Stretch the top border gently over the board and secure with 5mm/¼in staples into the back of the board.

6 Pull the lining over the back of the board, turn under the top edge and pin to the fabric at the top. From the right side, check that the borders are an equal size and straight. Hem or staple the lining along the top edge.

7 Fold over the fabric at the short end of the board and hold the end at right angles. Turn under the raw edges and pin. Using a curved upholstery needle, hand stitch the main fabric to the lining along the corner seam.

8 Pin a strip of loop Velcro along the top edge and hand stitch along both sides. Cut a 15cm/6in-wide pelmet board to fit inside the pelmet, at the top, then stick hook Velcro to the front and side edges. Secure with staples every 5–8cm/2–3in.

draped swag and tails

The simplest form of swag and tails is a trapezoid panel of fabric long enough to drape between hold-backs, with the tails hanging down each side. It looks most elegant when the top edge is fixed to a pelmet board and the tails fall over hold-backs on either side of tall narrow windows, such as French doors.

calculating the fabric

The two measurements required are the finished drop of the curtains and the length of the pelmet board, which usually extends 10cm/4in on each side of the window. Use these measurements to make a pattern for the swag following the instructions in the introduction to this chapter.

you will need

- **pattern**
- **fabric**
- **contrast fabric**
- **curtain weights and chain**
- **fabric tape**
- **pelmet board covered with calico**
- **staple gun**
- **sewing kit**

tip for draped swag and tails

Make matching hold-backs using either the main fabric or the contrast lining.

1 Using the pattern, cut out the swag shape in the main and contrast fabric adding 1.5cm/⅝in seam allowance all around. Make sure the fabric is the right way up, with the pelmet edge at the top, and centre any pattern before cutting. Place the two fabrics right sides together and stitch around the edge, with 1.5cm/⅝in seam allowance leaving a gap at the top edge for turning. Trim across the corners to reduce bulk.

2 Press the seams open, reaching as far as possible into the corners. Turn the swag through. Roll the seams until they are right on the edge and press. Drop a weight into the end of the tails and slip-stitch the gap closed.

3 Transfer the dotted line on the pattern to the wrong side of the swag. Insert pins along this line then tack (baste) to mark the line.

4 Pleat the swag along the tacked lines, beginning at the front edge and forming concertina (accordion) pleats about 10cm/4in deep across the fabric. Tie the pleats on the tacked line loosely with a piece of fabric tape. Pleat the other end in the same way.

5 Make the pelmet board following the guidelines in the introduction. Cover the pelmet board in calico or spare curtain fabric and fit in position. Attach the hold-backs to each side of the board.

6 Lift the swag into position so that the ties are behind the hold-backs. Staple the top edge of the swag to the top front edge of the pelmet board. Pull out the tapes and gently twist the swag behind the hold-backs until the tails are facing forward as shown.

1

2

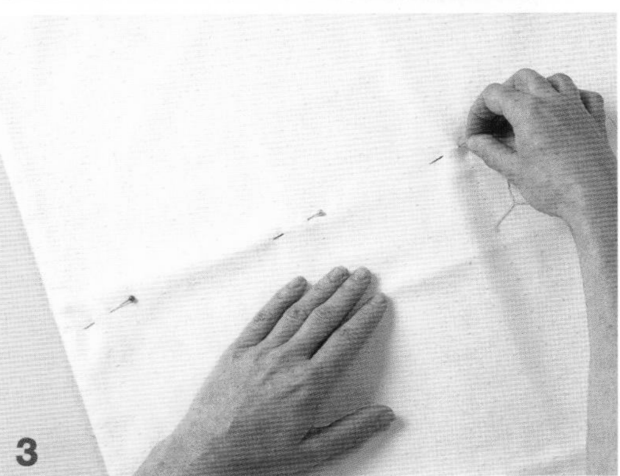

3

VICTORIA SEBAG-MONTEFI

stiffened tie-backs

Stiffened tie-backs are the most common way of holding back curtains. They are made from buckram, a stiffened hessian (burlap) that is lightweight, holds its shape well, and can be designed in a variety of shapes. Make several tie-back templates, marked with the size and the length of trimming required, and to try them on your curtains to help you decide the ideal shape.

you will need

- pencil and paper
- starched hessian (burlap) buckram
- interlining
- fabric
- flanged cord
- brass curtain rings
- sewing kit

tip for stiffened tie-backs

Piping can be used as an alternative to flanged cord.

1 Make a paper template and position it on the hessian (burlap) buckram, along the straight grain. Draw two shapes in pencil and cut out. Dampen the buckram by dipping it quickly into lukewarm water then place the shapes on interlining. Press with a hot iron to seal.

2 Allow the buckram to dry, then cut out the shapes in interlining, cutting close to the edge with no seam allowance.

3 Place one shape, interlining side down, on the wrong side of the fabric and draw along the top edge. Move the shape down about 5mm/¼in and draw round the remaining outline. Mark an accurate 1.5cm/⅝in seam allowance and cut out along this line. Cut four in total.

4 To make the front of each tie-back, cut a piece of cord to fit around the edge. Pin it to the right side of a fabric shape, beginning at the top edge and pinning it along the seamline. Snip into the flanged edge (cord tape) to allow the cord to bend around the corners.

5 Tack (baste) the flanged edge, close to the cord. Check that the tacking stitches follow the marked seamline on the wrong side. Flatten one end of the cord and oversew to the fabric.

6 Trim the other end of the cord to length and flatten it. Place it next to the oversewn end so that it looks like a piece of uncut cord. Tack both ends securely.

7 With right sides together, tack another shape to the front. Stitch round the edge, leaving a long gap at the bottom for inserting the buckram. Trim the seams to reduce bulk and notch the curves. Turn right side out.

8 Push the buckram inside, keeping the seam allowances to the back. Pull the lower edge to the reverse side and slip-stitch the backing fabric just inside the cord. Sew curtain rings on the back at each end.

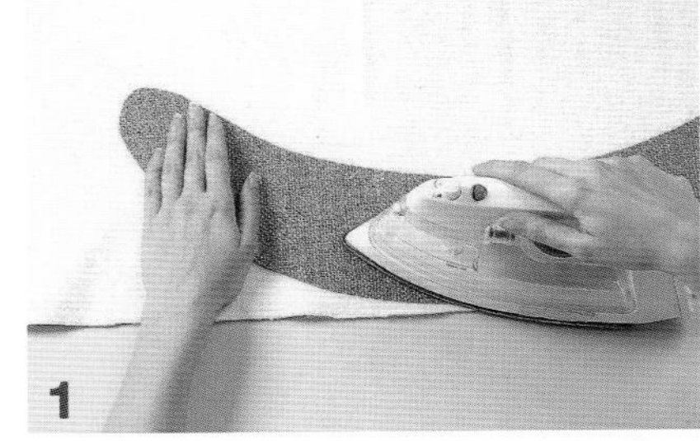

1

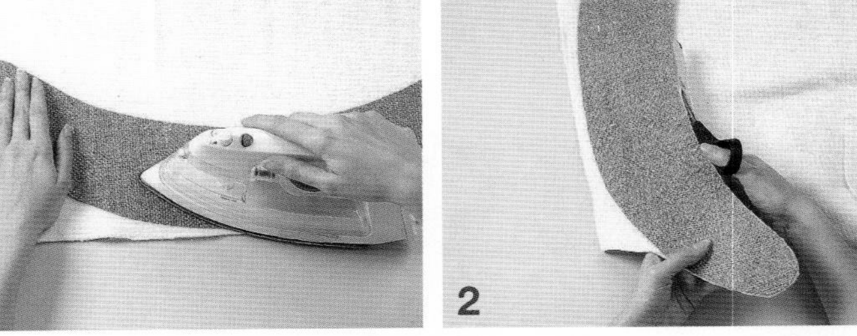

2

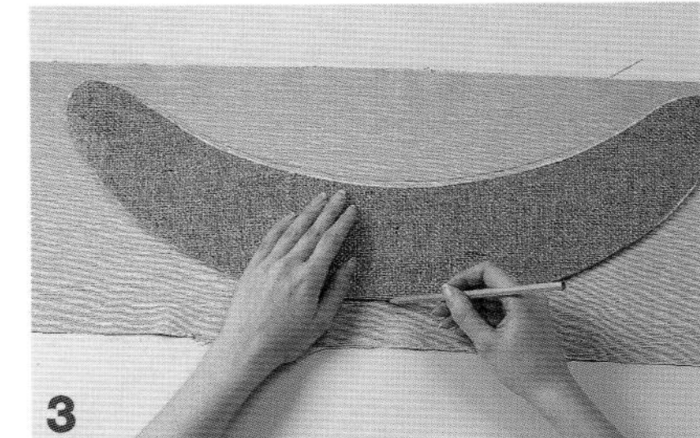

3

4

5

6

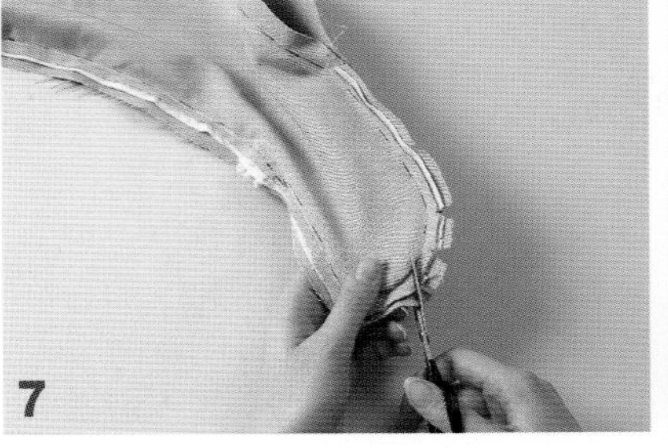

7

8

binding stiffened tie-backs

This alternative finish complements curtains with a contrast border down the leading edge of each curtain. The shape is slightly different, with a loop fastening instead of curtain rings, but the preparation is the same as for stiffened tie-backs.

you will need

- starched hessian (burlap) buckram
- interlining
- fabric and contrast
- sewing kit

tip for binding stiffened tie-backs

Add a matching border to the curtain for a co-ordinated look.

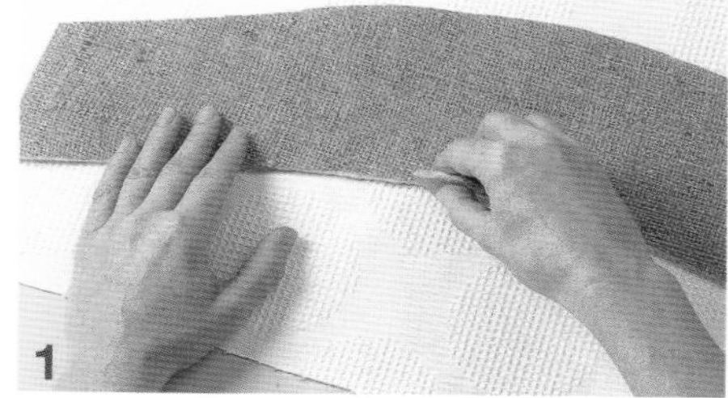

1

2

1 Follow the instructions for the stiffened tie-backs to cut the buckram and attach the interlining to the buckram and cut out. Draw along the top edge of the main fabric and move the template down about 5mm/¼in before completing the shape. Add 1.5cm/⅝in seam allowance to each end. For each tie-back, cut out two lining shapes, adding a seam allowance to all edges.

2 Using contrast fabric, cut sufficient 5cm/2in-wide bias strips to fit twice the length of each tie-back. With right sides together pin strips along the top and bottom edges of one fabric shape for each tie-back to make a binding and stitch in place.

3

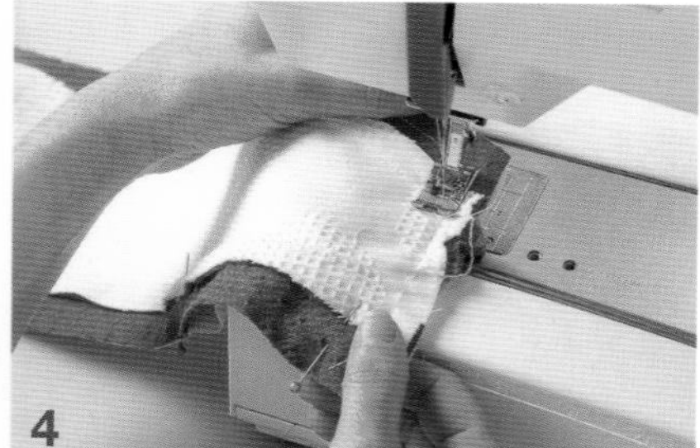

4

5

3 For the hanging loop, cut one strip of bias binding 8cm/3in long. Fold the long edges into the centre and press. Fold in half along the length to make a narrow strip, press and stitch along the edge. Form a loop and pin the short ends to one end of the tie-back, so that when it is folded back it faces up at the same angle as the tie-back. Make another for the other end. Make two for the other tie-back.

4 With right sides together, pin the lining fabric tie-back shape to the first shape. Stitch around the edge, leaving a large gap along the bottom.

5 Trim across the corners and turn through. Tuck the buckram inside, keeping the seam allowances to the back. Pin and slip-stitch the gap.

plait (braid) tie-backs

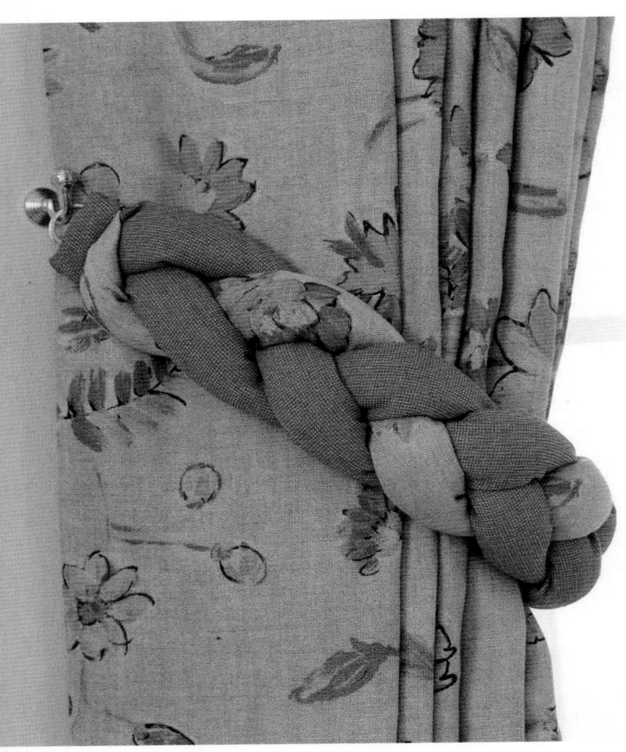

Use plaited (braided) tie backs to add a decorative feature to curtains. Tubes are made from rolls of wadding (batting) that are covered in fabric and stitched in one easy step. To see what the tie-back will look like, roll short lengths of wadding, cover them with fabric and plait them. Hold them up to the curtain and increase or decrease the wadding to suit your preference. Hold a tape measure around the curtain to find the required finished length.

you will need

- **100g/4oz wadding (batting)**
- **fabric to match curtains**
- **contrast fabric**
- **brass curtain rings or "D" rings**
- **sewing kit**

tip for plait (braid) tie-backs

Use a soft fabric that doesn't crease easily for this tie-back.

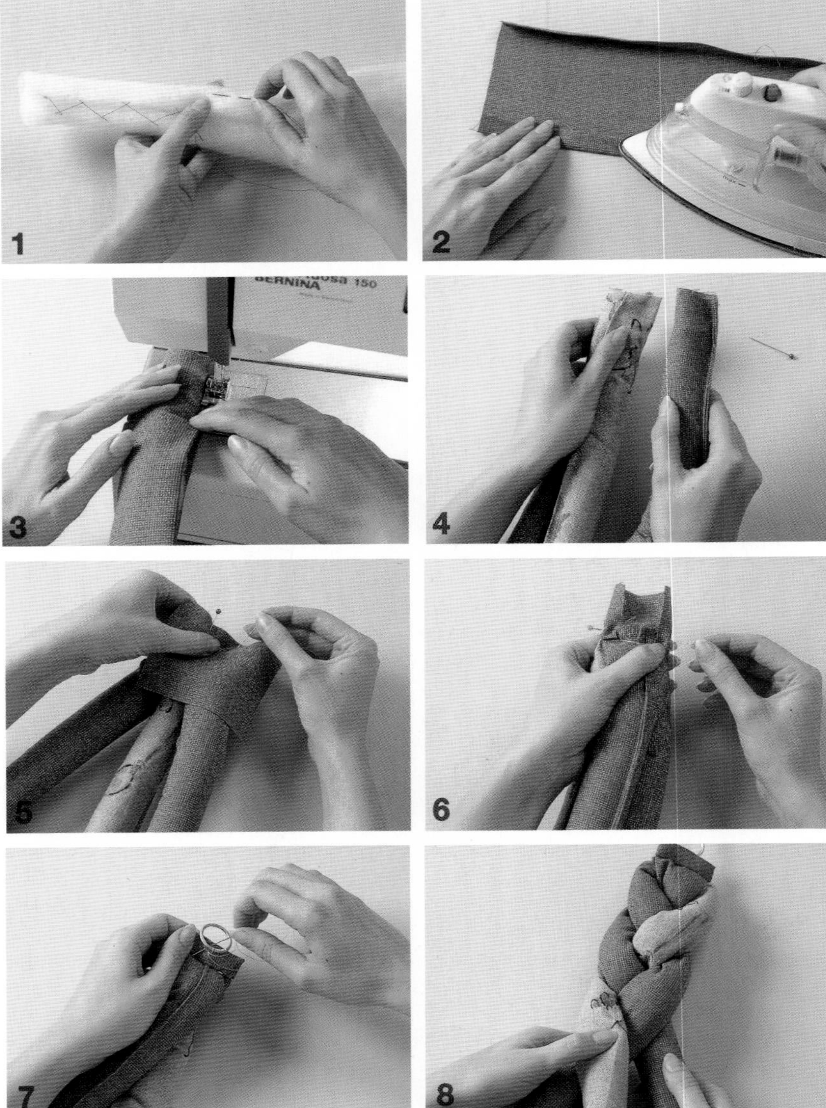

1 Cut 1.5m/1⅝yd strips of wadding (batting) the required width and roll up fairly tighly. Stitch along the edge with long herringbone stitches to secure. Make three rolls for each tie-back.

2 Check the width of fabric required to cover each roll and add 2cm/¾in seam allowance all around. Cut three strips of fabric each 1.5m/1⅝yd long, with two strips in contrast fabric. Press under 1cm/½in down each long side.

3 Wrap a strip of fabric around a roll of wadding, leaving 1.5cm/⅝in of fabric above the short end of the wadding. Pin the fabric together at the top. Holding the edges together, stitch a little at a time until the wadding roll is covered in fabric. Repeat to make three tubes.

4 Keeping the seams along the top, pin the three rolls together at one end, with the contrast in the middle.

5 Cut out a 5 x 8cm/2 x 3in rectangle of fabric for each end of the tie-back. Pin the rectangle across the end of the strips, right sides together, and stitch 1.5cm/⅝in from the edge.

6 Fold in the outside edges of the fabric rectangle and pin. Turn down the top edge to bind the raw edges neatly. Hem securely.

7 Sew a curtain ring or "D" ring on to the binding on the inside, so that half the ring is jutting out.

8 Attach the ring to the tie-back hook or to a fixed point, using a piece of tape. Working from the right side, plait (braid) the rolls of fabric so that the seams remain on the underside. Measure the length of the plait, and trim to size if required. Finish the end of the tie-back with a rectangle of fabric and curtain "D" ring to match the other end.

ruched tie-backs

Soft or sheer fabrics are ideal for this ruched tie-back. The effect is very delicate but the tie-back is quite sturdy as it has a stiffened interfacing inside. The softness comes from a layer of polyester wadding (batting), which supports the fabric and holds the ruching in place.

you will need

- **fusible pelmet-weight interfacing**
- **50g/2oz fabric-backed wadding (batting)**
- **lightweight fabric**
- **thin cord**
- **white "D" rings**
- **sewing kit**

tip for ruched tie-backs

If more fullness is required there can be less ruching on what will be the back of the tie-back.

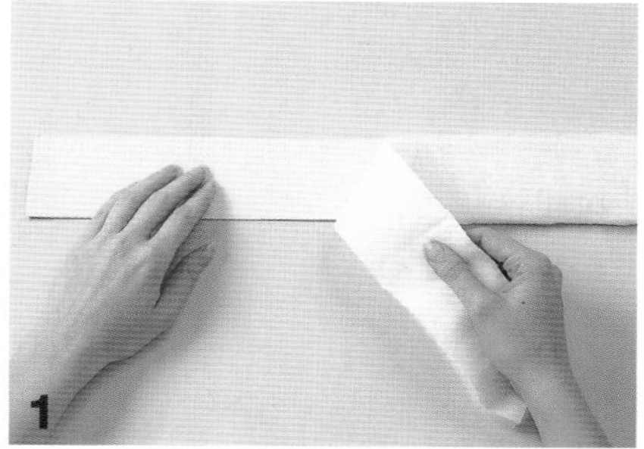

1

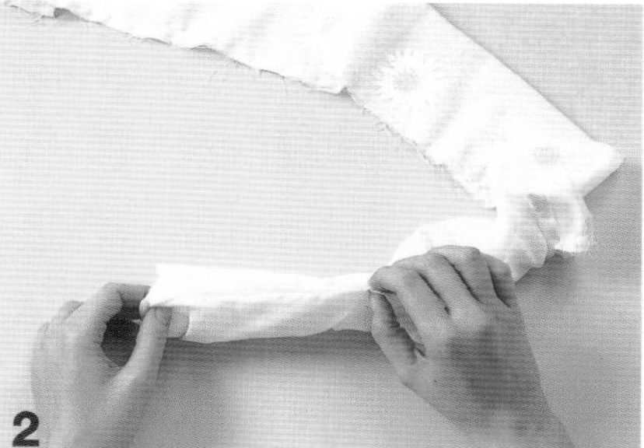

2

1 Decide on the length and width of the tie-back. Cut out a rectangle of fusible pelmet-weight interfacing and fabric-backed wadding (batting) for each tie-back. Place the wadding on the interfacing, turn them over and press gently with a steam iron to fuse the layers together.

2 Cut a strip of fabric three to four times the length and twice as wide as the tie-back, plus 1cm/½in seam allowances. Fold in half lengthways, with right sides together, and stitch a 5mm/¼in seam. Turn through the tube of fabric to the right side.

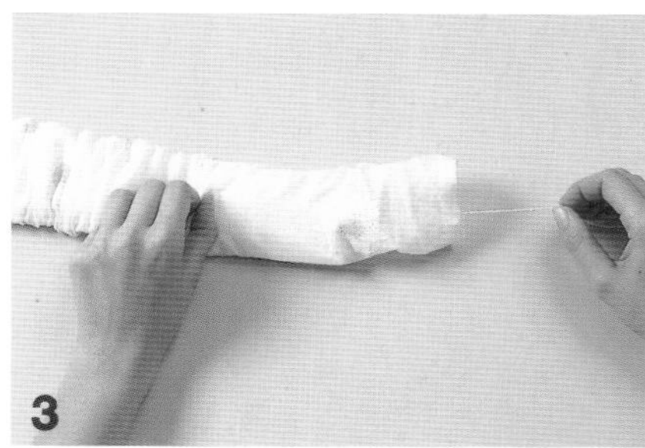

3

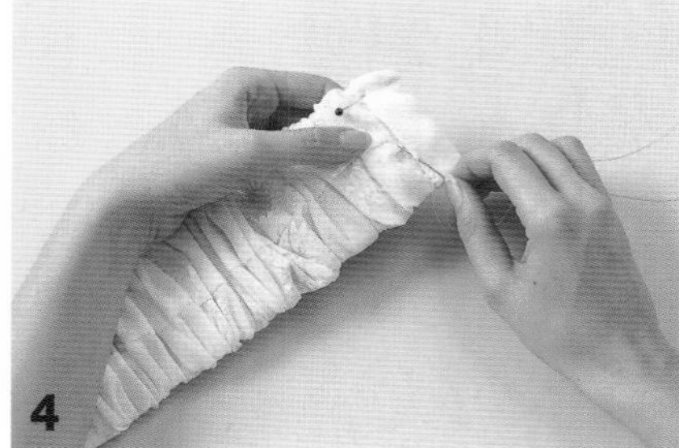

4

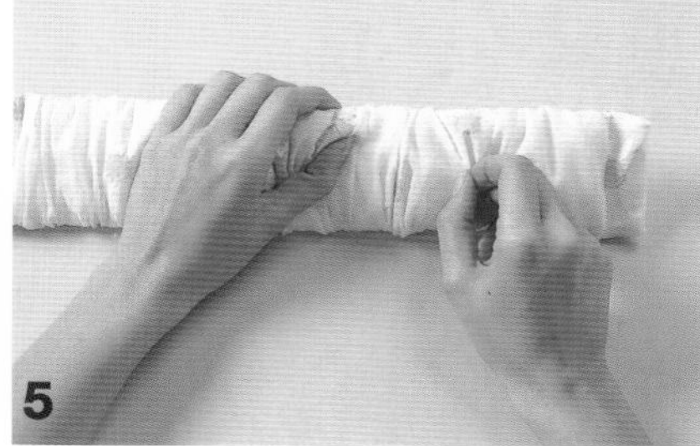

5

3 Stitch a length of thin cord on to one end of the interfacing. Feed the cord through the tube and hold it while gently pulling the fabric back along the interfacing. For the binding, cut a piece of double-thickness fabric 5 x 8cm/2 x 3in for each end of the ruched tie-back.

4 Pin across the end of the strip, right sides together, and stitch 1.5cm/⅝in from the edge. Fold in the outside edges and pin. Turn down the top edge to bind the raw edges. Hem the ends.

5 Adjust the gathers evenly along the length. Stitch a "D" ring to each end so that the ring juts out halfway.

pleated tie-backs

This elegant tie-back is another version of the stiffened tie-back, and uses binding to secure the pleats. It works best with crisp fabrics that can be pressed to hold a crease. You will need about ½m/½yd of fabric to make the pleated section for two tie-backs.

you will need

- fabric
- iron-on interfacing
- pencil or tailor's chalk
- starched hessian (burlap) buckram
- "D" rings
- sewing kit

tip for pleated tie-backs

Make sure the print is facing in the right direction before cutting the template shape.

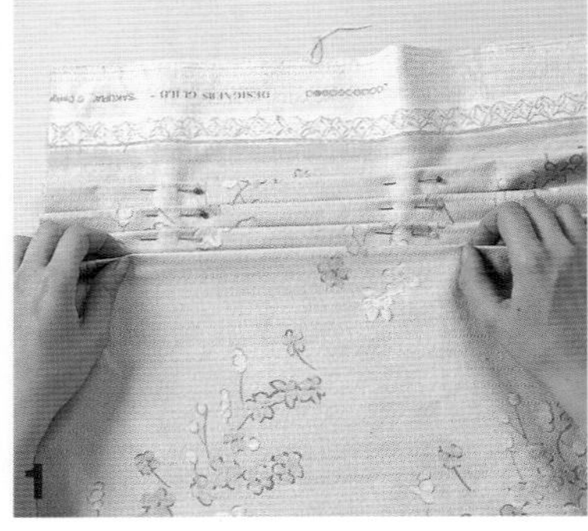

1

2

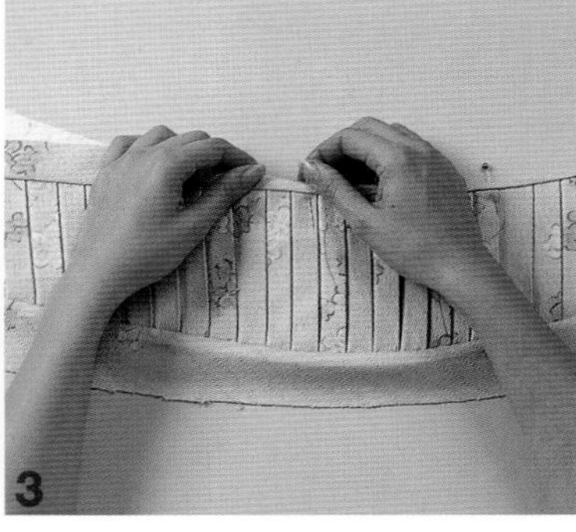

3

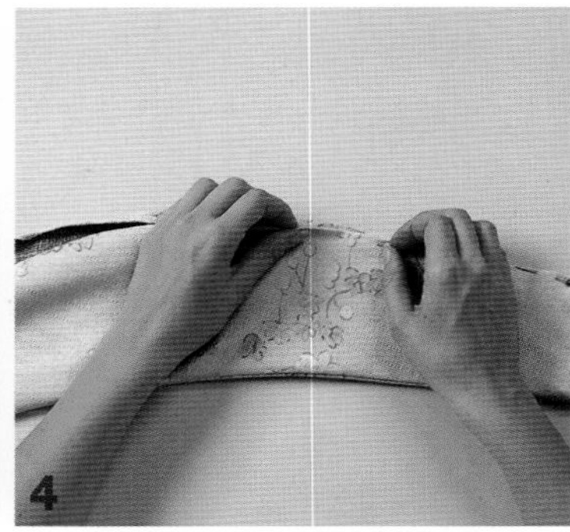

4

1 Fold the fabric into pleats of the size required. Measure the first few, about 1–2cm/½–¾in, then pleat the rest by eye if you feel sufficiently confident. Pin the pleats in several places along the length. Continue until you have sufficient pleated fabric for both tie-backs. Press the pleats, then stitch along the top and bottom edges and remove the pins. Support the pleats by pressing iron-on interfacing on the wrong side. Draw around your chosen tie-back template. Cut one shape for each tie-back in buckram and pleated fabric, adding seam allowances to the short ends only. Cut the backing fabric with seam allowances all round.

2 Cut 5cm/2in-wide bias strips of fabric for the top and bottom of each tie-back. With right sides together, pin and stitch along the top and bottom of the pleated shape.

3 Lay the pleated fabric over the interlined buckram. Fold the binding over to the reverse side and pin.

4 Press under the edges of the backing fabric shape and slip-stitch on to the reverse side of the tie-back, covering the raw edges of the binding. Sew a "D" ring to each inside end of the tie-back.

hold-backs

Hold-backs are an alternative way of holding a curtain to one side, although here they can be used to hold the fabric of the draped swag in place. They are available in a wide variety of shapes, often designed to match the finials on the end of curtain poles. This hold-back is rather like a covered button. The front disc (part of a kit) is covered with a circle of fabric, fitted to a thin stem and then screwed to the wall.

you will need

- pencil
- self-cover hold-back kit
- fabric
- strong sewing thread
- wadding (batting)
- double-sided tape
- sewing kit

tip for hold-backs

If the curtains or swag are patterned, make the hold-back in plain fabric.

1 Draw around the front of the hold-back on the fabric and cut out a circle 2.5cm/1in larger all around.

2 Work a line of running stitch around the edge of the circle, using a length of strong thread.

3 Cut a circle of wadding (batting) to fit over the front of the hold-back and stick in place with double-sided tape.

4 Place the hold-back disc face down on the fabric and pull up the threads around it. Sew in the ends securely. Assemble and fix the hold-back in place following the manufacturer's instructions.

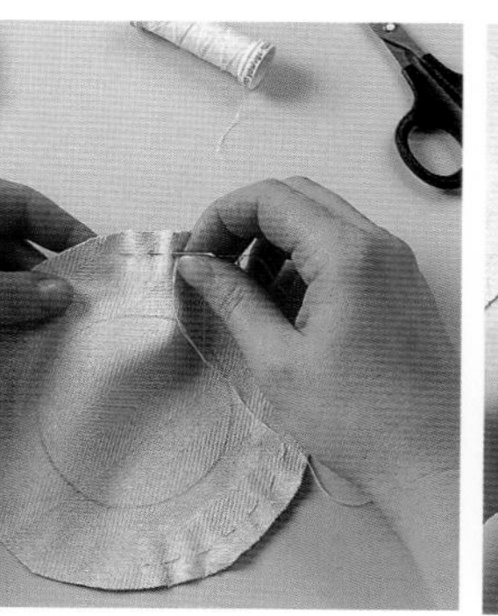

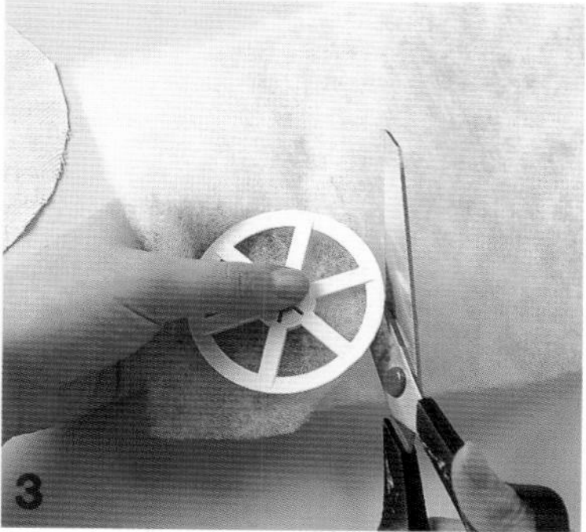

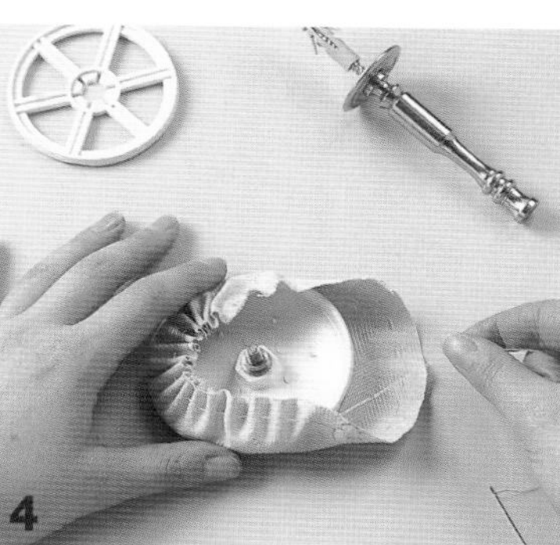

sheer curtain with heading tape

Sheer curtains are made in much the same way as ordinary curtains, although they are often left closed, to screen the sunlight or to provide privacy. Special lightweight tapes are available for sheer curtains, and are less conspicuous from the right side as they let the light through. If curtains remain closed all the time, there is no need for a curtain rail and the curtain can simply be attached to a strip of Velcro stuck along the top of the window frame. Sheer curtains do not normally have side hems or seams as the selvage is not conspicuous and hangs better than a stitched edge. Simply turn up the hem and attach the heading tape.

you will need

- **sheer fabric**
- **Velcro heading tape for sheer fabric**
- **sewing kit**

tip for sheer curtain with heading tape

Specialized Velcro heading tape is available in a variety of widths especially for this purpose.

1 Trim the fabric along a straight thread. Turn under an accurate double 5cm/2in hem along the bottom edge of the fabric and press.

2 Lift the fabric carefully on to the sewing machine and stitch the hem. Avoid using pins in case they mark the delicate fabric.

3 Cut the curtain to length and press the seam allowance to the wrong side. Pull the cords out at one end of the heading tape and fold the end over. Pin the tape just below the top of the curtain.

4 Fold the other end of the tape under and stitch the end. Stitch each long side of the tape, working both in the same direction.

1

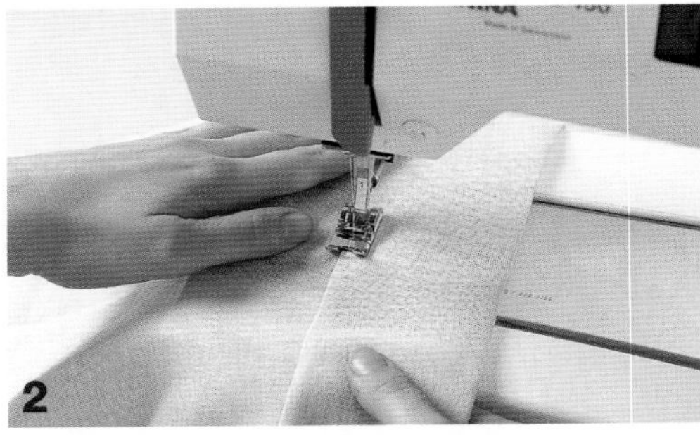
2

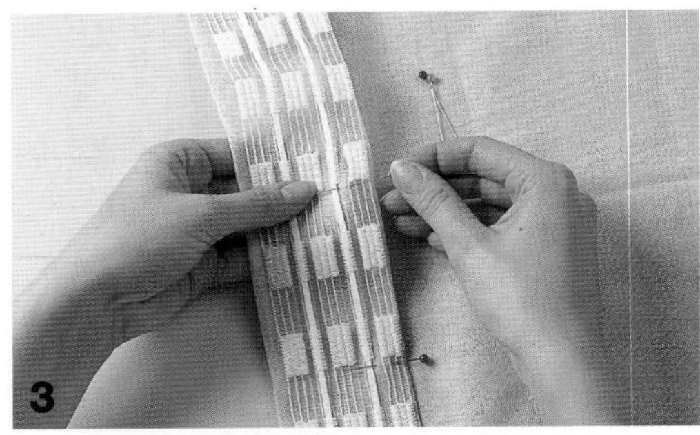
3

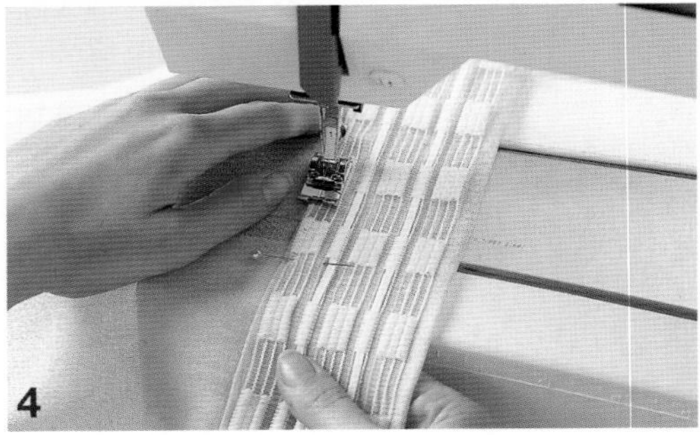
4

sheer flat curtain

This sheer flat curtain has less fullness in it than the sheer curtain made with a heading tape, and looks attractive with deep hems on all sides and mitred corners. Allow 1–1½ times the track length.

you will need

- **sheer fabric**
- **curtain clips**
- **sewing kit**

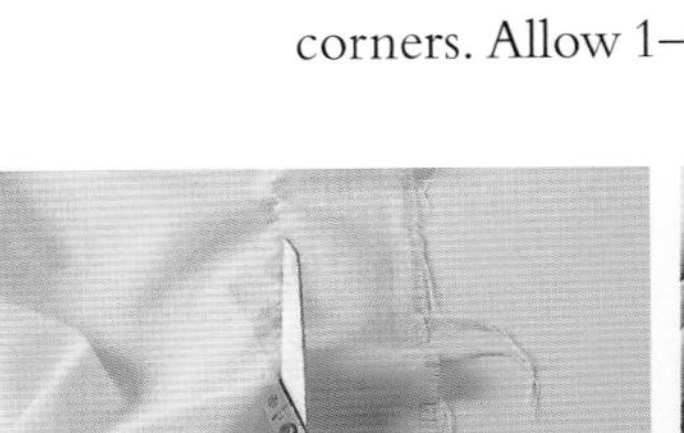
1

2

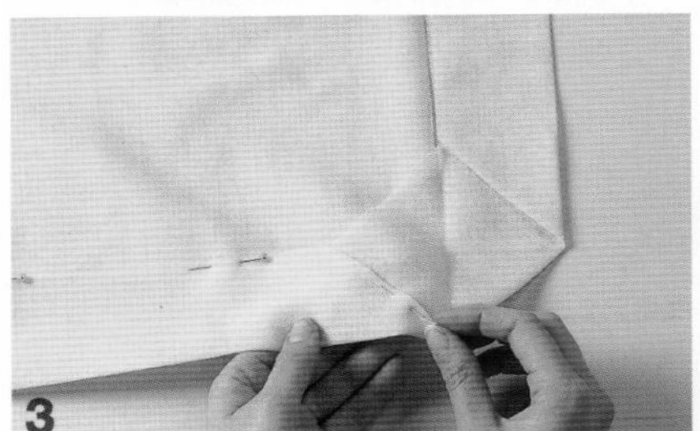
3

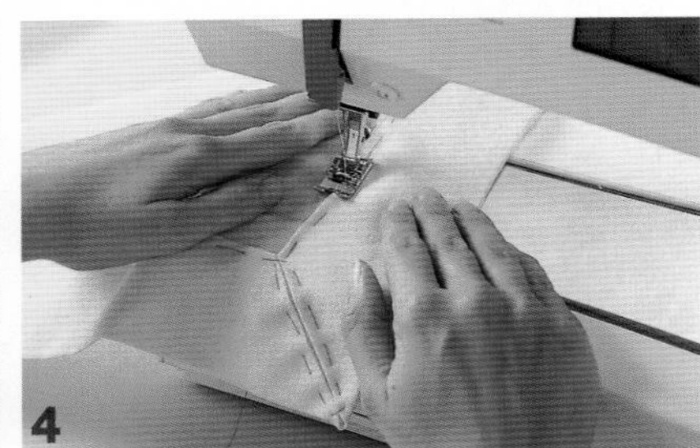
4

1 For a curtain with mitred corners, it is essential to straighten the fabric before cutting it. Pull a thread across one end of the fabric then cut along the line.

2 Press under a double 6cm/2½in hem along all edges, checking that the corners are absolutely square. Open out the hems and fold over each corner so that the point is level with the inside creases. Trim across the diagonal line.

3 Fold up the hems again, as for a double mitre (see basic techniques) and pin. Check that the corner comes to a neat point and that the edges of the mitre seams are level.

4 Tack (baste) the hem and mitred corners carefully, then stitch close to the inside edge. Slip-stitch the mitred corner and remove the tacking threads. To hang the curtains, space curtain clips evenly along the top of each curtain every 10–15cm/4–6in.

you will need

- **curtain weight chain**
- **sheer fabric**
- **Velcro (for a metal pole), hammer and panel pins (for a wooden pole)**
- **sewing kit**

draping a swag around a curtain pole

Although the fabric for this drape appears to be casually wrapped around the pole, it needs to be carefully arranged and fixed in position. On a wooden pole it can be pinned or stapled along the top, but on a metal pole Velcro is required.

To determine the approximate length of fabric required, drape a length of curtain weight chain around the curtain pole to achieve the desired drape. Buy a little extra fabric if possible. Drape the fabric around the pole. Adjust the folds and pin. Check the length of the tails and mark the ends of the fabric for trimming. Lift the swag off the pole and trim the ends. Turn under and hand stitch a narrow rolled hem along both ends of the fabric. Hand sewing gives a softer edge than machine stitching.

On a metal pole, arrange the swag and pin the pleats so that you can lift the fabric off and stitch loop Velcro on the inside. Mark the pole with tape and stick hook Velcro at the points marked.

On a wooden pole, tack (baste) the pleats ready for attaching to the pole with staples or a hammer and panel pins. Rearrange the swag over the pole.

left *This type of drape works well over a curtain pole to frame another curtain that sits inside the recess.*

basic shower curtain

above *Fit a curtain ring into each eyelet.*

Commercial shower curtains are generally a standard 180cm/72in square, which may not suit every situation. However, a basic shower curtain is very easy to make, in any size, using special waterproof fabric available in furnishing fabric departments. Test a small piece of the fabric to check that it can be pressed with a cool iron, otherwise use paperclips to hold the hem in place, instead of pins, for stitching. Join widths of fabric with a plain or welt seam.

you will need

- **waterproof shower curtain fabric**
- **curtain weight chain (optional)**
- **pencil**
- **hammer**
- **eyelet tool**
- **eyelets**
- **sewing kit**

tip for basic shower curtain

Buy either brass or silver eyelets to match the fabric and bathroom fittings.

1 Pull a thread across one end of the fabric and cut along the line to straighten. Measure and cut the length required, adding 10cm/4in hem allowance.

2 Using a cool iron, press under a double 4cm/1½in hem along the top edge and a double 1cm/½in hem along the bottom edge.

3 Stitch the top hem, using a slightly longer stitch than usual. Reverse stitch at each end. If you want to weight the shower curtain, tuck a length of curtain chain inside the bottom hem, then stitch, using a zipper foot.

4 Using a pencil, mark the position of the eyelets along the top edge of the curtain, spacing them about 10cm/4in apart.

5 Using a hammer and an eyelet tool, pierce holes at the marked points. Work on a solid surface, and if the fabric is difficult to cut, place a pad of newspaper underneath instead of the plastic disc supplied.

6 Insert the tube side of each eyelet from the right side and place a ring over the top. Carefully hammer the eyelet into position. Repeat along the top of the curtain.

CARGO

Roman blind

This is an elegant, tailored way to dress a window. It is a fabric panel with wooden dowels fitted into casings across the back, which pull up to make neat pleats as the blind is raised. A Roman blind is most successful made in crisp, firmly woven furnishing fabric, but it can also look stunning if it is made in sheer fabric with a solid, contrasting border.

calculating the fabric

Measure the required finished size of the blind and add 10cm/4in to both the length and width for seam allowances. The lining is the width and length of the finished blind, plus 6cm/2½in for each casing added to the length. The nylon cord is four times the length of the blind plus twice the width.

you will need

- **firmly woven furnishing fabric**
- **lining fabric**
- **pencil**
- **quilter's ruler (optional)**
- **Velcro**
- **7mm/5⁄16 in-wide wooden dowel**
- **3mm x 2.5cm/⅛ x 1in wood lath**
- **small plastic rings (2 for each casing)**
- **nylon cord**
- **sewing kit**

for hanging the blind

- **screw-eyes**
- **2.5 x 5cm/1 x 2in wooden batten, the width of the blind**
- **fixing brackets and screws**

tip for Roman blind

To hang the blind see the introduction to this chapter.

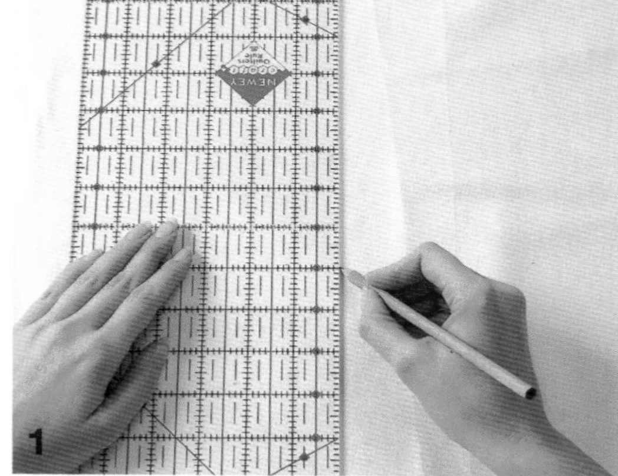
1

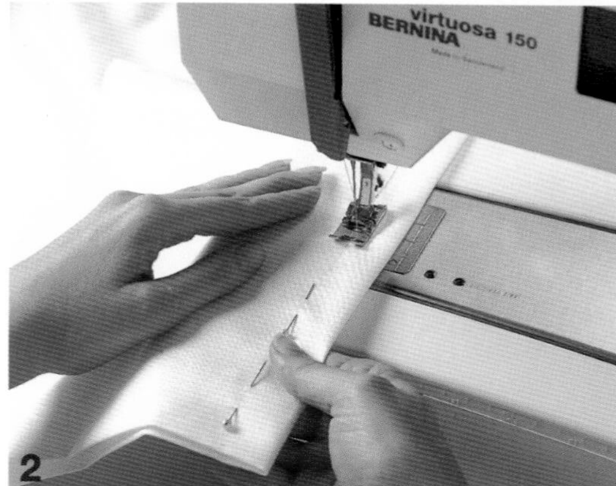

2

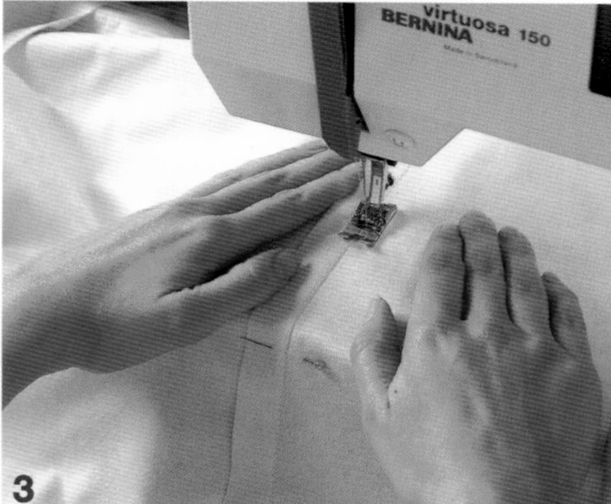

3

1 Cut out the main fabric and lining. Draw a pencil line horizontally across the lining fabric, 25cm/10in from the bottom edge. Mark a casing line 6cm/2½in above it. Continue marking the lines and casing lines 25cm/10 in apart. A quilter's rule is ideal for accurate marking.

2 Press under a 2.5cm/1in turning down both side edges of the lining. With wrong sides together, fold the lining, pinning each pencil line to the casing line above it. Stitch along the pinned line, reverse-stitching at each end for strength. Press the casing to one side.

3 Press under 5cm/2in down both sides of the main fabric. Pin the lining in the centre on the reverse side of the fabric. Stitch on top of the previous casing stitches, reverse-stitching at each end.

▷

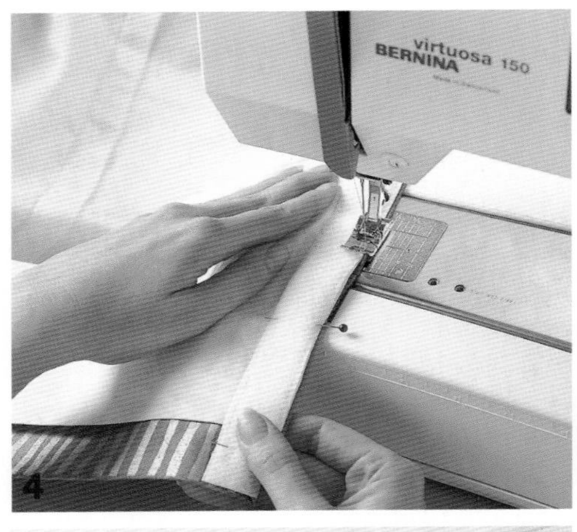

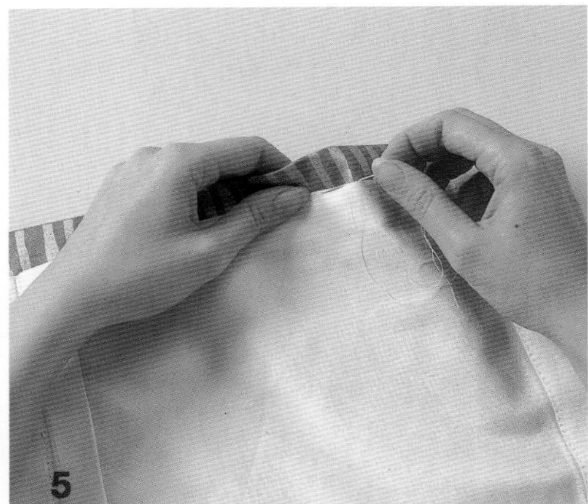

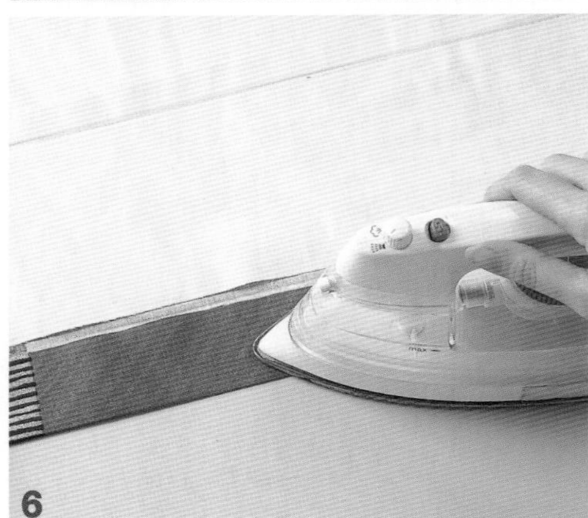

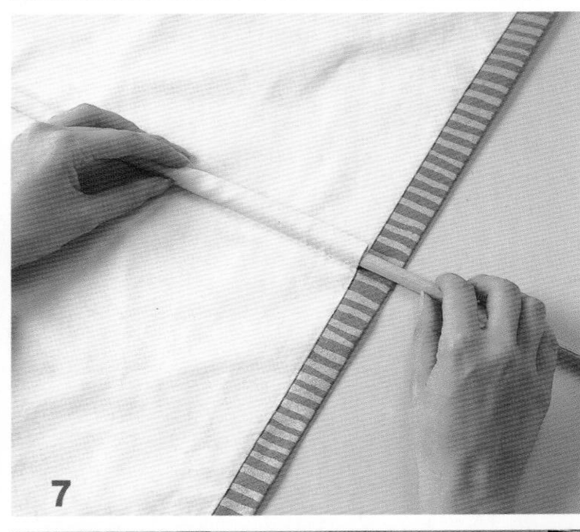

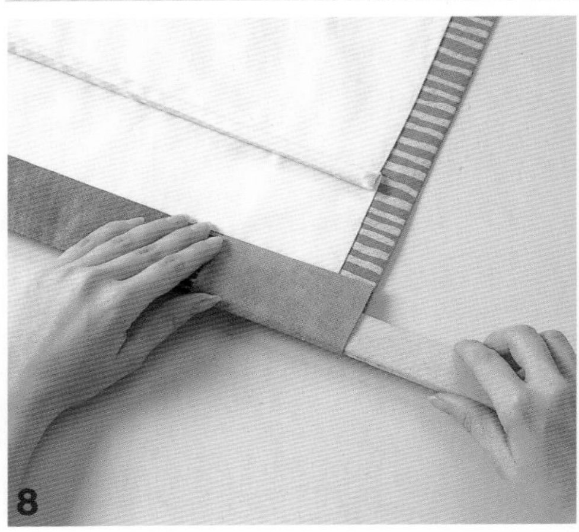

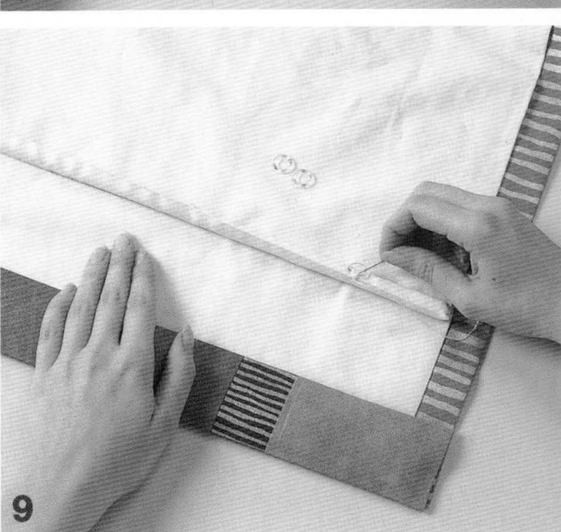

4 Turn over 2cm/¾in along the top edge and pin a strip of loop Velcro on top. Stitch along the top edge of the Velcro, then slip-hem the lower edge to the lining fabric only.

5 Slip-hem the side seams of the lining, taking care not to stitch through to the right side.

6 Trim the lining 8cm/3in from the bottom edge. Turn up and press a double 4cm/1½in hem along the bottom edge of the blind. Hem the blind, stitching into the lining only.

7 Cut the dowel 2cm/¾in shorter than the casing length. Insert one through each casing, then stitch the ends.

8 Cut the wooden lath 2cm/¾in shorter than the blind width. Slot it through the bottom hem, then stitch the ends.

9 Hand sew two plastic rings on to each casing, each one 10cm/4in in from each side. Cut the nylon cord in half. Thread one end of the first piece of cord down through one set of rings, and tie it securely to the last ring. Repeat with the other piece of cord.

below *Vertical stripes are an ideal choice for the simple folds of Roman blinds.*

London blind

A London blind is flat along the top edge, but has inverted box pleats down each side. The blind looks effective made in a vertically striped fabric, with the pleats opening to reveal an interesting colour or pattern as the blind is pulled up. The amounts of fabric quoted below include some flexibility so that you can make the best use of the fabric. Bear in mind that if the pleats begin approximately 15cm/6in from the side edge of the blind, the centre of each pleat will be twice that distance, i.e. 30cm/12in, from the side edge.

above *Arrange the folds neatly once the blind is pulled up.*

calculating the fabric

The main fabric is cut 13cm/5in wider than the batten width, with another 61cm/24in added to the width for the pleats. Add 4cm/1½in to the length for seam allowances. The lining is the same length and 7cm/2¾in narrower.

Take a tape measure with you when you are buying the fabric, and choose one that can be folded down a stripe or that will show a pattern inside a pleat.

For each length of cord used, allow twice the length plus one width.

you will need

- **fabric**
- **lining fabric**
- **Velcro**
- **small plastic rings**
- **nylon cord**
- **sewing kit**

for hanging the blind

- **screw-eyes**
- **2.5 x 5cm/1 x 2in wooden batten, the width of the blind**
- **fixing brackets and screws**

1 Cut out the main fabric and lining fabric. Pin right sides together, and stitch the side seams. Press the seams open and centre the lining on the main fabric. Stitch along the bottom edge and turn through. Press the edges.

2 To mark the position of the pleats, insert a pin 15cm/6in in from the side seam and another two pins each 15cm/6in apart. With pins mark a pleat to match on the other side.

3 Matching the outside pins, fold the blind right sides together and measure 20cm/8in from the top edge. Tack (baste) and stitch the pleat seams, reverse-stitching at each end.

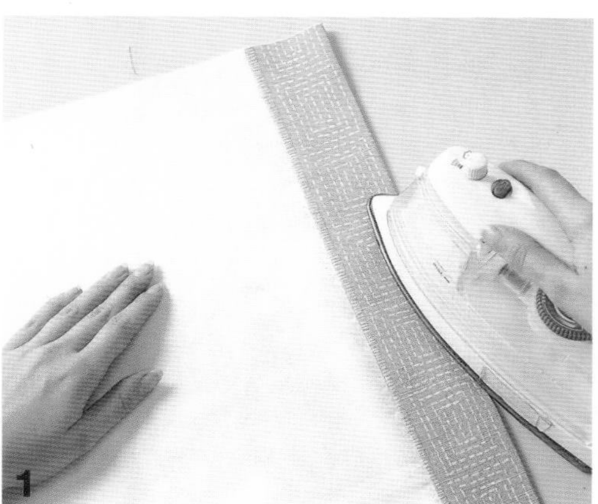

1

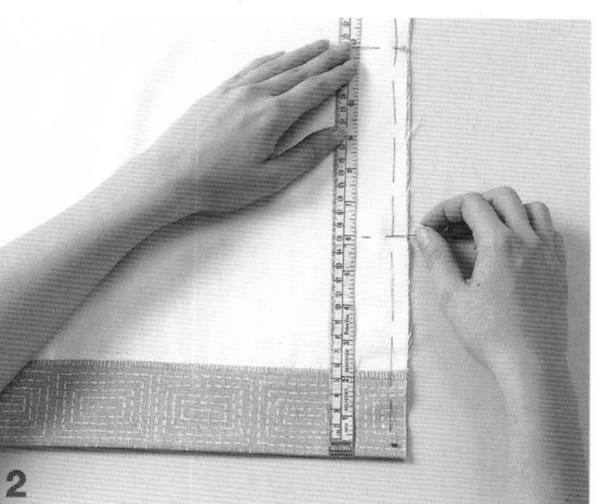

2

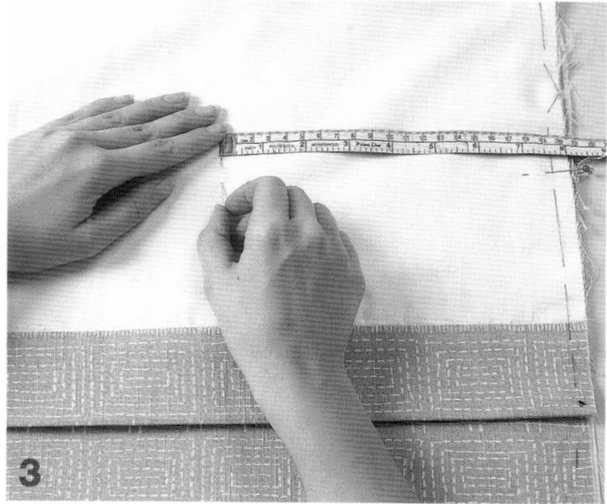

3

▷

4 Open out the pleats to form inverted box pleats and tack (baste) along the top edge. Pin the pleats from the right side and press. Press again on the wrong side.

5 Fold over a 2cm/¾in turning across the top of the blind and press. Stitch a length of Velcro tape along the top edge. Slip-hem the lower edge of the Velcro to the lining only.

6 Hand stitch a small plastic ring in the centre of each pleat on the lining side, 5cm/2in from the bottom edge. Repeat every 10–13cm/ 4–5in all the way up the blind.

7 Cut two equal lengths of nylon cord and thread one through each row of rings.

8 Tie the end of each cord securely to the bottom ring.

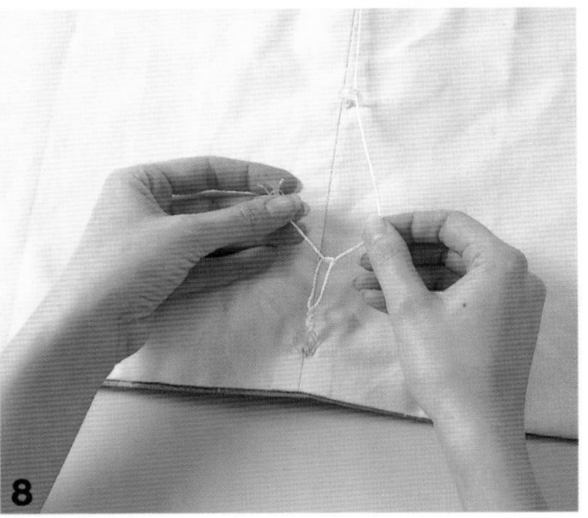

tips for London blind

To hang the blind see the introduction to this chapter.

Pin the pleats in position before pulling the blind up for the first time.

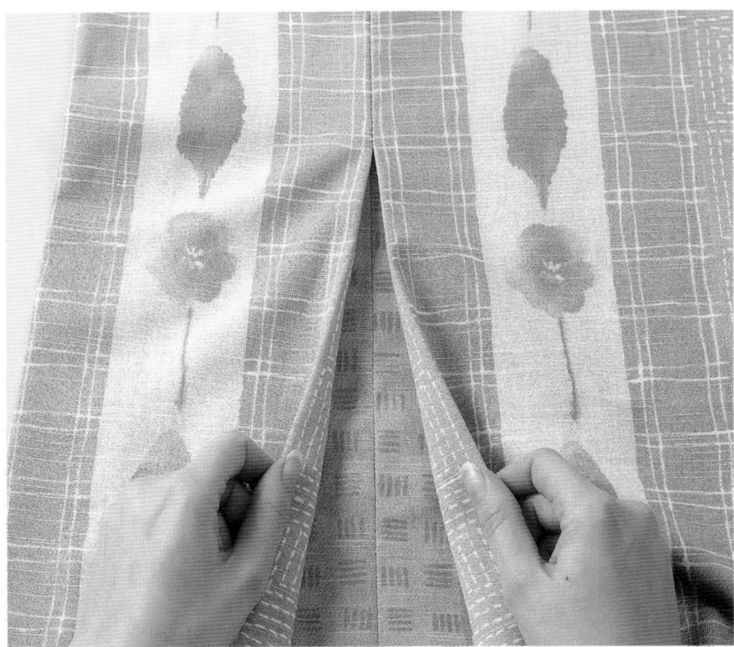

above *If the fabric isn't wide enough and needs to be joined, position the seam down the centre of the pleats.*

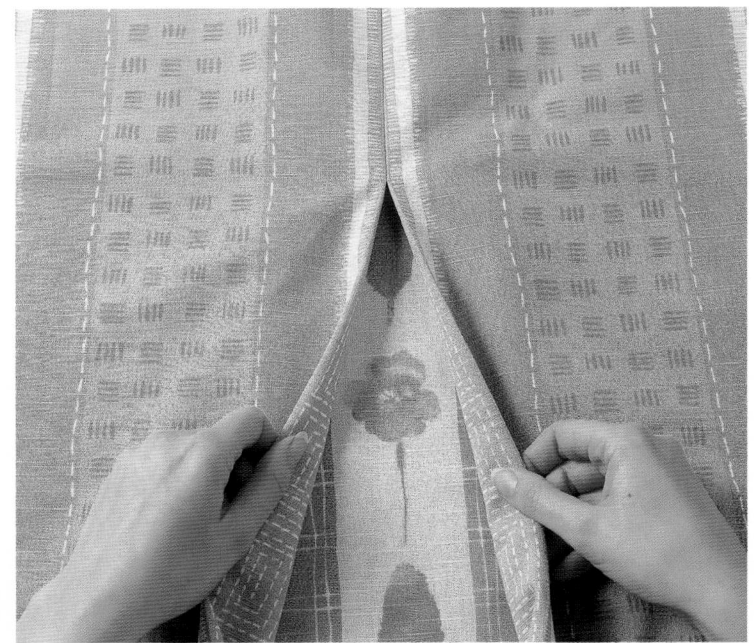

above *Where possible, create the pleats so that an attractive motif shows when the blind is pulled up.*

Austrian blind

An Austrian blind is gathered across the top edge with heading tape, which allows the fabric to fall into soft, scalloped folds when the blind is raised. It looks rather like a curtain when it is let down. Its soft appearance lends itself to frills or fringing, which can be added down the sides as well as along the bottom, as here. Choose a soft, bouncy fabric that resists creasing.

calculating the fabric

Measure the track width and blind drop to the top of the frill. Allow 2–2½ times fullness across the width adding 3cm/1¼in for side hems. Add 5cm/2in to the blind drop for the length. See step 1 for the frill. For each length of cord used allow twice the length plus one width.

you will need

- **fabric**
- **lining fabric**
- **Austrian blind tape**
- **8cm/3in-wide pencil pleat heading tape**
- **nylon cord**
- **sewing kit**

for hanging the blind:

- **screw-eyes**
- **Austrian blind rail or curtain track and 2.5 x 5cm/1 x 2in wooden batten, the width of the blind**

tip for Austrian blind

To hang the blind see the introduction to this chapter.

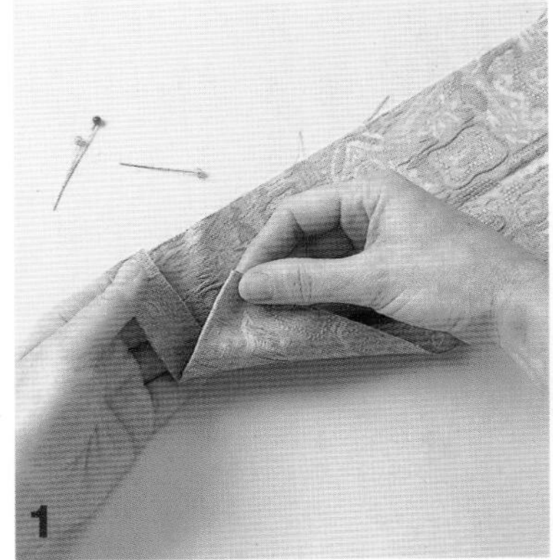
1

2

1 Cut out the main fabric and lining. For the pleated frill along the bottom edge of the blind, cut a strip of main fabric 13cm/5in wide and at least twice as long as the width of the blind. Press under 1cm/½in at each end to the wrong side and fold in half lengthways.

2 Place the strip along the bottom edge of the main fabric and 1.5cm/⅝in in from one side edge. Pin the strip into small pleats, about 1–2cm/½–¾in deep. Measure the first few pleats then work by eye until the pleats go all the way across the fabric, stopping 1.5cm/⅝in from the side edge.

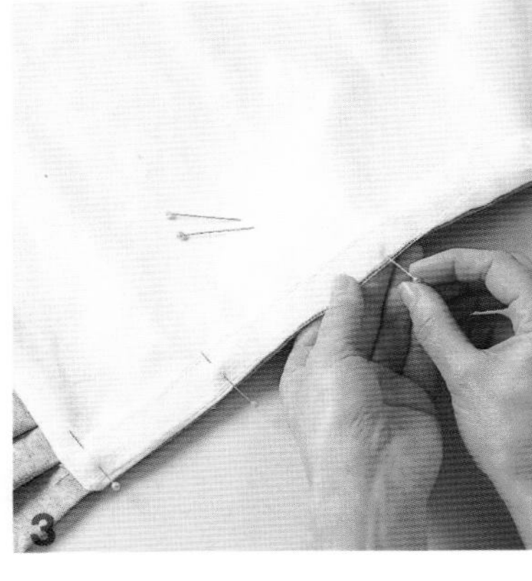
3

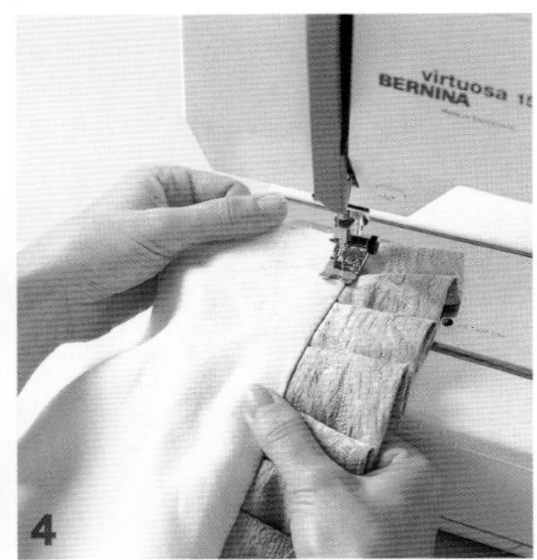

4

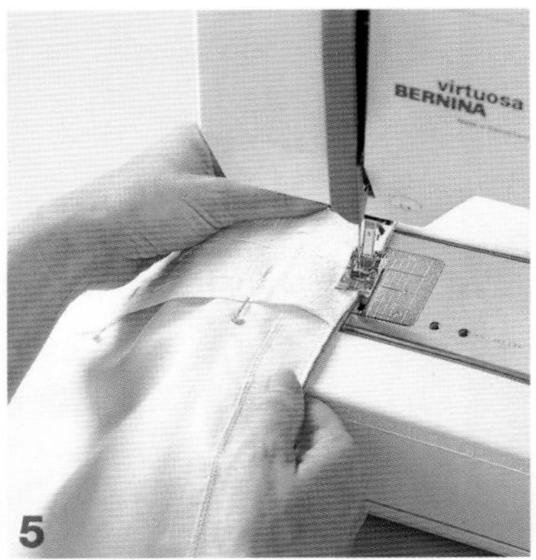

5

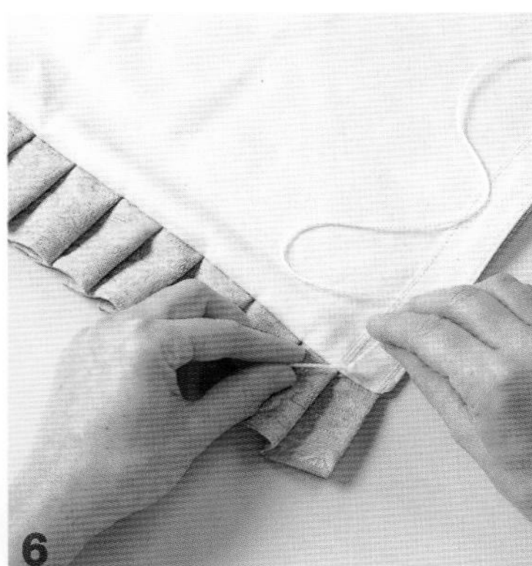
6

3 With right sides together, pin the lining fabric over the top of the pleats. Stitch down the sides of the blind and across the bottom. Trim across the corners, turn through and press. Pin a length of Austrian blind tape down each side of the blind. Space further lengths 50–60cm/20–24in apart.

4 Stitch the Austrian blind tape to the blind, stitching both sides of the tape in the same direction. Fill the spool with a thread colour that matches the main fabric and use a top thread to match the lining.

5 Fold over a 2cm/¾in turning across the top of the blind and press. Pin a length of pencil pleat heading tape 5mm/¼in from the top edge and stitch round all sides, leaving the tape cords free at one side.

6 Thread a length of nylon cord down each Austrian blind tape, going through a loop every 10–13cm/4–5in. Tie the cords securely to the last loop. Hang the blind from a special Austrian blind rail, or alternatively fit a wooden batten with screw-eyes behind a curtain track.

roller blind

Roller blind kits are available from department stores, and contain everything except the fabric. Ready-stiffened fabric for roller blinds is available, but if you want to use your choice of fabric it will need to be straightened, then sprayed with fabric stiffener before cutting to size. Avoid heavyweight or loosely woven fabric. Home-made roller blinds are suited to small or medium-size windows that require just one width of fabric.

measuring up for the blind kit

If the blind is to fit inside a recess, measure the exact width with a metal tape and deduct 3cm/1¼in for the blind mechanism. If it is to hang outside the window, add an extra 5cm /2in to each side of the recess so that it will completely cover the space. Buy a roller blind kit the exact width if possible, or get a longer one and cut it to length.

calculating the fabric

The width of the blind is the length of the roller, allowing for the end fixtures. There is no allowance for side seams as the stiffened fabric will not fray. Add 30cm/12in hem and roller allowance to the length. If the blind is to finish below the windowsill, add on another 5cm/2in.

you will need

- **closely woven furnishing fabric**
- **fabric stiffener spray**
- **quilter's ruler (optional)**
- **rotary cutter (optional)**
- **roller blind kit**
- **pencil**
- **long ruler**
- **double-sided tape**
- **sewing kit**

tip for roller blind

Always cut the fabric after spraying as it may shrink considerably.

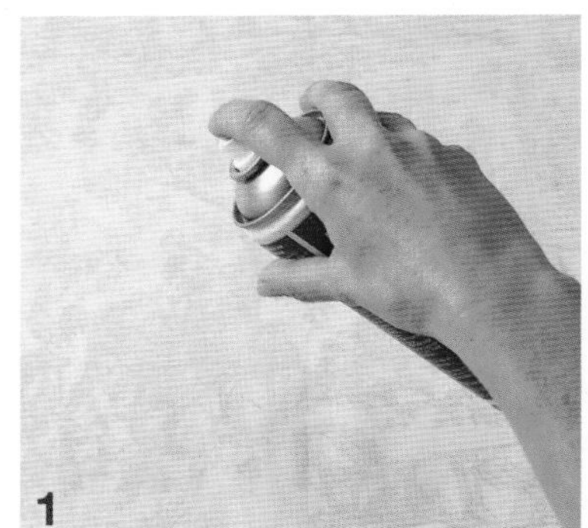

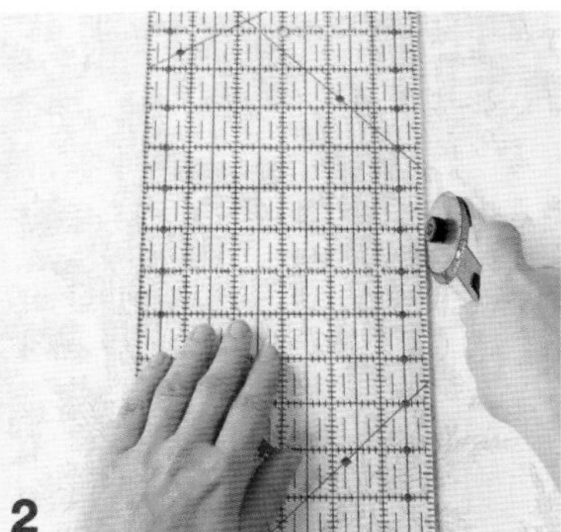

1 Pull a thread at one end of the fabric and cut along the line to get the straight grain. Fold the fabric in half lengthways. If the corners don't meet exactly, straighten the fabric by pulling it on the diagonal or pinning selvage to selvage with the cut edges aligned and steam pressing it. Press the fabric. Following the manufacturer's instructions, spray it lightly with fabric stiffener horizontally and vertically on both sides to achieve a complete and even coverage.

2 Leave the fabric to dry, then press it, and cut to size. A quilter's ruler and rotary cutter are the ideal method to get square corners and straight edges with minimal handling of the fabric. Trim off the selvages and align the markings on the ruler with the cut edge. Cut across at right angles to the correct length.

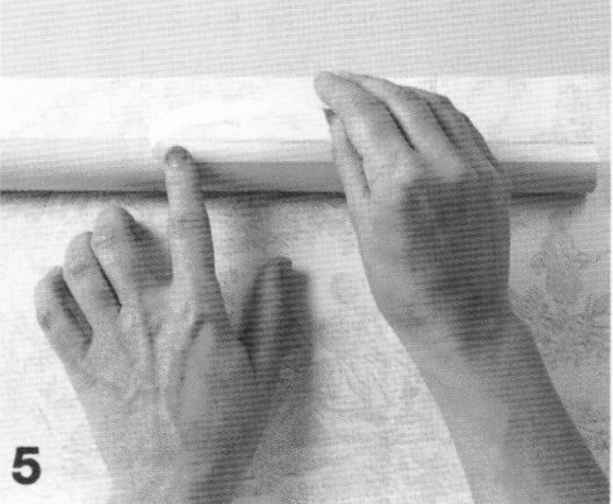

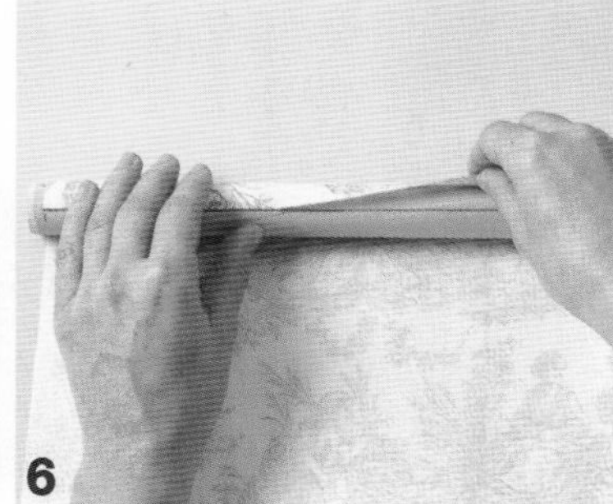

3 Fold over and press a double 4cm/1½in hem along the bottom edge. Stitch. Cut the wooden lath in the blind kit 2cm/¾in shorter than the finished width of the blind and slot it through the hem. Stitch the ends of the hem to secure. If a cord-holder is included in the kit, attach it in the centre of the lath on the right side.

4 Cut the roller 3cm/1¼ in narrower than required to allow for the blind mechanism. So that the blind will roll straight, it is essential to mark a straight line down the centre of the roller, using a pencil and long ruler.

5 Stick a length of double-sided tape along the pencil line and then peel off the protective backing paper.

6 Place the roller across the wrong side of the fabric, 2–3cm/¾–1¼in from the top. Check that it is in the centre then stick the top edge of the fabric to the double-sided tape exactly along the marked line. Attach the spring mechanism and fitments to the ends of the roller. Attach the brackets to the recess or wall, and fit the blind according to the manufacturer's instructions.

far left *Toile de jouy* fabric is used to co-ordinate bed linen with other soft furnishings in the room.
top left Plain white bed linen can be transformed with beautiful embroidery. Here single rose motifs have been used alongside pretty garlands to make a complete set.
below left Plain pillowcases can be personalized with simple motifs. For comfort, keep the embroidery away from the centre where your face touches the pillow.
right Mixed check fabrics can be made into a simple quilt in a weekend to make a very practical bedcover for a child's room.

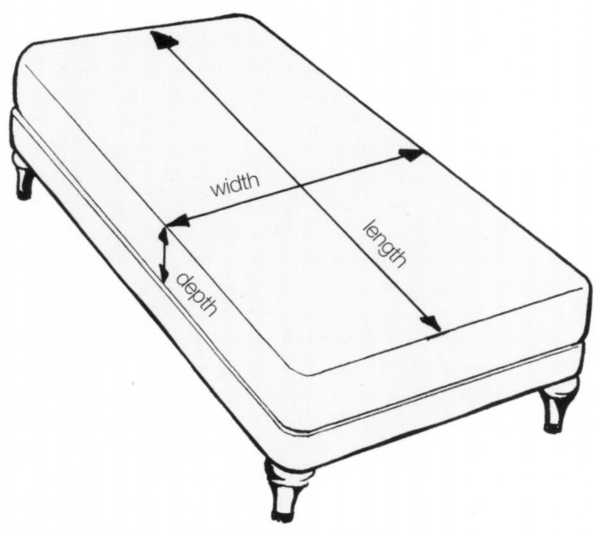

standard bed and cot sizes

Bed sizes vary considerably between countries, but as a guide the following were used for the projects.

Single bed	90 x 190cm/3 x 6½ft
Small double bed	135 x 190cm/4½ x 6½ft
Standard double bed	150 x 200cm/5 x 6½ft
King-size bed	180 x 200cm/6 x 6½ft
Standard cot	56 x 118cm/22 x 46in
Continental cot	60 x 120cm/24 x 47in
Extra-large cot	63 x 127cm/25 x 50in
Cot bed	70 x 140cm/27½ x 55in

basic pillowcase

The basic pillowcase is made from a single strip of fabric that is simply hemmed, folded and stitched down both sides. The pillow is tucked under the flap on the inside to hold it firmly and neatly in place. The basic pillowcase can be made in the same colour as the sheet or as a contrast and can be decorated with ribbon, embroidery or appliqué.

calculating the fabric

The length of the fabric is double the length of the pillow with 20cm/ 8in added for hem and flap allowance. The width of the fabric is the width of the pillow with 3cm/1¼in seam allowance added.

you will need

- **pillow**
- **fabric**
- **sewing kit**

tip for basic pillowcase

Add ribbon or other trimmings before you stitch the side seams.

1 Press and stitch a double 5mm/¼in hem at one short end of the fabric and a double 2cm/¾in hem at the other end.

2 Fold the narrower hem end over to make a 15cm/6in flap with the right side facing out. Pin across the hem.

3 Fold the pillowcase in half crossways with wrong sides together. Pin and stitch a 5mm/ ¼in seam down both sides.

4 Press the seam open and turn through. Stitch an 8mm/⅜in French seam (see basic techniques).

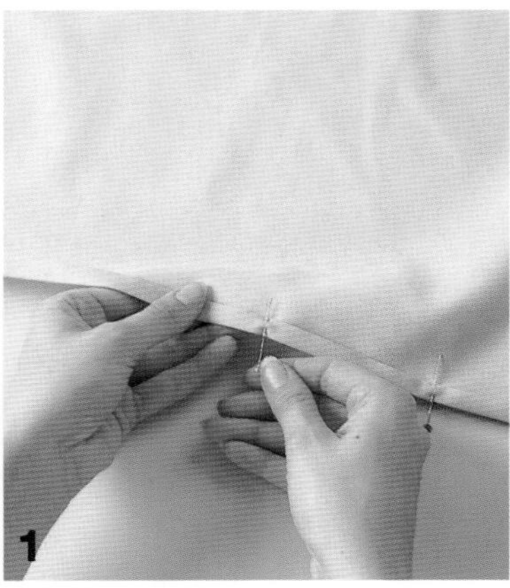
1

2

3

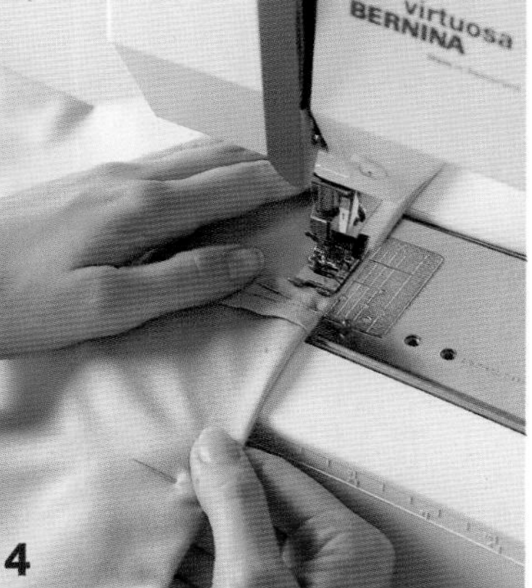

4

pillowcase with a border

This pretty pillowcase is simply the basic pillowcase with a decorative contrast border added before the pillowcase is made up. Narrow piping can be added between the border and the main pillowcase or the border can be embroidered by hand or machine.

calculating the fabric

The width of both fabrics is the width of the pillow with 3cm/1¼in seam allowance added. The length of the main fabric is 10cm/4in less than double the length of the pillow. The depth of the contrast border fabric is 33cm/13in.

you will need

- pillow
- main fabric
- contrast fabric
- sewing kit

tip for pillowcase with a border

Using flat fell and French seams hides any raw edges and makes the pillowcase harder wearing.

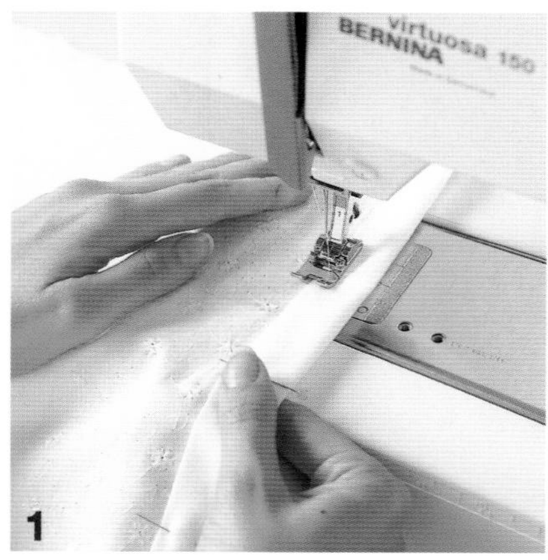

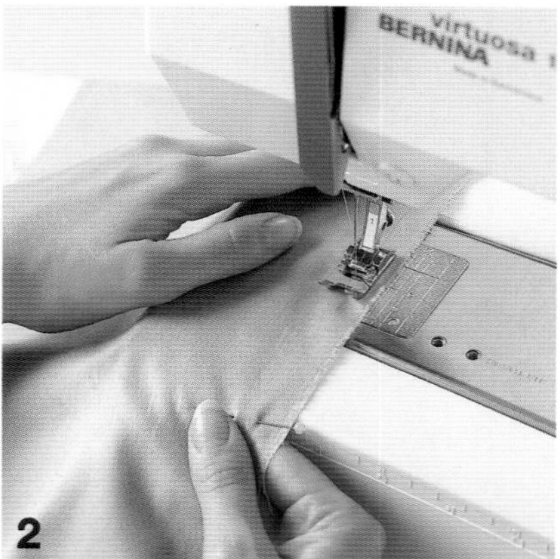

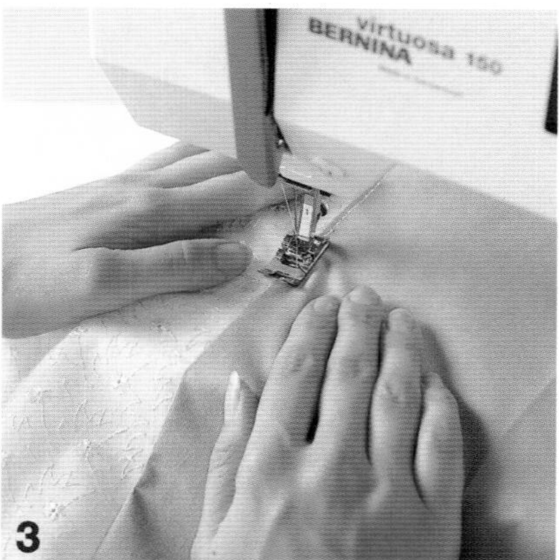

1 Press and stitch a 2cm/¾in double hem on one short edge of the main fabric and make a 5mm/¼in double hem on one longer edge of the contrast fabric.

2 Pin the raw edges of the two pieces right sides together and stitch a 1.5cm/⅝in seam. Press the seam towards the darker fabric. Trim the underneath seam allowance to 5mm/¼in.

3 Turn the other edge of the seam allowance under and press to prepare a flat fell seam (see basic techniques). Stitch the edge of the seam or use one of the decorative embroidery stitches on the machine. Complete this pillowcase as a basic pillowcase making a 15cm/6in flap on the contrast fabric and stitching the sides with French seams.

buttoned pillowcase

Buttons make an attractive addition to a pillowcase but as they are hard and uncomfortable to lean against, must be kept well away from where your head might lie. To solve this problem, add an attractive border to the outside edge of the pillowcase.

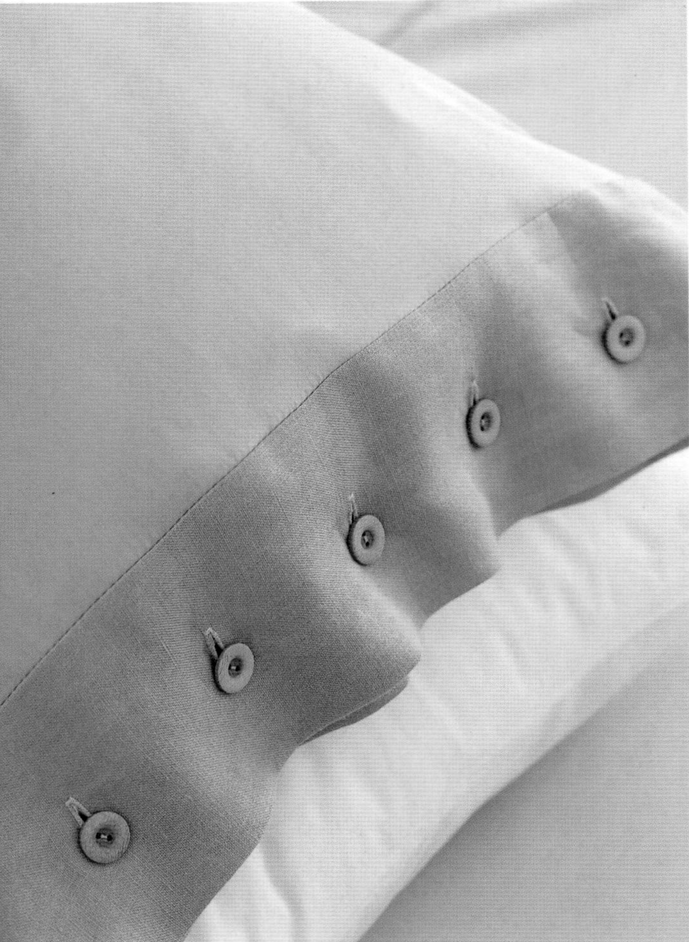

calculating the fabric

Cut the main fabric for the pillowcase the length and width of the pillow, adding 3cm/1¼in seam allowance to each measurement. Cut two pieces for the button border 23cm/9in long and the same width as the main fabric.

you will need

- pillow
- main fabric
- contrast fabric
- buttons
- sewing kit

tip for buttoned pillowcase

If you can't find buttons to match, cover buttons in a contrast fabric.

1

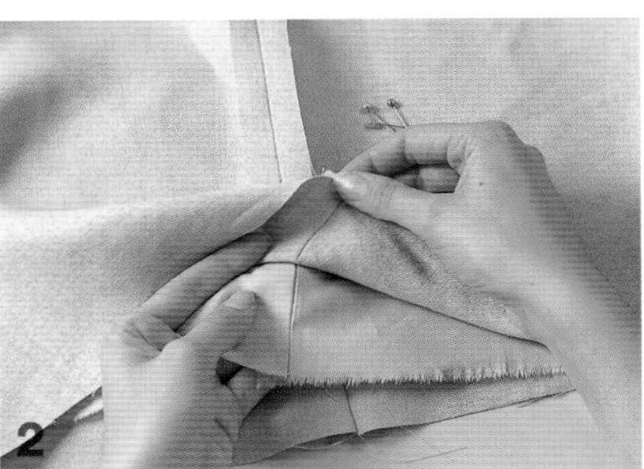

2

1 With right sides together, join the side seams of the border panels with 1.5cm/⅝in flat seams. Press open. Fold the main fabric in half and stitch together along the long edges.

2 Turn the pillowcase right side out. Place the border on top with right sides together. Match the side seams and pin, then stitch around the top edge. Press the seam towards the border.

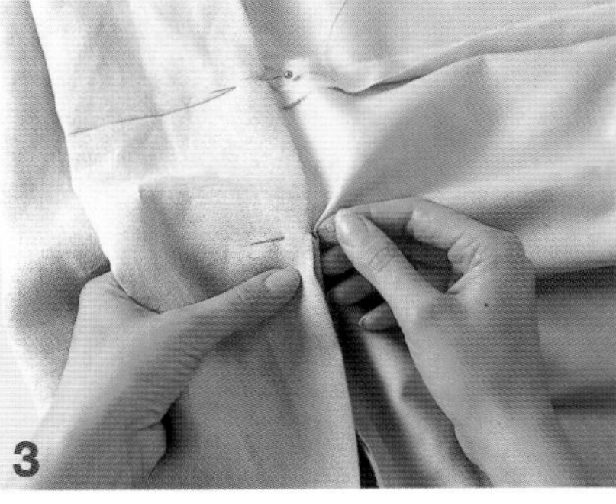

3

4

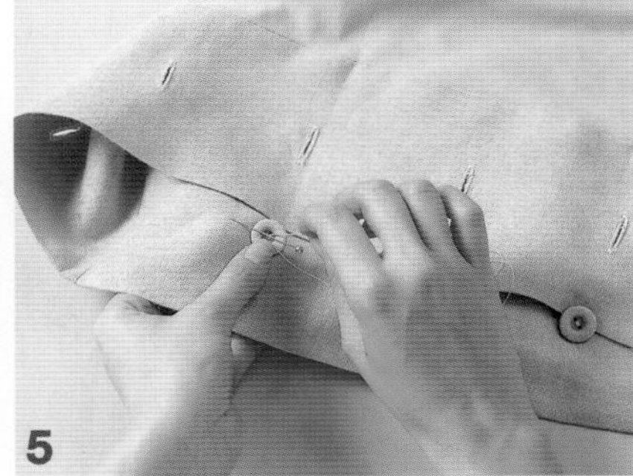

5

3 Turn in a 1.5cm/⅝in hem on the raw edge of the border. Fold over the edge of the border to meet the stitching on the inside. Pin and tack (baste) in position. Hem the border to the stitching.

4 Insert pins along the centre of the border. Measure and mark the buttonholes with tacking thread.

5 Make machine buttonholes on the top of the border using a toning thread. With sharp, pointed scissors, slit the buttonholes. Sew the buttons in the corresponding position on the inside back edge of the border. Stitch over a pin to create a shank behind the button (see basic techniques).

tied-edge pillowcase

Ties add an unusual touch to a simple pillowcase design. Vary the look by making the ties wide or narrow and alter the length so that they will tie into a simple knot or make a pretty bow. You could make ties from contrasting fabric or ribbon.

calculating the fabric

Add 3cm/1¼in to the width of the pillow and 23cm/9in to double the length of the pillow.

For the ties shown here you will need 40 x 50cm/16 x 20in of fabric.

you will need

- pillow
- main fabric
- sewing kit

tip for tied-edge pillowcase

For an alternative look use a contrast pillowcase over the pillow.

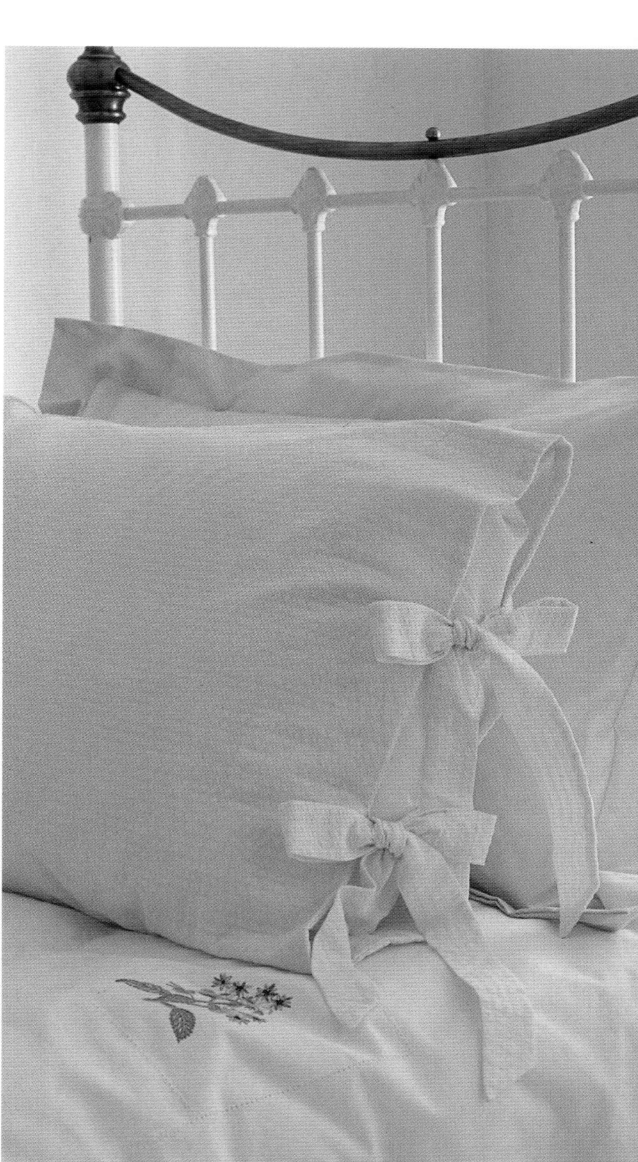

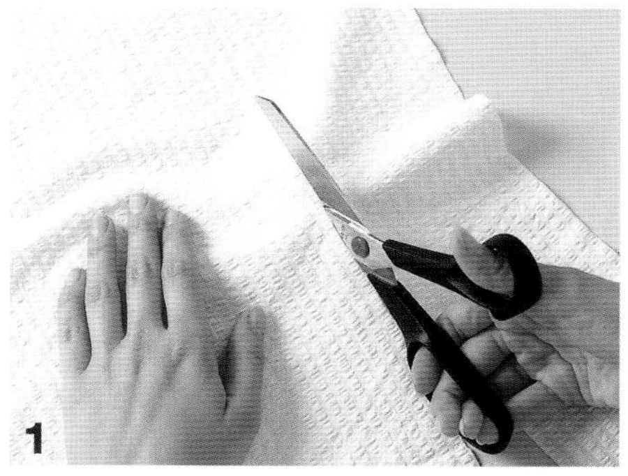

1

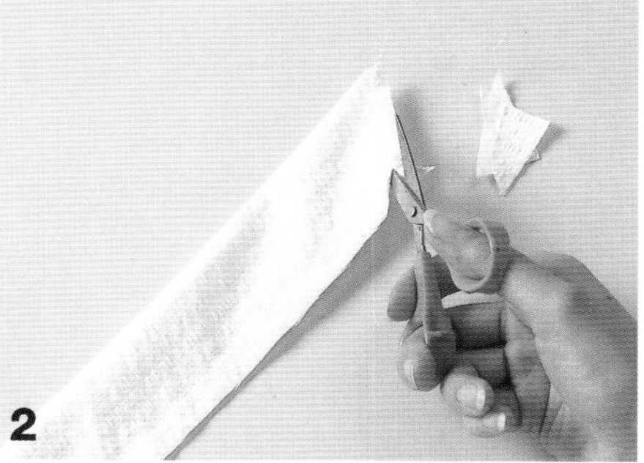

2

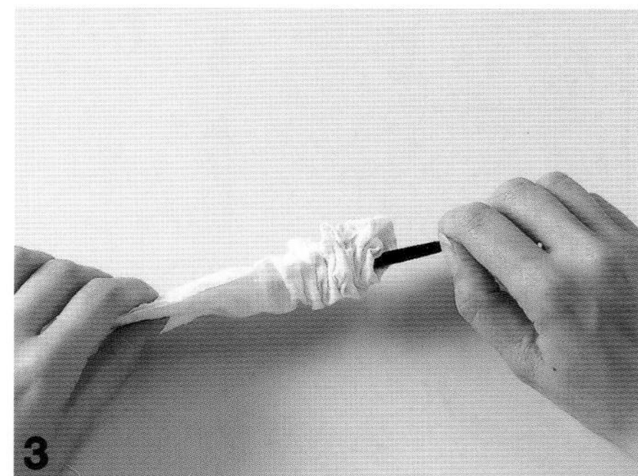

3

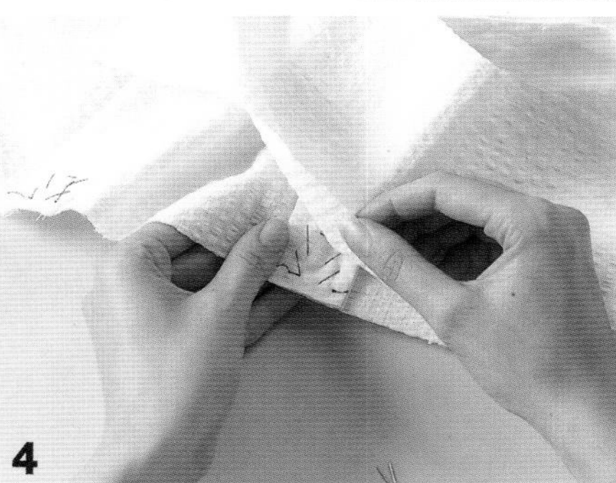

4

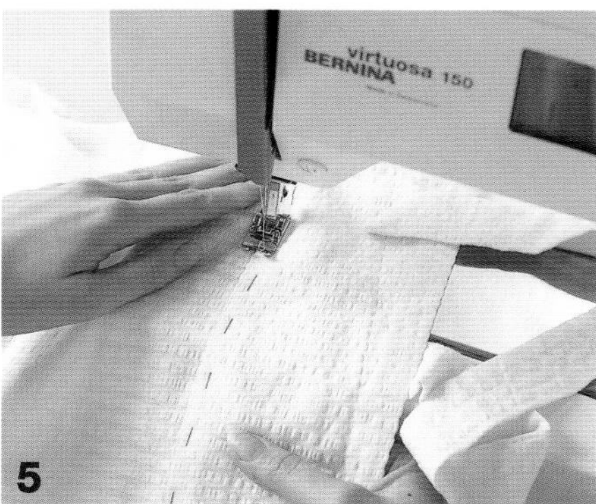

5

1 Cut four ties each 10 x 50cm/4 x 20in lengthways down the fabric. Fold the main fabric in half and stitch the sides with French seams (see basic techniques). Cut off the top 10cm/4in and put to one side for the facing.

2 Fold the ties in half lengthways with right sides together. Stitch down the long side and diagonally across one short end with a 1.5cm/½in seam. Trim the point to reduce bulk.

3 Turn the tie through. Ease out the point and press flat.

4 Tack two ties equal distances from the centre point on one side of the pillowcase with raw edges aligned. Match the ties on the other side. Pin the facing over the ties with right sides together. Match the seams and stitch.

5 To finish, turn a small hem on the raw edge of the facing and stitch the hem in place.

Oxford pillowcase

An Oxford pillowcase has a flat border all the way round that makes the pillow look fuller and more substantial. The border can be added in a contrast fabric but this simple method looks quite stunning made in a sheer fabric with a contrast basic pillowcase inside.

calculating the fabric

Cut the width of each piece 13cm/5in wider than the pillow. The front panel is 13cm/5in longer than the pillow. The back panel is 10cm/4in longer than the pillow and the flap is 30cm/12in deep.

you will need

- pillow
- organza
- sewing kit

tip for Oxford pillowcase

If you find sheer fabric difficult to stitch on your machine, cut strips of tissue paper and stitch through the paper to complete the seams. Tear off the paper.

1 Pull a thread and cut along the gathers to ensure the fabric is cut straight. Cut all three pieces from the fabric with the lengthways straight grain running down the pillow.

2 Pin and tack (baste) a 2cm/¾in double hem along one short edge of the back panel and along a long edge of the flap. Stitch each hem close to the fold.

3 Place the hemmed flap panel on top of the front panel with the wrong sides together and pin. Arrange the back panel on top and tack all the way around.

4 Stitch a 9mm/⅜in seam and trim to 3mm/⅛in. Trim across the corners. Press the seams open as far into the corners as possible.

5 Turn the pillowcase through and roll the edge between your fingers. Tack the edge to hold the fabric flat.

6 Measure 5cm/2in from the needle and stick a piece of masking tape on to the sewing machine to mark the distance. Top-stitch the border using the tape as a guide.

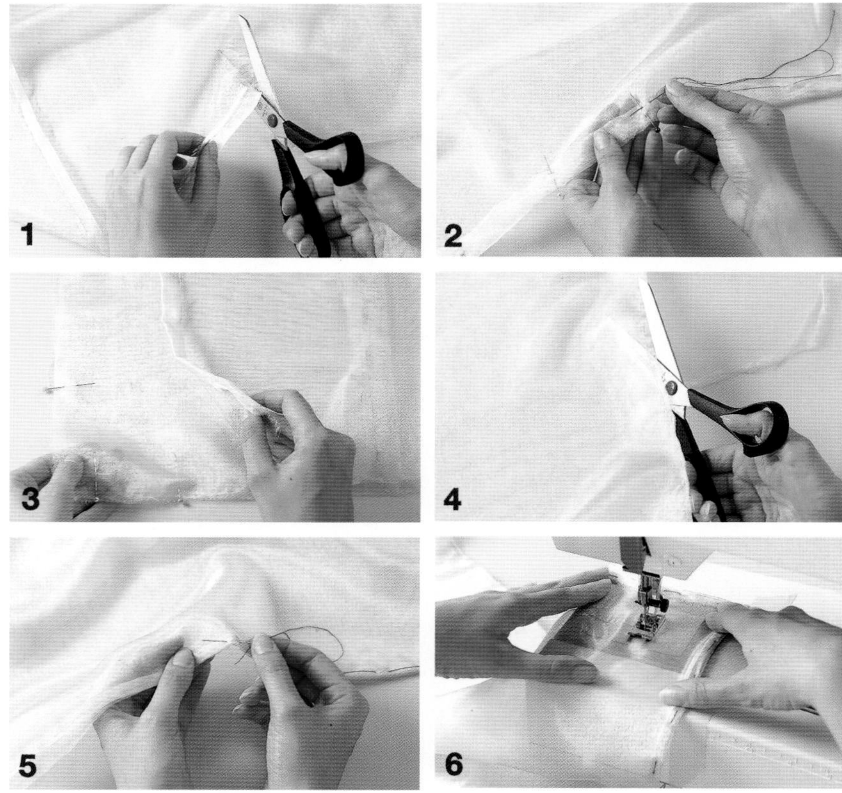

ruffled pillowcase

The ruffle is made of the same fabric as the body of the pillow, but it could be made from a contrast colour or fabric type. The ruffle can be decorated with ribbon or lace before gathering. The pillow can be embroidered with a monogram or embroidery.

calculating the fabric

Cut the width of each piece 3cm/1¼in wider than the pillow. The front panel is 3cm/1¼in longer than the pillow. The back panel is 5.5cm/2¼in longer than the pillow and the flap is 25cm/10in deep. The length of the ruffle is twice the length and twice the width of the pillow. The width of the ruffle is twice the required finished depth plus 3cm/1¼in seam allowance.

you will need

- pillow
- main fabric
- sewing kit

tip for ruffled pillowcase

If you want to add embroidery, it is much easier to do this before the pillowcase is made up.

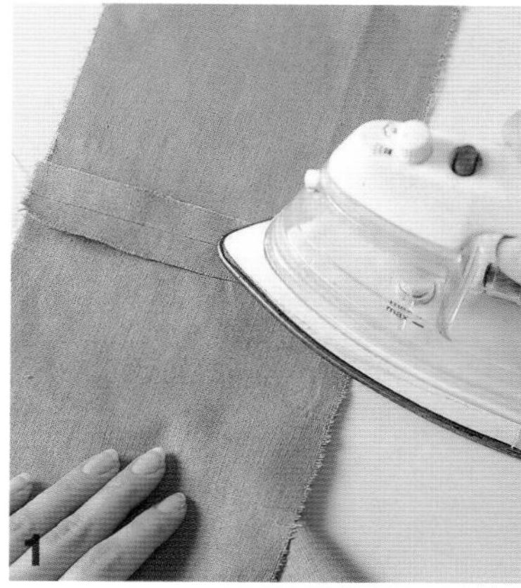

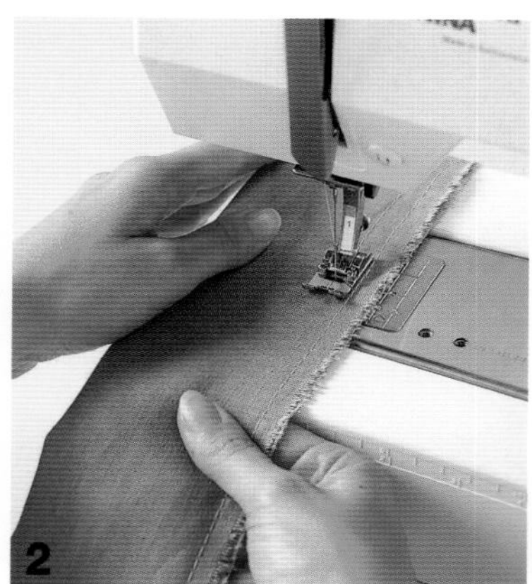

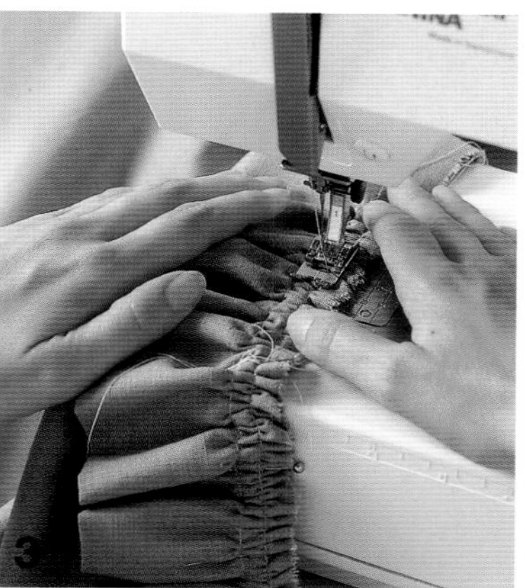

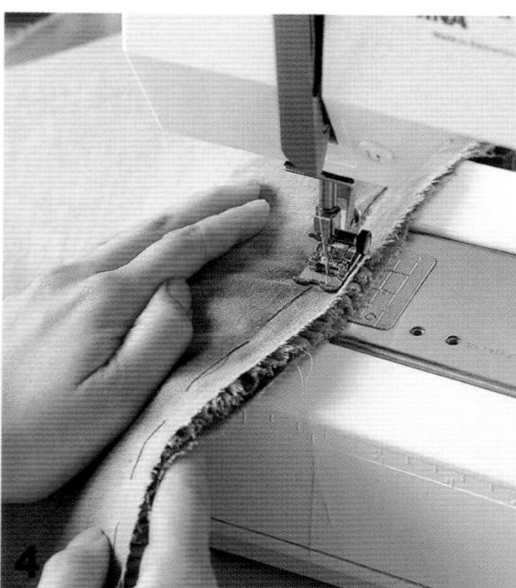

1 Cut sufficient strips of fabric to make the ruffle and join with flat seams. Join the strips into a complete circle. Press the seams flat.

2 Fold the ruffle lengthways with the seams to the inside and raw edges aligned and press. Fold the ruffle in four widthways and press to mark. Unfold, then work two rows of machine gathers along the raw edge, stopping and cutting the thread at each pressed mark. Knot one lot of thread ends in each quarter.

3 Mark the centre of each side on the front of the pillowcase and pin the joins in the gathers at these points, with raw edges aligned. Pull up the gathers evenly and tack (baste). Stitch the gathers 1cm/½in from the edge.

4 Make a 2cm/¾in double hem across each back piece on one side. Pin the main piece to the right side of the front and pin the flap on top, sandwiching the ruffle between the raw edges. Stitch around the edge. Trim and turn through.

flat sheet

Flat sheets are versatile and can be used as a bottom or top sheet. When used as a top sheet, the top hem can be decorated with a piped edge, embroidery or a trimming. This will be visible when the sheet is folded over the bedcover or blanket.

above *Piping adds an unusual finish to the edge of a sheet.*

calculating the fabric

Measure the length, width and depth of the mattress. To work out the fabric size in each direction, add twice the mattress depth to the length and width, then add 50cm/20in to tuck in.

you will need

- **sheeting**
- **piping cord or ribbon (optional)**
- **sewing kit**

tip for flat sheet

You can make the two bottom corners fitted (see fitted sheet).

1 If the fabric is the width required leave the selvage down the sides; otherwise, stitch a 1.5cm/⅝in double hem down each side.

2 Along the bottom, make a 2.5cm/1in double hem and on the top edge press and stitch a 8cm/3in hem.

3 On the top edge stitch another row 6mm/¼in from the first to make a casing. Thread fine piping cord through the channel.

4 Alternatively finish the edge of the top hem with a pretty ribbon.

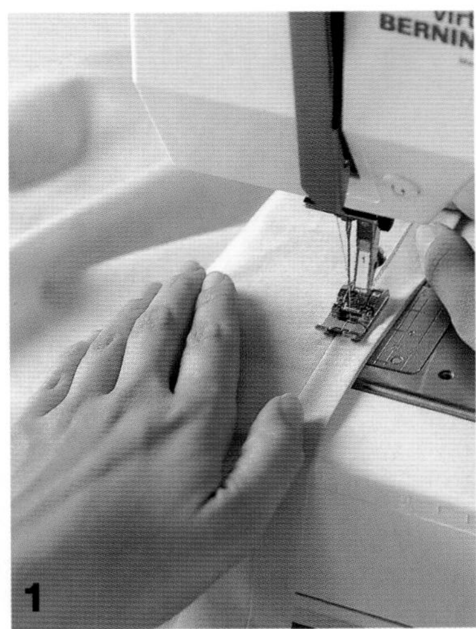

1

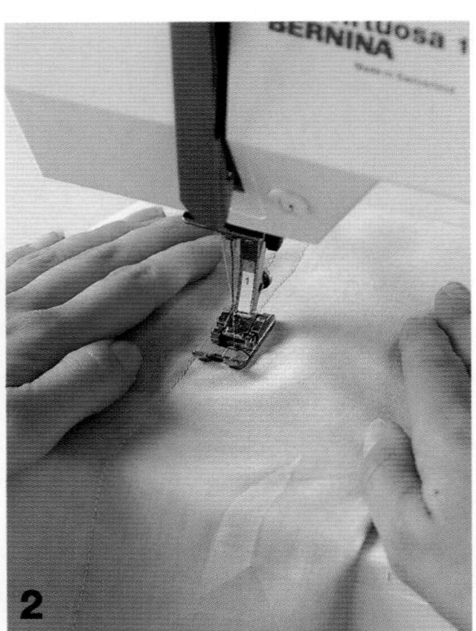

2

3

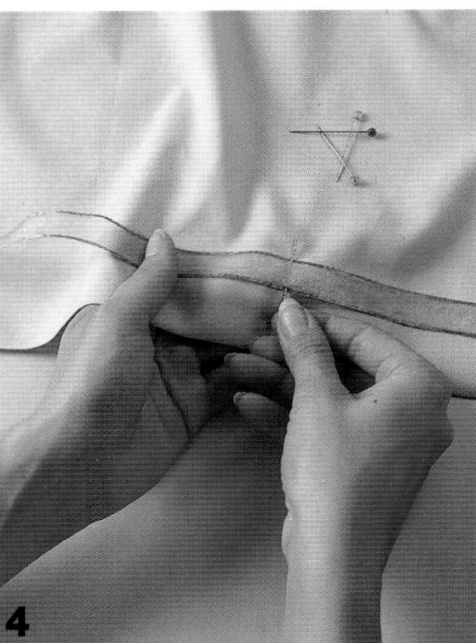
4

box pleat valance (dust ruffle)

The box pleat valance (dust ruffle) is the most formal of the valances and looks particularly stylish in a crisp cotton or linen. Box pleats are essentially two knife pleats facing each other. The box pleats do not have to meet fold to fold, but can be narrow and spaced to give a lighter, jauntier appearance.

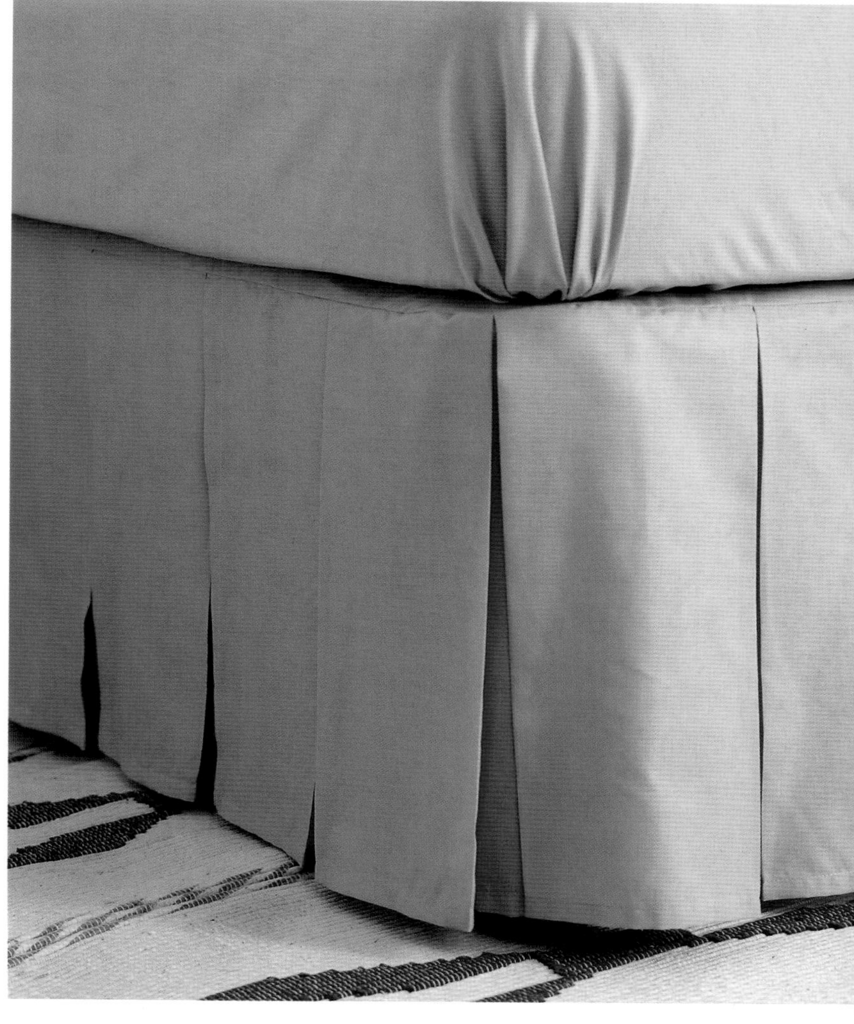

calculating the fabric

Measure the length and width of the mattress. To make the flat base add 3cm/1¼in to the width and 3.5cm/1½in to the length. For the depth of the skirt, measure from the bottom of the mattress to the floor and add 5.5cm/2¼in. For the length of the skirt add twice the length to the width and multiply by three then add 6cm/2½in.

you will need

- **sheeting**
- **sewing kit**

calculating the pleats

Draw a diagram of the bed and work out how many and what size of pleat will fit across the base of the bed so that a pleat lies on each corner. The front of the pleat from fold to fold is the pleat width. Half that measurement is the pleat depth on the back.

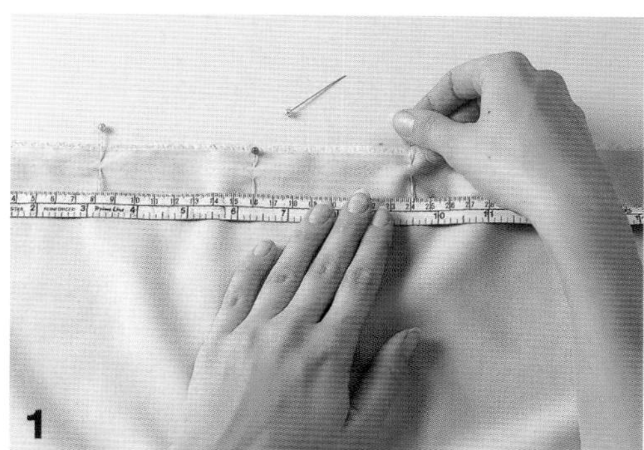

1

1 Cut sufficient strips of fabric for the skirt and tack the seams. At one end, mark 3cm/1¼in for the side hem. Begin to mark the pleats beginning with a full pleat width and then two half widths. Continue along the full length of the skirt, marking the hem allowance at the other end. Any joins should be down the centre of two half widths. Adjust the length of the panels accordingly. Join the seams with French seams (see basic techniques).

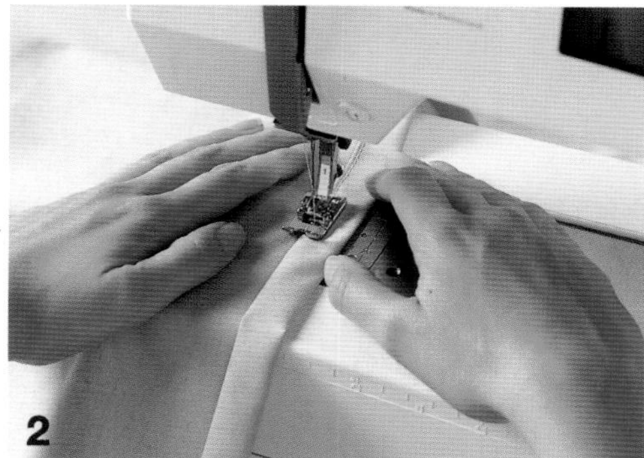

2

2 Turn up a double 2cm/¾in hem and stitch. Cut the fabric to fit the mattress base and round off the corners as for the corner pleat valance.

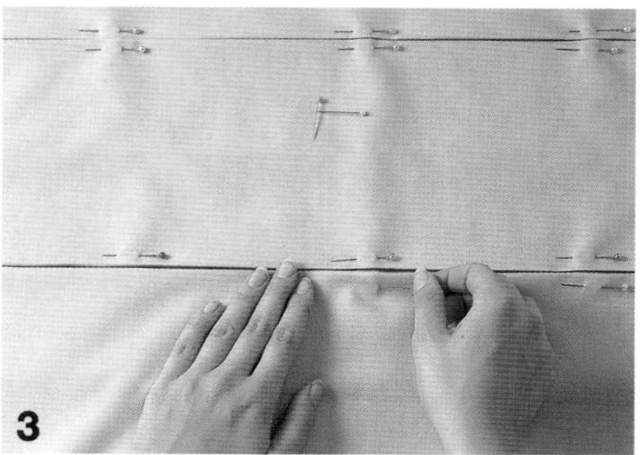

3

3 Fold the pleats carefully so that the straight grain of the fabric runs down the edge. Press with a steam iron and then pin and tack (baste) each down its length. Complete as for the corner pleat valance.

duvet cover

One of the problems when making a duvet cover is finding fabric, other than standard sheeting, that is wide enough to make the front in one panel. Fabric can be joined with flat seams equally spaced down each side of a larger centre panel or with a single offset seam trimmed with piping.

you will need

- **main fabric**
- **piping cord**
- **fasteners such as buttons or popper (snap) tape**
- **sewing kit**

tip for duvet cover

Wash fabric before cutting out in case it shrinks.

1 Cut two panels for the front of the duvet cover so that the seam lies about one-third of the way across. Cover a length of piping cord to fit the length of the duvet cover and tack (baste) down the inside seam on one of the panels.

2 Pin the other panel on top and stitch close to the piping using a zipper foot. Press the seam allowance to one side. Join widths if required to make the back panel.

3 Turn and press a double 2.5cm/1in hem along the bottom edge of the back and front panels of the duvet.

4 To fasten the duvet with ties, cut four ties each 8 x 46cm/3 x 18in. Fold the strips in half lengthways and stitch a seam down the side and along the bottom. Turn the ties through and press. On the front and back bottom edges of the duvet, mark 30cm/12in from each side edge. Space two ties equally between the markers on the duvet front and back. Tuck the short raw edge of the ties into the hem and fold back over the seam. Pin in place.

5 Stitch the hem and the tie at the same time, stitching close to both folds.

6 With wrong sides together, pin the back and front of the duvet together. Stitch together around two long sides and the top using a 5mm/¼in seam. Press the seam open and turn through. Complete the French seam with a 9mm/⅜in seam allowance. Stitch 30cm/16in in from each side across the bottom of the duvet.

7 Alternatively, cut the popper (snap) tape 50cm/20in narrower than the width of the duvet. Centre the popper tape on the hem of one panel. Fit the other half on top, pin to the second hem and pull the tape apart. Stitch the popper tape and the hems at the same time. Stitch across the hems 25cm/10in from the edge of the duvet.

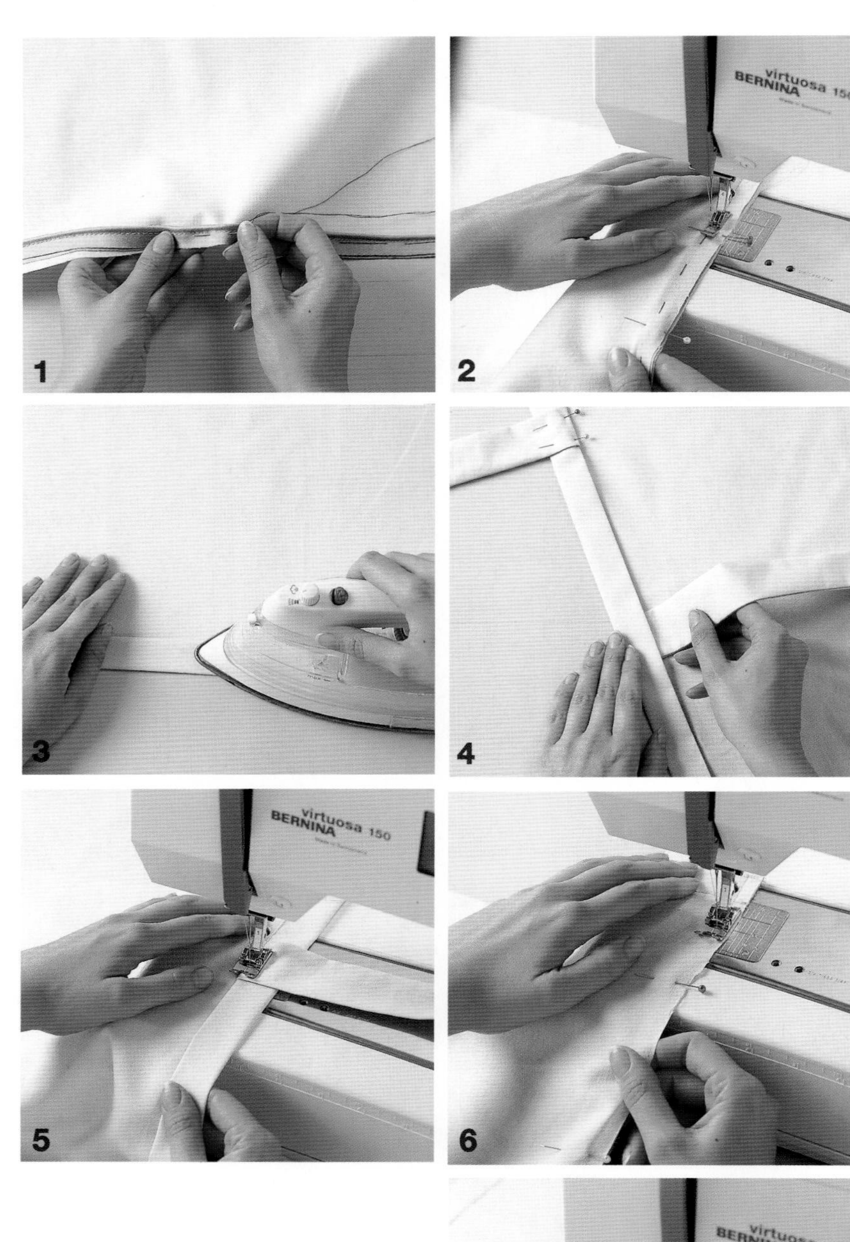

front envelope opening duvet cover

An envelope opening allows you to use a more unusual fabric for the front of the duvet cover because the textured surface doesn't lie next to your skin. The more suitable sheeting fabric can be used for the back and flap. The flap can be fastened with poppers (snaps) or pretty buttons and ribbon loops.

above *Use pretty buttons to finish.*

calculating the fabric

All panels are the width of the duvet plus 3cm/1¼in seam allowance. Cut the front panel the same length as the duvet plus 7cm/2¾in hem and seam allowance. Decide on the depth of the envelope flap and add this measurement to the length of the duvet back, adding 7cm/2¾in hem and seam allowance.

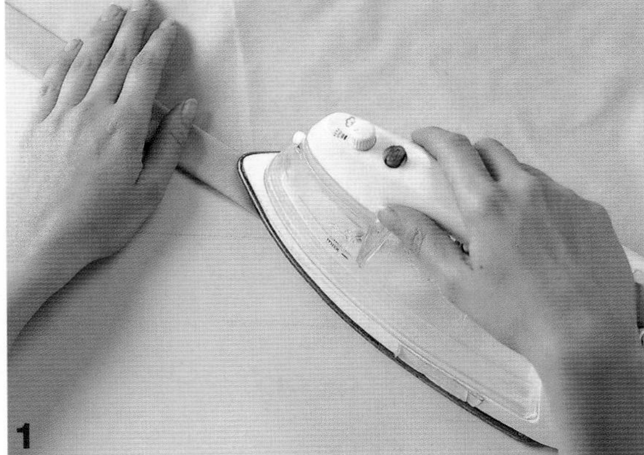

1

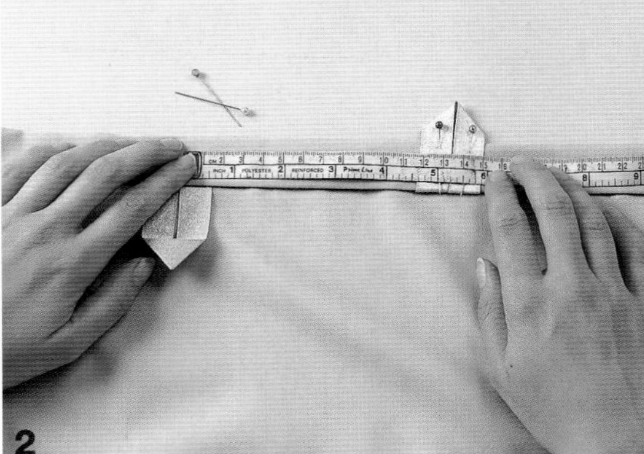

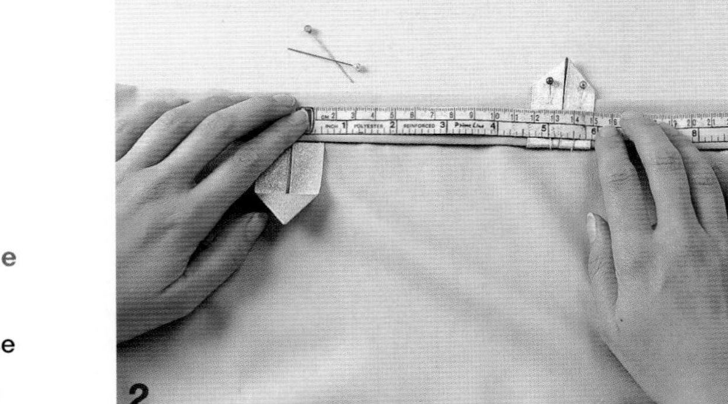

2

you will need

- **main fabric**
- **contrast fabric**
- **ribbon**
- **lightweight interfacing**
- **buttons**
- **sewing kit**

tip for front envelope opening duvet cover

Check that the fabric you use is suitable for a duvet cover.

1 Press a 2cm/¾in double hem across the bottom of the envelope flap. Press and stitch a 2cm/¾in double hem across the top of the main front panel.

2 For a single duvet, cut eight pieces of ribbon approximately 15cm/6in long for the button loops. Fold and press the ribbons to make a point as shown. Spacing the loops evenly across the duvet, tuck the raw ends under the hem and fold each back on itself and pin.

3 Stitch along the bottom edge to secure the ribbon loops of the hem. Add ribbon to the front of the hem. Stitch from the right side down each edge of the ribbon.

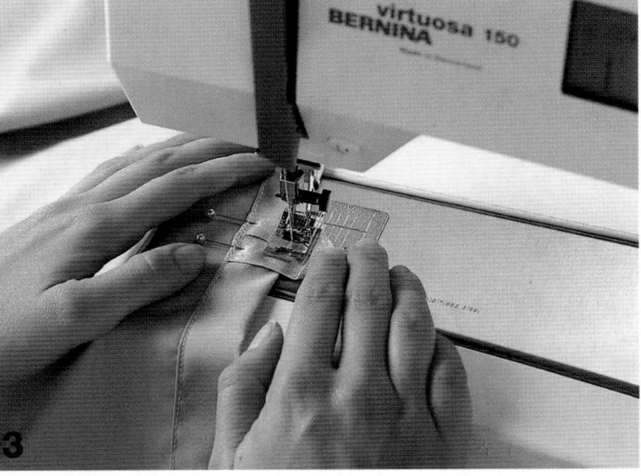

3

4

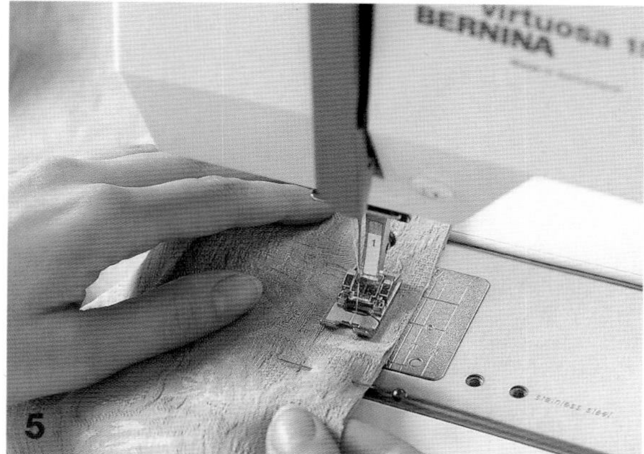

5

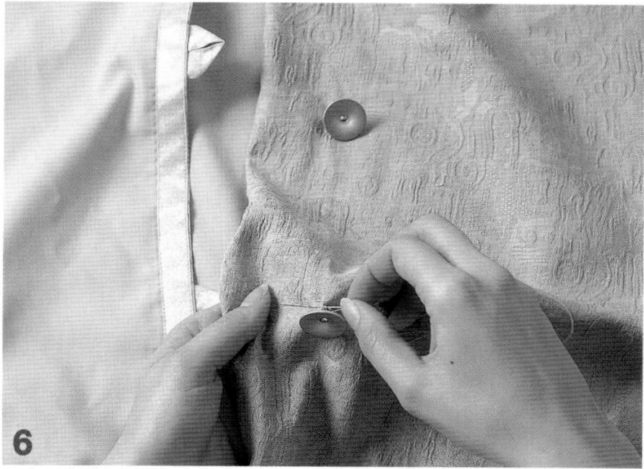

6

4 Lay the back panel with right side up and fold the flap over. Place the main panel on top with right side down.

5 Stitch the side seams and along the bottom, reverse-stitching at the top for extra strength. Zigzag-stitch the seams and turn the cover through.

6 Mark the position of the buttons on the front of the duvet. Press a square of interfacing behind each mark to strengthen the button fastening. Stitch the buttons in place.

fleece throw

A warm fleece throw is the simplest way to provide some extra warmth in the cold winter days. The edge of the fleece can be bound with a contrast fabric that complements the bed linen. Join the binding strips on the diagonal, preferably where the seam will be hidden in the mitre corners.

calculating the fabric

The length of the binding strips is twice the length and twice the width of the throw, plus seam allowances for joining strips and mitring corners.

you will need

- **fleece**
- **contrast lightweight fabric**
- **ribbon**
- **sewing kit**

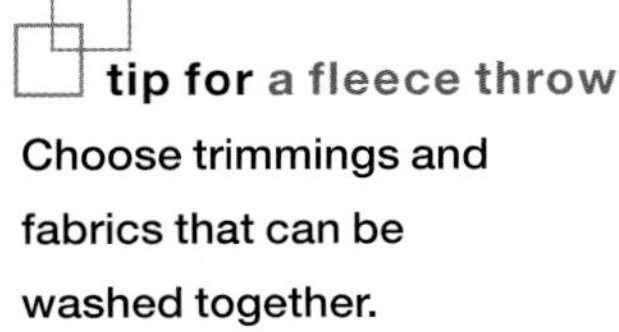

tip for a fleece throw

Choose trimmings and fabrics that can be washed together.

1

2

3

1 Cut the selvages off the fleece fabric. Cut the fleece to the exact size you require.

2 Decide on the width of the binding and cut four strips twice the finished width plus 3cm/1¼in seam allowance. Fold the strips in half widthways and press.

3 Open out the binding strips. Place the fleece right side up on top of one binding strip so that the edge of the fleece is level with the pressed crease. Pin and tack (baste) the fleece to the binding along the first side and close to the fold. Turn the fleece and binding over.

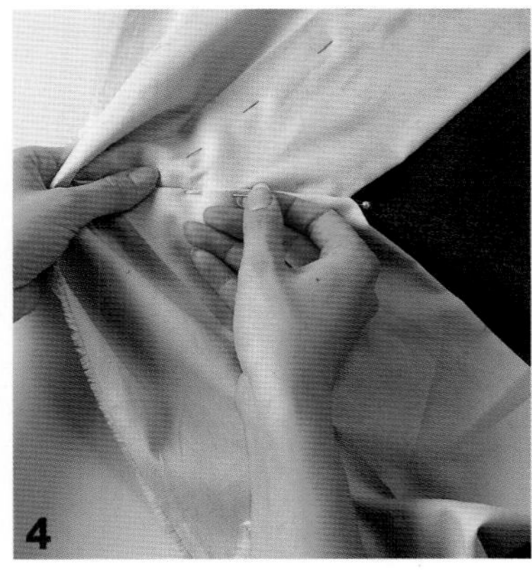

4

5

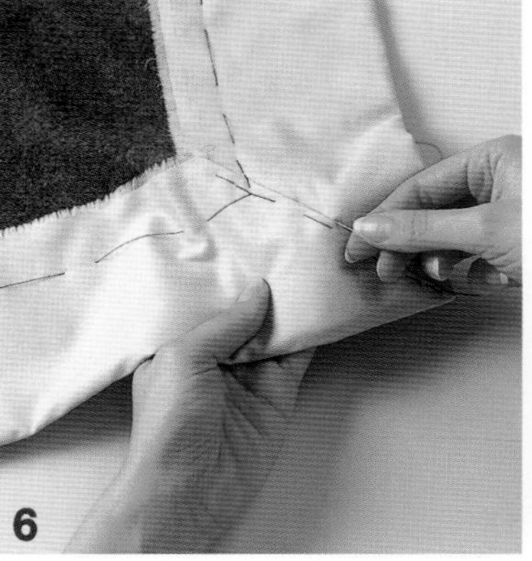

6

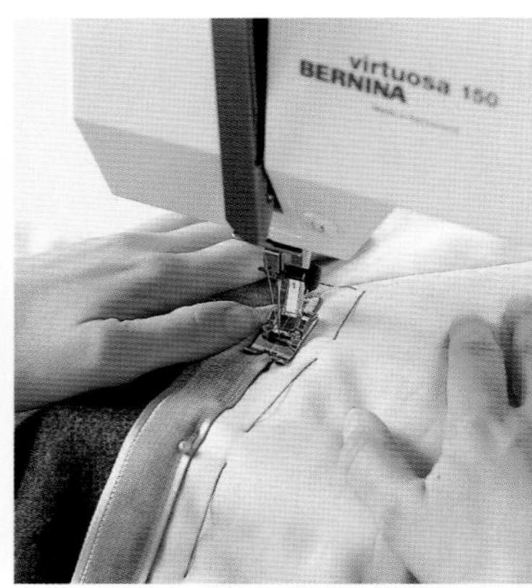

4 Turn under 1.5cm/⅝in along the front edge of the binding. Fold the binding over to make a neat mitre at the corner. Continue pinning and tacking the binding until all four sides and corners are complete.

5 Turn the throw over and fold the binding over to the right side. Fold the binding over at the corners to make a neat mitre.

6 Tack along the edge of the binding all around the throw. Slip-stitch the mitred corners in place on both sides and along the binding edge on the reverse.

7 Pin the ribbon to the front of the throw so that it overlaps the raw edge of the binding. Mitre the corners neatly. Stitch down each side of the ribbon. Stitch both sides in the same direction to prevent the ribbon twisting.

quilted bedspread

This quick and easy patchwork quilt can be made in a weekend. The large panels of mixed blue-and-white fabric give the quilt a classic look and the layers are simply tied together at intervals. Achieving a random look to the quilt is not as easy as you might think. Lay out the cut squares and rectangles on the floor and rearrange until you achieve a colour and fabric balance.

calculating the fabric

Measure the bed and allow 30–50cm/12–20in for an overhang on the sides and end of the quilt. You will need at least five different fabrics for the quilt top. Work out how many square metres/yards will fit on the quilt and buy sufficient fabric allowing a little extra for seam allowances. The wadding (batting) has to be slightly larger than the finished quilt size and the backing fabric, 16cm/6¼in larger all round.

you will need

- **selection of cotton fabrics in a similar weight for the patches**
- **fabric for the borders**
- **backing fabric**
- **50g/2oz wadding (batting)**
- **quilting pins**
- **crochet cotton**
- **sewing kit**

tip for quilted bedspread

If required, join widths of wadding with herringbone stitch.

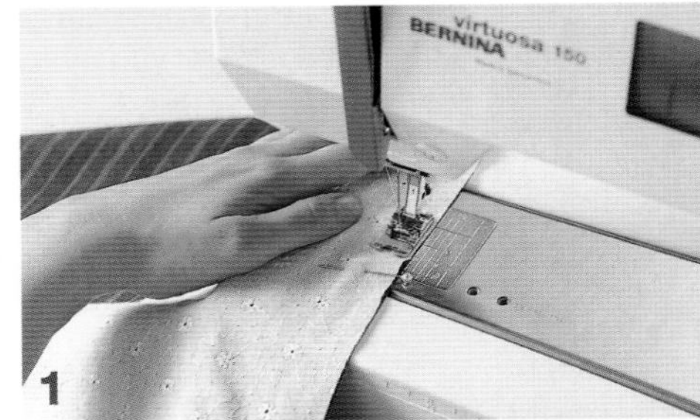

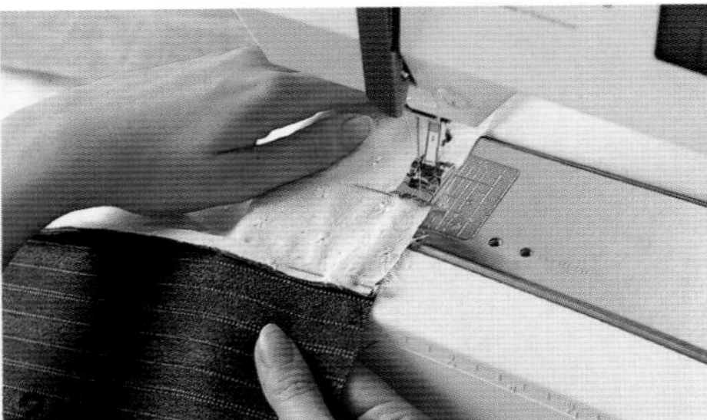

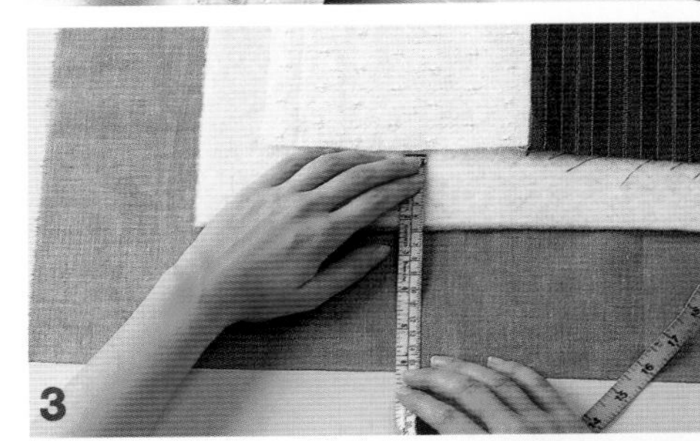

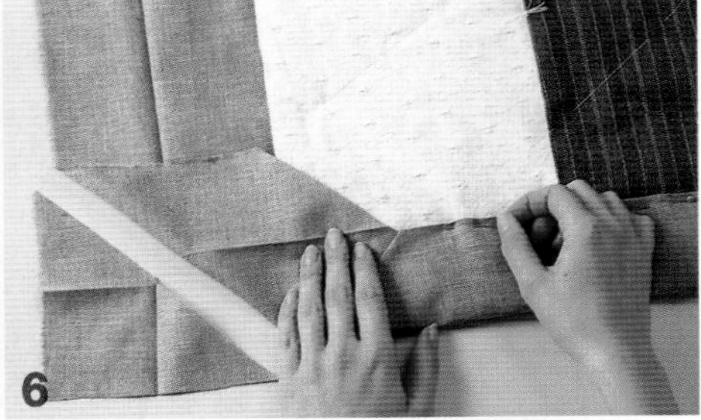

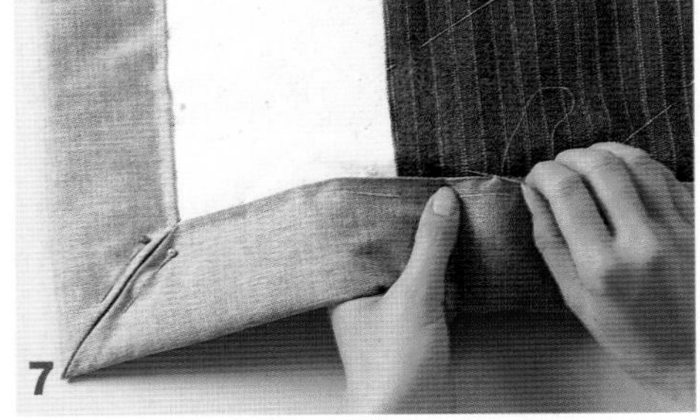

1 To plan the panels for the quilt front, take 16cm/6¼in from the proposed width of the quilt and divide by three. Add 12mm/½in to this for the centre panel and add 9cm/3½in for the two outside panels. Cut squares and rectangles of different fabrics to these widths and sew together with 5mm/¼in seams.

2 Press the seams towards the darker fabric. Pin the three rows together and stitch with 5mm/¼in seams. Press the seams towards the darker side. If necessary, snip into the seam and press different sections in opposite directions. Press the quilt top.

3 Place the quilt backing on a clean, flat surface. On top centre the wadding (batting). Centre the quilt top on the wadding and smooth out. Check that the backing is 15cm/6in from the raw edge of the quilt top.

4 Beginning in the centre and working out in a ray pattern, tack (baste) the layers together with long stitches. Measure and mark the position of the ties so that they are regularly spaced over the quilt – about 15–20cm/6–8in apart. Using crochet cotton take a small stitch through all layers, leaving a 10cm/4in tail. Take a back stitch, then bring the needle out at the front. Tie the ends in a reef (square) knot.

5 Trim the wadding only to match the quilt top. Fold the raw edge of the backing in to meet the raw edge of the quilt top and press the edge.

6 Open out the hem. Trim across the diagonal line. Fold the corner at the pressed crease lines. Refold the binding to make a double hem with a neat double mitred corner (see basic techniques).

7 Slip-stitch the edge of the binding to the quilt top. For a more secure finish, the edge of the binding can be stitched through all layers with a decorative row of white running stitch. Slip-stitch along the mitred corners to complete the quilt.

bed drape

This lovely decoration gives a stunning look to a bed. Sheer fabric is gathered on to a hoop, which can be attached to the wall or suspended by cord from the ceiling. The ideal cane to use is kooboo cane, which is very pliable and can be bent into a circle.

above *Very flimsy, lightweight fabrics may need curtain weights to hold them in place.*

calculating the fabric

Measure from the proposed height of the hoop down to the floor and add 10cm/4in seam allowance. Allow 3–4 widths of fabric to give sufficient fullness, especially if the bed has a headboard.

you will need

- **sheer fabric**
- **pliable cane to make into a ring**
- **strong cord or neutral colour adhesive tape**
- **ribbon (optional)**
- **cord for hanging**
- **sewing kit**

tip for bed drape

For a different effect decorate the hoop with extra twisted fabric.

1 Press under an 8cm/3in hem along the top edge of each fabric width and stitch. Stitch a second row to make a casing deep enough to fit the cane hoop. Cut the cane to the required length, shaping the ends at an acute angle. Thread the cane through the casing.

2 Bend the cane into a circle, overlapping the cut ends. Bind the ends securely together with strong cord or adhesive tape. Tie a length of cord at the gap between each width of fabric. (The cord should be long enough to reach the ceiling.)

3 Check the length of the drape then stitch a 5mm/¼in double hem along the bottom edge. If desired, attach a ribbon bow at the front. Tie the cords at the required height and suspend from the ceiling.

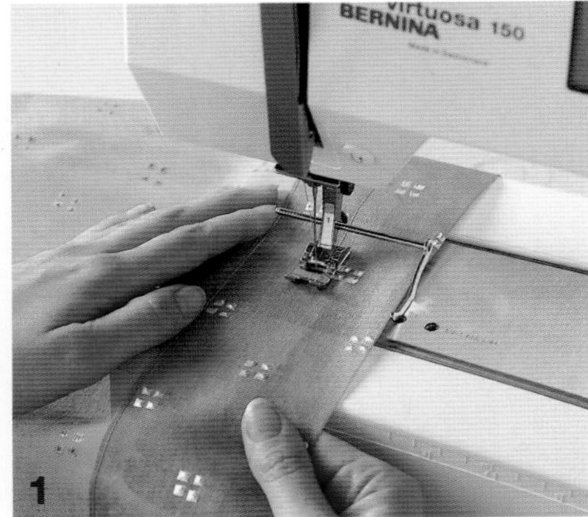

1

2

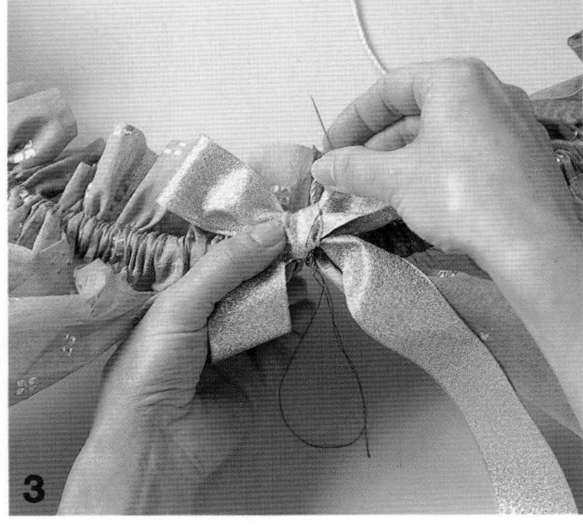

3

a flat canopy for a bed

A flat canopy is a more dramatic way to decorate a four-poster bed. The fabric softens the hard frame of the bed and creates a tent-like, intimate effect, as the "ceiling" is lowered. The canopy hangs down to the bottom of the mattress at the head of the bed, over the top of the bed frame and down a short distance at the foot of the bed. The amount the drape hangs at the foot depends on the depth of the bed frame. Tie the canopy with ribbons and insert curtain weights in the front two corners so that it hangs straight.

calculating the fabric

Drape a long piece of rope or chain weight over the ends of the bed posts or along the side of the bed to find out what length of fabric is required to drape from one end to the other. Add the short drop at the front and the distance from the bedpost to the mattress at the head of the bed. The canopy can be as wide as the bed or a narrower strip as shown here.

you will need

- **main fabric**
- **ribbon**
- **curtain weights**
- **sewing kit**

tip for a flat canopy for a bed

Use Velcro on the posts to prevent the canopy slipping.

1 It is essential that the fabric is absolutely square before beginning to make a bed canopy. Pull a thread to straighten one end and fold the fabric in half lengthways – if the corners don't match pull the fabric on the diagonal until it is straight. You may need to work all the way down the fabric. Press the straightened folded fabric with a steam iron.

2 Cut two pieces of fabric the required size including a 1.5cm/⅝in seam allowance on all sides. With right sides together, stitch around all sides leaving a large gap for turning along the edge that will go behind the bed. Trim across the corners.

3 Trim the seams to 5mm/¼in and press open as far as possible into each corner. Turn the canopy through and roll the edges until the seam is exactly on the edge and press again.

4 Pin the ribbon down each side of the canopy. Place pins exactly on the edge as pins will mark satin ribbon. Leave enough ribbon at the foot end of the canopy to stitch on the other side of the overhang. Pin the ribbon in place on the underside of the canopy.

5 To fasten the canopy to the bed head, cut two lengths of ribbon each 1m/1yd long and fold in half. Stitch in place at the corners at the head of the canopy, in each corner, for example. The other end of the canopy will hang loosely over a pole or the bed post. Drop a curtain weight in to each front corner, then slip-stitch the gap closed.

6 Stitch down both sides of the ribbon. Stitch each side in the same direction to prevent the ribbon twisting. Fold the excess ribbon up on the other side and stitch so that you machine on top of the previous stitches.

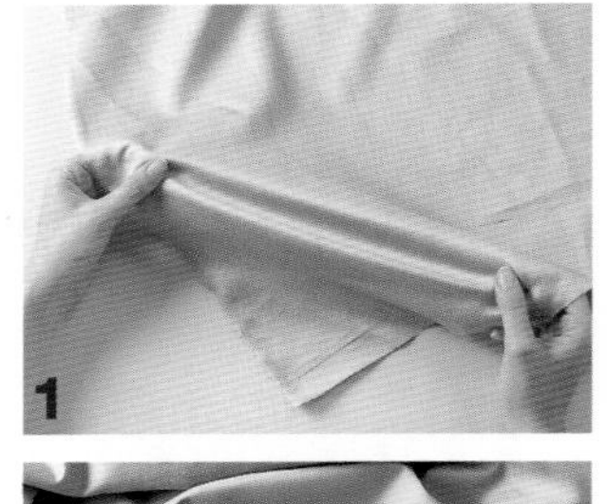
1

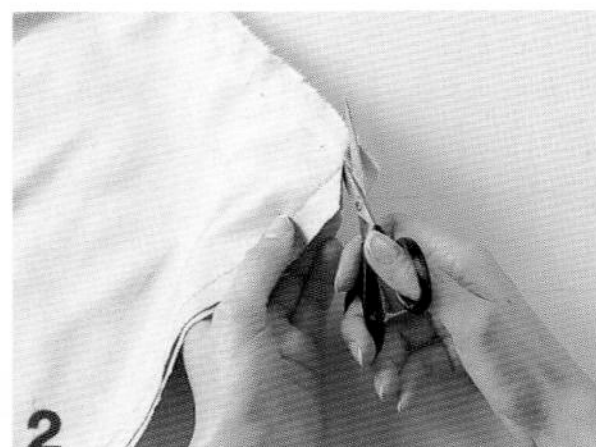
2

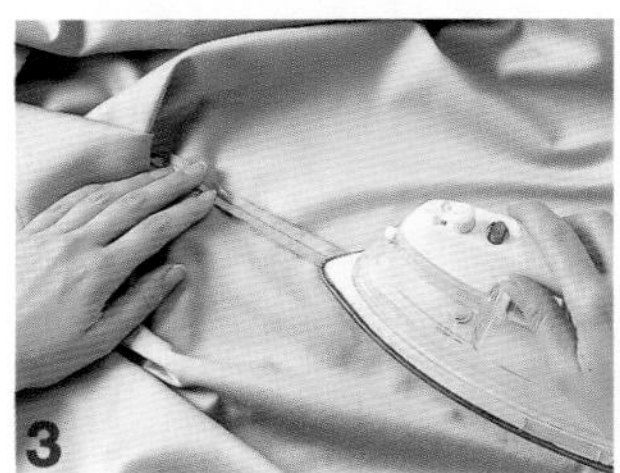
3

4

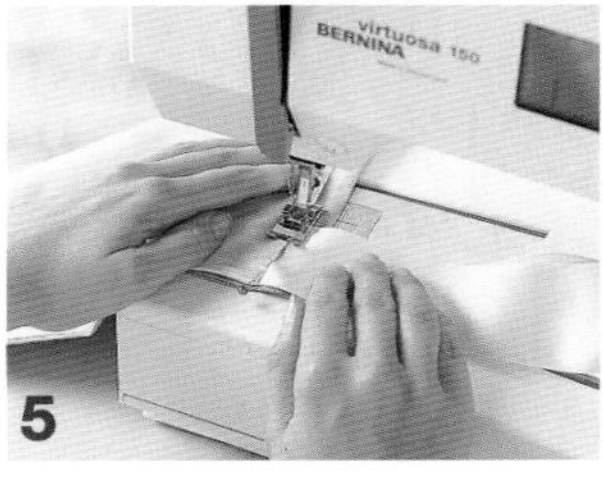

5

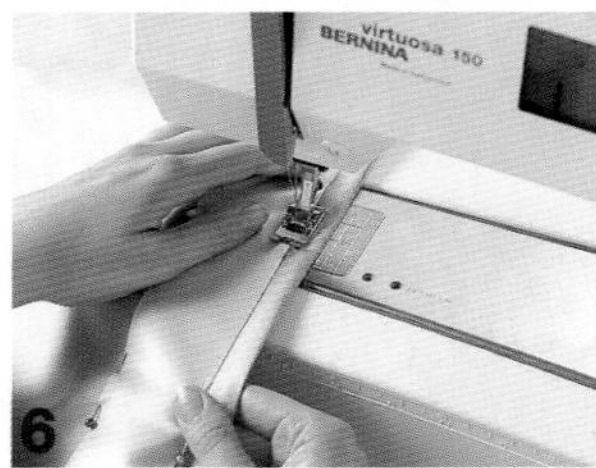

6

adding lace to a bed canopy

If the canopy is lined, the lace can be inserted between the fabric and the lining. If the canopy is a single layer, the lace should be attached with a type of lapped seam to hide any raw edges.

you will need

- **main fabric**
- **lace**
- **ribbon**
- **sewing kit**

tip for adding lace to a bed canopy

Lace-edged fabric looks particularly effective hanging from a corona.

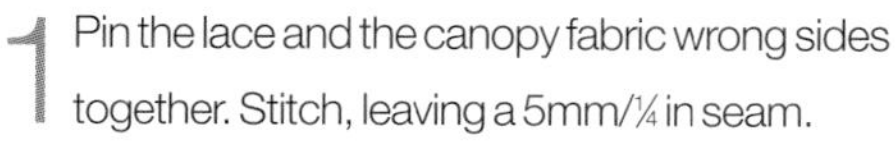

1 Pin the lace and the canopy fabric wrong sides together. Stitch, leaving a 5mm/¼ in seam.

2 Open the lace and fabric out and press the seam towards the canopy fabric.

3 Pin a length of ribbon over the raw edges of the seam on the right side. Stitch down both sides of the ribbon, stitching each side in the same direction to prevent puckering.

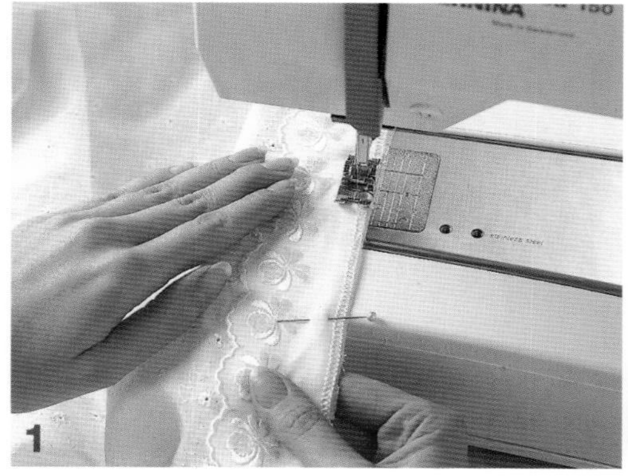

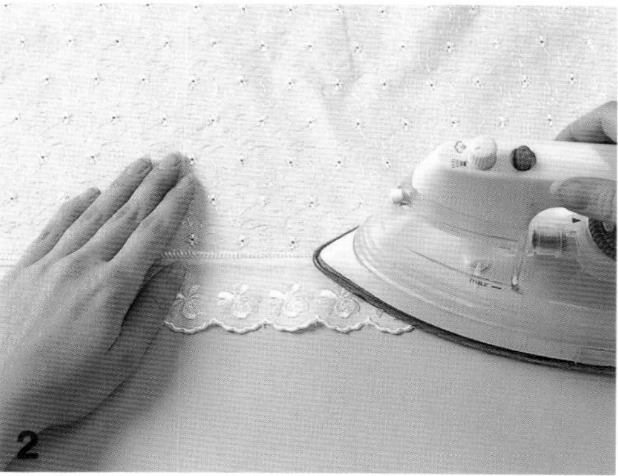

a corona with fixed drapes

A corona looks extremely impressive, but in fact it is simply a curtain and a pelmet attached to a semi-circular pelmet board. Here a soft, lace-trimmed valance covers the top of the curtain, which hangs from hooks underneath pelmet board. The curtain can simply drape down either side of the bed, or can continue across the back of the bed as well.

you will need

- pencil
- wooden board for the corona base 25 x 12.5 x 2.5cm/10 x 5 x 1in
- jigsaw
- sandpaper
- staples and staple gun
- adhesive Velcro
- hammer
- galvanized staples
- fabric
- Velcro heading tape
- lace
- curtain hooks
- sewing kit

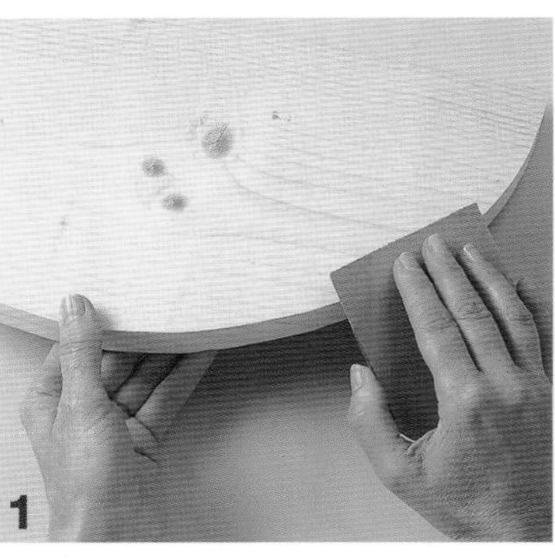

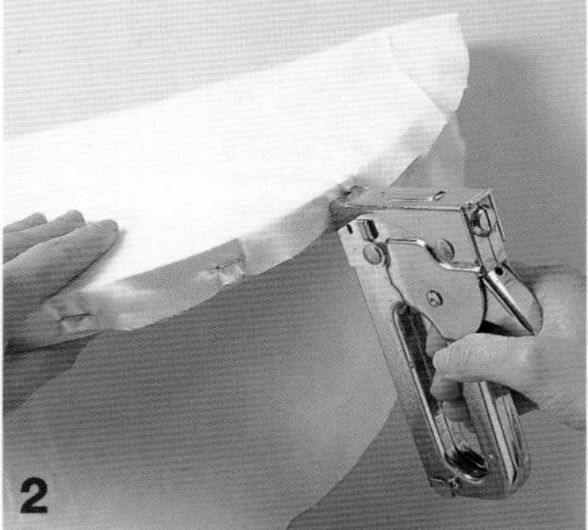

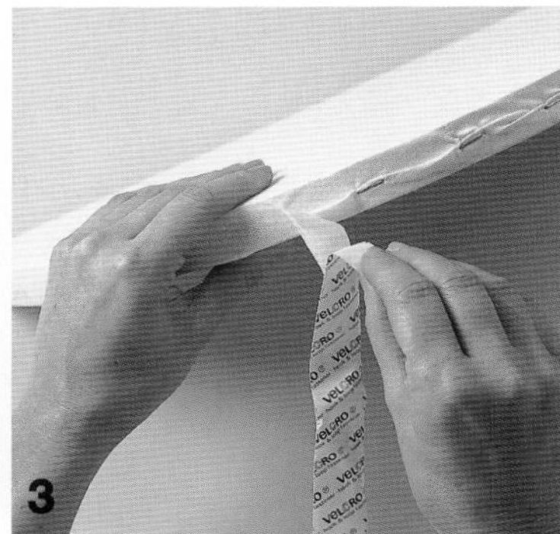

1 Draw a semi-circular pattern the required width of the corona on to a piece of wooden board, with the depth from the straight edge about 25cm/10in. Cut out with a jigsaw and sand the edges.

2 Using a staple gun, cover the board with fabric, stapling into the curved edge.

3 Adhere the hook side of Velcro tape around the curved edge, ensuring it is firmly stuck. Secure with staples.

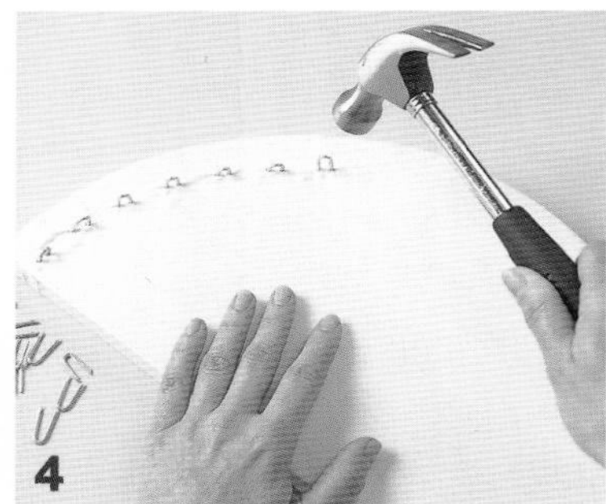

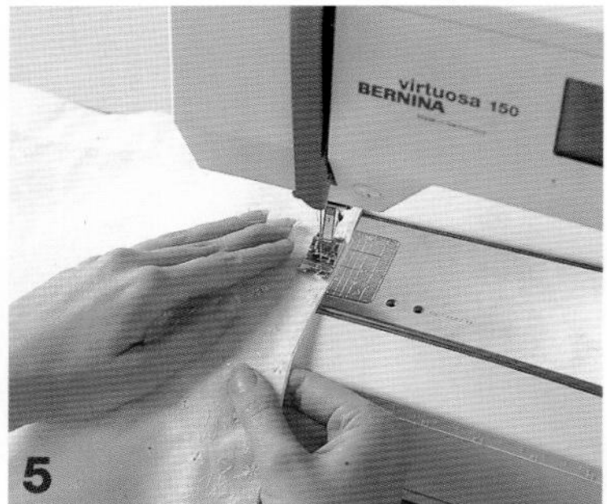

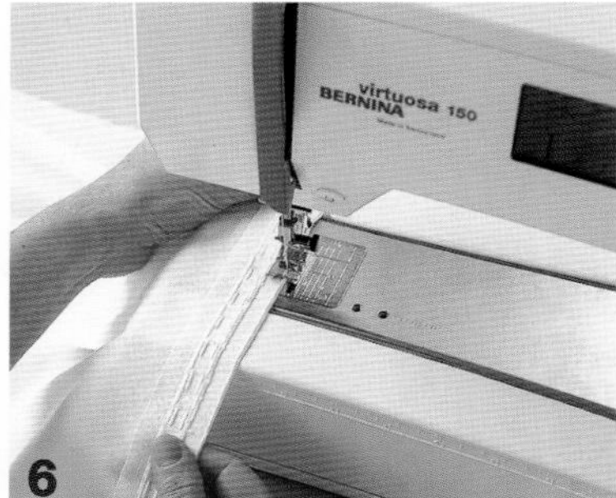

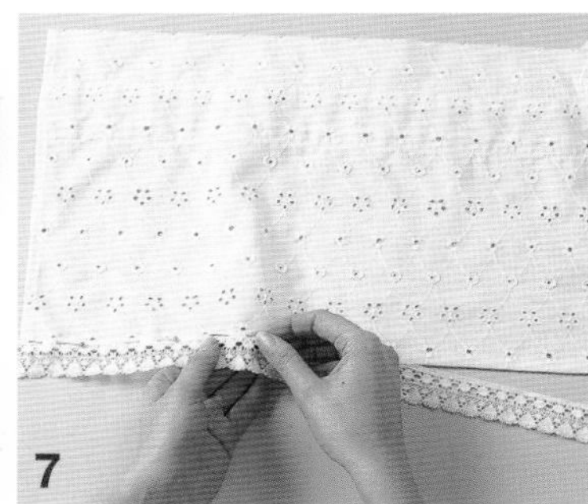

4 Hammer galvanized staples all the way around the underside of the board, about 2.5cm/1in from the edge. Leave gaps and attach two brackets to the straight edge for fixing the corona to the wall.

5 Cut the valance (dust ruffle) fabric three to four times longer than the curved edge of the board, adding 7cm/2¾in seam allowance to the depth. Press under 6cm/2½in to the wrong side along the top edge. Stitch a 5mm/¼ in double hem along each short side edge. Press any seams open.

6 Pin a 5cm/2in-wide Velcro heading tape along the top of the valance, 5cm/2in from the pressed edge. Trim the tape at the end of the valance and fold under the raw end. Tuck the ends of the tape cords underneath at one side and leave loose at the other. Stitch round the edge of the tape.

7 Press under a 5mm/¼in hem along the bottom edge. Pin lace to the right side of the edge and stitch in place. Draw up the tape cords to fit the corona board and attach the valance to the Velcro.

to make the curtain

Measure around the whole corona board and make a curtain two to three times wider. Stitch a simple 2.5cm/1in-wide heading tape along the top edge. Insert one curtain hook for each galvanized staple and gather the curtain to fit. Beginning in the middle of the curved edge of the board, hang the curtain on to the corona.

tied headboard cover

A tied cover is the simplest type of cover for headboards. It is essentially a flat piece of fabric that is tied at the sides with ribbon bows. This style of cover is only suitable for square or rectangular shaped headboards.

above *Sheer ribbon adds a feminine touch.*

calculating the fabric

Measure the width of the headboard and add 3cm/1½in seam allowance. Measure from the base of the headboard over the top and down the other side.

you will need

- slim, squared-up headboard
- main fabric
- contrast lining
- plate
- tailor's chalk
- bias binding
- ribbon
- sewing kit

tip for tied headboard cover

Join the binding with a diagonal seam.

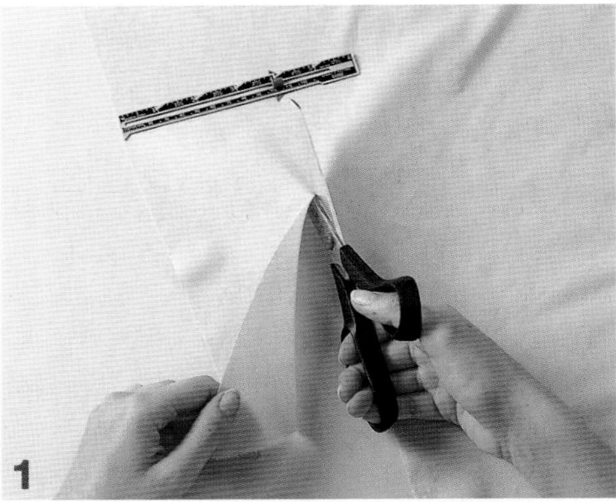

1

2

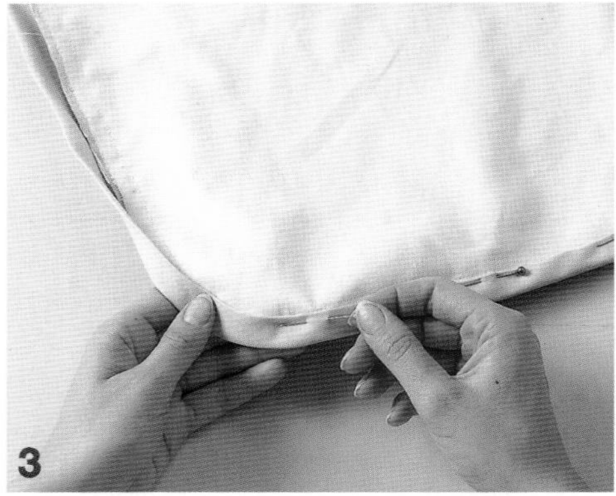

3

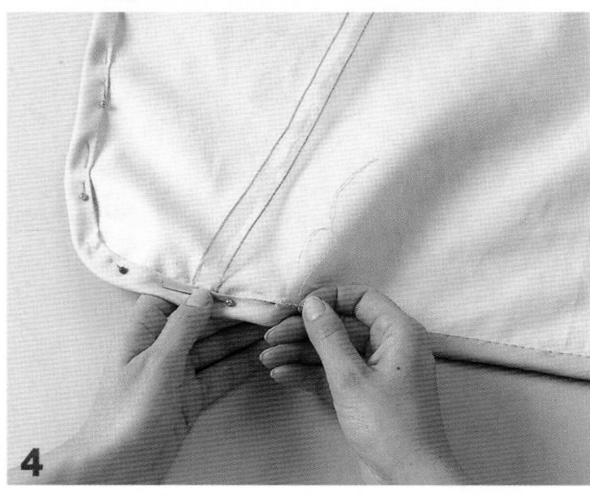

4

1 Cut one piece of main fabric and one in a contrast lining. Put a plate at each corner and draw around the curve with tailor's chalk, from raw edge to raw edge. Place the lining and fabric wrong sides together and tack (baste) around the edge. Cut and join sufficient strips of bias binding, 9cm/3½in wide, to fit around the cover.

2 With wrong sides together, fold the bias strip in half lengthways and press. With raw edges aligned pin and tack the binding to the right side of the cover. Stitch 1.5cm/⅝in from the edge.

3 Turn the binding to the wrong side and pin in place, easing binding round the corners neatly.

4 To make the ties, cut 12 lengths of ribbon, each 40cm/16in. Fold the cover in half. At each side measure and mark about 10cm/4in from the top and bottom of the cover and in the middle. Tuck a piece of ribbon inside the binding at each mark and pin. Slip-stitch the binding to the lining, securing the ribbon in the stitching.

shaped headboard cover

This type of cover is suitable for a fairly slim headboard as it is made without a gusset. The thin wadding (batting) covers any buttons or padding on the original headboard.

you will need

- 50g/2oz wadding (batting)
- felt-tipped pen
- main fabric
- contrast fabric
- piping cord
- ribbon
- sewing kit

tip for shaped headboard cover
Use a flanged cord instead of piping for a different effect.

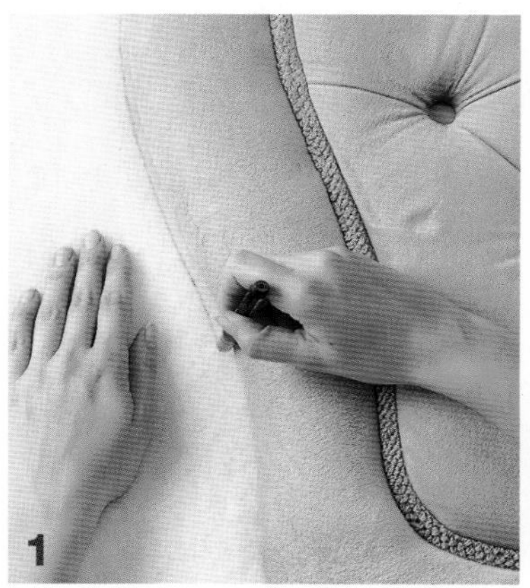

1

2

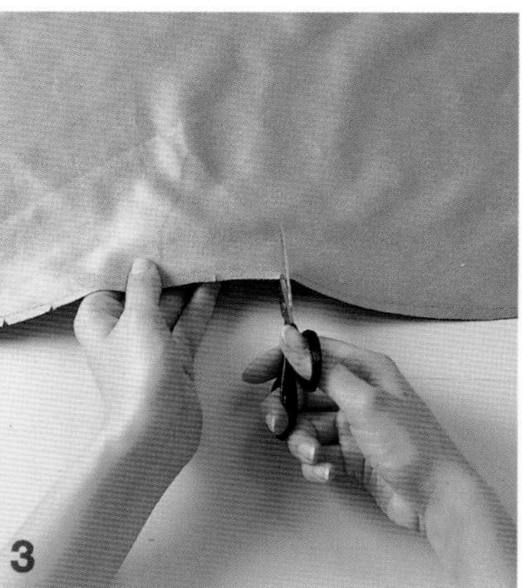

3

4

1 Place a large piece of 50g/2oz wadding (batting) on a flat surface. Place the headboard on top. Draw around the edge with a felt-tipped pen, adding 0.5–1cm/¼–½in on all sides. Cut out, adding a 1.5cm/⅝in seam allowance around the edge. Cut two pieces each of wadding, main fabric and lining the same size.

2 Cover sufficient piping cord to fit around the curved edges of the headboard. Pin each piece of wadding to the wrong side of a piece of main fabric. Tack (baste) and stitch the piping round the curved edge. Stitch the second side on top.

3 Stitch the lining sections together and trim the seams. Snip the inward facing curves and notch the outward curves of the lining and headboard cover.

4 Slip the llining over the wadding side of the headboard cover. Cut four lengths of ribbon each 25cm/10in, and pin between the layers along the bottom edge, two on each side. Match the side seams. Pin then stitch around the bottom edge, leaving a large gap for turning. Turn through, tuck the lining inside and slip-stitch the gap closed. Slip the cover over the headboard and tie the ribbons.

box-style headboard cover

This style of cover has a gusset to fit a deep headboard with a square edge. The piping adds an interesting detail and defines the shape of the cover. If using a patterned fabric, the gusset will have a seam in the centre at the top so that the pattern matches down the sides.

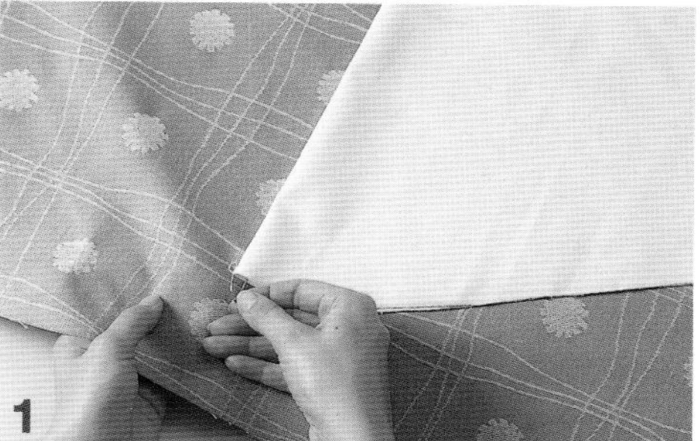

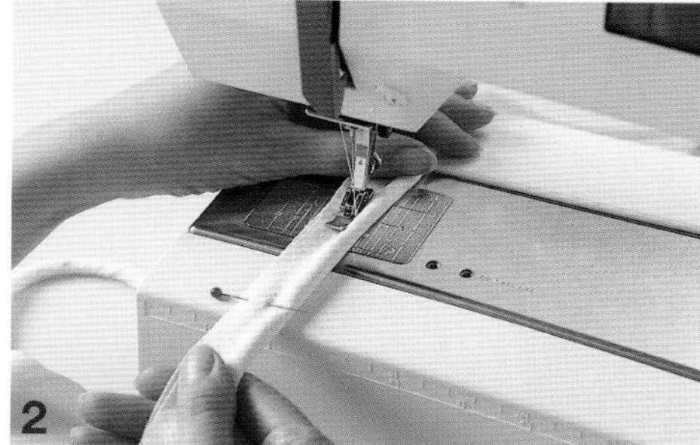

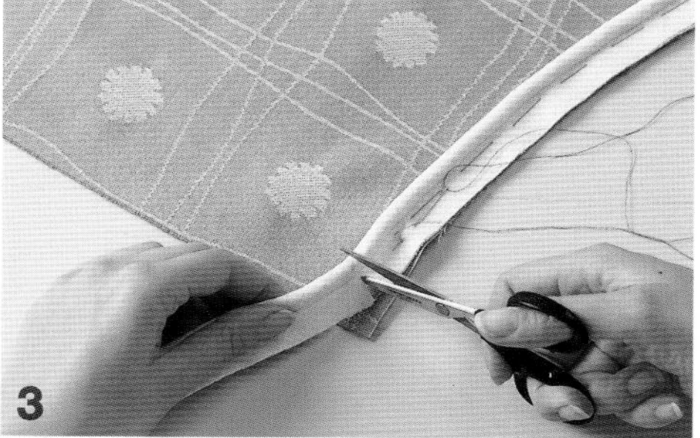

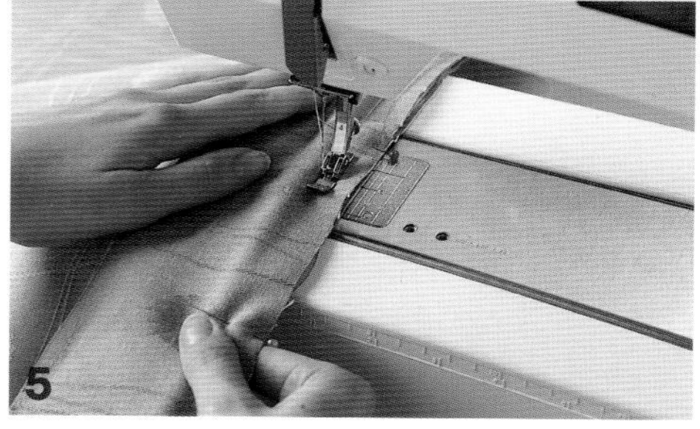

you will need

- **pencil**
- **calico for template**
- **main fabric**
- **piping cord**
- **contrast fabric for piping**
- **fusible bonding web (optional)**
- **sewing kit**

1 Make a template from calico by drawing around the headboard. Cut the template out adding a 1.5cm/⅝in seam allowance around the edge. Fold the template in half and position the fold down the centre of any pattern. Open out and pin in position.

2 Cover sufficient piping to fit around the edge at the front and back of the headboard cover.

3 With raw edges aligned, pin and tack (baste) the piping around the edge of the cover. Snip the piping at the corners so that it fits smoothly.

4 Cut the gusset the width of the sides, adding 3cm/1¼in seam allowance. On patterned fabric, cut the gusset in two pieces. Pin in position, matching the pattern from the bottom edge up to the centre on each side. Sew the centre seam.

5 Stitch the gusset as close as possible to the piping on the headboard front using a zipper foot attachment. Pin the back cover to the other side of the gusset, matching the corners, and stitch in place. Turn up the bottom hem and slip-hem or stick with fusible bonding web. Add ties at the bottom if required.

cot (crib) quilt

A baby needs to be warm but not too hot – duvets are not suitable and many quilts are rather bulky. This simple quilt is light and easy to wash and it keeps its shape because of the machine-quilting stitches.

calculating the fabric

Measure the inside of the cot, allowing 50cm/20in at the top for the baby's head. Add 8cm/3in allowance to each side.

you will need

- **lightweight cotton fabric**
- **50g/2oz wadding (batting)**
- **contrast fabric for the frill**
- **backing fabric**
- **sewing kit**

tip for cot (crib) quilt

You could use ribbon or lace to make the frill.

1 Place the fabric right side up on top of the wadding (batting) and pin in place. Tack (baste) the layers parallel to the sides as well as diagonally.

2 Fit a quilting foot and a quilting guide to the sewing machine. Set the guide to stitch rows 3–4cm/1½–1¾in apart. Begin in one corner and stitch diagonally across the quilt.

3 Turn the quilt and stitch back in the other direction to make a diamond pattern. Use your hands to guide the fabric so that no tucks form in the quilt top.

4 Decide on the depth of the pleated frill. Cut bias strips, twice the desired finished width, adding 3cm/1¼in seam allowance. You will need 2–3 times twice the length plus the width.

5 Pin the frill along the sides and bottom edge of the quilt. Make the pleats by eye, folding and pinning them in place. Adjust any that are not quite straight. Stitch the frill in place.

6 Place the lining on top and pin and stitch in place around the edge leaving a gap along the bottom edge. Trim across the corners and turn the quilt through. Press the top edge with a cool iron and top stitch the top edge. Slip-stitch the gap.

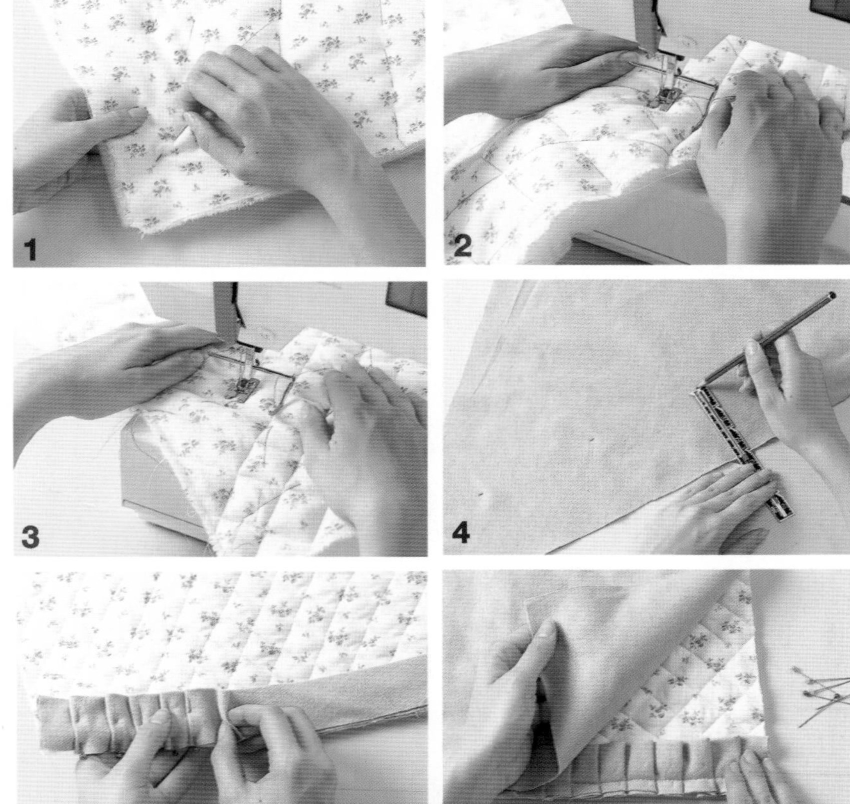

lined baby basket

There is so much paraphernalia for babies that you can never have enough storage. Make a pretty quilted liner for a layette basket to match the cot (crib) quilt and use it to store baby clothes or nappy changing materials.

calculating the fabric

Measure the inside bottom of the basket, adding 1.5cm/⅝in seam allowance to each edge. Measure the height of the basket and around the outside top edge for the side panels.

you will need

- **fabric**
- **50g/2oz wadding (batting)**
- **contrast fabric for frill and ties**
- **bodkin or rouleau turner**
- **sewing kit**

tip for lined baby basket

Use ribbon or lace for the frills and ties for a more delicate effect.

1 Cut a piece of fabric and wadding (batting) larger than the inside measurements of the sides of the basket you want to line. Machine quilt in a diamond pattern (see cot quilt). Tuck the panel into the basket inside out and pin a seam down one corner. Pin darts down the other corners. Stitch the darts.

2 Pin and stitch the pleated frill along the top edge of the right side of the fabric, with raw edges aligned (see cot quilt). With right sides together, stitch lining the same size as the quilting along the frill edge. Open the quilting and lining out and fold crossways with the frill facing the lining. Stitch a seam on the quilted side only. Fold the lining to the outside and slip-stitch the seam. Stitch the frill ends together.

3 Fold a 1m/1yd strip of 3cm/1¼in wide fabric in half and stitch 6mm/¼in from the folded edge. Turn the tube through using a bodkin or rouleaux turner. Cut the rouleau in half. Tie knots in the end and stitch the middle of each piece to the end of the basket liner.

4 Tie the rouleaux through the basket handles in a pretty bow. To complete the basket, cut a piece of wadding to cover the base of the basket and cover with fabric. Tuck into the base of the basket.

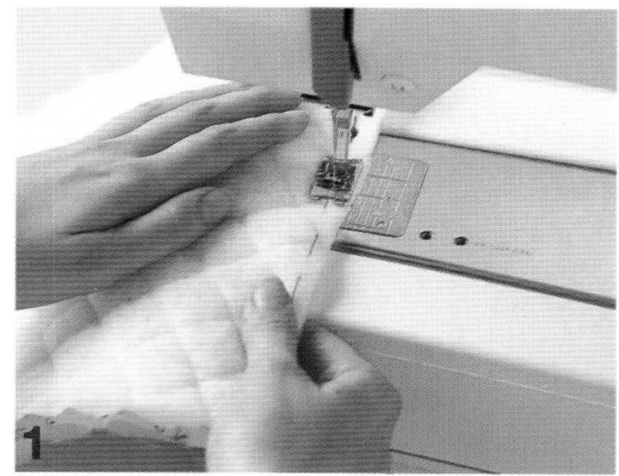
1

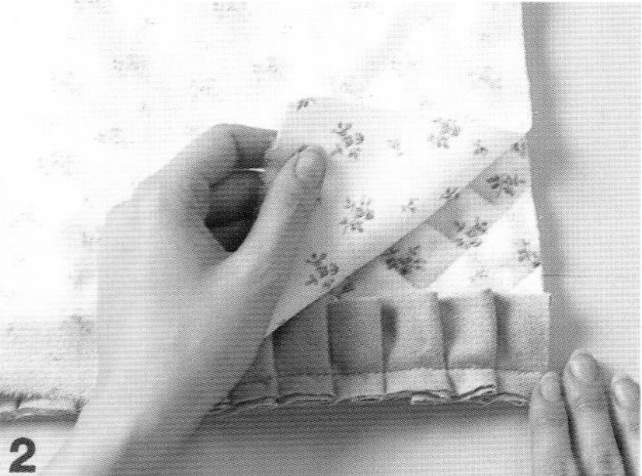
2

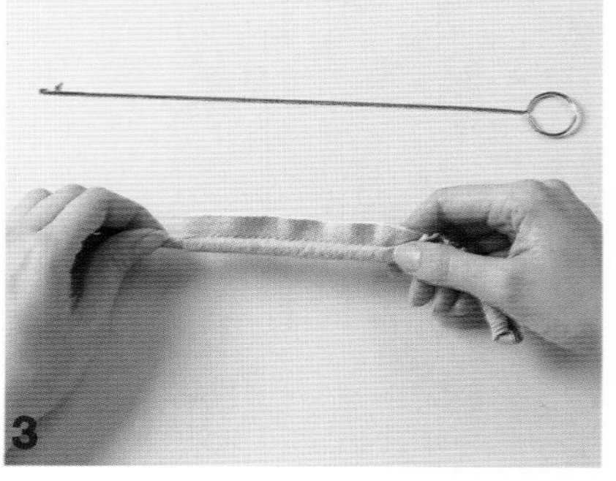
3

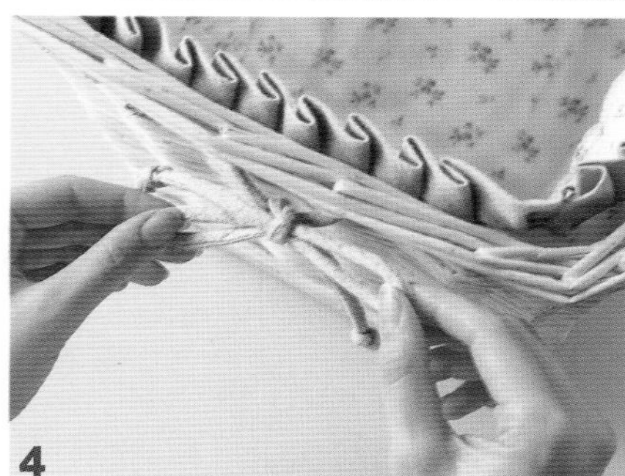
4

covering a Moses basket

A Moses basket is an ideal temporary bed for a newborn baby. The sides of the basket protect the baby from draughts while allowing air to circulate through the weave.

you will need

- **Moses basket**
- **150g/6oz wadding (batting)**
- **lightweight cotton fabric**
- **ribbon for the bows**
- **lace for edging**
- **5mm/¼in elastic**
- **sewing kit**

to cover the basket

1 Cut a piece of 150g/5oz wadding (batting) the depth of the basket, adding 10cm/4in to turn over the top edge and long enough to fit around the inside of the basket, adding 5–10cm/2–4in for ease. Cut into the wadding at each side of the handles and cut across between the slits level with the top of the basket.

2 Measure right around the top of the basket. Cut a strip of fabric one and a half times the length plus 3cm/1¼in seam allowance and 66cm/26in deep. The depth measurement includes a generous tuck-in allowance. Fold the fabric in half crossways. To shape the cover, mark 10cm/4in along the bottom edge from the fold and cut diagonally to the top edge. Stitch a French seam (see basic techniques). Shape and stitch the seam at the other end of the cover in the same way.

3 To make the outside frill, turn up a 10cm/4in hem along the lower edge of the fabric and press. Stitch the hem and then stitch again 1cm/½in from the first line of stitching to make a casing for the elastic, leaving a gap at the seam to thread the elastic through later. Turn under and stitch a 1cm/½in double hem along the bottom edge.

4 For the holes for the handles, measure the width of the handles and add 2.5cm/1in for ease (a).

5 Measure the height of the basket at its lowest (b) and highest (c) point. Measure the basket from the top centre round the side to the handle. Multiply this measurement by 1.5 to find the distance (d) to mark the handle from the top French seam.

6 Lay the cover flat with a French seam at each end and the hem at the top. Insert a pin the distance (d) from the right seam and the measurement (b) down from the hem edge.

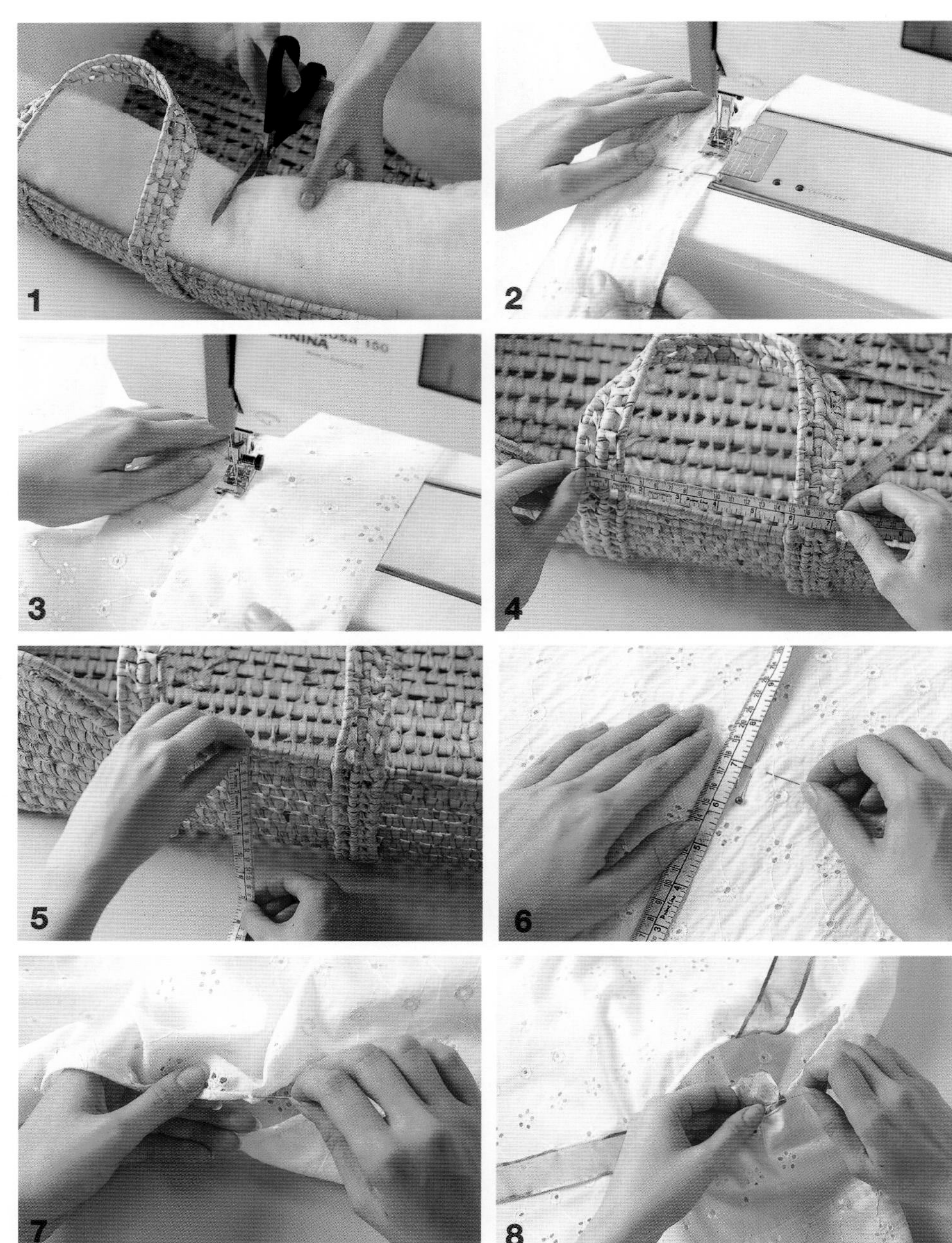

7 Mark the other end of the handle hole, measurement (a) across to the left, and distance (c) down from the hem edge. To make the handle holes, cut a sloping oval between the marks about 5cm/2in wide through both layers. Turn under the raw edges around each to make a narrow rolled hem and slip-stitch.

8 Cut two 30cm/12in lengths of ribbon and hand stitch to the middle of each side of the handle hole.

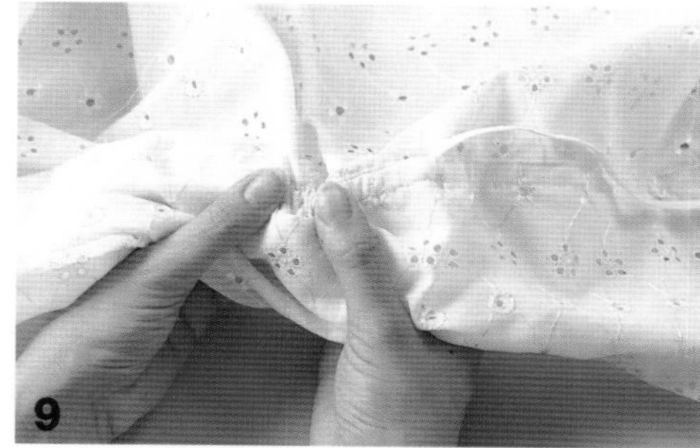

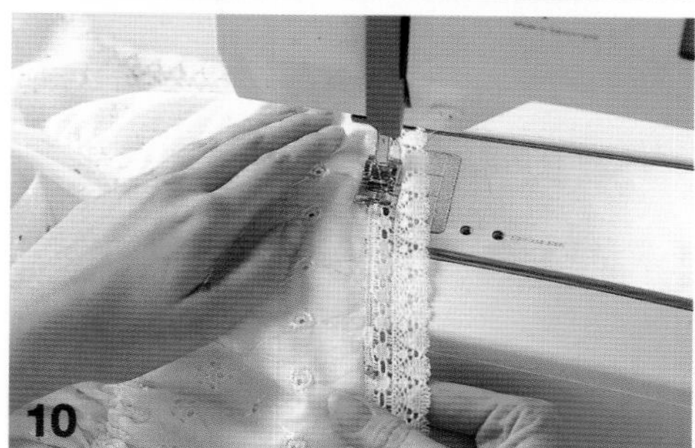

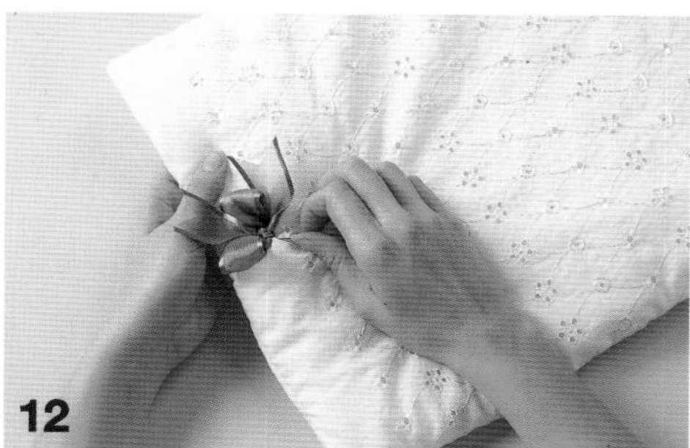

9 Cut a piece of elastic, 10cm/4in shorter than the circumference of the basket and thread through the casing. Tie the ends securely and tuck inside the casing. Slip-stitch the gap.

10 Pin lace around the edge of the frill and stitch. Insert the wadding (batting) into the basket. Fit the cover over the handles with the frill on the outside and arrange the gathers evenly.

11 To make a matching quilt, remove the mattress and draw around it. Add 1.5cm/⅝in all round for seams and cut out. Lay the fabric right sides together with the wadding on top and pin. Stitch around the edge, leaving a gap on one side for turning through.

12 Trim the wadding neatly and notch the curves. Turn the quilt through, pushing out the corners and slip-stitch the gap. Tie a ribbon bow and stitch it to the top of the quilt. Tie three ribbon bows and stitch one to the top of the quilt and one at each end of the Moses basket.

table linen

Table linen can be practical or luxurious and made in either plain fabric or something quite exquisite, depending on how you intend it to be used. Choose easy-care cotton fabrics for everyday use, but look for more luxurious fabrics and trimmings for special occasions. There are so many kinds of table linen that can be used to make your table look really special, including fine cottons and linens or rich velvets for a Christmas table setting. Use simple quilted mats for family meals, formal white linen to cover a long table for a buffet, or make a set of specially decorated napkins for a dinner party. Simple appliqué makes a table runner look unique and makes ordinary cotton look special.

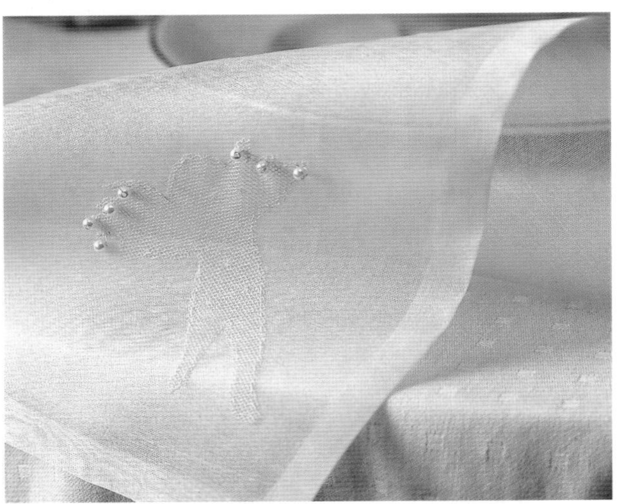

above left Add a subtle decorative touch using appliqué and pearl beads on crisp, sheer fabrics to make a stunning table runner or set of place mats.
centre above Blue-and-white check seersucker fabric makes a delightful and easy-care tablecloth for the breakfast table.
above right Pure raw and bleached linen are timeless fabrics that look stunning on any table. Drawn thread work is the traditional technique for hems and decoration.
centre left Choose co-ordinating velvet ribbons to tie around exotic brocade napkins instead of napkin rings for a special dinner party .
below left Napkins do not have to be made in plain fabrics. Pre-pleated and other textured fabrics add contrast to smooth china plates.
right Exotic fabrics and trimmings transform a plain table for a special occasion.

Whether for everyday use or a special occasion, table linen is primarily designed to protect the table from spillages, knocks and hot dishes. This doesn't mean necessarily that the fabrics need to be particularly heavyweight, as the table itself can be protected with a heat-resistant material or pad hidden under a pretty tablecloth. Nevertheless, table linen must be practical and has to be suitable for cleaning. The more often it is used, the easier it should be to wash and press. Indeed easy-care items that don't need to be ironed are the most suitable for everyday use.

There are lots of different ways that you can cover a table. As well as a tablecloth, there is the table runner, which is a strip of fabric that lies along the centre of the table. A table runner can act as a continuous tablemat down the centre of the table at a dinner party or be left to decorate the table during the day.

Tablemats are, at their simplest, a rectangle of fabric large enough to hold a dinner plate but can also be padded or quilted to protect the table from heat. It depends on the material your table is made from. Thin tablemats can always be used over a tablecloth with a heat-resistant cover underneath, but simple quilted tablemats that can be washed and quickly tumbled dry are more suitable for family meals.

Napkins are simply squares of fabric. Make them in a generous size, as they are much more practical. Although normally only used for special occasions nowadays, you might find that a set of easy-care napkins for family meals would reduce your clothes washing.

rectangular tablecloth

The deep border adds weight around the edge of this linen tablecloth, which helps to keep it flat and prevents it from slipping off the table. Make it in easy-care fabric for everyday dining, or in linen for special occasions or as a day cover for the table top.

calculating the fabric

Measure the length and width of the table, then subtract 11 cm/4½in from each measurement to allow for the border. Add twice the desired overhang to each measurement.

you will need

- **fabric**
- **contrast fabric**
- **sewing kit**

tip for rectangular tablecloth

Make sure the border and main fabrics are compatible for laundering.

1 Cut out the main fabric. For the border, cut four strips of contrast fabric 28cm/11in wide and 22cm/9in longer than the main fabric. Fold in half lengthways and press. Open out the folds.

2 With right sides together and raw edges aligned, centre the border strips along the edges of the main fabric. Stitch from the main fabric side, beginning and finishing 1.5 cm/⅝in from the corner.

3 At each corner, fold one border on top of the other then fold the border diagonally to mark the stitching line. Stitch from the corner of the main fabric out to the foldline in the centre of the border.

4 Trim the seam and press. Fold the border fabric to the wrong side and mitre the corner, trimming the excess fabric at each side of the diagonal seam. Stitch or slip-stitch the reverse side hem. Slip-stitch the mitred corner to complete the tablecloth.

circular tablecloth

Circular tablecloths can be made any size, to fit your table. A cloth for a dining table should hang down to the level of your knees when sitting at the table, but bedside or living room tablecloths often reach the floor. If the fabric isn't wide enough join an equal amount to each side, leaving the main width of fabric in the centre, to make the seams less obvious.

calculating the fabric

Measure the diameter of the table and add twice the proposed overhang to this measurement plus 5cm/2in seam allowance. This is the tablecloth diameter. Cut a square of fabric 5cm/2in larger than this to allow plenty of room for marking the circle.

you will need

- **fabric**
- **string**
- **pencil**
- **contrast fabric**
- **sewing kit**

tip for circular tablecloth

Stitch around just inside the marked line before cutting to prevent the edge stretching.

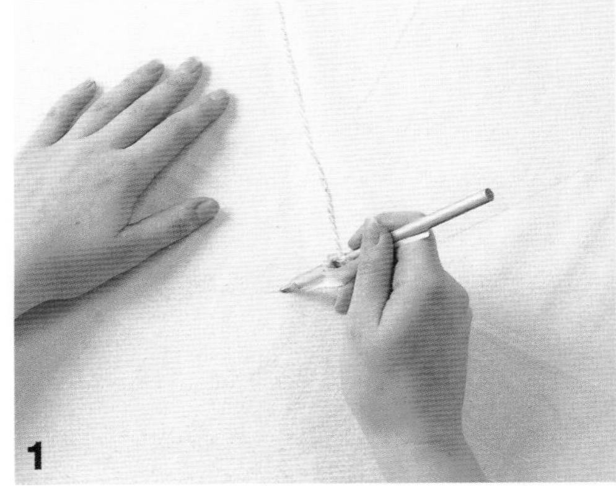
1

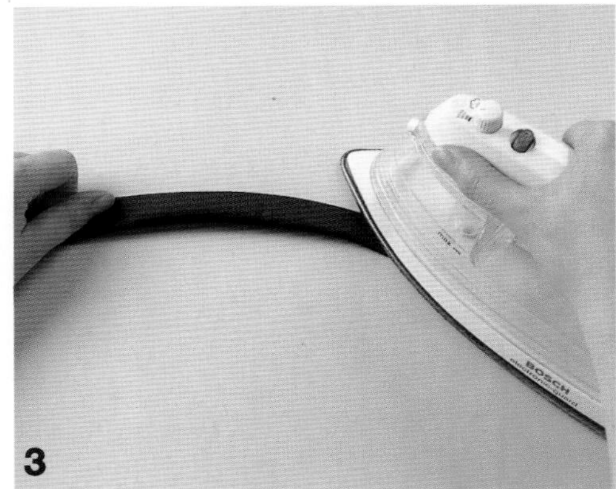
3

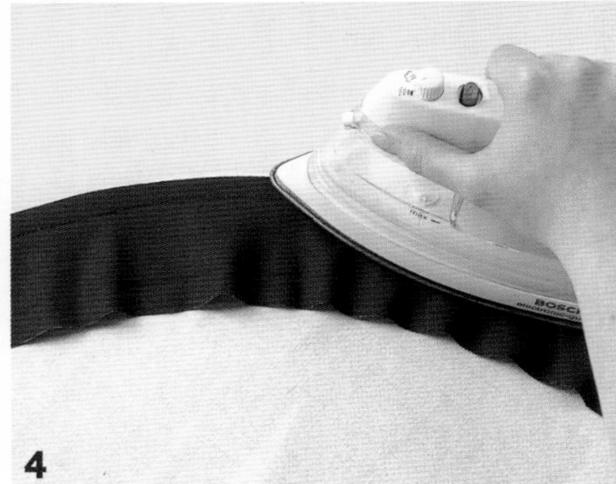
4

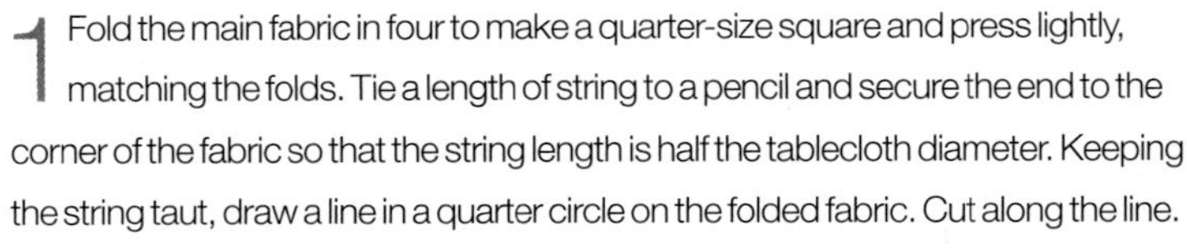

1 Fold the main fabric in four to make a quarter-size square and press lightly, matching the folds. Tie a length of string to a pencil and secure the end to the corner of the fabric so that the string length is half the tablecloth diameter. Keeping the string taut, draw a line in a quarter circle on the folded fabric. Cut along the line.

2 To work out the circumference of the tablecloth, multiply the diameter of the cloth by 3.14. Using contrast fabric, cut and join sufficient bias strips, 8cm/3in wide, to make a binding long enough to go around the tablecloth edge.

3 Press the binding strip in half lengthways with wrong sides together, then press the raw edges into the crease. Fold again and press the strip into a gentle curve.

4 Open out one edge of the binding and pin it around the edge of the tablecloth, with raw edges aligned and right sides together. Join the ends of the binding with a diagonal seam. Stitch the binding along the first crease. Press.

5 Turn the binding to the wrong side of the tablecloth and pin. Hem the cloth, stitching into the previous stitches. Press on the wrong side with a steam iron.

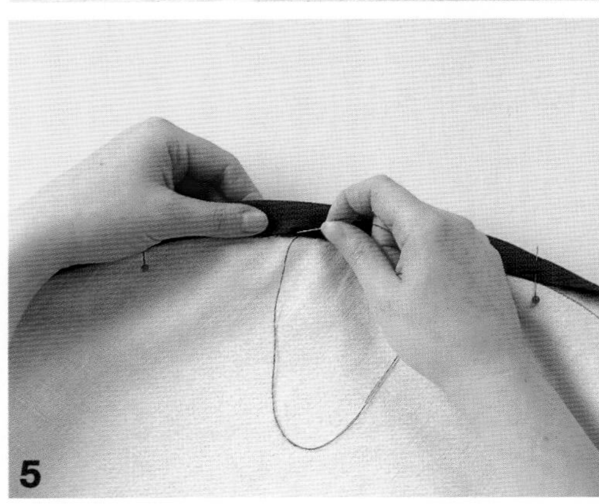
5

bound-edge napkins

A contrast binding is a classic way to finish the edge of a napkin. Use a fairly thin fabric for the binding so that the corners are not too bulky and can be easily stitched in place by machine. This is a very simple project to tackle.

calculating the fabric

Allow a 38cm/15in square of fabric for each napkin. You will need a 16 x 40cm/6 x 16in piece of fabric for the binding.

you will need

- fabric
- contrast fabric
- sewing kit

tip for bound-edge napkins

Trim the seam allowance on the binding at the corners to reduce bulk.

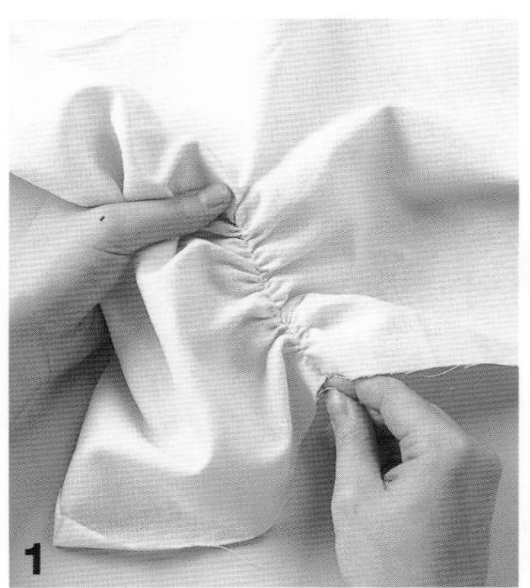

1

2

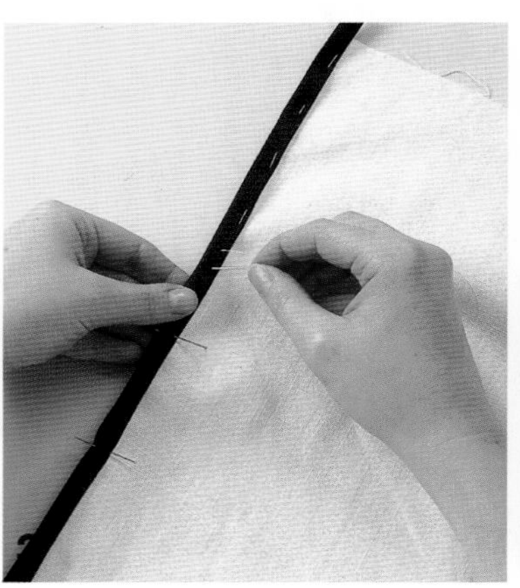

3

4

1 To cut the main fabric, snip into the selvage and pull a thread, then cut along the line. Measure 38cm/15in intervals along the selvage and repeat the process. Measure along the cut edge and pull a thread to complete the squares.

2 For each napkin, cut four binding strips each 4 x 40cm/1½ x 16in from contrast fabric. With wrong sides together, press the strips in half lengthways, then fold the raw edges into the centre and press again.

3 Tuck a strip of binding down two opposite sides of the napkin and tack (baste) in place, checking that you catch the binding on the wrong side in the stitching. Stitch close to the inside folded edge.

4 Trim the binding flush with the edge of the napkin. Pin the other two pieces of binding in place. Turn the short ends in at the corners and tack. Stitch as before, reverse-stitching at each end.

quilted placemats

Placemats are very practical for everyday eating as they can be washed quickly ready for the next meal. Any washable fabric is suitable but pre-shrink it before making up the mats. If you are using a patterned fabric, position the template so that the pattern appears in the centre of the mat.

you will need

- **pencil and paper**
- **fabric**
- **25g/1oz wadding (batting)**
- **contrast fabric**
- **quilter's marker pencil or quilting guide**
- **sewing kit**

tip for quilted placemats
Use a large plate to mark the rounded ends.

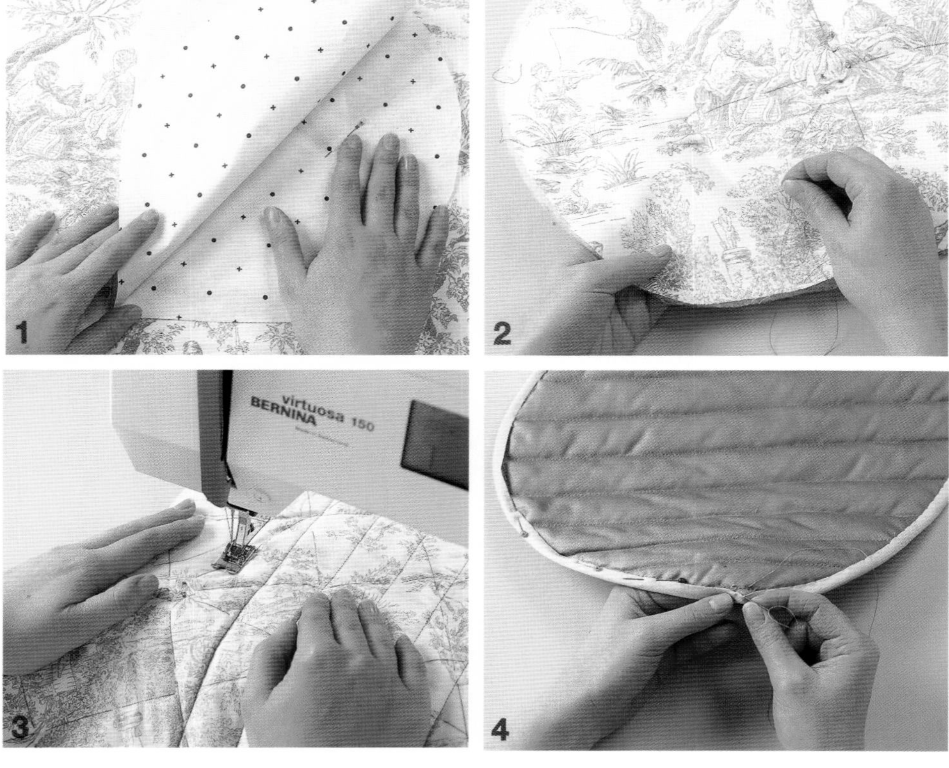

1 Make a paper template the size and shape of the mat required. The mats shown here are 30 x 40cm/12 x 16in. For each mat, cut one piece from fabric, wadding (batting) and contrast backing. Centre any fabric design.

2 Layer the three fabrics with the main fabric on top, and the contrast fabric at the bottom, both right side out, and the wadding (batting) sandwiched in between. Working with the main fabric uppermost, tack (baste) lines radiating out from the centre of the mat. Then tack straight lines across and down each mat.

3 Draw a line diagonally across the middle of the mat with a quilter's pencil. Draw further lines 3cm/1¼in apart. Stitch along the lines using a quilting foot. You can use a quilting guide to space the lines instead of marking.

4 Cut and join sufficient 4 cm/1½in-wide bias strips to fit around each mat. Turn in 7mm/⅜in along one long edge. With raw edges aligned, pin the binding around the edge of the right side of the tablemat and join the ends with a diagonal seam. Stitch in place 7cm/⅜in from the raw edge. Press to the wrong side. Slip-stitch the folded edge in place so that it hides the line of machine stitching.

beaded table runner

A table runner is simply a strip of fabric that runs along the centre of the table. Fusible bonding web is a quick way to attach simple appliqué shapes to the fabric and the beaded fringe adds the ultimate finishing touch.

calculating the fabric

Measure the length of the table, adding twice the overhang and 3cm/1¼in seam allowances. The width is a personal choice depending on the width of the table.

you will need

- **fabric**
- **organza**
- **pencil**
- **fusible bonding web**
- **beading needle**
- **large seed beads**
- **slightly larger pearl beads**
- **sewing kit**

tip for beaded table runner

Add further shapes in the middle of the runner to make a pretty table centre.

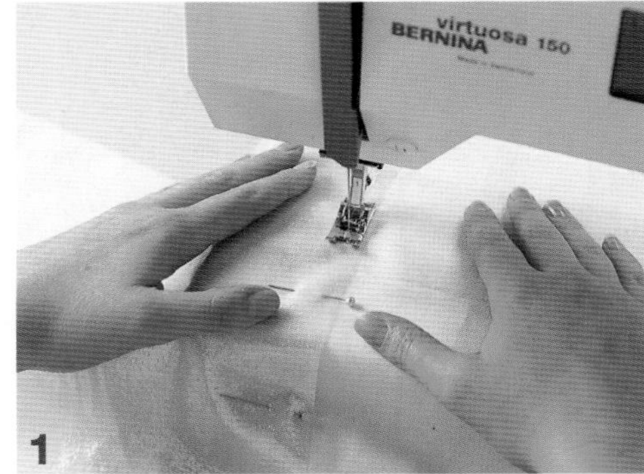

1

2

3

4

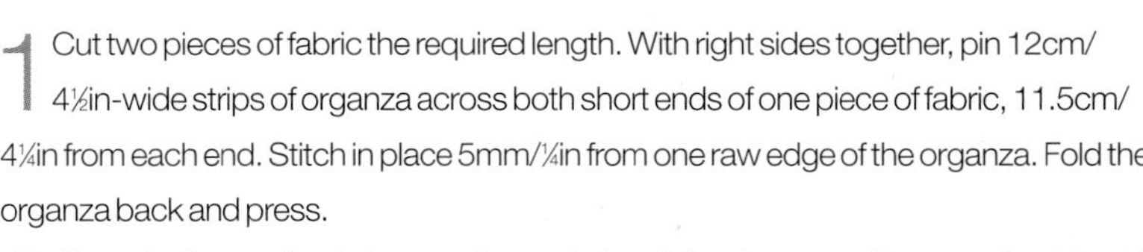

1 Cut two pieces of fabric the required length. With right sides together, pin 12cm/4½in-wide strips of organza across both short ends of one piece of fabric, 11.5cm/4¼in from each end. Stitch in place 5mm/¼in from one raw edge of the organza. Fold the organza back and press.

2 To make the appliqué shapes, draw spiral and star shapes on the paper backing of fusible bonding web. Press the webbing on to organza, using a cool iron. Cut out the shapes.

3 Peel off the backing paper and arrange the shapes on the main fabric just inside the organza borders. Press with a cool iron so that they stick to the fabric. Catch the shapes around the edges with tiny hand stitches.

4 To line the table runner, pin the two pieces of fabric right sides together, and stitch around the edge, leaving a gap for turning. Trim across the corners and turn through. Slip-stitch the gap.

5 To make the bead trim, attach a double length of thread in one corner of the table runner using several small back stitches. With a beading needle, thread 16–20 large seed beads on to the thread, followed by a slightly larger pearl bead. Pass the needle back down the seed beads only and stitch in the thread end in the table runner seam. Add matching lengths of beads equally spaced along the hem at each end of the table runner.

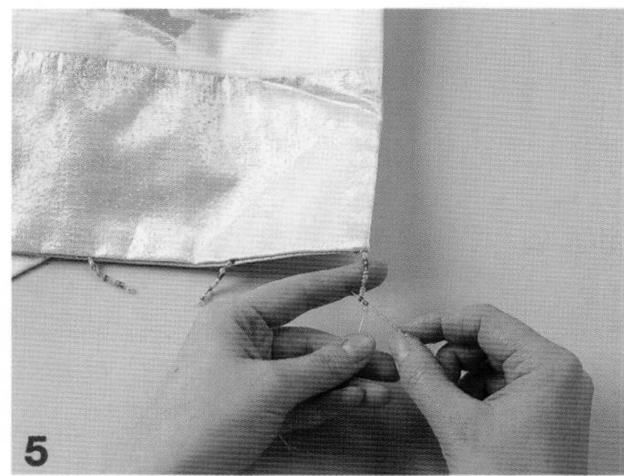

5

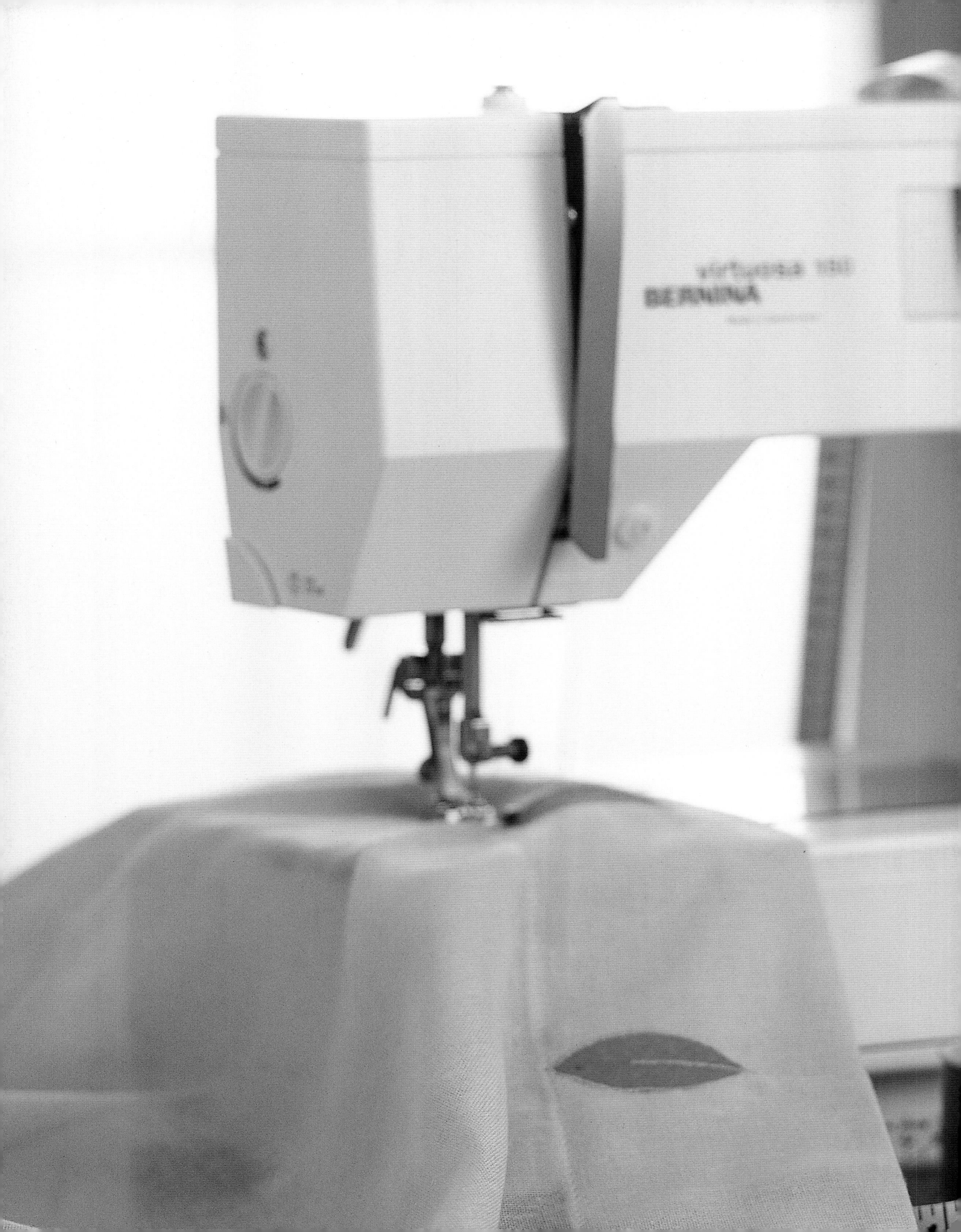
BERNINA

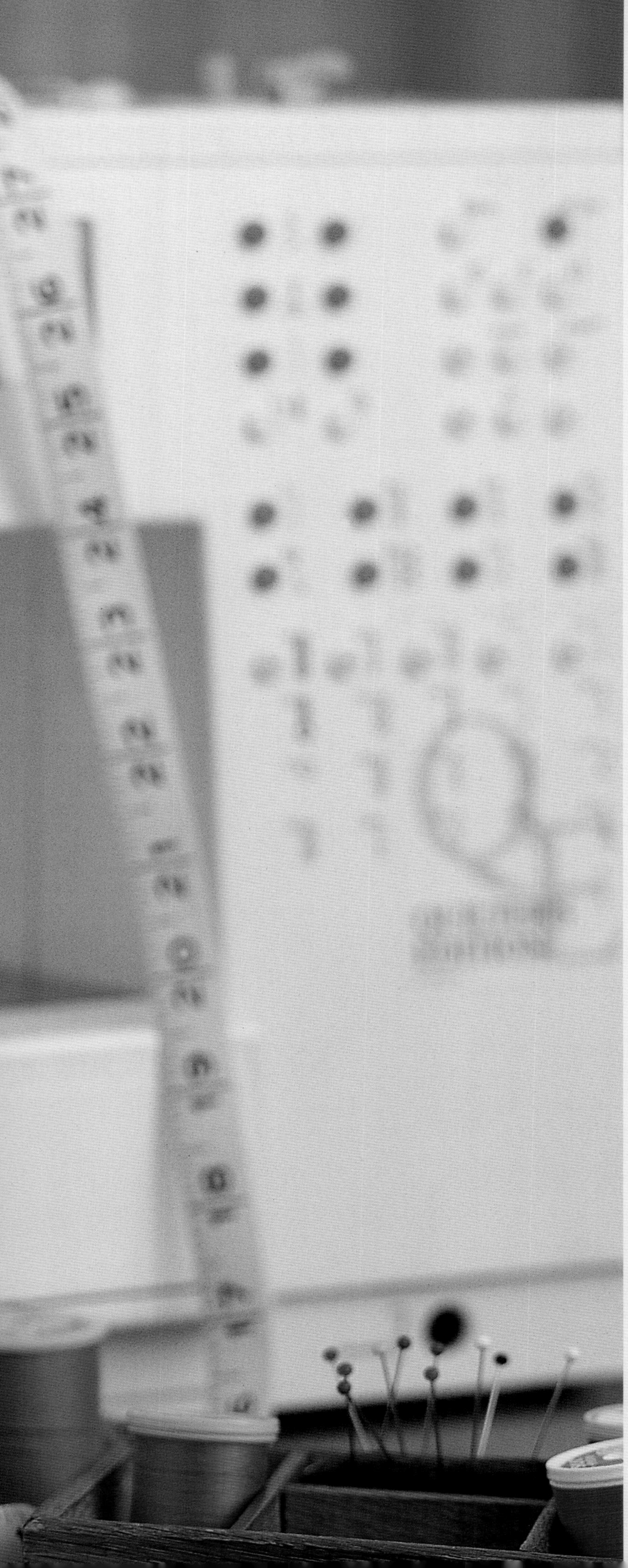

5 basic techniques

Technique makes the difference between something that looks average and something that looks immaculately tailored, with a crisp, professional finish. Take time to learn the basic techniques in the following pages – they will help you achieve perfect results that you can be proud of.

the sewing kit

You will probably have much of this equipment already in your sewing box. Check that the scissors you use for cutting fabric are perfectly sharp and do not use them for any other purpose.

1 Bodkin
Used to thread elastic, cord or ribbon through casings.

2 Dressmaker's carbon and tracing wheel
Used together to transfer markings to the wrong side of the fabric. Select carbon paper that is close in colour to the fabric colour but still visible. Always use white carbon paper on white fabric (it shows as a dull line).

3 Fabric markers
A pencil is suitable for marking most hard-surfaced fabrics and can be brushed off with a stiff brush. A vanishing-ink pen will wash out in water or fade. Use a tracing pen to draw a design on waxed paper and then transfer it to the fabric by ironing over it.

4 Fusible bonding web
This glue mesh is used to stick two layers of fabric together. It is available in various widths. The narrow bands shown here are useful for heavyweight hems and facings, and the wider widths are used for appliqué.

5 Hand-sewing needles
"Sharps" (medium-length, all-purpose needles) are used for general hand sewing. For fine hand sewing, use the shorter, round-eyed "betweens". Hand-sewing needles are numbered from 1–10, with 10 being the finest.

6 Pincushion
Useful for holding pins and needles as you work.

7 Dressmaker's pins
Use normal household pins for most sewing, and lace pins for delicate fabrics. Glass-headed pins are easy to see.

8 Quilter's tape
Used to mark very accurate seam allowances. The tape is 5mm/¼in wide but can be placed further from the raw edge to stitch wider seams.

9 Rouleau turner
A metal tool used to turn through rouleau loops.

10 Safety pins
Use to hold thick layers of fabric together.

11 Scissors
You will need a large pair of drop-handle (bent-handle) scissors for cutting out fabric, a medium pair for trimming seams or cutting small pieces of fabric, and a small pair of sharp, pointed embroidery scissors for cutting threads and snipping into curves. Never cut paper with sewing scissors as it dulls the blade.

12 Seam ripper
A small cutting tool for undoing machine-stitching mistakes. Also useful for cutting buttonholes.

13 Tape measure
Buy a 150cm/60in tape with metal tips in a material such as fibreglass that will not stretch. A small metal ruler with an adjustable guide is useful when pinning hems, tucks and buttonholes.

14 Tailor's chalk
Used to mark fabric. Keep the edge sharp by shaving it with medium scissors. Test on the right side of the fabric to ensure it will brush off.

15 Thimble
Worn on the middle finger of your sewing hand to prevent accidental needle pricks when hand sewing.

16 Sewing threads
For best results, choose a thread that matches the fibre content of the fabric. Use a shade of thread that matches the fabric. If there is no match go one shade darker. Use strong thread for furnishing fabrics and for hand quilting. Tacking (basting) thread is cheaper and poorer-quality. Use strong buttonhole twist or linen thread for buttonholes.

17 Tissue paper
When machine stitching delicate fabrics, tack (baste) strips of tissue paper to each side of the seam and stitch as normal. Tear the tissue paper off afterwards.

16
17
2
13
4
12
1
5
15
2
9
11
3
8
3
6
7
14
10

the sewing machine

For soft furnishings, a sturdy flat-bed sewing machine is the most suitable kind but any ordinary domestic machine can be used.

Balance wheel
This controls the sewing machine. On manual machines, turn the wheel to lower the needle.

Bobbin winder
This allows you to fill the bobbin quickly and evenly.

Foot control or knee control
This starts, stops and controls the speed at which the machine stitches.

Needle clamp
This secures the shaft of the needle into the machine.

Needle plate
The needle plate surrounds the feed teeth and has a hole for the needle.

Presser foot
This holds the fabric flat on the needle plate so that a stitch can form.

Stitch length control
Use this to alter the length of straight stitches and the density of zigzag stitch.

Stitch width control
This controls the amount the needle moves sideways. Use a suitable presser foot so that the needle doesn't break as it swings from side to side.

Thread take-up lever
This feeds the correct amount of thread from the spool down through to the needle.

Tension regulating dial
The tension dial alters the tension on the top thread.

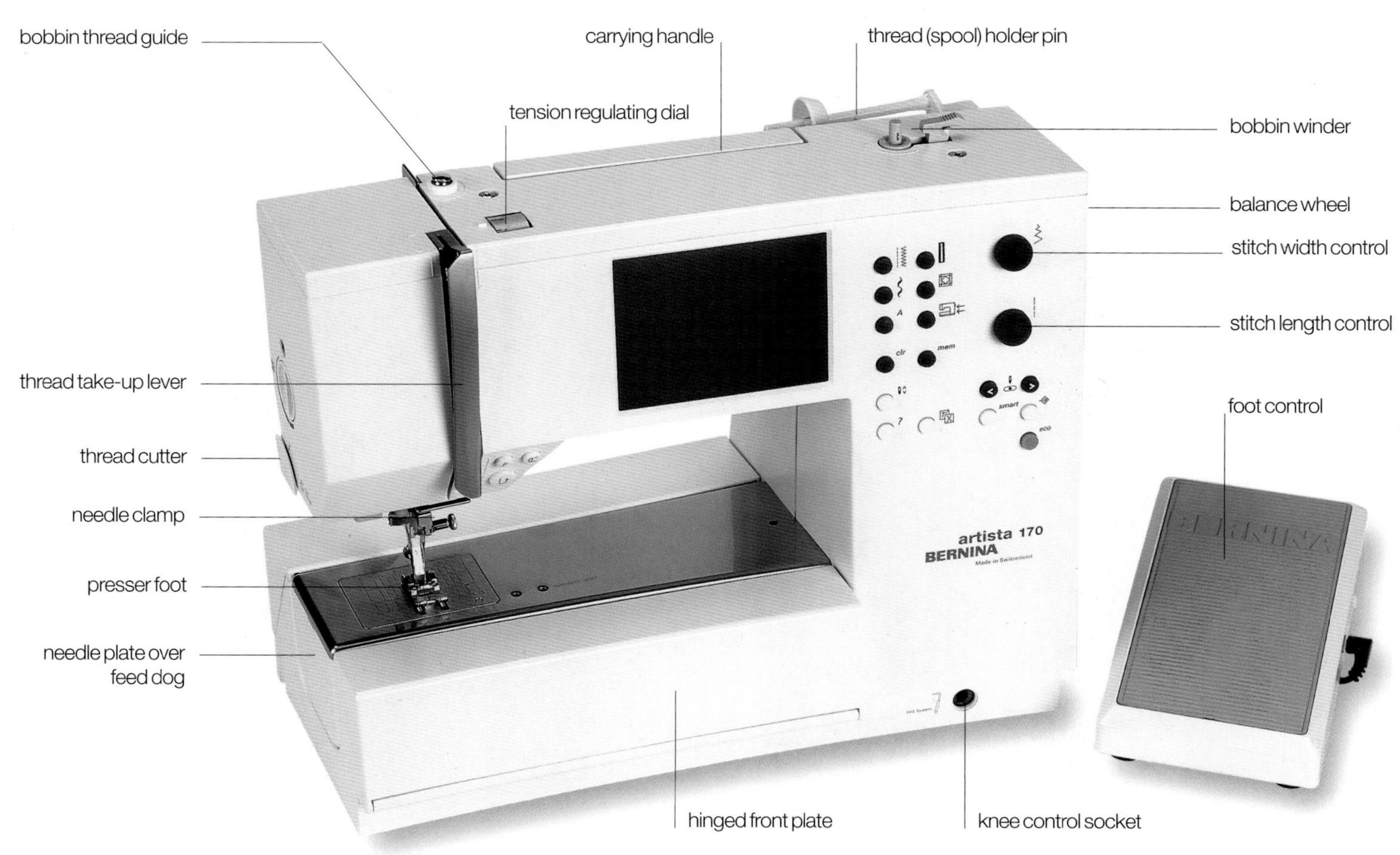

Thread cutter

This is situated at the back of the sewing machine for cutting threads.

Thread (spool) holder pin

This holds the reel (spool) of thread when filling the bobbin and stitching.

MACHINE NEEDLES

Always select a machine needle to suit the fabric and the thread you are using; this will reduce the possibility of the needle breaking.

Universal needles

Universal sewing machine needles range in size from 70/9, used for fine fabrics, to 110/18, used for heavyweight fabrics. Size 80/12 is ideal for a mediumweight fabric. Keep a selection of needles to hand and change the needle when using a different weight of fabric. A fine needle will break if the fabric is too thick, and a large needle will damage a fine fabric.

Embroidery needles

These needles have larger eyes than normal to accommodate a wide range of decorative threads (floss). Keep a separate needle for each type of thread because the thread creates a groove on the needle that will cause other threads to break.

Top-stitch and jean-point needles

Special top-stitch needles have a very large eye to accommodate a thicker thread, although top stitching can also be worked using the same thread as the main fabric. Jean-point needles have a specially elongated sharp point to stitch through heavyweight fabrics.

Fitting the needle

Machine needles can only be fitted one way as they have a flat surface down one side (the shank) and a long groove down the other side (the shaft). When the needle is inserted, this groove should line up directly with the last thread guide. When the machine is in use, the thread runs down the groove and scores a unique channel into the metal. So when you change thread, you should change your needle, too.

zipper foot

clear-view foot

general all-purpose foot

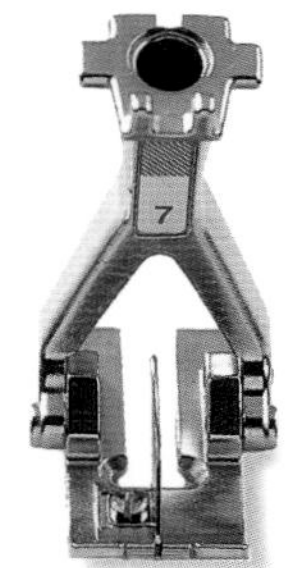

buttonhole foot

MACHINE FEET

All sewing machines have interchangeable feet for different types of sewing. These are designed for particular functions such as stitching close to a zipper or piping cord. The most common ones are illustrated here, but you can buy other specialist (specialty) feet.

General-purpose foot The basic metal general-purpose foot is used for all general straight and zigzag stitching on ordinary fabrics.

Clear-view foot Similar to the general-purpose foot, this foot allows you to see where you are stitching. It can be cut away or made from clear plastic. Use for machine quilting or appliqué.

Zipper foot This allows you to stitch close to the zipper teeth, and to piping cord. On some, the needle can be adjusted to sew on either side. A special zipper foot is available for invisible zippers.

Buttonhole foot This foot has a metal strip to guide rows of satin stitch forwards and backwards, leaving a tiny gap between for cutting the buttonhole.

STITCH TENSION

A new sewing machine should have the tension correctly set, with the dial at the marked centre point. Try out any stitches you intend to use on a sample of the fabric.

To check the tension, bring all the pattern and zigzag dials back to zero and set the stitch length between 2 and 3 for normal stitching. Place a folded strip of fabric on the needle plate, lower the needle into the fabric and sew a row of straight stitches. These should look exactly the same on both sides.

Altering the tension

To tighten the tension, turn the dial towards the lower numbers; to loosen it, turn towards the higher numbers. This will automatically affect the tension of the thread coming through the bobbin case. If the top tension dial is far from the centre, the spring on the bobbin case is probably wrong.

Only alter the lower tension as a last resort. You should be able to dangle the bobbin case without the thread slipping through. Shake the thread and the bobbin case should drop a little. Turn the screw on the side of the bobbin case slightly to alter the tension. Test the stitching again on a sample of fabric and alter the top tension this time until the stitches are perfect.

maintenance and trouble-shooting

Like a car, a sewing machine will only run well if it is used frequently and looked after. Cleaning is essential when you change fabrics, especially from a dark to a light-coloured one. Remove the sewing machine needle. Use a stiff brush to clean out the fluff (lint) along the route the top thread takes through the machine. Unscrew the needle plate and brush out any fluff from around the feed teeth. Remove the bobbin case to check that no thread is trapped in the mechanism.

above *Immaculately-tailored seams will ensure your soft furnishing items last longer as well as look better.*

Oil the machine from time to time, following the instructions in your handbook. Only use a couple of drops of oil. Leave the machine overnight with a fabric pad beneath the presser foot, then wipe the needle before use. Some new machines are self-lubricating. Even if you take good care of your machine, problems can occur. Some of the more common problems are listed below.

The machine works too slowly

The machine may have two speeds and may be set on slow. More likely, it hasn't been used for a while and oil could be clogging the working parts. Run the machine without a needle for a minute to loosen all the joints. Check that the foot control is not obstructed. As a last resort, ask a dealer to check the tension belt.

No stitches form

Ensure that the bobbin is full and inserted correctly. Check that the needle is facing in the right direction and threaded from the grooved side.

The needle doesn't move

Check first of all that the balance wheel is tight and that the bobbin winder is switched off. If the needle still doesn't move, the problem may be caused by thread trapped in the sewing hook behind the bobbin case. Remove the bobbin case and take hold of the thread end. Rock the balance wheel backwards and forwards until the thread comes out.

left *A professional look to soft furnishings is a result of seams stitched with perfect tension and no puckers.*

MATCHING STRIPES AND CHECKS

The pattern repeat on check fabrics is more distinct and not as large as other fabrics, but the seams are more of a challenge to match. In some cases it is sufficient to match the pattern horizontally only, but with the large expanses of fabric used in soft furnishing it is essential to match vertically as well. The following method can be used for all striped, checked and patterned fabrics. It ensures that the pattern continues across a curtain or tablecloth, matching exactly at the seam.

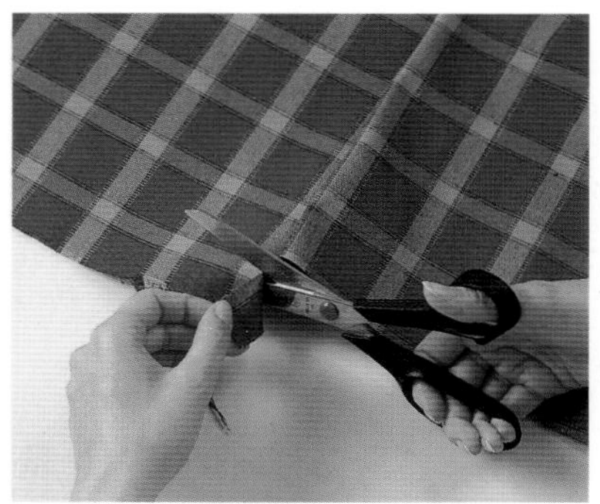

1 Cut the centre panel, then match the fabric horizontally down the seams. Cut off the excess fabric.

2 Turn over and press the seam allowance on one edge. Pin the folded edge to the next length of fabric, matching the pattern horizontally and vertically.

3 Slip-tack (baste) the seam from the right side by slipping the needle along the fold, then taking a similar-size stitch through the other fabric. The seam can then be stitched as normal.

USING PATTERNS FOR EFFECT

Soft furnishings can be very striking when the pattern or stripe is used to accentuate a decorative feature. Avoid problems by choosing the fabric carefully.

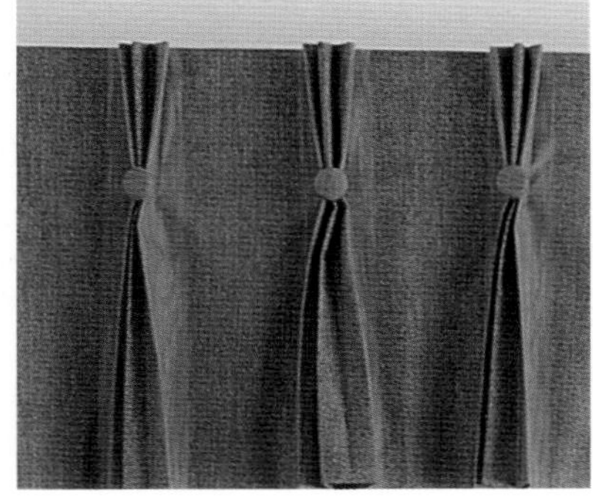

1 Hand-stitched triple pleats work perfectly with this vertically striped fabric. The spacing of the pleats can be adjusted to suit the width and spacing of the stripes.

2 Triple pleat tape on the other hand pulls the fabric up so that a different stripe pattern appears on each group of pleats. A pencil pleat tape would be a better choice.

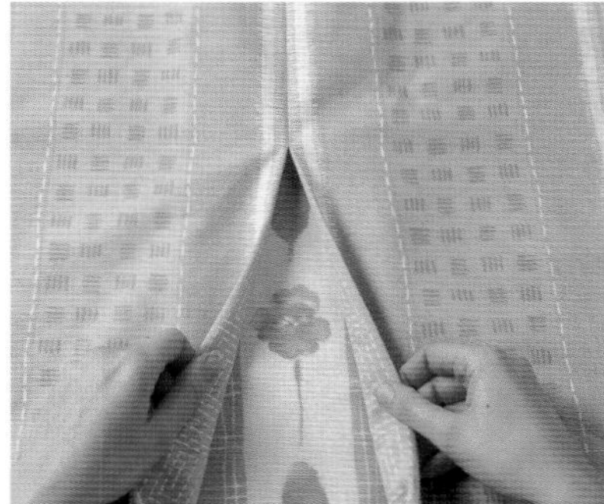

3 London blinds have a deep box pleat either side that opens as the blind is pulled up. The pansy pattern on this striped fabric has been placed in the centre of the pleats to accentuate this feature.

USING NAP FABRIC

Nap fabrics are fabrics that can only be cut and hung in one direction. If the fabric has a one-way design, it is obvious which way it has to be cut. Pattern pieces for pile fabrics, such as corduroy or velvet, must be cut facing the same direction. These fabrics catch the light in a certain way and look much darker when the pile is facing up and lighter when facing down.

right *The direction of the nap can be determined by running your hand over the surface.*

making seams

Various seams are used in different soft furnishing projects, depending on whether the finished item needs to be strong, to withstand frequent washing or to be purely decorative.

FLAT SEAM

This is the basic seam used in most soft furnishing projects. The size of the seam allowance varies, but is usually 1.5cm/⅝in. Even if the seam will be trimmed, stitch a wider seam and trim it to get a stronger join.

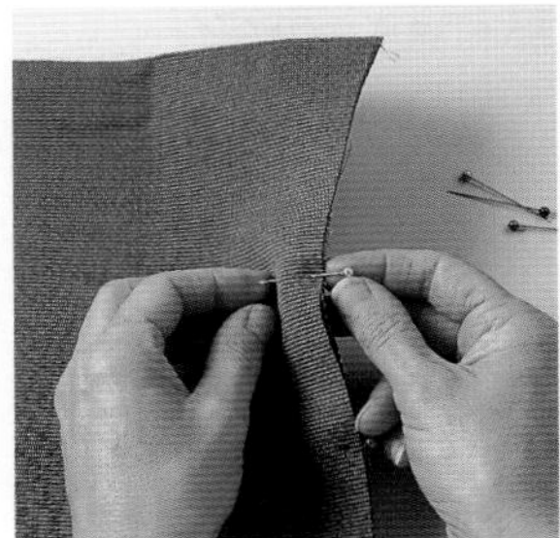

1 Pin the two layers of fabric together, matching the raw edges carefully.

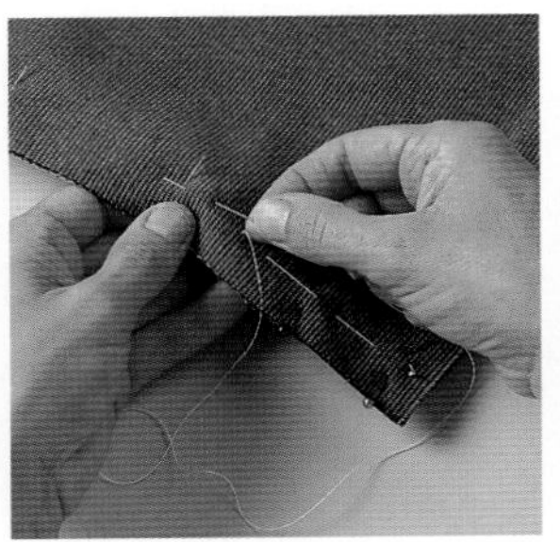

2 Tack (baste) 1.5cm/⅝ in in from the edge. If the fabric is fairly firm, it is possible to stitch across the pins without the need for tacking.

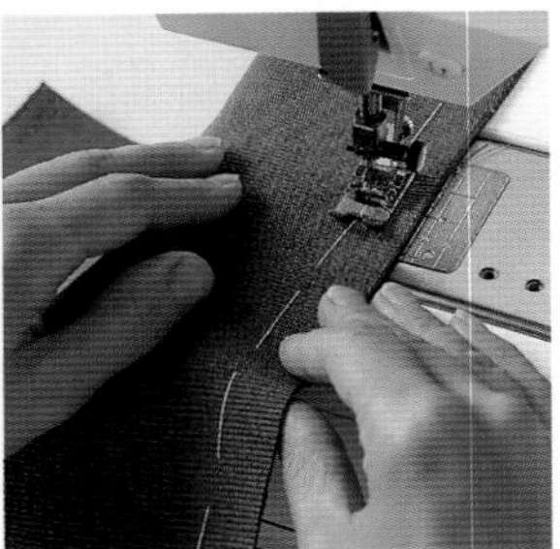

3 Stitch along one side of the tacking thread. Press the seam open. Zigzag-stitch or overcast the edges to prevent fraying.

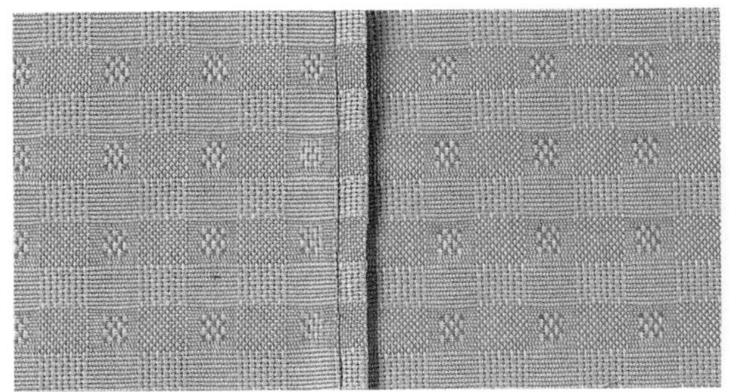

FRENCH SEAM

A French seam is suitable for lightweight fabrics. It is used on bed linen to make strong seams that will not fray. The finished width of the seam can be narrower on fine fabrics.

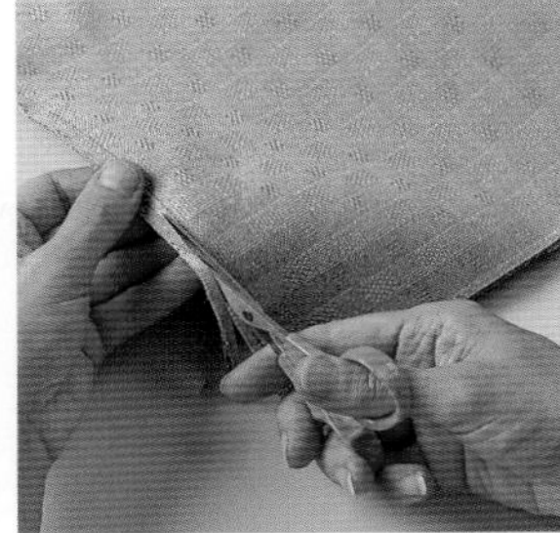

1 Wrong sides together, stitch a 7mm/⅜in seam. Trim to 3mm/⅛ in.

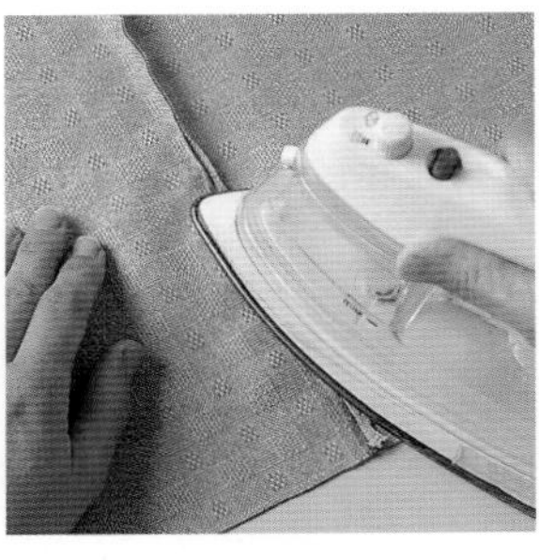

2 Press the seam open. This makes it much easier to get the fold exactly on the edge at the next stage.

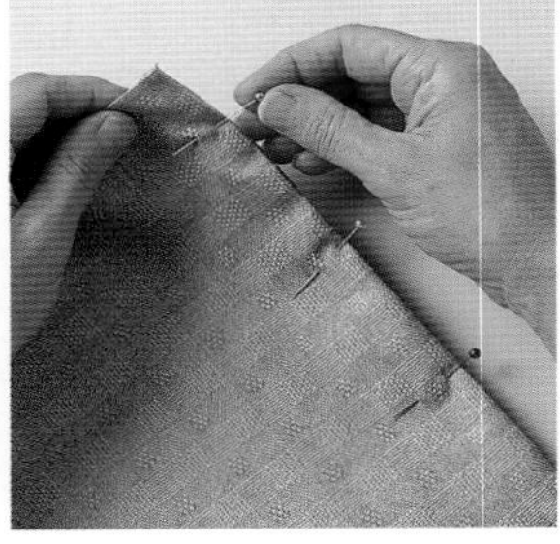

3 Fold, enclosing the raw edges, and press. Pin the seam and stitch 5mm/¼ in from the edge. Press to one side.

LAPPED SEAM

This seam is ideal for joining fabric that requires accurate matching as it is stitched from the right side. Plan carefully when cutting out pattern pieces in order to make the seam as inconspicuous as possible.

1 Turn under 1cm/½ in along a straight thread and press.

2 Lay the pressed edge on top of the other piece of fabric. Pin along the fold, carefully matching the design.

3 Tack (baste) the fabric if it is slippery, otherwise stitch carefully over the pins, close to the fold. For extra strength and decoration, top-stitch a further row 5mm/¼ in away.

FLAT FELL SEAM

This is the traditional seam used for denim jeans. It is a strong seam that can be washed and wears well, as all the raw edges are enclosed. It is most suitable for mediumweight fabrics.

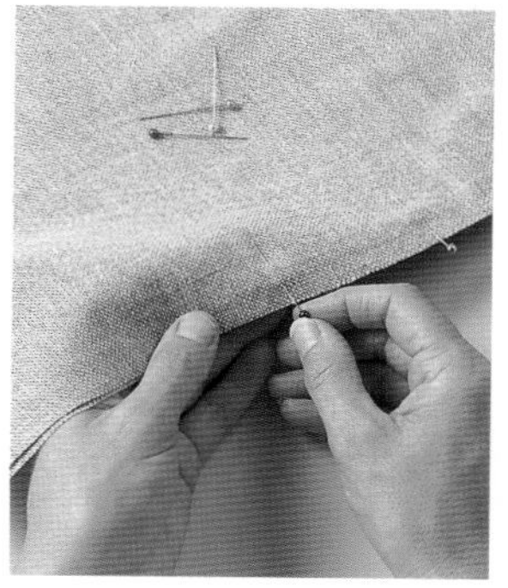

1 Pin the fabric right sides together and stitch a plain 1.5cm/⅝in seam. (For the traditional finish with two rows of stitching showing, begin with the fabric wrong sides together instead.)

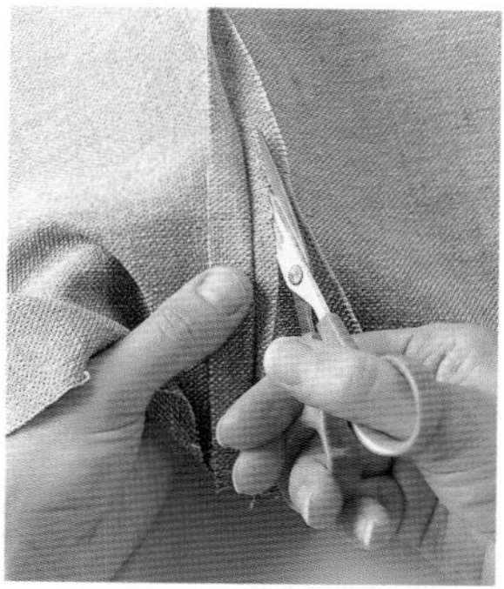

2 Trim one side of the seam allowance to 3mm/⅛in. Press the wide seam allowance over the trimmed edge.

3 Turn under the edge of the larger seam allowance and pin then tack. Stitch close to the edge of the fold.

ENCLOSED SEAMS

Seams that are enclosed (for example, inside a cushion cover) do not need to be finished, but in order to achieve a neat line when the cover is turned through they should be trimmed carefully. Bulky seams should be layered. Curved seams and corners need to be trimmed, and also snipped or notched into the seam allowance.

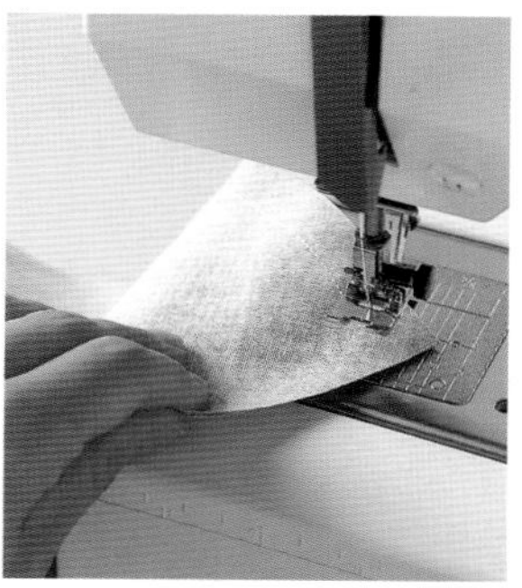

1 Stitch around a curved edge, using the lines on the needle plate as a guide for stitching. When you get to the corner, leave the needle in the fabric and rotate the fabric until the next seam is lined up.

2 Snip into any inward-facing points or curves to within one or two threads of the stitching. Trim the seam allowance to 5mm/¼in.

3 Cut across any outward-facing points. If the fabric is medium- or heavyweight, trim the seam allowance on either side slightly as well.

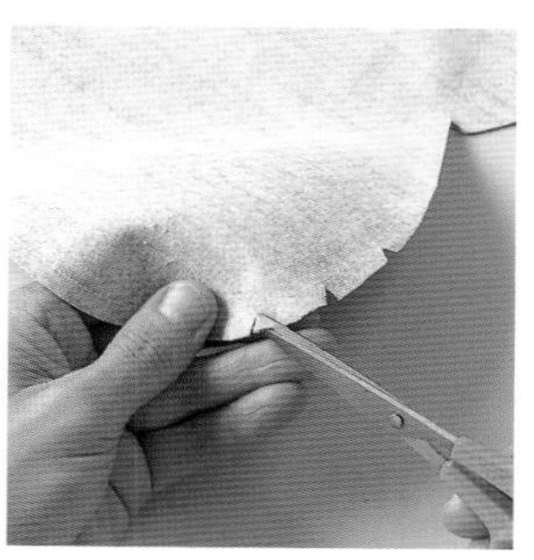

4 Notch the outward-facing curves. Cut notches closer together on tight curves, and every 2.5–5cm/1–2in on shallow curves.

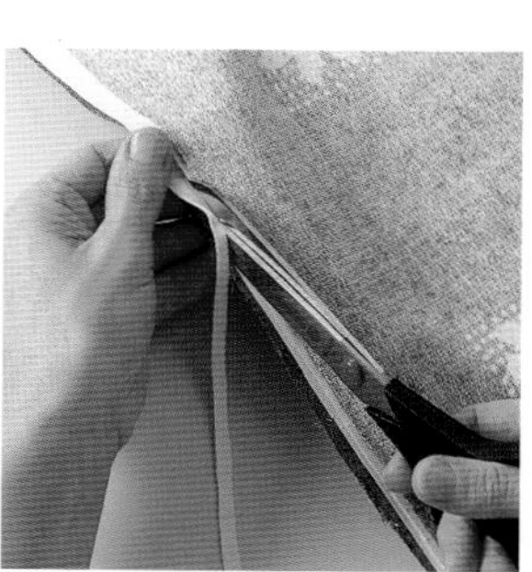

5 If the seams have been stitched with multiple layers of fabric, trim them to reduce bulk. Grade the seam allowances so that the edge that is next to the right side is the largest.

mitring corners

Mitring is the neatest way to finish corners on soft furnishings. The type of mitre used depends on the item and the type of fabric. The majority of curtains use an uneven mitre but sheer curtains use a double mitre. Double mitres are suitable for sheer fabric, or the turned-in hem edge will be visible through the hem.

SINGLE MITRE

Use a single mitre on firm, closely woven fabrics, where the shorter turning inside the hem edge will not show through, even against the light.

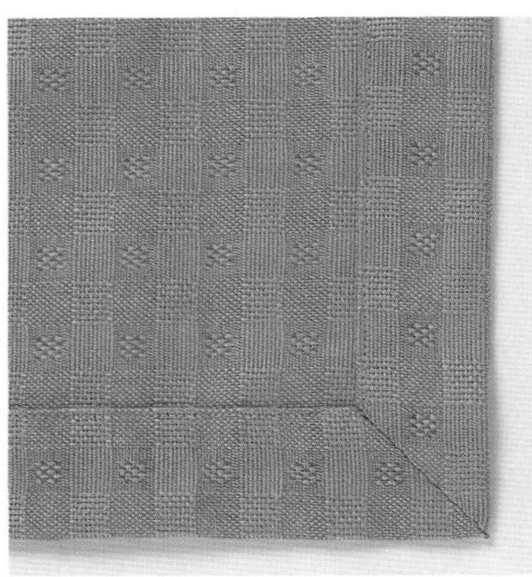

1 Trim the fabric along the straight grain. Turn over and press the hem allowance.

2 Open out the hem and press the corner over on the diagonal, exactly where the folds cross. Trim this flap to 5 mm/¼ in.

3 ◁ Press a 5mm/¼ in turning along the edge of the hem, including along the diagonal line. Fold the hem over and pin in place. Tack (baste) then stitch along the inner edge of the hem.

4 ▷ Slip-stitch the diagonal seam of the mitre closed as shown.

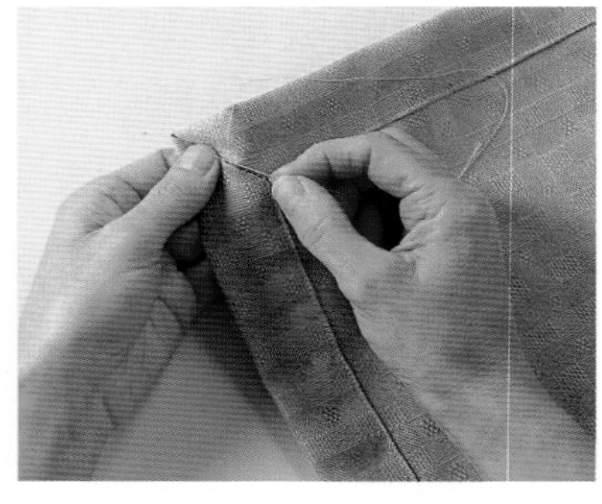

UNEVEN MITRE

The uneven mitre is used almost exclusively for curtain hems. The fabric isn't trimmed before folding. The extra weight helps the curtain to hang straight.

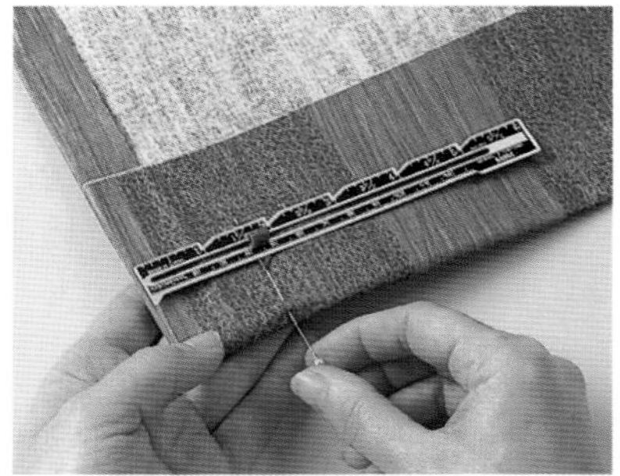

1 Fold and press a 2cm/¾in double hem down each side and a double 8cm/3in hem along the bottom. Pin the point where the bottom hem meets the side hem. Open the hems, pin 4cm/1½ in from the edge.

2 Fold over the corner between the pins diagonally and press flat.

3 Refold the side and bottom hems to make a neat uneven mitre and pin. Slip stitch the mitre.

DOUBLE MITRE

Use a double mitre on sheer or lightweight fabrics, and on the edge of flat curtains or blinds where the light will shine through the fabric.

1 Trim the fabric along the straight grain. Fold and press a double hem on each edge of the fabric.

2 Open out the double hem and fold the corner over on the diagonal, exactly where the outside folds cross. Trim this flap to 5mm/¼ in.

3 Refold the double hem and pin the mitred corner neatly. If the diagonal raw edge is showing, open up the corner and trim. Finish as for the single mitre.

RAW EDGE MITRE

This basic mitre is used if the back of the fabric will be lined. The lining is slip-stitched into position in the middle of the hem to cover the raw edges.

1 Trim the fabric along the straight grain. Fold and press the hem allowance, then open out.

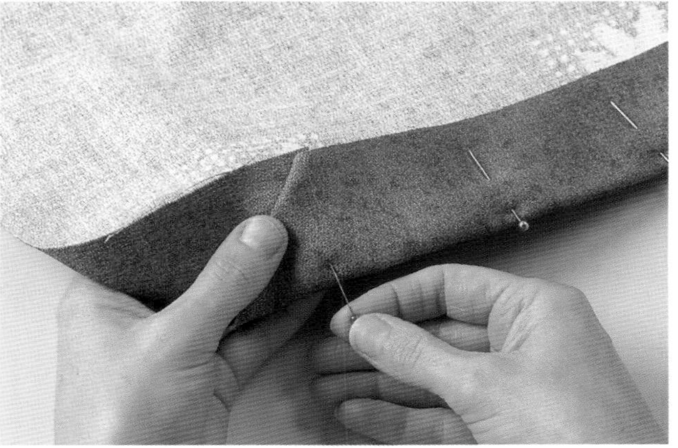

2 Press the corner over diagonally, exactly on the pressed crease. Refold the hem and pin. Slip-stitch the mitre.

right *Mitres can be used as an integral part of the project design. This curtain makes good use of a fabric that is attractive on both sides.*

turning hems

A hem is the most common way to finish the side and bottom edges of soft furnishings. Machine-stitched hems are usually quite acceptable on simple unlined curtains and modern slipcovers, but more elaborate fabrics and curtains in a more formal style should really be hand stitched.

Hems can be either single or double. A single hem has a single layer of fabric, with the raw edge turned under or finished by zigzag stitch or overcasting. A double hem has a double turning, with the raw edge lying inside along the bottom fold. It is used when the fabric is translucent, or to add weight to a curtain.

MACHINE-STITCHED HEM

This is usually narrower for side hems and deeper for a bottom hem. It is used mainly with light- and mediumweight cotton or linen fabrics. Fold and pin a single or double hem depending on the type of fabric. Stitch along the edge of the fold from the reverse side.

MACHINE-ROLLED HEM

This is used to finish the edge of sheer or lightweight fabrics. Fold a narrow 1cm/½in single hem and stitch along the fold. Trim close to the stitching, fold again then stitch on top of the previous stitching.

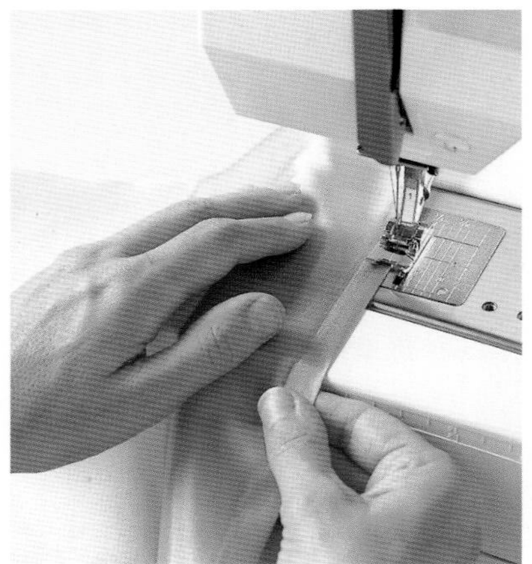

MACHINE BLIND HEMMING

This is quick and easy once you have adjusted the needle position. Tack (baste) the hem 5mm/¼in from the upper fold. Fit the special foot into the machine and fold the hem back under the main fabric along the tacked line. Select the blind hemming stitch and take a few stitches. Alter the width of the needle swing so that you catch only one or two threads of the main fabric.

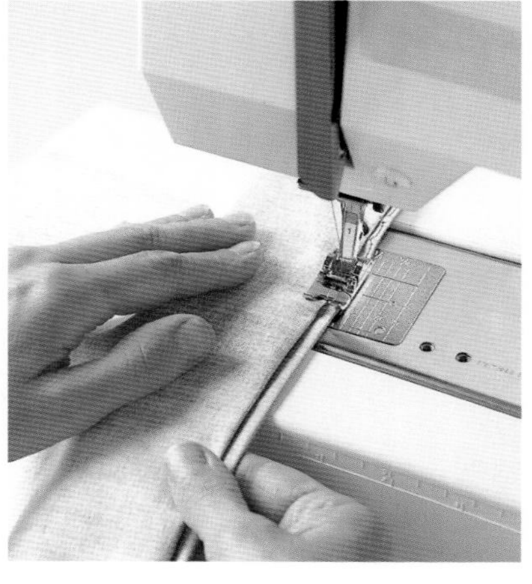

HERRINGBONE STITCH

Herringbone stitch is a stable hemming stitch usually worked on lined and interlined curtains, especially if the fabric is quite thick. Beginning at the left, take a back stitch into the hem and then further to the right take another back stitch into the main fabric or interlining. Work from right to left if you are left-handed.

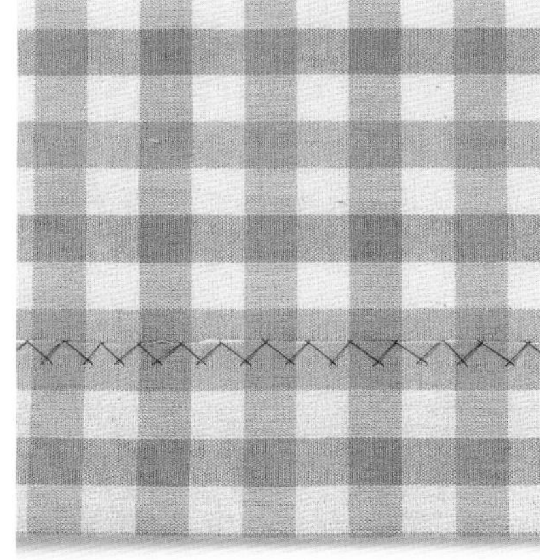

HAND HEMMING

This tends to produce a ridge on the right side of the fabric, so it is most often used to stitch bindings or facings in place. The stitches are stronger when worked into the stitching on the reverse side. Pick up one or two threads of fabric or a machined stitch then take a small diagonal stitch into the hem.

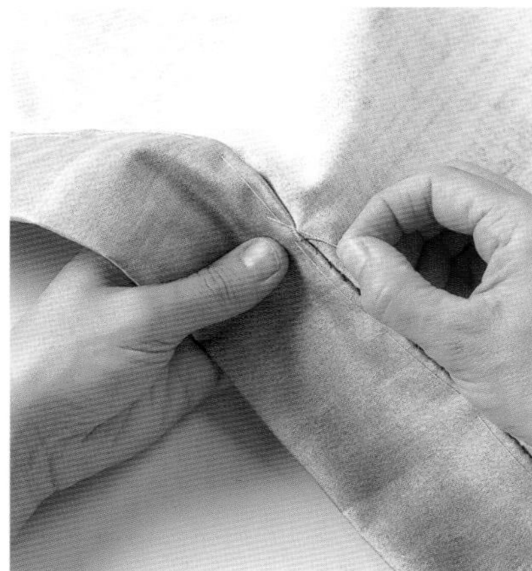

SLIP HEMMING

This hand stitch is one of the most common hem finishes, used on light- and mediumweight fabrics. Work the stitches fairly loosely so that there is no ridge on the right side. Pick up one or two threads of fabric, then slide the needle along inside the hem for 5–15mm/¼–½in.

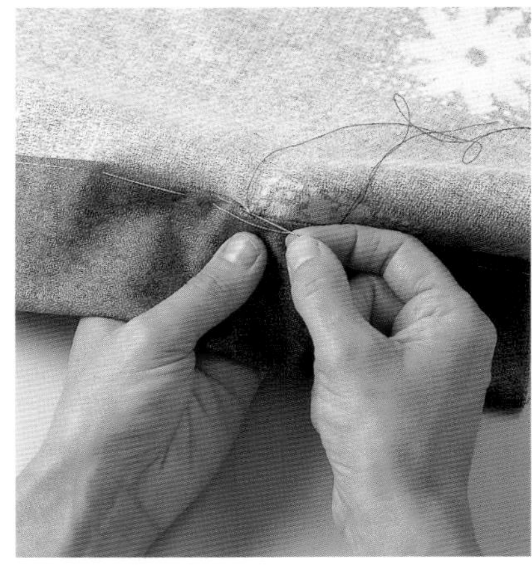

HAND BLIND HEMMING

This is worked in a similar way to slip hemming, but there is less risk of a ridge on the right side as the stitching is worked between the layers of fabric. Tack (baste) 5mm/¼in from the edge of the hem. Fold the edge of the hem over and hold with your thumb. Pick up one or two threads of fabric and then take one or two stitches into the hem.

preparing bias strips for piping and binding

Piping and binding add extra style to many soft furnishings projects, giving them a truly professional look and lifting them out of the ordinary.

Piping is most often used to accentuate and define the edge of shaped objects such as chair seats and cushions. Plain white piping cord is available in various widths, ready to be covered with co-ordinating fabric or a contrast fabric. Patterned fabrics look particularly effective when one of the colours is picked out in the piping. The strips of fabric used to cover the piping cord are usually cut on the bias, but checked and striped fabrics are often cut on the straight grain to ensure that the pattern matches exactly. The covered piping cord is then sandwiched between the fabric layers of the chair seat or other item, and stitched into the seam to give a neat finish.

MAKING A BIAS STRIP

This method is suitable for small projects that require a fairly short bias strip, or where it is crucial to match a checked or striped pattern at the join.

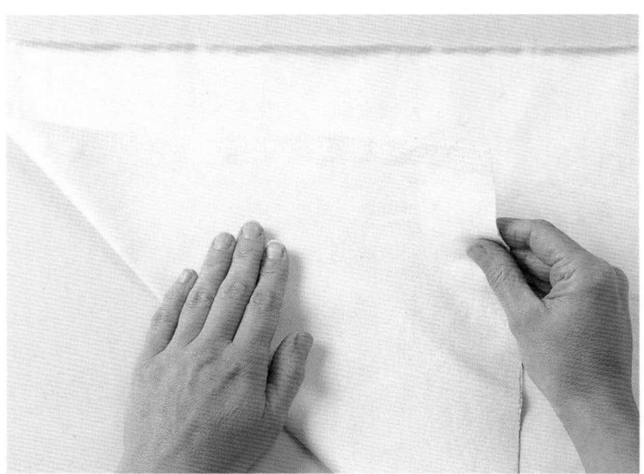

1 Fold the fabric across at 45° so that the selvage is parallel with the straight grain running across the fabric.

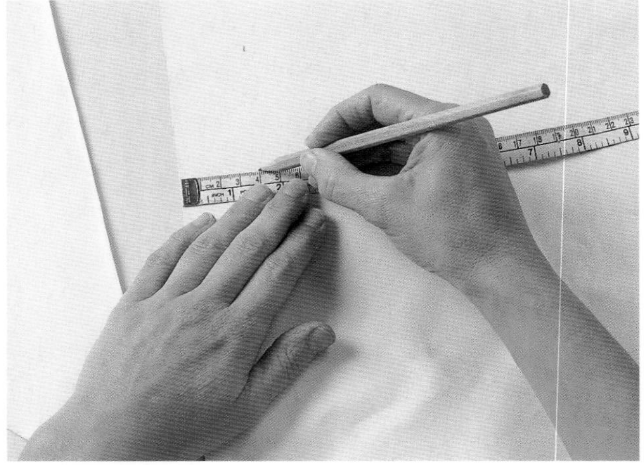

2 Press the diagonal line then open it out. Cut along this line. Decide on the width you wish the bias strip to be, and mark lines across the fabric, using a pencil and ruler. Cut sufficient strips to complete the project.

3 Join the strips by overlapping the ends at 45°. Pin, then stitch between the small triangles of fabric.

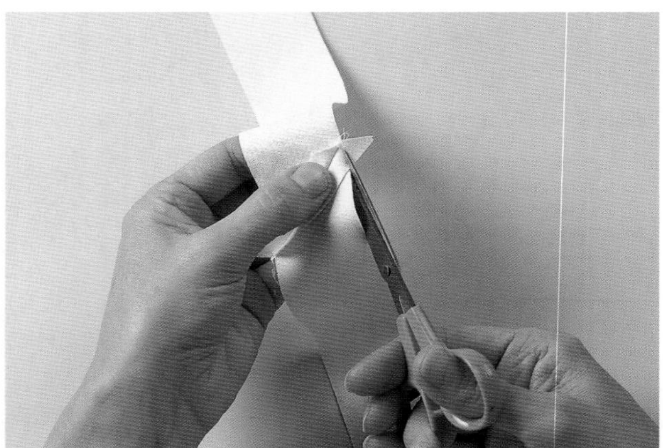

4 Press the seam open and trim off the jutting-out triangles. Join sufficient strips for the project in the same way. Steam-press the fabric to remove some of the excess stretch.

MAKING A CONTINUOUS BIAS STRIP

Larger soft furnishings projects may require several metres (yards) of piping or binding, in which case you will need to make a continuous bias strip.

1 Cut a large square of fabric and fold it in half diagonally. Cut across this line.

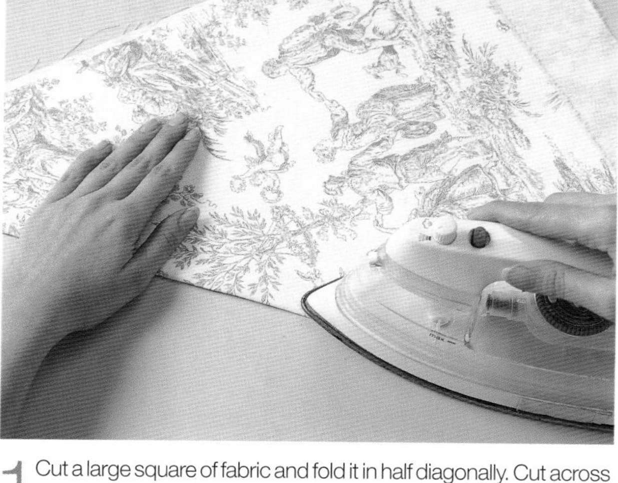

2 Pin the two short edges together, right sides facing. Stitch the seam 5mm/¼ in from the raw edge. Reverse-stitch at each end to secure the seam. Press the seam open.

3 Place the fabric wrong side. Draw parallel lines the required distance apart across the fabric, using a pencil and ruler. Press down hard with the ruler to prevent the fabric from stretching.

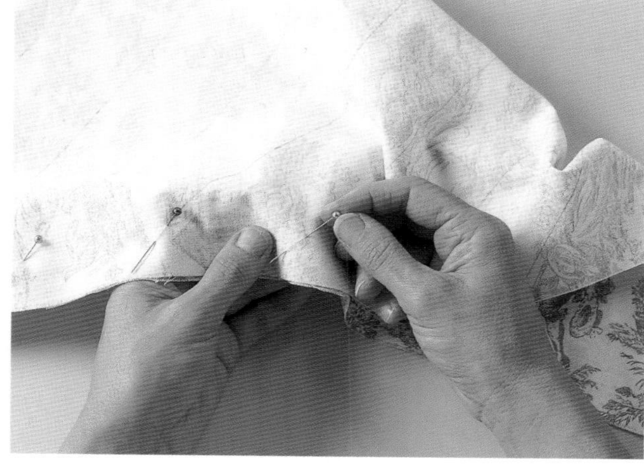

4 Right sides facing, pin the diagonal edges to make a tube. Offset the edges so that the first line below the corner is level with the opposite edge of the fabric. Stitch the seam and press open.

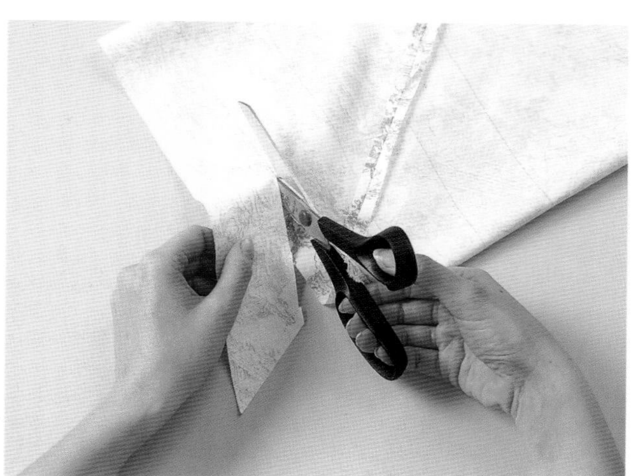

5 Cut the fabric tube into a continuous strip, beginning at one corner and cutting along the marked lines.

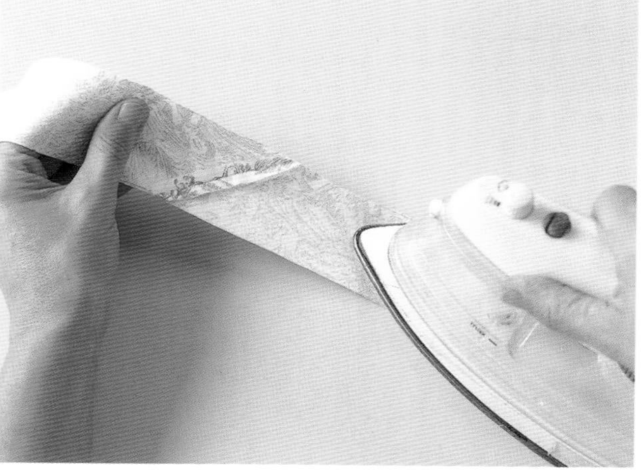

6 Press the bias binding with a steam iron, pulling it slightly to remove the stretch.

PIPING

Piping cord is available in a wide range of gauges, each of which will create a different effect. In general, the heavier-weight the fabric, the thicker the piping cord you should use. There are several different types of piping cord, the traditional cord type and the man-made kind, with a smooth outer surface that is more suitable for lightweight or sheer fabrics.

right *A range of cotton piping cords.*

Applying piping

1 Cut bias strips of fabric wide enough to fit around the piping cord, leaving the required seam allowance flat. Measuring accurate seam allowances will make the piping much easier to position and stitch later on.Cut and join sufficient strips of fabric for the project (see section on preparing bias strips). Press the strips to remove some of the stretch. Fold them over the piping cord and pin in place.

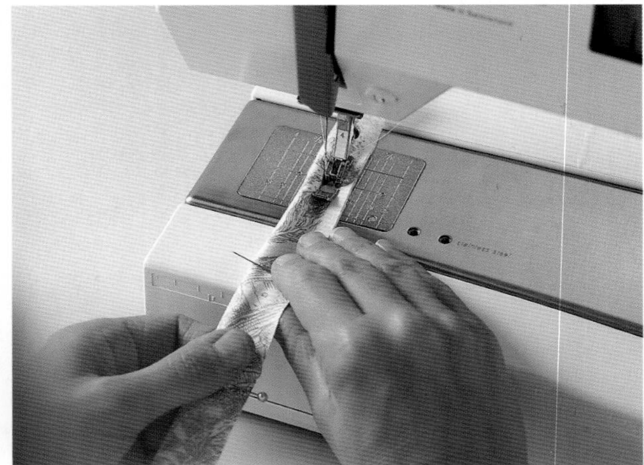

2 Fit a zipper foot to the sewing machine. Stitch as close to the piping cord as possible, removing the pins as you go. You can move the needle across slightly so that it stitches at the very edge of the zipper foot.

3 Pin and tack (baste) the piping to the edge of the main fabric. If the bias strips were cut to the correct width, the seamlines will be accurate.

4 Place the second layer of main fabric on top and pin. Tack if the fabric is slippery. Stitch as close as possible to the piping cord, moving the needle over if required.

JOINING AND FINISHING PIPING

Piping cord is quite bulky and must be trimmed if it crosses a seam, or if you need to join two ends of cord together. The piping can simply be "run off" the edge of the fabric where the seamlines cross, or where a join will be inconspicuous. Alternatively, the bias strips can be seamed and the cord trimmed so that the join is not noticeable.

Simple join

This method is quick and ideal to use if the join will be in an inconspicuous place such as the bottom of a cushion. Use this method to run piping cord off a slipcover seam to reduce bulk before a zipper is stitched in place. Open out the ends of the piping and trim the cord so that the ends will meet. Fold the bias strip back over the cord and pin it flat on to the seam allowance. Overlap the other end and tack (baste) along the edge of the cord. Cut the ends of the piping cord so that the zipper foot does not run over it as you stitch.

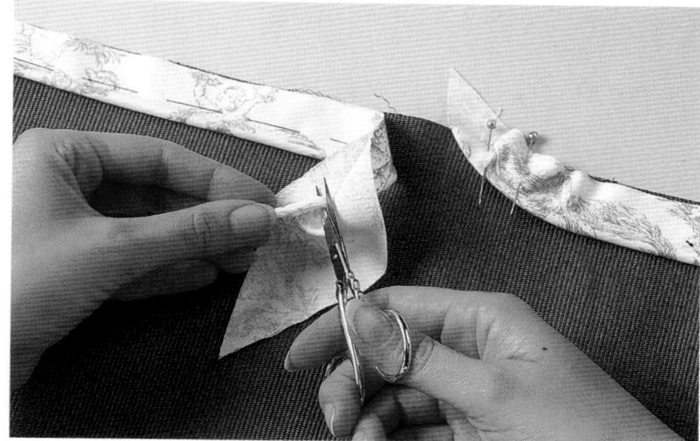

Seamed join

1 Open out the ends of the piping strips and pin together with a diagonal seam so that it fits the gap. Stitch the seam and trim to 5mm/¼in. Press open.

2 Overlap the piping cord and trim the ends to different lengths. Refold the bias binding and tack (baste) in place.

right *Piping is used to accentuate the shape of these bold patterned cushions.*

BINDING

Binding is used to cover raw edges. It can be used to finish soft furnishings such as table linen, blinds and curtains. The width of the binding can vary from 5mm/¼in to several centimetres/inches.

Single binding

Cut strips of binding fabric on the straight grain for straight edges, or on the bias if the edge is curved. Join both straight and bias strips on the diagonal.

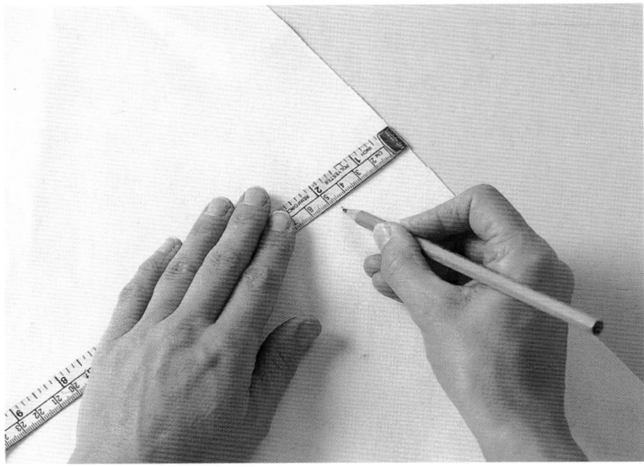

1 Cut strips of binding fabric four times the finished width, adding 3–5mm/⅛–¼ in ease, depending on the thickness of the fabric.

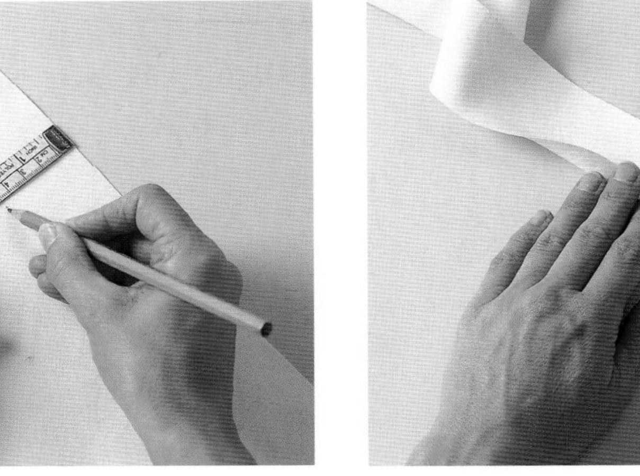

2 Fold over and press one-quarter of the width along one side of the binding. Fold the other side in, leaving a slight gap in the centre, and press.

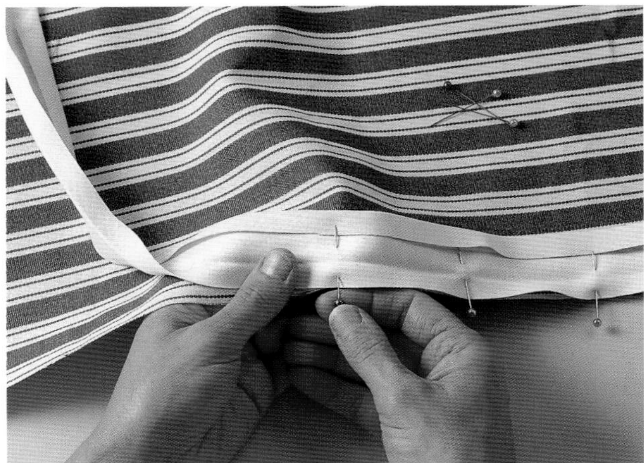

3 Open out one side of the binding and pin along the edge of the main fabric, right sides together. With deeper binding the seam allowance will be much wider than normal.

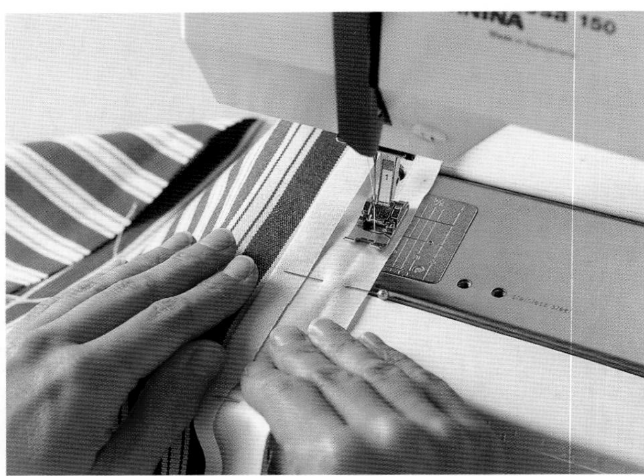

4 Stitch along the foldline, removing the pins as you reach them.

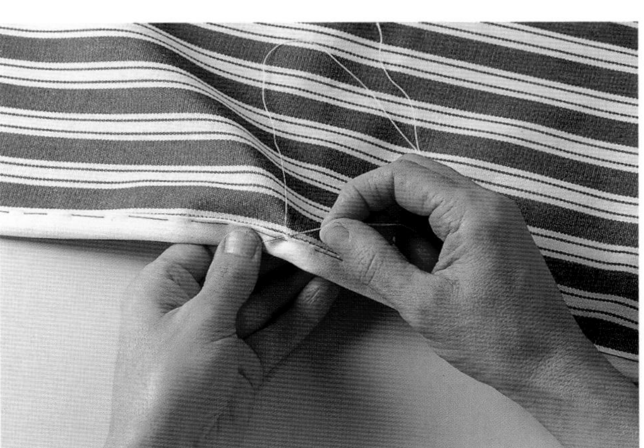

5 Fold the binding over to the reverse side and tack (baste). Hem the binding into the machine stitches. Alternatively, stitch by machine from the right side. Check that the stitching will catch the underneath edge before beginning to stitch.

Curved edges

Cut strips of binding fabric on the bias and join as required (see section on preparing bias strips). For a large item, such as a circular tablecloth, fold the binding and press it into a similar-shaped curve to make the fitting easier. This example has a scalloped edge.

1 Fold and press the bias binding. Open out one edge and pin around the curve of the fabric. Place the pins closer together on a tight curve.

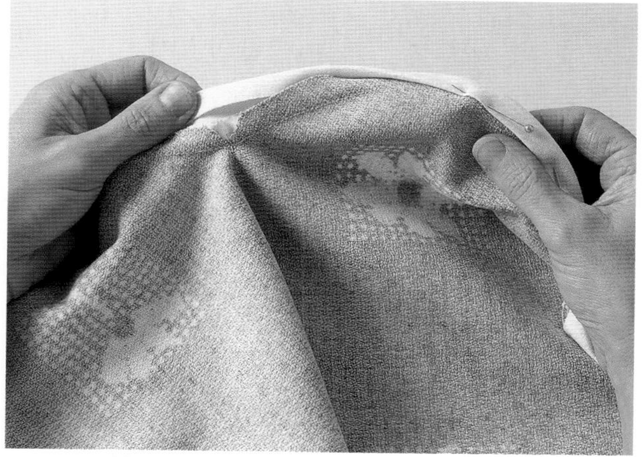

2 Stitch the binding. Keep the needle in the fabric at the point between the scallops and rotate for the next scallop. Once complete, fold the binding to the reverse side.

3 At the point between the scallops, fold the binding into a neat tuck and then pin. Hem the binding into the stitching and slip-stitch the tucks.

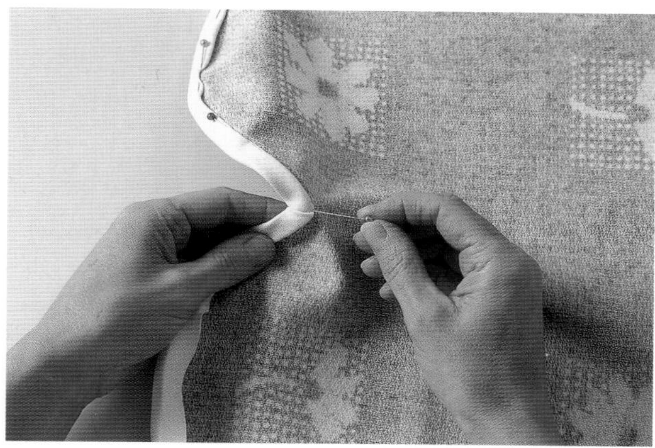

left *At the tuck remove the excess fabric so that the binding can lie flat on an inward facing point.*

Double binding

This quick method is more suitable for binding with lightweight or sheer fabrics. The finished binding will be stronger and less translucent.

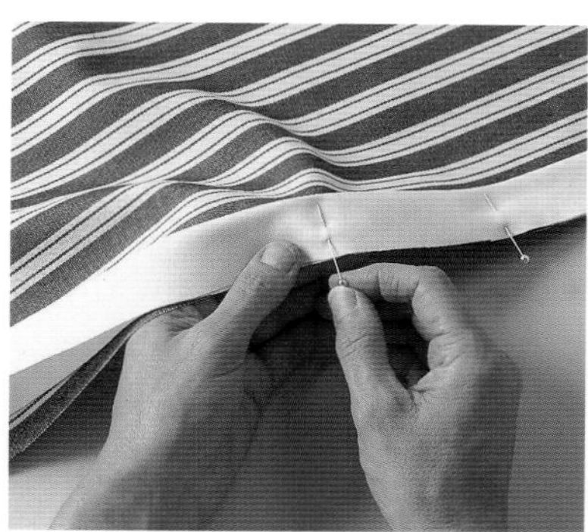

1 Cut and join bias strips of fabric six times the finished width required, adding another 3mm/⅛ in for ease. Fold the strip in half and pin along the right side of the fabric.

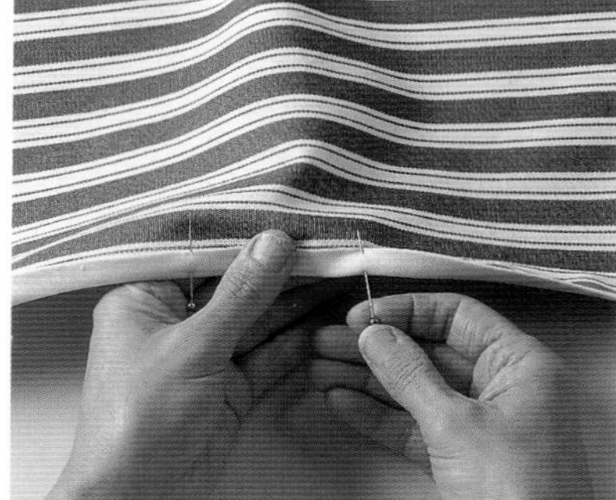

2 Stitch along the seam allowance, which should be the same width as the finished binding. Turn the binding to the reverse side and pin.

3 Tack (baste) the binding, then hem into the stitches. Alternatively, use a machine and stitch from the right side.

fastenings

These are generally used on fitted items such as cushions, slipcovers and bed linen, which need to be removed from time to time for cleaning purposes. Some fastenings are strong, some can be fitted invisibly but still allow quick-and-easy opening, and others are purely decorative. The type of fastening you choose will depend on the style, position and size of the opening, and also the look you prefer.

VELCRO

This clever invention is made in two parts – one part is covered in plastic hooks and the other has a soft loop pile. The two pieces stick together firmly but can be easily pulled apart. It is quite a bulky but neat fastening, often used for heavyweight cushion covers and strong enough to support the weight of a curtain pelmet or valance. Self-adhesive Velcro is available for attaching to wooden pelmet boards or window frames. For extra security it can be stapled in place.

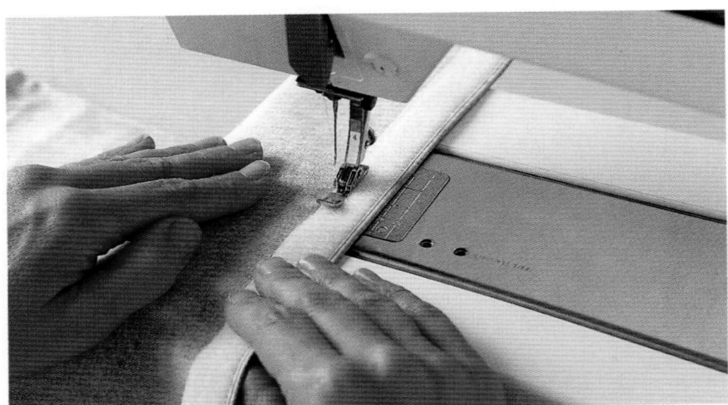

1 Use the soft loop side of Velcro for the top edge of the opening. Turn over and press a 1.5cm/⅝in seam allowance then pin the Velcro along the edge. Stitch down both edges.

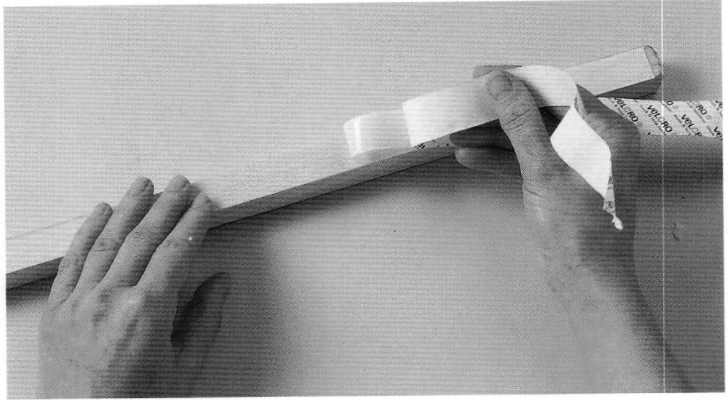

2 Velcro can be used to attach blinds, curtains and valances to a window or pelmet board. Attach the self-adhesive hooked side of Velcro along the edge of the pelmet board, or batten. If the curtain or blind is very heavy, insert staples at regular intervals to make it more secure. Stitch the soft side of the Velcro to the blind or pelmet.

EYELETS

Eyelets are now available in a range of sizes and colours. They are used to fasten simple curtains to a curtain pole, and are an integral part of the fastening for a reefer blind. They can also be used as a decorative stud to hold two seams together permanently. Work on a solid surface otherwise the two sections of the eyelets will not come together neatly.

1 Fold and stitch a double hem, wide enough to fit the eyelets comfortably. Mark the spacing of the eyelets with pins. Use the special tool to cut a hole at each mark.

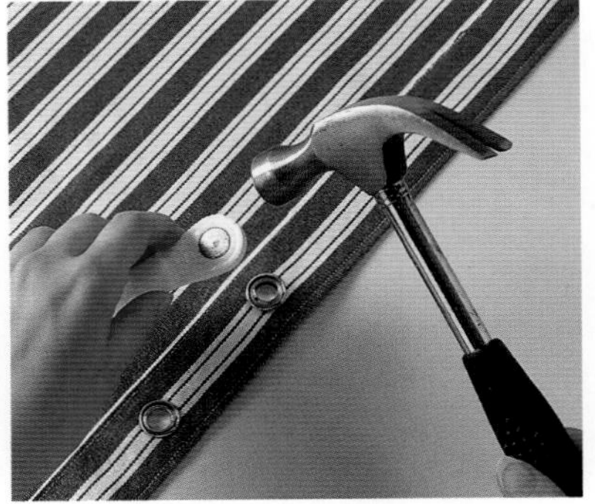

2 Insert the tube section from the underside and drop the ring on top. Hammer into position, using the special tool provided.

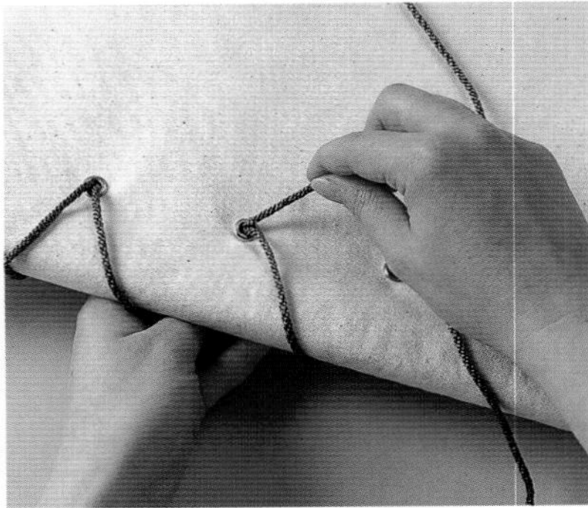

3 Eyelets were used to fasten the canvas around the bar of this deckchair. The eyelets were fitted through all layers at once. The cord is purely decorative.

POPPERS (SNAPS)

These are ideal for quick access. They are available as single fasteners or on a tape. Apart from two lines of stitching, the tape is not visible from the right side of the project. Single fasteners should be chosen carefully to suit the style of the soft furnishing. Poppers are a quick and easy method of fastening that are useful for items that are frequently laundered.

Popper (snap) tape

This is most often used for duvet covers to close a wide gap along the bottom edge. It is sold by the metre in large department stores.

1 Press under a 1.5cm/⅝ in turning along the edge, or for a stronger opening, make a double hem the same width as the popper (snap) tape. Peel the tape apart and pin one side to the edge of the opening.

2 Stitch down both sides of the tape, using a zipper foot so that you can stitch either side of the studs. Pin the other side and check the position of the poppers (snaps) before stitching. Close the poppers and stitch across each end.

Single poppers (snaps)

Single poppers (snaps) are now available in a wide range of sizes, styles and colours to suit any fabric or item of soft furnishing. They are sold complete with a special tool and fitting instructions. Use the steps below as a pictorial guide.

1 Fold and stitch a double hem wide enough to fit the poppers comfortably. Plan the spacing of the poppers and mark their position with pins. Insert pins in the opposite side of the opening to match.

2 Sort the popper pieces into types. There are generally two parts for the top stud and two for the lower stud. Insert the correct two parts for the top into the tool.

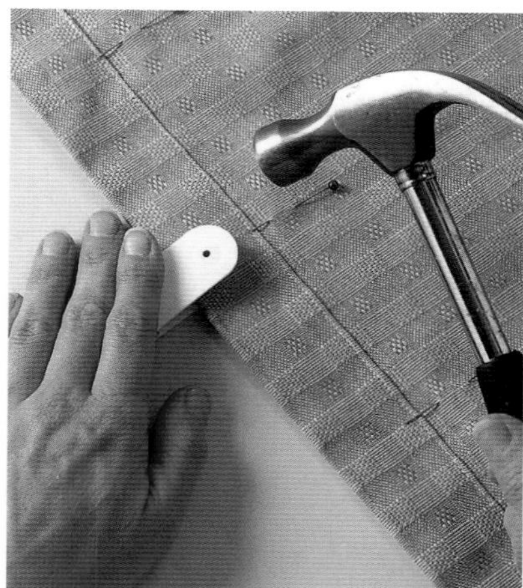

3 Place the tool over the hem, with the top of the stud next to the right side. Hold in place and hit the tool quite hard with a hammer. Fit the rest of the poppers (snaps), then fit the lower studs on the opposite side, checking that the poppers are the right way up and will fasten.

buttons and buttonholes

This traditional fastening can be purely functional or a decorative part of the item. For example, buttons at the bottom of a duvet cover can be quite plain, whereas used on an envelope opening on the front of the duvet cover they will be a decorative feature. As a rule, match the buttonhole thread to the fabric rather than the button.

MEASURING THE BUTTON

1 Measure a flat button from side to side and add 3mm/⅛ in ease allowance. The allowance is so that the button will fit through the buttonhole.

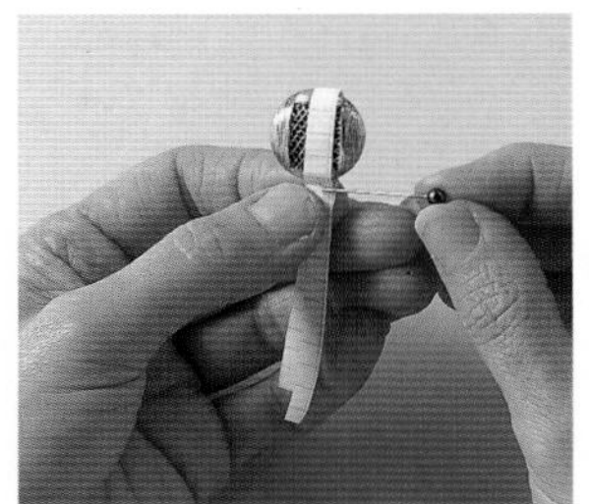

2 To measure a thick or shaped button, cut a thin strip of paper and wrap it around the button. Mark with a pin and open out. Add 3mm/⅛ in ease.

MARKING THE BUTTONHOLE

The direction of the buttonhole depends on where any strain will be applied. The button should pull to one end of the buttonhole in the direction of the strain. If the buttonhole is stitched in the wrong direction, it could open out and the button may pop out.

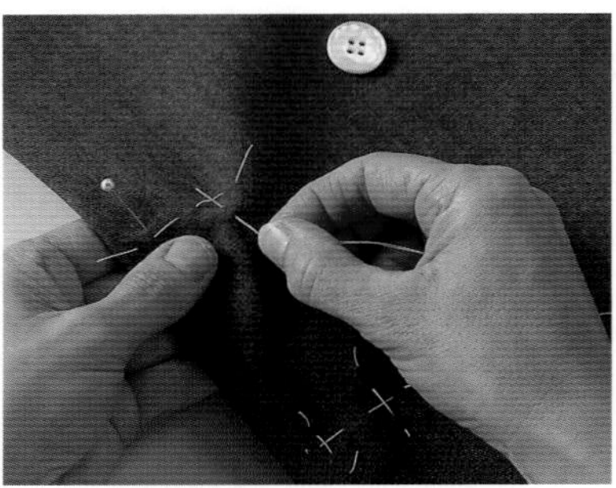

1 Mark the spacing of the buttonholes. Tack (baste) a line at each mark, along the straight grain. Mark the button length with pins, then tack. The end of the buttonhole must be at least half the length of the button away from the fold.

2 Set the sewing machine for buttonholing and fit the correct foot. Stitch the four sides of the buttonhole, changing direction exactly on the tacked lines. Finish with a few tiny straight stitches to secure the threads. Work all the buttonholes at the same time.

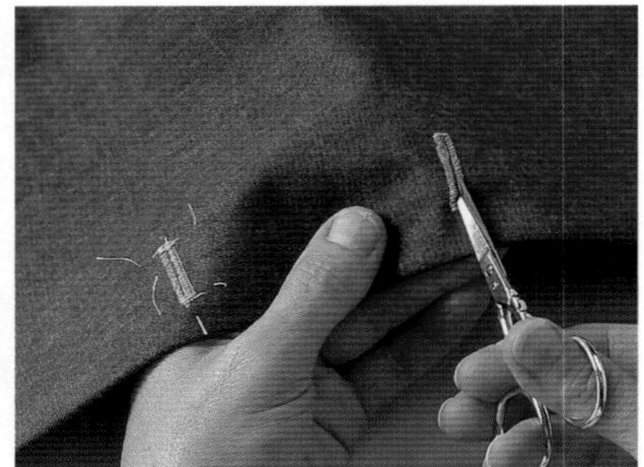

3 Remove the tacking thread. Cut along the centre of the buttonhole, using small pointed embroidery scissors or a seam ripper, taking care not to cut any stitches.

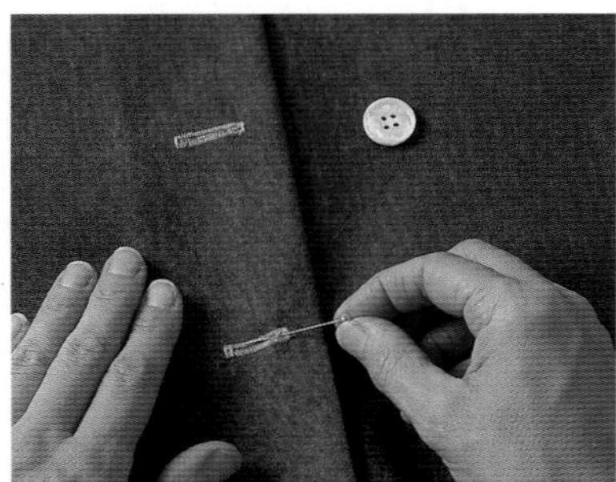

4 Line up the two sides of the openings and mark the position of the buttons with a pin. The button centre should be 3mm/⅛ in from the end of the buttonhole.

5 To make a shank, place a pin across the top of the button and stitch over the top. Remove the pin and wrap the shank with thread. Take the thread to the back and buttonhole-stitch the thread bars.

6 Covered buttons have a shank already on the underside and can be stitched straight on to the fabric.

COVERING BUTTONS

Buttons covered in the same fabric as the project look very professional. Self-covered button "blanks" are available in a range of sizes. Metal buttons are only suitable for soft furnishings that will be dry cleaned – use plastic buttons if the item will be washed. Both types of button can be used for either of the methods outlined below.

Traditional method

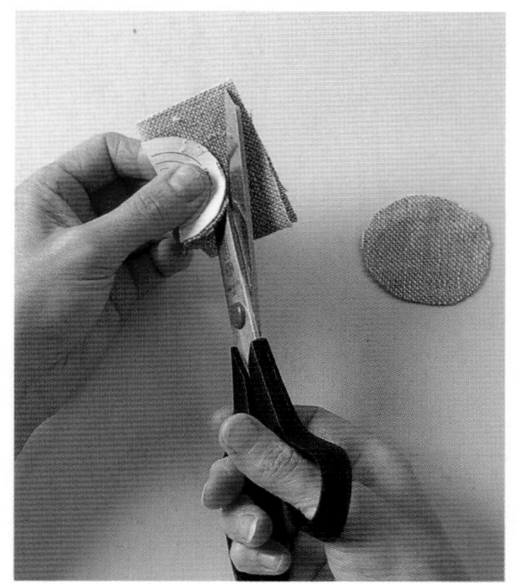

1 Trace or cut the appropriate-size circle from the back of the button kit packet. Cut the required number of circles out of fabric. If the buttons are loose, you will need to cut the circle 5–7mm/¼–⅜ in larger than the button.

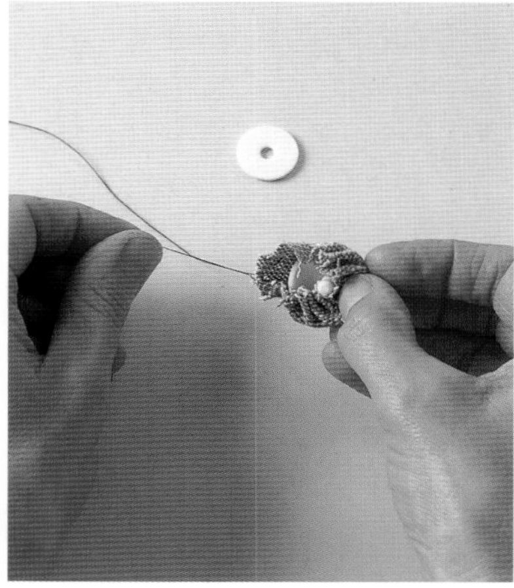

2 Tie a knot in the end of the thread. Sew a line of running stitches around the edges of the fabric circle, leaving a long tail of thread. Hold the button in the centre of the circle and pull the thread up tightly.

3 Arrange the gathers evenly and tie off. Fit the back of the button over the shank and press firmly into position. If the fabric has a pattern, check it is in the right position before fitting the back.

Using a special tool

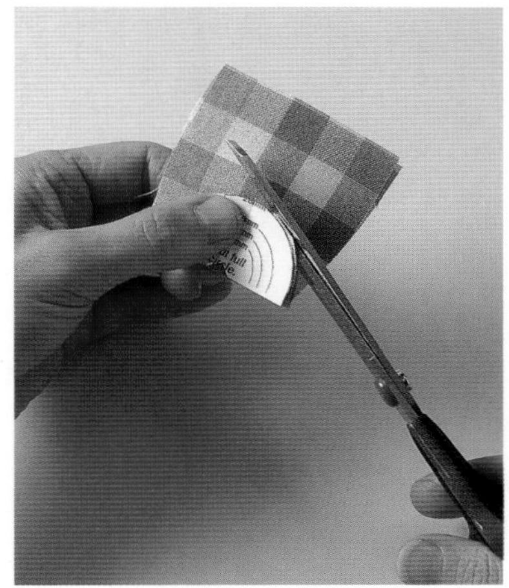

1 Cut the circle for the button the correct size. If there is a pattern, ensure that it is centred and matches all the other buttons.

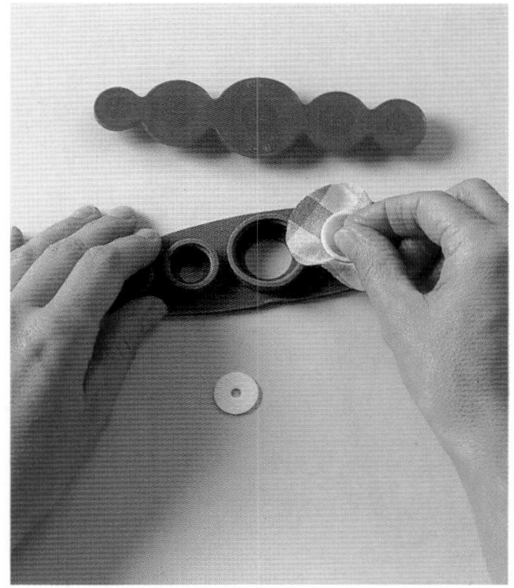

2 Lay the fabric circle on top of the appropriate hole on the base of the tool. (The sizes are marked.) Push the button down into the hole, making sure the fabric edges all face into the centre.

3 Fit the back over the shank. Position the top of the tool over the base and push down firmly. Ease the completed button out of the tool.

zippers

Zippers are one of the strongest kind of fasteners and are used for many soft furnishings. A dressweight zipper should be sufficient for most soft furnishings. There are several different ways to insert a zipper, and the method you choose will depend on its position. Fitted well, a zipper should be inconspicuous.

SEMI-CONCEALED ZIPPER

This is the easiest way to fit a zipper. It is called the semi-concealed method because the zipper teeth are visible between the folds of fabric. Use it to insert a zipper in a seam, or along the gusset of a box-style cushion.

1 Position the zipper along the edge of the opening and mark each end with a pin. Stitch the seam from the pin to the edge of the fabric at both ends.

2 Sew a row of small, even tacking (basting) stitches between the stitched seams. Press the seam open.

3 Open the zipper and place the teeth on one edge along the seam. Pin and tack 3mm/⅛ in from the outside edge of the teeth.

4 Close the zipper. Pin and tack the second side in the same way. Fit the zipper foot in the machine. Working from the right side, stitch just outside the tacking thread line. Begin partway down one side of the zipper.

5 At the corner leave the needle in the fabric and rotate, ready to stitch across the end of the zipper. Count the number of stitches into the centre and stitch the same number out the other side.

6 Remove the tacking thread from around the stitching, then snip and pull the tacking thread from the centre of the seam.

CONCEALED ZIPPER

This is a quick-and-easy way to fit a concealed zipper. The zipper is inserted to one side of the seam so that the teeth are covered with fabric.

1 Place the pattern pieces right sides together and mark the ends of the zipper with pins. Stitch the seams from the pins to the outside edge.

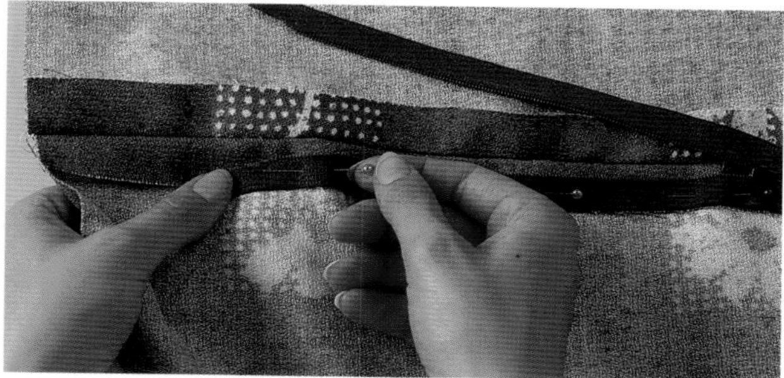

2 Sew a row of small, even tacking (basting) stitches between the stitched seams. Press the seam open. Pin the zipper with the teeth in the centre of the seam. Tack 3mm/⅛ in from the teeth.

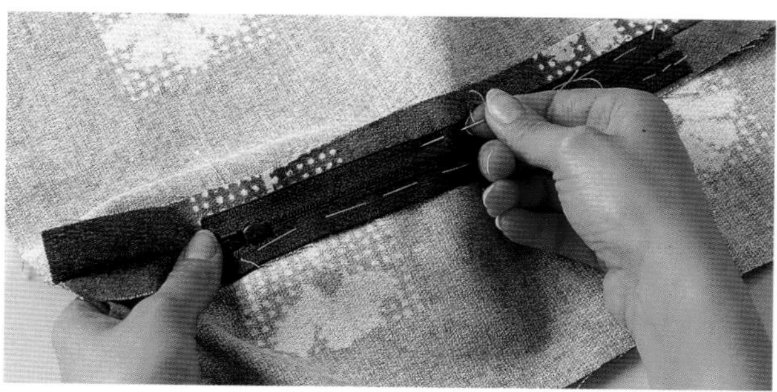

3 Close the zipper and tack the other side to match. Fit the zipper foot in the machine.

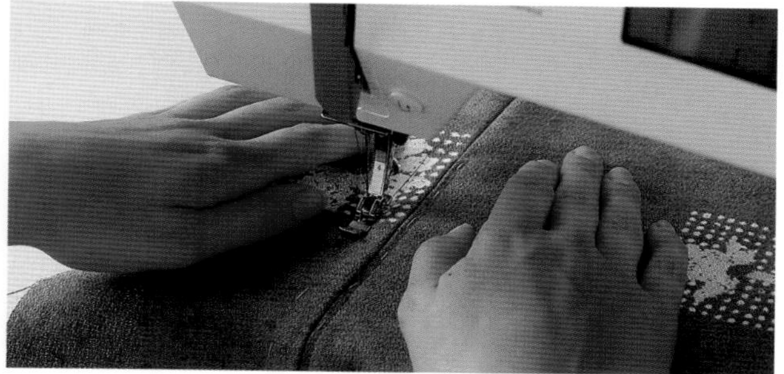

4 On the right side, stitch close to the fold on the lower edge and just outside the tacks on the upper side. Remove the tacks.

FITTING A ZIPPER BEHIND PIPING CORD

This method is often used for cushions or slipcovers with piping. The zipper is tucked in behind the piping and is almost invisible.

1 Make the piping and tack (baste) on to the front panel of the item. Tack the zipper, face down, along the seam allowance.

2 Fit the zipper foot in the machine. Open the zipper and stitch 3mm/⅛ in away from the zipper teeth. Stitch halfway down.

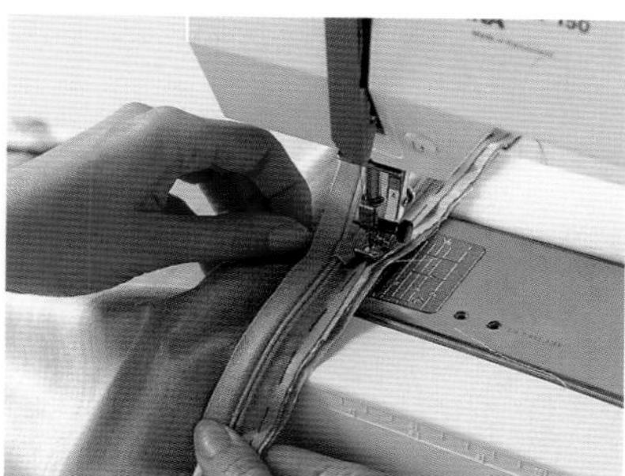

3 Lift the presser foot and close the zipper, easing the slider under the foot. Stitch the rest of the way down the zipper.

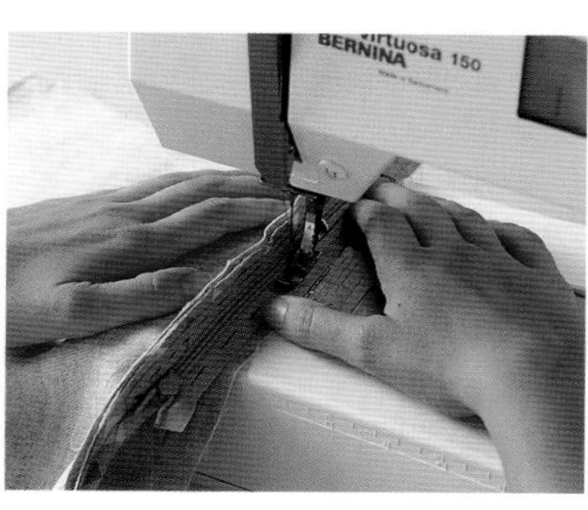

4 ◁ Pin and tack the other side of the zip. Stitch 3mm/⅛ in away from the teeth, lowering the slider as before.

5 ▷ Pin and tack the seams at either end of the zipper and stitch.

hand stitching

The majority of soft furnishings are stitched by machine, but there is often also a need for some temporary or permanent hand stitching. Temporary stitches such as tacking (basting) are used to hold fabric in position before stitching and are usually removed later. Permanent stitches include hemming and hidden stitches such as lock stitch, which is used to support curtain linings and interlinings.

TACKING (BASTING)
Work small, even tacking (basting) stitches along seams to secure before stitching. Longer, uneven tacking stitches are used to stitch substantial distances, for example, when temporarily stitching a lining before lock stitching.

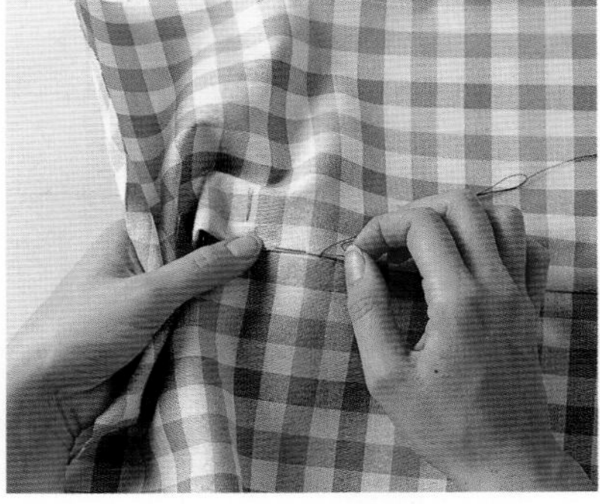

SLIP TACKING (BASTING)
This is worked from the right side of the fabric. Turn over and press one seam allowance. Match the pattern along the seam and pin. Work small, even tacking (basting) stitches alternatively along the fold and then into the fabric.

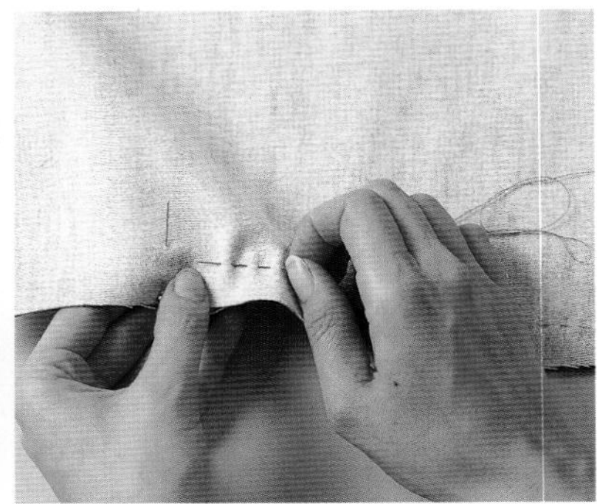

RUNNING STITCH
This stitch is so called because several stitches are "run" along the needle at one time. Keep the spaces and stitches the same size. It is used for awkward seams where there is no strain.

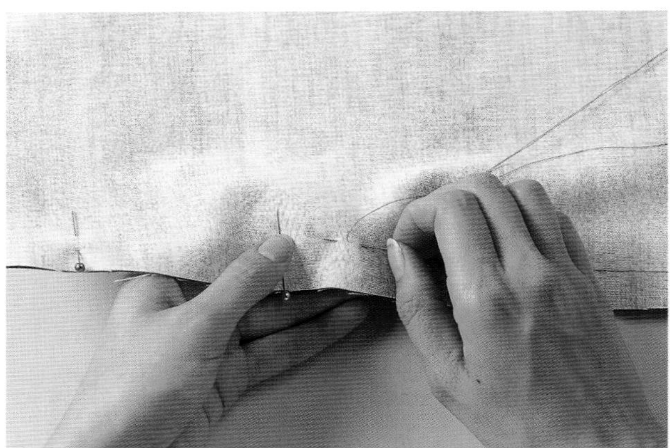

BACK STITCH
This strong stitch is used to complete seams that would be difficult to reach by machine. Half back stitch is similar but stronger – work it in the same way as back stitch, but taking a small stitch only halfway back to the previous stitch.

HERRINGBONE STITCH
This is often thought of as an embroidery stitch but it is also useful in soft furnishings. It can be worked in small stitches instead of hemming, or as much larger stitches to hold layers of fabric together when making curtains.

hand embroidery

Personalize your soft furnishings with simple embroidery and appliqué techniques to make them unique. If the item is three-dimensional, decorate the fabric before making it up. Flat curtains and table linen can be made up first and embroidered later.

Simple embroidery stitches such as running stitch and chain stitch are often the most effective. Either of these stitches can be worked, to great effect, in a design across the bottom of plain curtains. The spirals below are worked in running stitch.

1 Draw spirals freehand along the bottom of the curtains, using tailor's chalk or a vanishing fabric marker pen if it shows up on the fabric.

2 Using a single ply thread, stitch along the lines with small, even stitches. Leave a tail of thread at the beginning and end of each spiral, and sew in securely later.

INITIALS AND MONOGRAMS

Stitching an initial or monogram on to bed or table linen adds a distinctly personal touch. Enlarge text from magazines or use a computer font in a style that you like. Trace the letters individually and move about until the letters interlock, then trace the whole motif.

1 Open out the embroidery hoop by unscrewing it. Place the wooden hoop on a flat surface, place the fabric on top and then place the loop with the screw fitting over the top. Tighten the screw and at the same time pull the fabric taut.

2 Draw out the design and transfer to the fabric using dressmaker's carbon. Choose the stitches you would like to use.

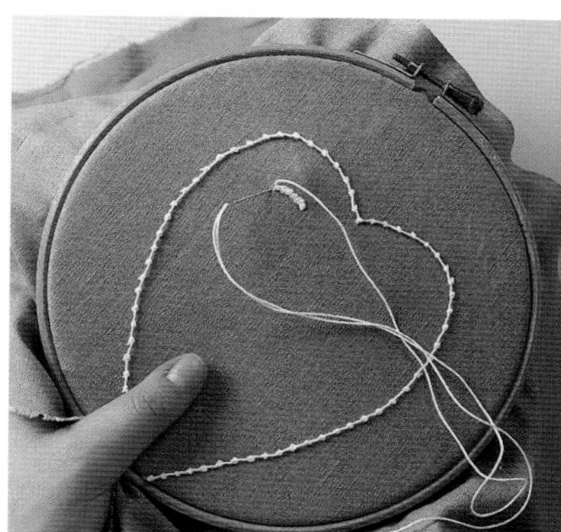

3 The heart is stitched in double knot stitch. Use satin stitch for the letters. For a slightly raised appearance, work chain stitch or running stitch underneath the satin stitch (padded satin stitch).

templates and patterns

Enlarge the templates to the required size by enlarging them on a photocopier. Alternatively, place a grid over the templates and on a larger grid plot the points where the template crosses the grid line. Join up the dots to make a complete shape.

The beanbag pattern below is intended as a visual guide, to be used when making up the project.

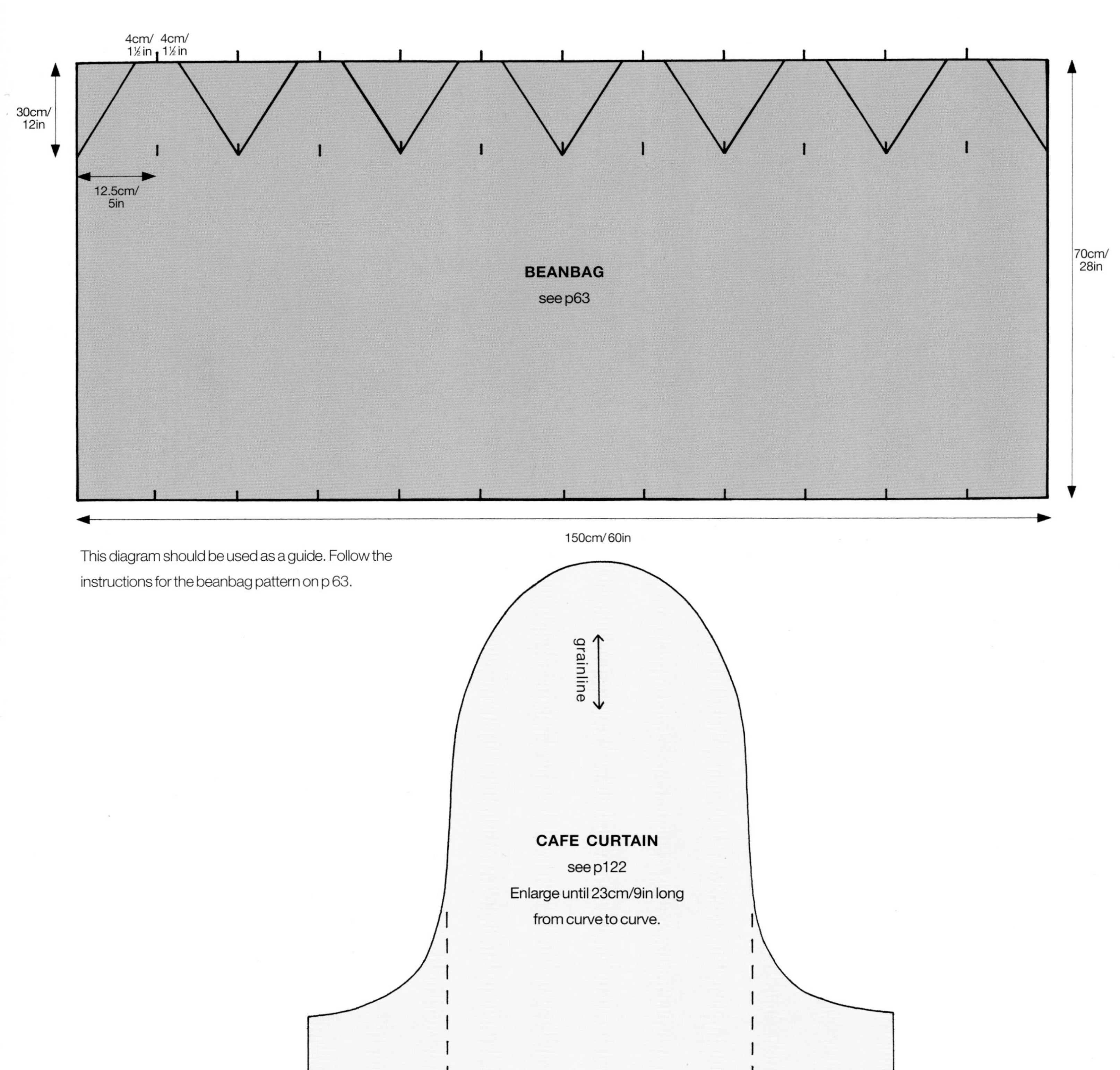

This diagram should be used as a guide. Follow the instructions for the beanbag pattern on p 63.

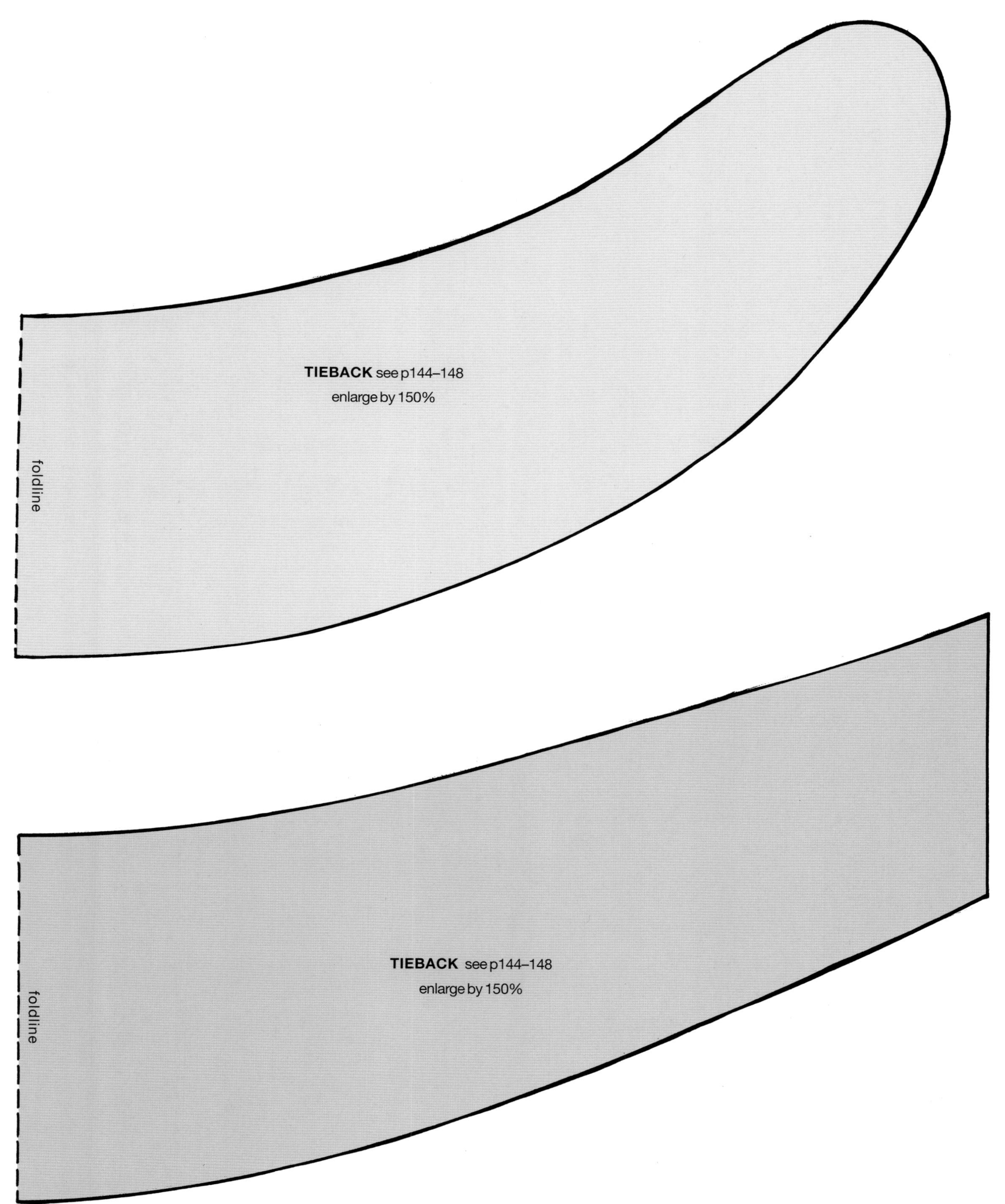
TIEBACK see p144–148
enlarge by 150%
foldline
TIEBACK see p144–148
enlarge by 150%
foldline

index

acknowledgements

Aero
374–379 King's Road
London, SW3 5ES
Tel: 020 7351 0511
for furniture

Alma Home
12–14 Greatorex Street
London, E1 5NF
Tel: 020 7377 0762
for leather and suede

Berwick Street Cloth Shop
14 Berwick Street
London, W1V
Tel: 020 7287 2881
for soft furnishing fabrics

Borovick Fabrics
16 Berwick Street
London, W1V
Tel: 020 7437 2180
for soft furnishing fabrics

Chest of Drawers
281 Upper Street
London, N1
Tel: 020 7359 5909
for pine furniture

The Cloth House
98 Berwick Street
London, W1V
Tel: 020 7287 1555
for soft furnishing fabric

The Conran Shop
81 Fulham Road
London, SW3
Tel: 020 7589 7401
for furniture

The Cube
14 Holland Street
London, W8
Tel: 020 7938 2244
for furniture

The Dining Chair Company
4 St Barnabas Street
London, SW1
Tel 020 7259 0422
for dining chairs, dining tables, sofas and stools

Fabric Warehouse
Packet Boat Lane
Cowley, Middlesex
Tel: 01895 448465
for soft furnishing fabric

Habitat
196 Tottenham Court Road
London, W1P 9LD
for furniture

The Iron Bed Company
580 Fulham Road
London, SW3
Tel: 020 7610 9903
for metal furniture

John Lewis
278–306 Oxford Street
London, W1A
Tel: 020 7629 7711
for soft furnishing fabric

McKinney & Co
The Old Imperial Gardens
Warriner Gardens
London, SW11 4XW
Tel: 020 7627 5077
for curtain accessories

Neal Street East
5–7 Neal Street
London, WC2
Tel: 020 7240 0135
for furniture and accessories

Ou Baholyodhin Studio
1st Floor Great Orex Street
London, E1 5NF
Tel: 020 7426 0666
for furniture

Same
146 Brick Lane,
London, E1
Tel: 020 7247 9992
for furniture

The Silk Society
44 Berwick Street
London, W1V
Tel: 020 7287 1881
for soft furnishing fabric

Thomas Dare
341 King's Road
London, SW3 5ES
Tel: 020 7351 7991
for soft furnishing fabric

V V Rouleaux
54 Sloane Square
London, SW1
Tel: 020 7730 3125
for ribbons and trimmings

Worlds End Tiles
Silverthorne Road
London, SW8
Tel: 020 7819 2100

Anness Publishing Ltd and the author would like to thank the following project makers:
Pat Smith of Classic Drapes tel: 0115 945 2210
for the curtains and blinds.
Low Wood Furnishings
tel: 01530 222246 for the three armchair covers.
Penny Mayor for the chair covers/tablecloth and napkin.
Sally Burton for the tablecloth, tablerunner and napkin.
Beryl Miller for the deck chair, director's chair, scallop chair, back pleat chair and two footstools.
Rita Whitehorn for the bed quilt.
Kath Poxon for the cot quilt.

The publishers would like to thank the following organisations and individuals who generously loaned images for inclusion in this book:
Alice & Astrid p22 bottom, p27 below right, p32 above.
Clare Taylor p4 top, p11 right.
Jennie Buckingham p24 above right.
KA International endpaper, p12 below left, p16 centre, p17 above, p19 below right, p30 bottom, p64 far left, p65 right, p96 above left, p 98 above left and below left.
Lucienne Linen p172 below left and p174 top.
Malabar p10 top and centre, p11 below right, p13 above left, p14 top and above left, p15 top right and centre right
Natasha Smith p24 above left, p33 left and p104.
Nordic Style p16 bottom, p19 right, p173 and p175 right.
prêt a vivre p11 below left, p13 above, p96 left below, p97 right and p102
Romo p2, p3, p13 below centre and below left, p21 right and above right, p22 top, p23 top and bottom, p25 top, p27 above, p30 top, p108 and p241.
Thomas Dare p12 top left, p14 below right and p32 above left.
Zoffany p125

Elizabeth Whiting Associates p12 centre left, p14 above, p15 right, p21 above left, p25 above, p27 below centre, p76 above and p125.
IPC Magazines pg 8–9 Hotze Eisma, p11 above left Dominic Blackmore, p12 above David Garcia, p.14 below left, Caroline Arber, p15 left Hotze Eisma, p15 above left James Mitchell, p17 above right Neil Mersch, p18 below right Andre Cameron, p19 below left Lucinda Symonds, p20 below right Winifred p20 left Simon Whitmore, Heinze, p22 centre Simon Whitmore, p31 Tim Imrie, p65 Hotze Eisma, p98 below Trevor Richards, p110, p174 far left Tim Evan Cook.